ON THE CASE: EXPLORATIONS IN SOCIAL HISTORY

Case files, records from all kinds of social, medical, governmental, military, and other agencies, become available to researchers when confidentiality ceases to be an issue. Such records are an important source for scholars in social history and related fields, providing insight not only into the lives of ordinary people but into the workings of the agencies that kept the records as well. Case files contain a wealth of information and challenge researchers by their complexity and the variety of approaches and methodologies their analysis demands. *On the Case* is a timely book intended to provide a forum for discussing the theoretical and methodological issues that arise in connection with the use of case files in research. The book brings together theoretical debates, new research, and new research methods and offers compelling illustrations of the drama, conflict, and power relations that the case file can capture.

This collection of essays features some of Canada's leading social historians. Readers will encounter an impressive array of case files, including psychiatrists' accounts of sexual deviants, employment records of sailors, state welfare and Indian Affairs reports, court records, the patient forms of hospital and asylum doctors, and state security files. While the contributors differ in choice of subject and approach, they share a commitment to the progressive traditions of social history. They recover the voices and actions of people – not only of those with power but also of those who seemingly have none.

Case files have proved crucial to scholars developing such new fields of historical study as sexuality, gay and lesbian lives, and domestic violence, and have reinvigorated work in more established fields of history such as immigration, security and intelligence, and the modern welfare state. *On the Case* is unique in offering new research as well as guiding readers through recent debates and the various theoretical and methodological challenges created by case files.

FRANCA IACOVETTA is a professor of history at the University of Toronto. She is the editor of *A Nation of Immigrants*, and co-editor of two series, Themes in Canadian Social History and Studies in Gender and History.

WENDY MITCHINSON is a professor of history at the University of Waterloo and author of *The Nature of Their Bodies: Women and Their Doctors in Victorian Canada*.

EDITED BY FRANCA IACOVETTA
AND WENDY MITCHINSON

On the Case:
Explorations in
Social History

UNIVERSITY OF TORONTO PRESS
Toronto Buffalo London

© University of Toronto Press Incorporated 1998
Toronto Buffalo London

Printed in Canada

ISBN 0-8020-4302-X (cloth)
ISBN 0-8020-8129-0 (paper)

Printed on acid-free paper

Canadian Cataloguing in Publication Data

Main entry under title:

On the case : explorations in social history

ISBN 0-8020-4302-X (bound)   ISBN 0-8020-8129-0 (pbk.)

1. Canada – Social conditions – Research.   2. Historical sociology –
Methodology.   3. Records – Canada.   I. Iacovetta, Franca, 1957–   .
II. Mitchinson, Wendy.

HN103.O52 1998   301'.07'22   C98-930801-4

This book has been published with the help of a grant from the Humanities and
Social Sciences Federation of Canada, using funds provided by the Social
Sciences and Humanities Research Council of Canada.

University of Toronto Press acknowledges the financial assistance to its
publishing program of the Canada Council for the Arts and the Ontario
Arts Council.

Contents

ON THE CASE: EXPLORATIONS IN SOCIAL HISTORY

Introduction

Social History and Case Files Research

FRANCA IACOVETTA and WENDY MITCHINSON

The historian's craft is comparable to the work of a detective 'on the case.' We check for clues about intriguing or informative events and people, track down leads in libraries and archives, and sometimes conduct interviews with 'eye witnesses' to the past. We examine diverse and fragmentary evidence, revise theories or common-sense assumptions against the materials gathered – all the while aiming to reach a resolution. But historians do not simply gather 'facts' about the past and tell them to others. We make choices about who and what we deem worthy of study and which questions we wish to explore. We hope to discover new things, but our gaze is also informed by our own world-view and social location and by compelling theories and analytical approaches. We read our sources carefully, paying attention to detail, nuance, and context, but we also assess them, deciding what to preserve or discard. And we assemble our findings on a topic into an intellectually coherent whole, even when we emphasize the messy or contradictory character of the past. The process is not a straightforward one, and few scholars, even as they interpret data and draw conclusions, would claim to have found 'the truth'; indeed, many historians today would reject the notion that the truth is there to be found.[1]

In this book we also use the phrase 'on the case' literally. All the authors focus on a particular type of source, namely case files or case records, in order to examine a variety of subjects and discuss theoretical and methodological issues that such sources raise. The term *case file*, broadly defined, refers to the records generated by political, social, legal, and other institutions entrusted with the task of categorizing and assessing certain populations, usually with the purpose of supervising, treating, punishing, servicing, and/or reforming individuals or groups deemed in some way deviants or victims.[2] Case files may be an administrative convenience and/or central to the workings, identity, and power of a bureaucracy. Unlike the census, case files are not always routinely generated and they usually contain a great deal of non-standardized verbal information, such as testimony.

Readers will encounter a wide range of case files in this book, including psychiatrists' case histories of sexual deviants, employment records of sailors, court proceedings and capital-offence case files, state welfare and Indian Affairs reports, refugee reception records, the patient records of hospital and asylum doctors, and state security files. The diversity itself suggests a significant aspect of our modern world – the desire to keep track of people and have a tracking record. The authors have mined these records in an effort to expose the words and actions of authorities and experts, and to recover the lives of the less powerful. A wide array of groups are studied. They include members of Protestant religious sects, the elderly, Native farmers on marginal lands, single mothers, refugee women, political activists, female hospital patients, and people who appeared in court: abused women, men arrested for assault and murder, girls charged with delinquency, and men accused of homosexual acts. The themes addressed are equally diverse: the rise of middle-class institutions during an era of capitalist transformation; state, moral, religious, and medical regulation of adults and children; constructions of femininity and masculinity; professionalization; the racialized character of laws and politics; state repression; and the subcultures of so-called deviants. The essays emerge from differing intellectual perspectives and research methodologies. Though all of them consider questions of theory and method, those in part 1 deal at length with these issues, while the remainder are demonstrations of case files research and have been grouped under broad thematic topics that reflect current research trends in social history. Together, the essays reflect the continuing energy and exuberance of Canadian social history and the concerns of those writing it. If some historians bemoan the loss of a unified vision of Canada owing to the diversity of peoples and themes being researched, an accusation hurled at social historians rewriting history from the vantage points of marginal groups, none of our contributors is among them. We happily accept responsibility for fracturing the Canadian 'story' by writing about people and events ignored in so-called national histories of Canada.[3]

Doing Case Files Research

Case files are not entirely new sources for historians, of course. Influential studies by European scholars such as Carlo Ginsberg and Natalie Zemon Davis revealed the significance of similar types of sources.[4] So did Joy Parr's pioneering work on British juvenile immigration schemes to Canada.[5] In recent years, growing numbers of scholars in Canada and elsewhere have become interested in case files research or collecting records that bear similarities (as well as differences) with modern case files.[6] Yet, despite this, scholars have lacked a forum to debate the merits (and potential pitfalls) of such work, discuss varying perspectives and approaches, and compare research findings with colleagues outside their specialized fields of study.

This volume began as a workshop of invited colleagues doing archives-based research with case files in a number of different fields. It offered a three-day forum for comparative analysis, debate, and feedback on each other's work. A serious dose of irony was injected into our discussions by Province of Ontario archivist Jack Choules, who noted that current interest in case files is occurring at a time when funding crises and lack of storage space mean that archives across Canada (and elsewhere) must consider the option of preserving only selective samples of legal, medical, and other case records. Selective preservation means a loss of valuable material; also, today's criteria of selection likely will not reflect all the concerns of subsequent generations. That historians cannot afford to be passive users of archives but should lobby for both preservation of records and access to restricted materials are points underscored in Gregory Kealey's essay on the origins of Canada's security system. Indeed, recent access to security records has helped to reinvigorate a topic once considered the prerogative of political historians.

Case files have a long history and are incredibly varied. Even in periods before the rise of modern casework methods we associate with twentieth-century health-care, social-work, and legal professionals, the materials generated by earlier record-keepers are familiar: serialized instalments of fragmentary information on specific individuals. Such elements are evident in the nineteenth-century Catholic nuns' registries used by Bettina Bradbury to reconstruct the institutional regimes of Montreal's elderly, and in the entries documenting the nineteenth-century Baptist and Methodist church misconduct trials examined by Lynne Marks. Frequently, the clients' voices and actions are evident in case file records, though they may appear in muted forms, such as witness courtroom testimony shaped by lawyers and procedural rules of evidence and summaries of interviews conducted by investigating officers. Such sources cannot be read as though they represented an unmediated text on a person's life. Often case files are not even single documents. For example, the legal 'dossier' usually is composed of different types of materials, such as trial transcripts, medical evaluations, psychiatric case histories, and perhaps letters of character or affidavits signed by the client or friends and family. As Steven Maynard observes, historians sometimes mistreat the case file as a monolithic whole, haphazardly pulling fragments of information and quotations from various parts of the file as it fits their narrative and interpretive slant. Different case files can contain different things. In some case files, intimate details of an individual's life are methodically recorded with clinical precision, while in other files, personal histories are brief or obscured by religious exhortations or the professional vocabulary of the authorities producing the records.

The creation of a case file implies the intervention of institutional and bureaucratic power into people's lives. The (usually middle-class) staff associated with these sources of power, whether professionals or volunteers, generally were concerned to resolve conflicts, bring their clients into conformity with dominant social and political norms, and/or punish political, sexual, and other transgressors. Whether dealing with 'public' or 'private' behaviour, the interface of such contact usually results in the institution 'taking over,' significantly shaping the environment and limiting the choices of the subject populations.[7] The irony is that it is not always clear why particular individuals ended up having a specific type of case file produced on them. Sexual deviants who found themselves in criminal courts could just as easily have been incarcerated in psychiatric hospitals or escaped detection altogether. Yet, whatever the specifics of any individual case, as Karen Dubinsky observes, case file records *are* qualitatively rich sources, which is why we are drawn to them. They reveal the vulnerability of many in the past, but also illustrate the resilience of individuals. In uncovering their agency we face a paradox: our legal obligations as researchers to protect the privacy of individuals in the past can lead us to write the marginal into history by writing their names and faces out of it. But even this problem is not uniform across sources. Collections of records with varying provenance have different restrictions. The holders of some files place little if any restrictions on their use, others insist on name changes, while still others require anonymity to the point that a reader cannot trace the person through footnotes back to the original records.

Historians have turned to case files because they offer us a rare window on human interactions and conflict. Complex power relations play themselves out at the local level, sometimes with unpredictable outcomes. If case files do not provide the client's unmediated voice, they help us explore still compelling questions, such as how certain populations became subject to the institutional power of medicine and the law, or how the ascendancy of industrial capitalist relations and middle-class hegemony in Western societies shaped institutional practices and everyday assumptions regarding appropriate conduct. These records can illuminate the ways in which dominant class, gender, and racial ideologies shaped official discourses and action, and relations between experts and clients. In still other cases, client voices are recorded, however distorted, leaving us to debate the status of transcribed interviews and court testimony.[8]

Social History, Past and Present

Social historians are not sole custodians of the case files in the archives, and we intend this book to be relevant to case files scholars in other disciplines. Still, we want to place these essays within the larger context of social-history scholarship to underscore the point that recent historical work with case files reflects both continuities and new trends in the field. Social history in Canada and elsewhere in the last three decades was largely committed to the recovery of the lives of those individuals and groups (including workers, women, farmers, and the poor) traditionally dismissed or ignored as marginal, inarticulate, and powerless. Influenced by the New Left and feminist politics of the 1960s and 1970s, the field's early practitioners launched an ambitious project to redefine who constituted legitimate historical subjects.[9] Younger scholars have inherited, as well as challenged, the questions and frameworks that have marked the field. In Canada, this large scholarly output, most of which dates from the 1970s,[10] has transformed the writing and teaching of history. Alongside the many studies in Canadian working-class, women's, immigrant, and family history,[11] important research exists on institutional populations, such as workhouse and asylum residents and prisoners,[12] and on the origins, the policies, and, to a lesser extent, the recipients of philanthropic or state welfare systems.[13] New specializations, such as gay/lesbian history, and animated debates over the role of theory, and which theory, to be used in history have helped ensure that social history remains a rich and rigorous field of enquiry.[14]

Notwithstanding social history's early association with neglected subjects, from the start scholars on the international scene were doing more than recovering individuals and groups. They explored critical historical processes – the transition from feudalism to capitalism, land-tenure systems and pre-industrial social relations, the rise of institutions – and how such developments reconfigured people's lives and options. Social histories of Canada produced in the last two decades similarly reflect a long-standing interest in the differential impact of economic transformations on women, workers, and families; daily life and conflict in pre-industrial and industrial settings; and mobility in rural and urban locales. Whether considering the class structure of commercial cities, rural or emigrant families 'on the move,' or early Quebec, these studies offered detailed household, business, and community reconstructions based on painstaking statistical gathering and demographic modes of analysis.[15] While some works were criticized, quite rightly, for lack of attention to gender differences and women's lives in particular, continuing important work in these areas attests to the need to revisit such topics.

The family, for example, receives attention here in several essays, all of them informed by feminist analyses that seek to disentangle the family, to recognize it as a flexible institution but also as an arena of negotiation and conflict among members with unequal resources. Annalee Golz's analysis of the scripted language of battered wives who exposed their abusive men in nineteenth-century Ontario courts, Franca Iacovetta's discussion of working-class parents who used the family court to punish disobedient daughters, and Marlene Epp's study of post-1945 Mennonite refugee women and the various people who formed their 'grab bag' families suggest how the insights of women's and gender history have helped to rewrite (dis-aggregate) family-history. Often drawing on case files, recent scholarship on marital cruelty and domestic conflict are valuable correctives to a family history literature that once focused largely on the cooperative aspects of family-based economic strategies of survival and success.[16] Marks's effort to map the transitions from premodern (church-based) to modern (state-based) forms of regulating people's behaviour also reflects an ongoing interest in charting the implications for family relations and other aspects of everyday life of major societal transformations. In addressing issues of conflict within religious communities, she draws on sources that religious historians have largely neglected, and contributes towards a developing social history of religious activity.[17] Robin Brownlie's study of government plans to transform World War One Native veterans into 'petty patriarchs' of agriculturally settled families charts some depressingly predictable features, including parsimonious state officials and patronizing Indian agents.[18] But her analysis of Native men's rejection of the Indian agents' disparaging profiles reveals little-explored aspects of Native masculinity that incorporated notions of breadwinner and family provider.

Since the 1970s, social historians in Canada and abroad have also been interested in the campaigns that accompanied the rise and ascendancy of the middle classes. Such an interest was evident in the early 'social control' literature that probed the programs of middle-class reformers involved in movements as seemingly diverse as schooling reform and delinquency laws, temperance and prohibition, female suffrage, sabbatarianism, eugenics, regulation of prostitution, charity-giving, and state welfare.[19] While this scholarship told us considerably more about the anxieties, activities, and limitations of bourgeois reformers and civic authorities than about the targets of reform, some efforts were made to understand how the working classes and poor responded to these innovations. Given the current preoccupation of many case files scholars with probing both the processes by which the state and regulatory agencies intervened in people's lives and how people resisted or negotiated such intrusions, the value of this earlier work should not be forgotten. Either implicitly or explicitly, several essays in this collection, including those by Eric Sager, Kealey, Maynard,

Margaret Little, Golz, Iacovetta, and Geoffrey Reaume and Lykke de la Cour reveal the influence of earlier Marxist-inspired studies of state power. Scholars of capitalist state formation and the concomitant creation of a moral culture infused by bourgeois values, and of the ideological power of the legal system, highlighted the processes whereby the state and its related agencies could rule effectively over a citizenry without persistent recourse to coercion. They did (and do) so by legitimizing certain behaviours and ideas and encouraging conformity to them. Such ideological processes, if need be, could be enforced through repression and punishment.[20] The 'dossier' can be seen as the product of authorities exercising power over their citizens, or of a dialectic encounter between experts backed by state, medical, or religious power, and clients possessing far fewer resources. It thus offers us a way of examining in specific contexts the complex power dynamics that characterized relations between dominant and subordinate groups. Sager's discussion of the non-coercive means by which British imperial authorities maintained supervision over work crews aboard ocean-going ships is one such example. Others examine how family, households, religious and secular courts, welfare offices, and hospitals became dramatic sites of contestation. The degree of intrusion and coercion, the moral and social pressures to conform, link all the papers. Scholars using any set of case files must understand how the institution producing them exercised its power.

An interest in how state institutions both imposed conformity and encouraged its citizens to censor voluntarily their actions has links with Gramsci's notion of hegemony, a concept on which several authors draw. It is an explanatory tool for understanding how state-sanctioned ideas and behaviours that actually reflect and serve the interests of the dominant classes can take on a status as the 'natural' order of things or be internalized by many (though never all) of its citizens as appropriate.[21] Though perhaps leery of the overdrawn conspiratorial tone present in some earlier analyses, many contemporary historians have shared similar research goals. And, of course, social historians of various persuasions have always hoped to find resistant and alternative actions of those who opposed the mainstream. Here, Wendy Mitchinson's discussion of the physical pain that many Canadian women endured before seeking medical aid and James Walker's examination of Chinese restaurant owner Quong Wing's stand against labour laws prohibiting his hiring of white women offer analyses of how competing claims about rights and entitlement can inform community standards. They plot the defiance of modest citizens who, as in the case of women patients, tried to influence their encounters with doctors or, as in Wing's case, challenged a democratic liberal society to live up to its rhetoric of rights and tolerance.

Also revealing some important continuities with earlier literatures on reform and social control is recent work in the area of moral regulation. These scholars are particularly interested in exposing the processes whereby certain behaviours and values become marginalized as deviant while others are legitimated as moral, at least on the part of mainstream society. This literature has been influenced by Michel Foucault, whose work shifted the lens from state formation (the focus of many Marxist scholars) to the ways in which state power infiltrated civil society, defining standards of conduct and otherwise shaping social and moral behaviour. More particularly, he considered the rise of specialized expert discourses[22] within various professionalizing disciplines, such as medicine, psychiatry, and criminology, and their role in defining and enforcing proscribed sexual and non-sexual conduct.[23] As Carolyn Strange observes, Foucault argued that these new scientific discourses supplanted earlier religious and 'superstitious' authority not because they discovered previously unknown truths but, rather, because they succeeded in constructing new ways of distinguishing truth from falsity, natural from the unnatural. Angus McLaren's reading of the British Columbia murder trials explores contemporary notions of acceptable and unacceptable forms of masculine aggression. Little, Epp, de la Cour/Reaume, Golz, and Iacovetta do the same for sexual and other transgressors. Several authors, including Maynard and Strange, have taken up Foucault's analysis of the dossier and his famous axiom, that knowledge is power, as a way of exploring the competing truth claims and expert opinions that shaped criminal case histories. Strange's essay challenges us to resist the temptation to read 'the truth' in the remarkably rich and compelling materials contained in the capital-offence case files of convicted murderers. Maynard illustrates how Ontario psychiatrists actively constructed and pathologized men's homosexual experiences into cases of insanity, perversion, and criminal behaviour. These discursive practices, he adds, were steeped in and generated relations of power that could be used to limit homosexual men's freedom. Significantly, none of the essays on regulation have adopted a dichotomous position in favour of Marx or Foucault, or between discourse analysis and materialist approaches, preferring instead to integrate useful insights from these and other perspectives.

Where the social-control literature was weakest was on the question of women and gender, and the differential impact that the state, law, and professions could have on female and male clients. Historians of women have documented how gender mediated class and power relations, developing analytical frameworks that acknowledged patriarchal forms of oppression as well as female agency – that is, women's capacity to pursue choices and strategies amid constrained and bleak conditions. The continuing importance of female agency as a descriptive and analytical tool in women's history links all of the essays here dealing with women's and girls' lives. But perhaps the most explicit assertion of the theme of the agency of the oppressed is in de la Cour's and Reaume's descriptions of how psychiatric patients, in this instance both women and men, defied medical authorities by constructing their own definitions of illness and developing their own social practices within the asylum. That medical history has long produced 'top-down' approaches celebrating professional, institutional, and therapeutic developments partially explains why recent contributions to this field so strenuously stress patient agency.[24]

Contributors addressing the dialectical tensions between oppression and the agency of women and other marginal groups have drawn on a diverse scholarship. Particularly influential, however, as Dubinsky's afterword notes, is Linda Gordon's work on domestic violence and on the welfare state. Her *Heroes of Their Own Lives* argues that women social-welfare clients, more than simply relinquishing autonomy in return for material assistance, were active players, sometimes inviting, sometimes resisting agency intervention, and thus shaping the nature of 'the social control experience.'[25] For several contributors, but especially Little in her essay on single-mother welfare recipients, Gordon's modified social-control model is important. Little's portrayal of the travelling caseworkers who evaluated the eligibility of poor women in southern Ontario also reminds us that our studies of marginal people cannot simply dismiss the social-control agents as 'unwelcome intruders' into our research.[26] Nor can we treat them in monolithic terms, as simply the faceless agents of the state or patriarchy. Their varied backgrounds, front-line work, relations with superiors, and other features must also be scrutinized. The relationship of power is always a dynamic one. And if agents were not monolithic, neither were the institutions they represented, some of which created enduring regimes while others failed to do so.

Reading Case Files after 'The Linguistic Turn'

In exploring poorly understood populations, processes, and phenomena, the pioneering generation of social historians were optimistic about the potentially transformative impact their work might have on historical practice and understanding. They set into motion an ambitious project. More than thirty years of scholarly output has not erased the central epistemological challenges facing researchers in the field, namely: how do we interpret the experiences, strategies, and perceptions of those women, men, and children who did not leave behind their own written record and who appear in the historical record only fleetingly and usually as the objects or targets of more powerful others? Complicating matters is the nature of our evidence, which usually does not come in the form of private diaries or other first-hand accounts of those whose lives we hope to illuminate. Observations, reports, surveys, and other records are generated by outsiders, be they middle-class reformers, professional social experts, and officials connected with growing state bureaucracies and social institutions. (Of course, elite diaries and journals also raise challenges.) Even the records produced by what we might call plebian organizations, such as trade unions, were often penned by elites rather than rank-and-file women and men. As Parr put it, social historians, then and now, face the twin challenges of understanding the observers and of mining effectively their observations for the observed.[27]

In recent years, postmodern and post-structuralist theorists have not only aggressively visited these epistemological questions; some have questioned the foundations of established historical practice and the status of historical evidence by rejecting the premise that we can arrive at a definitive meaning for any document or text we read. If social historians want to view the past from the people's perspective, postmodernists warn, we must be aware of the dangers of essentializing 'the people,' whether they be women or men, old or young, Black or white, and so on. The quicksand of linguistic meaning makes it difficult to know what such terms mean. For example, to whom does 'people of colour' refer: does such a group exist, divided as they surely must be by gender, class, age, ability, religion, and other distinctions? Some post-structuralist critics also boldly denied the possibility of our truly knowing the material reality of the past, and called upon historians to employ the literary tools of discourse analysis to deconstruct the multiple, competing, and fractured meanings of categories, texts, and identities, and to give up the struggle to discern objective conditions or structures. Such critiques provoked angry responses from Marxists and historical materialists, resulting in heavily polarized debates in which scholars have presented discourse analysis and materialist approaches as mutually exclusive.[28] Social history became characterized by 'the conceptual opposition of representation and reality.'[29] Scholarship based on case files generated some of these polarized debates, including the polemical exchange between Linda Gordon and Joan Scott over Gordon's use of the case files of child-protection agencies.[30] More recently, however, some scholars, including historians of women and sexuality, have moved beyond a dichotomized debate by suggesting how a sensitivity to representation, discourses, and the fractured nature of experience and identity can be integrated with materialist and feminist analyses of class, patriarchy, and power.[31]

This book does not offer easy answers to current debates regarding historical practice after 'the linguistic turn.' Many of our contributors are clearly influenced by linguistic theories that have heightened awareness of the meaning of words and concepts and the difficulties of ever knowing their essential meaning.

Several essays probe the meanings of complex terms such as race, illness, sexuality, and family. The concern about essentializing or generalizing groups is addressed in some articles through attention to the individual. The narrative line is strong in the stories of people that so many of the contributors delight in recounting. Yet out of those specific stories, generalizations are drawn and need to be drawn. As Jane Roland Martin has argued, 'if categories exist that do not conceal difference, they will be so specific as to stultify intellectual inquiry.'[32] While some authors remain committed to Marxist (in the case of Kealey and Iacovetta) or neo-Marxist (Sager) approaches, none finds a need for blanket dismissals of new approaches, especially when current notions about the decentred nature of power and competition over meanings can be integrated into class analyses of power, ideology, and resistance. Others, including Strange, offer concrete suggestions as to how post-structuralist insights can generate new questions. She uses the capital-offence case files to illustrate 'the textual production of truth,' and invites us to see the case file as a textual artefact of competing truth claims and narratives by the various parties involved. Maynard's analysis of psychiatric case histories offers another effort to work through 'the material-idealist impasse' by situating expert discourses within their larger social and material context – a feature that distinguishes several other contributions. Still other authors have not felt compelled to respond directly to postmodern critiques, in part because debates regarding the limitations of sources or interpretive challenges raised by our sources are not new to historians.[33] It may even be counter-productive to expect more of case files than of other types of historical records, since the challenges they raise for us may differ in degree not kind.

Case Files in Context

Historians are practitioners of an imperfect craft. Yet, none of us feels compelled to abandon the archives or quit the trade. Case files are not clear windows on the past, but they can be read in judicious ways. They expose interesting, indeed fascinating, things about the past, even if they cannot provide us with answers to our original questions. While offering different solutions, all the contributors agree that a central challenge concerns inherent biases in the records. As Sager notes, they describe certain people in words and categories that serve the official purposes of other people. They not only represent the views, perceptions, and responses, but also the prejudices and ideological lens, of the gazer. Neither is any collection of cases the universe of files. How effectively can we read such records 'against the grain,' that is, for reasons other than those the record-makers intended and for the clients' voices? If, as Foucault suggested, such records represent a kind of archives of repression, then can researchers use them in subversive ways? How do we discern the patient's perspective, the battered wife's strategies, and the bad girl's street culture when little of the evidence available comes to us directly from these people? In response, the authors have advocated different methods, including quantitative and qualitative forms of data analyses. But all have acknowledged that we must be clear about the linkages between a particular set of records and the larger institution and record-keepers producing them. Whether tackling a sample of records or a sensational single case, we need a sense of the whole in order to make sense of the part we are examining, to be able to talk about its typicality (or not), and whether it is illustrative of certain historical patterns.

For some, this task meant reconfirming a long-standing methodological premise in social history, namely, understanding the records' provenance – their nature, structure, and original purpose. Case files reflect the workings of bureaucracies and authorities intervening in people's lives; we thus need to clarify where the files fit within their appropriate institution, the intent of the file-makers, and the various contexts in which the files are produced. This point is made explicitly in essays that are otherwise quite dissimilar in method and approach. In drawing a statistical profile of the labour contracts signed by sailors who joined Britain's ocean-going ships, Sager explains how any viable assessment of these contracts requires understanding how they fit into Britain's imperial strategy, and how sailors' defiant actions provoked particular state responses. Maynard reminds us that we need to be aware that the case file, as well as the discreet materials (including psychiatric case histories) that constitute it, each have a history. Epp demonstrates how probing the context in which a set of case records is produced can lead us to discern discrepancies in evidence, contested definitions, and even the wilful distortions created by the record-keepers. All the essays act as a caution against the easy assumption that we can merely read off the case file all that is required to know about a given subject. The richness of these records does not free us from the search for contextualizing and corroborating evidence.

Issues of representativeness and selection are crucial when faced with case files. What is the most appropriate way to proceed: exploring the most interesting or illustrative cases or applying random sampling techniques? Do we adopt a narrative framework in which the stories occupy centre stage, or do we collect and describe quantifiable material? How do we generalize or make comparisons among cases when every story is in some respects unique? Again, the book offers differing approaches. The most obvious difference concerns quantitative versus qualitative approaches – a debate that is nicely encapsulated in the Sager and Strange pieces. But even here, dichotomized positions are avoided. Sager's call for social-science techniques in history makes some points on which all contributors agree – the dangers of implicit quantification, for instance, and the need for methodological pluralism – and is fully consistent with a Foucauldian analysis of state regulation. Strange and Dubinsky offer some differing insights, but both caution against naive interpretations and call for a greater sensitivity to language, scripted narratives, and the production of the records.

Historians and historical social scientists have long grappled with the challenges of interpreting and evaluating texts. Even the current heated battles over the status of historical evidence do not negate the immense contributions made by several generations of social historians to the shape of history and historical knowledge. Today, few Canadian historians would teach a history that entirely ignores women, workers, Natives, and racial-ethnic minorities. We know about the struggles and accomplishments of ordinary and non-privileged people, be they skilled artisans demanding the nine-hour day in the 1870s, Jewish communist women staging consumer boycotts during the 1920s, or working mothers stretching limited family budgets across time and household. While the contributors differ in choice of subject and methodological and theoretical orientations, we share a basic commitment to the original and enduring aims of social history – writing people's history and thereby rewriting all history. While our individual essays differ in their focus on the powerful or marginal, we confirm the progressive impulses and humanist tradition of social history, its commitment to politically engaged scholarship, its optimistic reading of the agency of the oppressed, and its potential for arming us with the critical intellectual tools for affecting social change.

Notes

1 This debate has a history: consider, for example, E.H. Carr, *What Is History?* (Middlesex 1967); Peter Novick, *That Noble Dream: The 'Objectivity Question' and the American Historical Profession* (New York 1988); and Joy Parr, 'Gender History and Historical Practise,' *Canadian Historical Review* 76:3 (1995).

2 We have not placed quotation marks around terms such as deviant, experts, and knowing, but we view them as ideologically charged terms requiring critical dissection.

3 Michael Bliss, 'Privatizing the Mind: The Sundering of Canadian History, the Sundering of Canada,' *Journal of Canadian Studies* 26:4 (Winter 1991–2); for a critique, see responses in ibid., 27:2 (Summer 1992); Ruth Roach Pierson, 'Colonization and Canadian Women's History,' *Journal of Women's History* 4:2 (Fall 1992); and Veronica Strong-Boag, 'Contested Space: The Politics of Canadian Memory,' *Journal of the Canadian Historical Association*, new series, 5 (1994).

4 Davis's *The Return of Martin Guerre* (Cambridge, Mass., 1983), a masterful study of
   peasants and gender relations, isolated the illuminating single case; her *Fiction in the
   Archives: Pardon Tales and Their Tellers in Sixteenth-Century France* (Cambridge,
   Mass., 1988 [1987]) showed the folly of reading legal records as unmediated texts.
   Cultural historian Carlo Ginzburg 'found' heretics and pagans in the Roman inquisi-
   tion records by noting the discrepancies between the inquisitors' questions and the
   respondents' replies; see *The Cheese and the Worms: The Cosmos of a Sixteenth-
   Century Miller* (New York 1976).
5 'Introduction,' *Labouring Children: British Immigrant Apprentices to Canada,
   1869–1924*, 2nd ed. (Toronto 1994)
6 Examples in women's history include Linda Gordon, *Heroes of Their Own Lives:
   The Politics and History of Family Violence: Boston, 1880–1960* (New York 1988);
   Constance Backhouse, *Petticoats and Prejudice: Women and Law in Nineteenth-
   Century Canada* (Toronto 1991); Wendy Mitchinson, *The Nature of Their Bodies:
   Women and Their Doctors in Victorian Canada* (Toronto 1991); and Karen Dubinsky, *Improper Advances: Rape and Heterosexual Conflict in Ontario, 1880–1929*
   (Chicago 1993).
7 Thanks to Jim Phillips, a workshop participant, for this and other insights.
8 Davis, *Fiction*; William Cronin, 'A Place for Stories: Nature, History, and Narrative,' *Journal of American History* 29 (1992); essays in this volume. On voice in oral
   history see Ronald J. Greele, ed., *Envelopes of Sound* (Chicago 1975); Sherna Gluck
   and Daphne Patai, eds, *Women's Words* (New York 1991); and Mary Crnovich, ed.,
   Gossip: A Spoken History of Women in the North (Ottawa 1990).
9 For example, E.P. Thompson, *The Making of the English Working Class* (London
   1963); Eric Hobsbawm, *Labouring Men* (London 1964); Michael Anderson, *Family
   Structure in Nineteenth-Century Lancashire* (Cambridge 1971); John R. Gillis, *Youth
   and History* (New York 1974); Herbert Gutman, *Work, Culture and Society in Indus-
   trializing America* (New York 1977); Louise A. Tilly and Joan W. Scott, *Women,
   Work and Family* (New York 1978); Raphael Samuel, *People's History and Socialist
   Theory* (London 1981); Tamara Hareven, *Family Time and Industrial Time* (New
   York 1982); Joan Kelly, *Women, History and Theory* (Chicago 1984); and Davis,
   Martin Guerre.
10 Early works include Gregory S. Kealey and Peter Warrian, eds, *Essays in Canadian
   Working-Class History, 1850–1985* (Toronto 1976); Susan Mann Trofimenkoff and
   Alison Prentice, eds, *The Neglected Majority: Essays in Canadian Women's History*,
   2 vols (Toronto 1977; 1985); Linda Kealey, ed., *A Not Unreasonable Claim: Women
   and Reform in Canada, 1880s–1920s* (Toronto 1979); Joy Parr, ed., *Childhood and
   Family in Canadian History* (Toronto 1982); Michael S. Cross and Gregory S. Kealey, eds, *Readings in Canadian Social History*, 5 vols (Toronto 1982–4).
11 Recent historiographical treatments of the now vast, and overlapping, literatures on

workers, women, and immigrants include Craig Heron, 'Towards Synthesis in Canadian Working-Class History: Reflections on Bryan Palmer's Rethinking,' *left history* 1 (1993); Heron, 'Working-Class History,' in Doug Owram, ed., *Canadian History: A Reader's Guide*, vol. 2 (Toronto 1994); and Gail Cuthbert Brandt, 'Postmodern Patchwork: Some Recent Trends in the Writing of Women's History in Canada,' *Canadian Historical Review* 72:4 (Dec. 1991); Wendy Mitchinson, 'Women's History,' in Owram, *Reader's Guide*; Diana Pedersen, ed., *Changing Women, Changing History*, 2nd ed. (Toronto 1992); and Franca Iacovetta, 'Manly Militants, Cohesive Communities, and Defiant Domestics: Writing about Immigrants in Canadian Historical Scholarship,' *Labour/Le Travail* 36 (Fall 1995). Earlier important works in family history include Parr, *Childhood and Family*; Bettina Bradbury, 'Pigs, Cows, and Boarders: Non-Wage Forms of Survival among Montreal Families, 1861–1891,' *Labour/Le Travail* 14 (1984); John Bullen, 'Hidden Workers: Child Labour and the Household Economy in Early Industrial Ontario,' *Labour/Le Travail* 18 (Fall 1986); and David Gagan, *Hopeful Travellers: Families, Land, and Social Change in Mid-Victorian Peel County, Canada West* (Toronto 1981); more recent studies are Bettina Bradbury, *Working Families: Age, Gender, and Daily Survival in Industrializing Montreal* (Toronto 1993); and Bradbury, ed., *Canadian Family History: Selected Readings* (Toronto 1993).

12 To take one example, crime, even a highly selective sample for the period 1970s–1990s, suggests the diversity of subjects and approaches: Rainer Baehre, 'Origins of the Penitentiary System in Upper Canada,' *Ontario History* 69:3 (Sept. 1977); H.J. Graff, 'Crime and Punishment in the Nineteenth Century: A New Look at the Criminal,' *Journal of Interdisciplinary History* 7:3 (Winter 1977); Paul Bennett, 'Taming "Bad Boys" of the "Dangerous Class": Child Rescue and Restraint at the Victoria Industrial School, 1887–1935,' *Histoire sociale/Social History* 21:41 (May 1988); Greg Marquis, 'Working Men in Uniform: The Early Twentieth Century Toronto Police,' *Histoire sociale/Social history* 20 (Nov. 1987); Judith Fingard, *The Dark Side of Life in Victorian Halifax* (Porter's Lake, NS, 1989); Carolyn Strange, *Toronto's Girl Problem: The Perils and Pleasures of the City, 1880–1930* (Toronto 1995); John Weaver, *Crimes, Constables and Courts: Order and Transgression in a Canadian City, 1816–1970* (Montreal and Kingston 1995).

13 A sample includes Stephen Speisman, 'Munificent Parsons and Municipal Parsimony: Voluntary vs Public Poor Relief in Nineteenth Century Toronto,' *Ontario History* 65:1 (1973); Judith Fingard, 'The Poor in Winter: Seasonality and Society in Pre-Industrial Canada,' in Cross and Kealey, *Canadian Social History* (1983); Veronica Strong-Boag, 'Wages for Housework: Mothers' Allowances and the Beginnings of Social Security in Canada,' *Journal of Canadian Studies* 14:1 (1979); Andrew Jones and Leonard Rutman, *In the Children's Aid: J.J. Kelso and Child Welfare in Ontario* (Toronto 1981); James Struthers, *No Fault of Their Own: Unemploy-*

ment Insurance and Public Policy (Montreal and Kingston 1988); Patricia Rooke and R.L. Schnell, *Discarding the Asylum: From Child Rescue to the Welfare State in English Canada* (Lanham, Md., 1983); Allan Moscovitch and Jim Albert, eds, *The 'Benevolent' State: The Growth of Welfare in Canada* (Toronto 1987); and Ruth Roach Pierson, 'Gender and Unemployment Insurance Debates in Canada, 1934–1940,' *Labour/Le Travail* 25 (Spring 1990).

14 On post-structuralism consider Bryan Palmer, *Descent into Discourse* (Philadelphia 1990); Mariana Valverde, 'Poststructuralist Gender Historians: Are We Those Names?' *Labour/Le Travail* 25 (Spring 1990); and Parr, 'Gender History.' On women's and gender history, the essays by Joan Sangster, Karen Dubinsky and Lynne Marks, and Franca Iacovetta and Linda Kealey, in *left history* 3:1 (Spring/Summer 1995) and 4 (Fall 1996); and the papers delivered by Nancy Forestell, Cecilia Morgan, Steven Maynard, and Madge Pon at 'Historians and the Politics of Masculinity' round table, Canadian Historical Association, St Catharines, June 1996. On Native agency, Mary Ellen Kelm and Robin Brownlie, 'Desperately Seeking Absolution: Native Agency and Colonialist Alibi?' and 'Responses [Douglas Cole and Jim Miller] and Reply,' in *Canadian Historical Review* 75 (Dec. 1994) and 76 (Dec. 1995).

15 For example, Michael Katz, *The People of Hamilton, Canada West: Family and Class in a Mid-Nineteenth-Century City* (Cambridge 1975); Louise Dechêne, *Habitants et marchands de Montréal au XVIIe siècle* (Paris 1974); Fernand Ouellet, *Histoire économique et sociale du Québec, 1760–1850* (Montreal 1966); Alan Greer, *Peasant, Lord and Merchant: Rural Society in Three Quebec Parishes, 1740–1840* (Toronto 1985); Allan Artibise, *Winnipeg: A Social History of Urban Growth 1874–1914* (Montreal and Kingston 1975); Bruno Ramirez, *On the Move: French Canadians and Italian Migrants in the North Atlantic Economy, 1860–1914* (Toronto 1991); T.W. Acheson, *Saint John: The Making of a Colonial Urban Community* (Toronto 1985); Margaret Conrad, ed., *They Planted Well: New England Planters in Maritime Canada* (Fredericton 1988); and Bruce Elliot, *Irish Migrants in the Canadas: A New Approach* (Montreal and Kingston 1988).

16 For example, James Snell, *In the Shadow of the Law: Divorce in Canada, 1900–1939* (Toronto 1991); Kathryn Harvey, 'To Love, Honour and Obey: Wife-Battering in Working-Class Montreal, 1869–79,' *Urban History Review* 19:2 (1990); Annalee Golz, '"If a Man's Wife Does Not Obey Him, What Can He Do?": Marital Breakdown and Wife Abuse in Late Nineteenth and Early Twentieth Century Ontario,' in Susan Binnie and Louis Knafla, eds, *Law, State and Society: Essays in Modern Legal History* (Toronto 1995).

17 Social histories of religion include George Rawlyk, *Ravished by the Spirit: Religious Revivals, Baptists, and Henry Alline* (Montreal and Kingston 1984); Marta Danylewycz, *Taking the Veil: An Alternative to Marriage, Motherhood, and Spinster-*

hood in Quebec, 1840–1920 (Toronto 1987); Ruth Compton Brouwer, *Women for God: Canadian Presbyterian Women and India Missions, 1876–1914* (Toronto 1990); and Lynne Marks, *Revivals and Roller Rinks: Religion, Leisure, and Identity in Late-Nineteenth-Century Small-Town Ontario* (Toronto 1996).

18 Studies revealing the poor treatment of Natives include Sarah Carter, *Lost Harvests: Prairie Indian Reserve Farmers and Government Policy* (Montreal and Kingston 1990); Jean Barman et al., eds, *Indian Education in Canada*, vol. 1 (Vancouver 1986); and J.R. Miller, ed., *Sweet Promises: A Reader on Indian–White Relations in Canada* (Toronto 1991).

19 The literatures on schooling and female suffrage are large: important works on Ontario education include Michael B. Katz and Paul Mattingly, eds, *Education and Social Change: Themes from Ontario's Past* (New York 1975); Alison Prentice, *The School Promoters: Education and Social Class in Mid-Nineteenth-Century Upper Canada* (Toronto 1977); Alison Prentice and Susan Houston, *Schooling and Scholars in Nineteenth-Century Ontario* (Toronto 1988); and Paul Axlerod, *Making a Middle Class: Student Life in English Canada during the Thirties* (Montreal and Kingston 1990); differing perspectives on suffrage include Veronica Strong-Boag, *The Parliament of Women: The National Council of Women* (Ottawa 1976); Carol Lee Bacchi, *Liberation Deferred? The Ideas of the English Canadian Suffragists, 1877–1918* (Toronto 1983); and Mariana Valverde, '"When the Mother of the Race Is Free": Race, Sexuality and Reproduction in First-wave Feminism,' in Franca Iacovetta and Mariana Valverde, eds, *Gender Conflicts* (Toronto 1992). On sabbatarianism and eugenics, consider Christopher Armstrong and H.V. Nelles, *The Revenge of the Methodist Bicycle Company: Sunday Streetcars and Municipal Reform in Toronto, 1888–1897* (Toronto 1977) and Angus McLaren, *Our Own Master Race: Eugenics in Canada, 1885–1945* (Toronto 1990), respectively. Works on prohibition include E.R. Forbes, 'Prohibition and Social Gospel in Nova Scotia,' *Acadiensis* 1 (1971); Wendy Mitchinson, 'The WCTU: For God, Home and Native Land. A Study in Nineteenth Century Feminism,' in Kealey, *A Not Unreasonable Claim*; Jan Noel, *Canada Dry* (Toronto 1995); and Sharon Ann Cook, *Through Sunshine and Shadow: The Woman's Christian Temperance Union, Evangelicalism, and Reform in Ontario, 1874–1930* (Montreal and Kingston 1995). The growing literature on prostitution includes John P.S. McLaren, 'Chasing the Social Evil: Moral Fervour and the Evolution of Canada's Prostitution Laws, 1867–1917,' *Canadian Journal of Law and Society* 1 (1986); and Andrée Lévesque, *La norme et les déviantes: Les Femmes au Québec pendant l'entre-deux-guerres* (Montreal 1989) (English trans. Y.M. Klein, Toronto 1994).

20 Influential texts include Philip Corrigan and Derek Sayer, *The Great Arch: English State Formation as Cultural Revolution* (Oxford 1985); Douglas Hay et al., eds, *Albion's Fatal Tree: Crime and Society in Eighteenth-Century England* (London

1974), especially Hay's essay; E.P. Thompson, *Whigs and Hunters: The Origins of the Black Act* (London 1975); Michel Foucault, *Discipline and Punish: The Birth of the Prison*, trans. A. Sheridan (London 1977); and his *The History of Sexuality*, vol. 1 (New York 1978). On Canada see Paul Craven, 'Law and Ideology: The Toronto Police Court, 1850–80,' in David Flaherty, ed., *Essays in the History of Canadian Law*, vol. 2 (Toronto 1983); Bruce Curtis, *Building the Educational State: Canada West, 1836–1871* (London 1988); Allan Greer and Ian Radforth, eds, *Colonial Leviathan: State Formation in Mid-Nineteenth-Century Canada* (Toronto 1992); and Mariana Valverde, ed., *Studies in Moral Regulation* (Toronto 1994).

21 Antonio Gramsci, *Letters from Prison*, trans. Lynne Lawner (New York 1973); L. Salamini, *The Sociology of Political Praxis: An Introduction to Gramsci's Theory* (London 1981)

22 Jeffrey Weeks's definition of discourse is 'a linguistic unity or group of statements which constitutes and delimits a specific area of concern, governed by its own rules of formation with its modes of distinguishing truth from falsity'; cited in Strange's essay in this volume.

23 Foucault, *Sexuality*; Valverde, 'Introduction,' *Moral Regulation*. See also Strange, *Toronto's Girl Problem*; Carol Smart, ed., *Regulating Motherhood: Historical Essays on Marriage, Motherhood and Sexuality* (London 1992); Dorothy Chunn, *From Punishment to Doing Good: Family Courts and Socialized Justice in Ontario* (Toronto 1992).

24 Canadian social histories of medicine include S.E.D. Shortt, ed., *Medicine in Canadian Society: Historical Perspectives* (Montreal 1981); Charles G. Roland, ed., *Health, Disease and Medicine: Essays in Canadian History* (Toronto 1984); Wendy Mitchinson and Janice Dickin McGinnis, eds, *Essays in the History of Canadian Medicine* (Toronto 1986); and Katherine Arnup et al., *Delivering Motherhood* (London and New York 1990).

25 Gordon, *Heroes of Their Own Lives*; Gordon ed., *Women, the State and Welfare* (Madison 1990); her 'Family Violence, Feminism and Social Control,' *Feminist Studies* 12 (Fall 1986)

26 Gordon, 'Social Control,' 454

27 Parr, 'Introduction'

28 See, for example, Joan Scott, *Gender and the Politics of History* (New York 1988); Denise Riley, *Uneven Developments: The Ideological Work of Gender in Mid-Victorian England* (Chicago 1988); Palmer, *Descent into Discourse*; the essays by Scott, Palmer, Gareth Stedman-Jones, and Christine Stansel, in *International Labour and Working-Class History* 31 (Spring 1987); the essays by Patrick Joyce, Geoff Eley and Keith Nield, and others in *Social History* 20:1 (Jan. 1995) and 20:3 (Oct. 1995); and essays by Kathleen Canning, Valverde, and others in *Signs* 19:2 (Summer 1994). A recent book that tries to clarify the different challenges to writing history is

Robert F. Berkhofer, Jr, *Beyond the Great Story: History as Text and Discourse* (Cambridge, Mass., 1995).

29 Regina Kunzel, 'Pulp Fiction and Problem Girls: Reading and Rewriting Single Pregnancy in the Postwar United States,' *American Historical Review* 100 (Dec. 1995)

30 While Scott claimed that such records could be understood only as linguistically constructed artefacts and meanings, Gordon argued that her files enabled her to recover the reformers' construction of domestic abuse and women's experience of violence. *Signs* 15:4 (Summer 1990). See also Dubinsky in this volume.

31 For example, Kunzel, 'Pulp Fiction'; her *Fallen Women, Problem Girls: Unmarried Mothers and the Professionalization of Social Work, 1890–1945* (New Haven and London 1993); Kathleen Canning, 'Feminist History after the Linguistic Turn: Historicizing Discourse and Experience,' *Signs* 19 (Winter 1994); Judith Walkowitz, *City of Dreadful Delight: Narratives of Sexual Danger in Late-Victorian London* (Chicago 1992); Strange, *Toronto's Girl Problem*; George Chauncey, *Gay New York* (New York 1994).

32 Jane Roland Martin, 'Methodological Essentialism, False Difference, and Other Dangerous Traps,' *Signs* 19:3 (Spring 1994), 636

33 See, for example, Bernard Cohn, 'History and Anthropology: The State of Play,' *Comparative Studies in Society and History* 22:2 (April 1980).

PART ONE
READING CASE FILES: CHALLENGES,
APPROACHES, METHODS

1

Stories of Their Lives: The Historian and the Capital Case File

CAROLYN STRANGE

There are two kinds of tales, one true and one false.

Socrates, in *The Republic*

Every word of this memoir is true.

James Ellroy, 'Dick Contino's Blues,' *Granta* 46 (Winter 1994)

True-crime writers establish their legitimacy simply by asserting the veracity of their stories, no matter how much they alter them through artistic licence. In contrast, criminal justice historians rarely proclaim that 'every word' in our 'stories' is 'true.' Ironically, making such claims would make readers suspicious. Instead, we qualify our interpretations with caveats about the incompleteness of the records, the biases of our sources, and (when we are honest) our own peculiar selection priorities. Even if we do not consider ourselves chroniclers of the truth, we state at least some things with confidence: person X really did kill person Y, and newspaper Z really wrote a column about it. Professional historians underline their commitment as truth tellers by planting footnotes that flag our journeys into the past. Should anyone care to question our claims, they need only tread the same ground.

Recently historians' flirtation with post-structuralist theory has left us considerably more reluctant to make even the most modest truth claims about the past.[1] Unlike Socrates, who philosophized that true stories could be distinguished from false ones, many historians, along with scholars in other disciplines, have their doubts. Indeed, the interest of post-structuralists in discourse over 'facts' is based on the assumption that trying to distinguish falsehood from veracity is not only fruitless but meaningless.[2]

In spite of these intellectual anxieties, historians' hearts still race when we uncover intriguing historical evidence, particularly what has previously been overlooked. Capital case files offer an example. These dossiers of legal evidence, maintained by the federal justice department and rigorously organized by the National Archives of Canada, document the fate of persons sentenced to death. As a historical data set, the case files inspire certitude: not only is the collection remarkably complete (ranging from 1867 to 1976, when capital punishment was abolished), but the vast majority of case files include all the information they were meant to contain about condemned persons: trial transcripts, judges' reports, justice department evaluations, and cabinet decisions. Individuals' files tell the stories both of those whose sentences were commuted and those who perished on the gallows. Remarkably few Canadian researchers have mined this rich vein of evidence (although several writers and film-makers have focused on noteworthy cases, such as those of Valentine Shortiss, Louisa Blake, Angelina Napolitano, and Leo Mantha, to say nothing of Louis Riel).[3] Encountering this evidence is like being dropped on the peak of a mountain blanketed in snow: these are records that historians dream of ploughing through.

I want to explore my own encounter with this evidence and to build on my experience of studying capital cases records to reflect on the confidence-inspiring nature of these files. As I will argue, it is tempting to believe that file contents represent the 'true' stories of people condemned to death. After all, they include not only official records, such as coroners' reports, but a range of material, including newspaper editorials, photographs, and letters and petitions. Compared to most other types of case files, they are amazingly rich in qualitative evidence, and as such they seem to be stories waiting to be written. Yet they are much more than raw material for 'true crime' stories. Reading the files as transparent tales of crime and punishment may satisfy our urge to construct coherent narratives, but it leaves critical methodological questions unaddressed. *How* should they be read? How much remains unknown? Most important, how was the information in the files interpreted and manipulated by historical actors who wielded the power to spare or execute people sentenced to death?

No one method could adequately analyse capital cases. Quantitative methodologies, such as Eric Sager discusses in this volume, allow us to evaluate broad trends, such as offenders' likelihood of execution based on their race, sex, class, age, and so forth.[4] But qualitative methodologies are more appropriate if we want to know how truth was asserted, disputed, and adjudicated in capital case dispositions. Cultural historians and scholars influenced by post-structuralist literary theory work with tools of textual analysis in order to question how apparently 'true' facts and events are constructed through language.[5] What does this mean for those studying case files? Approaching file contents as 'text,' we can see more than words or pictures on paper: we can analyse how meanings were organized and, furthermore, how meanings informed social action.[6] Capital case files are tangled texts, some recognizably modern (notably medical and psychiatric assessments) and others (juridical, religious, confessional) linked to long-established practices.[7] In this jumble were competing claims to the truth about convicted criminals. Sorting them out through case deliberations resulted in decisions either to hang or to commute. Unlike trials, in which the prosecution and the defence presented two opposing versions of cases, the post-conviction phase, in which the executive decided whether or not to let the law take its course, allowed a wide variety of claimants to introduce knowledge about events and characters. In this sense, the capital case file can be approached as a textual artefact of *competing* truths – multiple, discordant interpretations of condemned persons' lives.

To illustrate the merits of exploring case files' 'textuality' I will focus on one case, which in some respects is typical and in others unique. The circumstances leading up to the murder, a single woman's unwanted pregnancy, were depressingly common in early-twentieth-century Canada, where abortion was illegal and even information about birth control was prohibited. The fact that Mary Dolan and her paramour, Thomas McNulty, a married man, resorted to infanticide was certainly an atypical solution for persons in their predicament. Yet they were hardly the only ones in early-twentieth-century Ontario to consider it an option.[8] What made the case unusual was that both were convicted and sentenced to death for the full capital offence (rather than the lesser offence of concealment of birth).[9] Both received commuted life sentences – a less startling outcome given that no executions for infanticide had taken place since the mid-nineteenth century.[10]

If we want to understand how this case turned out as it did, we need to listen intently to the stories of the convicted persons' lives as they were told and retold by different narrators – some formal and authoritative, and others, without official standing, eloquent in their humility and awkwardness. Although we can gain an impression of how the case was decided, we still cannot speak with assurance about why it followed its particular course. Accordingly, we will not conclude with a definitive evaluation of the truths and lies of this 'he said, she said' crime. We can never satisfactorily penetrate the minds of the accused, but we can tune our ears to the many voices that struggled to be heard. In the process we can suggest why some stories about the crime and the defendants were considered truthful, while others were disbelieved or suppressed.

The Capital Case File as a Historian's Dream

Paradoxically, capital case files are first and foremost life stories. The official purpose of the capital case file was to provide the governor-general with a paper trail to help him (on the advice of cabinet) to decide who among the condemned would die and who would live. With the formation of a federal union in 1867, the national government assumed jurisdiction over criminal legal matters, including the review of every capital conviction in the provinces. Justice ministers (usually the prime minister himself in the first few decades of Confederation) were assigned the task of reviewing the records of each case to determine whether or not the royal prerogative of mercy was warranted. Since each person's fate was decided on a case-by-case basis, establishing a minimum standard of evidence rendered decision making marginally systematic. Justice Department regulations stipulated that before a decision could be made by the governor-general-in-council, several reports had to be sent to Ottawa: a verbatim transcript of the trial, the convicting judge's trial report, and his account impressions of the penalty's deservedness.

Even if case files contained nothing more than these required items they would be a boon to criminal-justice research. Few full trial transcripts have survived for any crimes other than capital ones; furthermore, judges' summaries and reports to the minister of justice dropped legalese in favour of full-blown narrative, often expressed in a conversational tone. Stripped of their stiffness, these statements seemingly lay bare the 'real' feelings of men who had no choice but to pronounce the death penalty, but who sometimes expressed personal reservations about its appropriateness for particular offenders. For historians resigned to making do with fragmentary sources, sources this rich understandably make us feel as if we have hit the jackpot of truth.

Aside from these required items the capital case file was a magnet for other texts that were produced incidently rather than in response to administrative directives. It was common for the Department of Justice to be sent coroners' reports and police accounts of prior criminal records. Coroners had wide latitude in questioning witnesses about the habits and relations of deceased persons and their suspected killers. More than accounts of death, capital case files provide portraits of both the victim and the accused in life. The great majority of killers were at least acquainted with, if not closely related to, their victims. At the turn of the century, as now, most people killed family members, lovers, friends, acquaintances, and peers. Police reports submitted after the conviction also provide background material that would have been dismissed as hearsay at the trial stage.

By the late nineteenth century, psychiatric assessments began to appear as well. In most cases, they were ordered by the Crown if prosecutors suspected that insanity might warrant a commutation. Only in the early twentieth century, as the criminal defence bar gradually professionalized, did defence lawyers begin to throw their resources into psychiatric evaluations of their clients.

Although psychiatrists deployed a professional, scientific discourse they did not always agree with each other, particularly when they were hired by legal adversaries. Thus, even those who operated within the same truth-seeking discourses could utter different truths.

As new medical and psychiatric experts took over from phrenologists and anthropometrists, they claimed to hold superior means of determining the truth about defendants' motivations. By the 1910s, psychiatrists began to make regular appearances in the post-trial phase as their profession grew in status. Their expertise rested on claims that they could uncover underlying causes of criminality, including degeneracy, alcoholism, religious mania, or pathological jealousy.[11] Not surprisingly, the growing professionalization of these truth assessors meant case file contents grew as well. Positioning themselves above the police, coroners, and jurors, psychiatrists typically asserted that they alone could explain why accused persons *really* committed crimes.

Petitions from relatives and concerned citizens offered compelling stories, albeit tales lacking the official cachet of judicial officers' and professionals' reports. Petitions were appeals for the life of the convicted person whose personal history (unfortunate, unremarkable, or exemplary) offered explanations for the crime and rationales for mercy. They came from everyone imaginable: ten-year-olds who wrote piteous, scrawled letters begging for their father to be released; prominent businessmen and clergy who lent their extravagant signatures to formally worded appeals; 'sob sisters' who could not bear to see handsome young men hanged; devout Christians who called upon the government to act mercifully; members of ethnic minorities who were desperate to protect one of their own from state violence; and feminists who called on men to act chivalrously toward women defendants. Petitions could be organized, containing up to tens of thousands of signatures, or they could be hastily written personal letters, naively addressed to the governor-general or the king. No matter what their form, they never reached the eyes of the monarch or his representative; unbeknownst to most petitioners, other than Crown and defence lawyers, they were processed along with the rest of the Ministry of Justice's correspondence. Nevertheless, all petitions, no matter what their source or form, eventually found their way into capital case files (sometimes filling several boxes).

Petitions can be read as counter-narratives set against the dominant narrative of conviction and condemnation.[12] To be successful, petitions for mercy had to reveal compelling truths about a condemned person's life. In some cases, casting aspersions on the victim's character helped to construct the defendant as a worthy recipient of mercy. Every petition attempted to alert the executive to something missed in the trial – either inadvertently, owing to a poor defence, or on account of strict rules of evidence. Petitions expressed an intuitive, subjective version of truth that could not be recognized formally at the trial stage. Here again the case files permit us to see beyond official courtroom evidence to the family background, medical conditions, money problems, mental aberrations, or good character of the condemned. Trials determined legal guilt or innocence, but petitions sought higher truths.

Case reports prepared for the minister of justice were unlike any other documents in the files because they summarized the file contents, including the nature and number of petitions received. The ministry section responsible for administering capital cases was the Remissions Branch, and its chief officer prepared summaries for the minister's and cabinet's review. In effect, these reports allow us to peep through the keyhole of the cabinet doors, even if we cannot throw them open. The remissions reports followed narrative conventions patterned after case-disposition protocols developed by the Home Office, the branch that dealt with capital cases in England.

In Canada these practices were upheld by Augustus Power, a lawyer and the first chief remissions officer in the Department of Justice. He headed the branch from the 1890s to the 1910s, eventually retiring in 1914. He put his personal stamp on the protocol that, for decades, would govern the preparation of reports to the minister of justice. Each remission officer's report began with a précis of the trial, setting the cast of victim, accused, lawyers, judges, and other actors, including petitioners, doctors, police officers, accused persons, and any other parties whose wishes and actions came to the attention of the ministry. After summarizing the trial transcript (the official story of crime and guilt), remissions officers introduced the judge's rendition of that same story, complete with his subjective assessment of witnesses' veracity, his interpretation of the accused's willingness or reluctance to testify, the quality of the defence, and his impression of the convicted person's moral responsibility. Judges' impressions of the trial and the condemned person were always highlighted in remissions reports since judges offered both expert knowledge of the law as well as their personal sentiments about culpability. In their private transmissions to the ministry, judges felt free to be opinionated, dismissing some killers as vicious while urging sympathy for prisoners whom they believed to be victims of circumstance. In the end, though, the report was a meta-narrative that combined elements from all the documents but positioned itself above them all. Remissions officers' reports were more than summary statements: they textually reconstituted each case into a form designed to guide the minister to execute or commute.

Reading capital case files this way hints that it might be possible to determine why the executive decided to hang some and spare others. But let us not forget cabinet privilege. The executive was resolutely tight-lipped when reporters,

Witnesses at Louis Riel's trial. (Archives of the History of Canadian Psychiatry and Mental Health Services, Griffin-Greenland slides, 1X-6)

petitioners, lawyers, and the condemned themselves pressed them to disclose how they reached their decisions. As a matter of unswerving policy, ministers of justice refused to explain why they decided to commute or execute decisions.[13] By comparing remissions officers' recommendations to the ultimate decision announced by ministers of justice we can see that cabinets rarely contradicted bureaucrats' suggested course of action. But we will never know why.

The Dilemma of Plenitude (or, the Capital Case File as a Historian's Nightmare)

Ironically, the richness and relative completeness of capital case files presents a problem: how to analyse so much data? what to exclude? One obvious solution to the dilemma of plenitude is to subject data to quantitative analysis. The National Archives of Canada has made this prospect more attractive by creating a data set of capital case files contents in DBase4 format. This makes it possible to generalize about a wide range of characteristics, including offenders' and victims' gender, age, race, occupation, marital status, and religion.[14] In addition, one can chart trends over time regarding different judges' conviction records, the jurisdictions in which offences took place, the types of weapons used, and the apparent motives for murders. With a data set of 1533 cases, and from eight to fifteen codable characteristics, quantitative analysis permits historians to determine changing trends both in the administration of justice and in the profile of relationships between victims and offenders. Quantitative analysis also allows us to contextualize individual cases. Thus far the most ambitious analyses of this nature have been conducted by Kenneth Avio, who has convincingly demonstrated that offenders' gender, ethnicity, and status, along with victim-offender relationships and the circumstances of the crime, swayed cabinets towards mercy or severity.[15]

Like any methodology, quantitative analysis has its pitfalls. Aside from the usual concerns about the reliability of the data and the appropriateness of specific statistical techniques, there is the seductiveness of numbers. Statistical sciences evolved in the same positivistic climate that gave rise to the case file method: both seek out facts and categorize, describe, and analyse them to determine truth. In statistics, numbers count: 'only the repetition of a particular social fact, its multiple occurrences, can give it meaning.' As François Ewald contends, 'the more frequently a particular sort of event occurs statistically, the more real it becomes ... Inversely, a single exceptional event counts for less in statistical terms because it occurs so rarely.'[16] Although statisticians do not necessarily examine facts as if they have 'no cause, or past, or future,' as Ewald claims they do, it is certainly true that data analysis can easily be skewed, both consciously and unconsciously, to produce spurious results. For instance, generalizations about long-term trends regarding capital case dispositions are always suspicious because information in late-nineteenth-century files is considerably sketchier than in mid-twentieth-century files.[17] Kenneth Avio has criticized quantitative studies that focus on one or two characteristics (such as gender or age) rather than engaging in multivariate analysis. The more sophisticated the analysis, the more reliable the results, but even Avio issues a caveat: '[T]he nature of the research requires scoring variables which are qualitative and, in certain instances, subject to personal interpretation.'[18] Given that people lived or died on the basis of these 'subjective' decisions, this is a telling warning indeed.

As much as quantitative analysis may paint a broad canvas of capital crime and justice, it can obscure the most compelling features of the files. Take motive. Many of the cases in the National Archives data set include entries under this category – motives such as jealousy, robbery, or the acquisition of insurance money. If we piece together the data, we can construct mini-narratives: nineteen-year-old William Bennett shot Bruce Leitch out of jealousy; twenty-year-old Frank McCullough shot a police constable in an 'attempt to escape'; showman Sidney Murrell, aged twenty-six, shot a man in the context of committing a bank robbery; Catherine Hawryluk, an eighteen-year-old, murdered her newborn twins.[19] In each of these cases, the motive is either stated or implied in the files. But what would we gain by quantifying motive? First, in recording motive from the transcript or the Remissions Branch report, we accept the official version of the case: the convicted person not only committed the act, but for *this* reason as opposed to others. Second, what do we learn by discovering that a young woman killed her newborns, or that a man was jealous of his former girlfriend's new husband? Can we pretend to get inside the head of a killer, let alone generalize about murderers' motivations? Is jealousy interpreted differently (by the principals, the court, the jury, the press, and the cabinet) when expressed by Aboriginals, Euro-Canadians, or Asians, or when manifested in men, as opposed to women? Are the rape-murderer's motivations assessed differently by a parish priest in 1872 than by a government psychologist in 1956? These questions are not meant to imply that we should abandon quantitative analysis, but that it is more appropriate to analyse evidence about which little doubt can be entertained, such as the identity of convicting judge, the time and place of the crime, the murder weapon, and the final case outcome.

Finally, quantitative methods lead us no closer than do qualitative approaches to solving the greatest mystery of all: the motives of cabinet members. We can say that, on balance, the executive discriminated in racist, classist, and ethnocentric ways. Yet these patterns were produced over years of ad hoc decisions made by a constantly shifting cast of men from different political parties, operating in the context of changing economic, political, and cultural circumstances. Examining specific cases is the only way to place a finer mesh over the statistical matrix of general tendencies. It is the closest we can come to understanding why and how cabinet members made life-and-death decisions.

The Textual Production of Truth

Wringing meanings from case files calls for alternative interpretive strategies. Qualitative methodologies are better suited to explore how 'facts' are distinguished from 'fiction' in textual forms. Using textual analysis, one can approach capital case files not only as material artefacts but as a discursive means of organizing knowledge and producing meaning.[20] File contents allow historians to trace how various players attributed meanings to particular aspects of cases, both those that emerged during trials and those previously undisclosed. In documenting deliberations over the fate of the condemned, case files recorded how discordance erupted between competing voices, each claiming to speak the truth about this person, this crime, and this punishment. Executive review seldom questioned trial verdicts, but it always involved arbitrating between opposing constructions of the truth and their relevance to the critical question: Should this condemned person live or die?

Before the 1940s no rules existed to help ministers decide whom to hang and whom to spare. However, in practice, Canadian cabinets generally rubber-stamped bureaucratic recommendations. The federal justice bureaucracy in turn followed precedents set in England. The English Royal Commission on Capital Punishment in 1867 had suggested that persons whom judges had recommended to mercy would normally be suitable subjects for commutation, and bureaucrats in the ministry adopted this guideline in Canada as well. In addition, rules of thumb operated on an informal basis. For instance, the very young, the very old, mentally deranged people, and pregnant women were typically spared the gallows. Aside from these exceptions, however, remissions officers operated according to the principle that each case was to be determined on its own merits. Consequently, the official interpretation of competing truth claims in case files literally spelled the difference between life and death.

The bureaucrat who collated the various documents in the files, and who prepared a summary report based on his evaluations of their contents, occupied a critical position as an arbiter of truth. Like a character in a Dickens novel, Augustus Power QC was aptly named for his role in the tragedies and comedies of capital case reviews during his long tenure as Canada's chief remissions officer. He and his underlings in the Remissions Branch of the Department of Justice were rarely overruled by cabinets unless enormous political pressure swayed the government in a contrary direction. Ministers of justice rarely read more than the remissions officer's report, and cabinet colleagues generally supported the ministers' recommendations. The remissions officer's report, then, was the most important document in case files because it summarized the other texts received in the period between sentencing and scheduled execution. More important, it positioned itself *above* the other materials through its authoritative claims to objectivity. In other words, this practice of summary report-writing was a means through which many voices, often in opposition, were reduced to one voice in a coherent case narrative.

Power and his associate officers were trained lawyers well versed in the legal matters discussed in transcripts and judges' reports. Stylistically, their reports were more than mere summaries of evidence and judges' impressions; rather they were legal texts that tied disparate narrative strands into an epitome. In these tales of crime and appropriate punishment, remissions officers' recommendations for or against mercy represented the punch line – the moral of the story. As we will see in the cases of Mary Dolan and Thomas McNulty, however, punch lines did not necessarily bring stories to an end.

Love, Betrayal, and Murder

On 7 December 1910 Augustus Power prepared a memorandum for Alan Aylesworth, the Dominion minister of justice, concerning the case of Mary Dolan, a young unmarried woman who was scheduled to hang a week later for the murder of her infant son.[21] The memorandum opened by stating her name, her crime, and the place and time of her conviction, then it quickly branched out in reference to the case of her co-accused, the man whom she claimed had fathered the child. The opening précis proceeded to mention that both the jury and judge had recommended mercy, the judge so enthusiastically that he 'took the somewhat unusual course of telling [the accused] that he agreed with the recommendation of the Jury.' Thus, before Aylesworth had finished the first paragraph, Augustus Power drew his attention to the judge's and jury's depiction of Dolan as a pitiable creature.

In fact, the memorandum regarding the Dolan case is atypical because the Crown and the defence essentially agreed that the defendant had committed the crime. The evidence was clear that the child was Dolan's, and that she had intentionally killed it, albeit under pressure from her married lover. The 'unlawful intimacy' between the twenty-four-year-old servant, the daughter of a respectable farmer, and Thomas McNulty, a forty-year-old tavern keeper, had undoubtedly inspired gossip in the small town of Orillia for years. In her confession to the murder, Dolan admitted that McNulty had earlier fathered another child, and that he had sent her to Buffalo to have it, forcing her to give it up for adoption. When she became pregnant again in the fall of 1909, she claimed that he had forced her to hide in an unheated barn, supplying her with barely enough food and water to live. Closer to her confinement, he sent her to a Toronto midwife, but he refused to give her the money necessary to dispatch their baby to an infants' home. In fact, he had suggested that she abandon the infant in Toronto; when she refused, he told her to do away with their son. Distraught, she took a train to Orillia on 26 March 1910, proceeded to a secluded area, and strangled her two-week-old son. After wrapping him in a blanket stuffed with rocks, she tossed the bundle over a bridge. Had fishermen not found the gruesome remains in a river four months later, she might never have been apprehended. But the open secret of the Dolan–McNulty affair soon put the spotlight on the couple.

Two highly experienced trial lawyers, T.C. Robinette for the defence and George T. Blackstock for the Crown, argued the case. The men conducted the trial amiably, as if it were a gentlemen's disagreement rather than an adversarial battle. Blackstock adopted an apologetic demeanour, openly expressing his concern that the men of the jury not consider that he enjoyed his role as prosecutor:

'It is my painful duty ... to lay before you one of the saddest and most distressing cases that it has ever been my misfortune to come into contact with. [And]
that, I am sure, will test your manhood and our feelings to the utmost limit.'
Urging the jurymen to rise above their 'profound sympathy for this poor young
girl,' he reminded them of their 'higher duty' to uphold the norms of a civilized
community. True, she was young and apparently guileless, but she had confessed that she had strangled the life out of her baby.[22]

T.C. Robinette, who had travelled from Toronto to Barrie to take on the case
pro bono, faced the task of defending a woman who had freely confessed to
murder. The wily Robinette had squeaked out of tighter corners than this in his
illustrious career.[23] His strategy was to complement Blackstock's characterization of the defendant by portraying her as a woman who had loved too much.
She had sinned, surely, but she had been forced by her cruel lover to destroy the
life she had yearned to nurture. Always on the cutting edge of medico-legal
knowledge, Robinette suggested that Dolan had been clinically depressed. Perhaps she was suffering the effects of 'puerperal insanity' (what we would now
term post-partum depression)? Maybe she was epileptic?[24] Ultimately Robinette emphasized that the case called for judgment based not on facts, but character: her lover, older and married, had abused her to hide his dishonourable
affair; unable to seek counsel for fear of exposing her shame, she reluctantly
obeyed his orders. According to the defence, this was not so much a crime as
the familiar, sad story of the woman scorned.

Pressed by Blackstock to do their duty, the jurymen decided that they had to
render a guilty verdict. However, their 'very strong recommendation to mercy'
enhanced Dolan's portrait as the weak puppet of an evil master. No doubt her
fainting spells on the stand lent theatrical flair to this courtroom drama. Judge
Britton, as Augustus Power later commented, took the extraordinary step of
endorsing the jury recommendation in open court. 'You went astray, but you
have paid very dearly for your moments of pleasure,' Britton commiserated
with Dolan. Echoing Blackstock's discomfort over prosecuting a woman on a
capital charge, Britton added that he too found the prospect of executing a
woman distressing. Pronouncing the death sentence was never agreeable, he
admitted, 'but it is the first time I have had the pain put upon me of passing sentence upon one of your sex.'[25] If the trial had not already staged the case as a
heterosexual melodrama, Britton's summation reminded the audience that gender relations would play a critical role in the post-trial phase. Distressed by the
prospect of hanging a woman (an event that had not occurred in Canada for
eleven years at that point), Britton, the jury, counsel, and spectators assumed
that the all-male executive would exercise its discretion to commute Dolan's
death sentence.[26]

The nineteenth-century psychiatrist at work. Dr A.H. Beaton in his office at the Orillia (Ontario) Asylum. (Archives of the History of Canadian Psychiatry and Mental Health Services, Griffin-Greenland slides, 8-0031)

Augustus Power's memorandum for the minister of justice reinforced these expectations of mercy. Unusual in its exclusion of counter-narratives, Power's report stitched together fragments from letters, police reports, petitions, and the trial transcript to compose a straightforward recommendation for mercy. In this most authoritative rendering of the tale, Mary Dolan's case was, according to Power, a 'pathetic' story of an 'unfortunate girl' who was more 'sinned against than sinning,' as she had been 'very heartlessly treated' by her paramour. Although Power typically cited his sources to establish critical distance between himself and the opinions of others, his reading of this case cohered so closely with that of Dolan's supporters that he freely plagiarized. One of the letters Power sampled had been sent by Mrs Blanche Johnson, the editor of the WCTU Sunday School quarterly and the Dominion Superintendent of the Salvation Army Rescue and Prison Board. Shortly after Dolan's trial she had written the minister of justice: 'I have visited this pitiful and broken-hearted creature [in jail] and while she has sinned previously she has been deeply sinned against.' In another letter on Dolan's behalf, a Vancouver shingle manufacturer surmised that she had been 'under the influence of a vicious man ... Was there ever a more pitiful case in the history of the Canadian Courts?'[27] In adopting these interpretations of the case as his own, rather than inserting them as quotes, Power legitimated their claim that McNulty ('who is a man about twice her age and the father of a family,' he added gratuitously) had been the guiltier party. Thus, executive-style justice could achieve what the judge and jury were not allowed: the opportunity to arrive at a more richly contextualized truth than evidentiary rules allowed.

Although the remissions officer's memorandum was distinguished in this case by the absence of counter-narratives, Power nonetheless discriminated tellingly in his sampling of texts and arguments. Competing truth claims circulated in the file and none but the story of the poor, sinned-against creature surfaced in the official report. Absent, for instance, were selections from a letter sent to the minister of justice by a correspondent who called herself 'Portia.' In her eyes, executing Dolan would be unjust, not because she was duped by a man, but because she did not deserve to be granted special consideration: '[S]he only did what thousands & thousands of other women have done only they did not wait so long. Every one knows that the birth rate both among married & unmarried women of all classes is suppressed & if every woman who has committed the same crime as Mary Dolan with so much less reason were hanged, there would be grave fears of exterminating the race altogether.' Waxing bolder, Portia uttered the words that may have been whispered in chambers and parlours, and sniggered in bar-rooms and farmers' fields: 'Is the child not better dead?' In Portia's eyes, Mary Dolan had effectively nipped an unpromising bud from an already-weak branch. In her estimation, 'children born under such unfortunate conditions are more likely than not to propagate a race of either weaklings or criminals.' This pseudo-scientific assertion, reinforced by medical reports of Dolan's defence of mental and physical weakness, failed to surface in Power's memorandum. For Power, conventional melodramatic tropes of seduced maidens and manipulative villains evidently rang truer than more modern, medicalized rationales for mercy. In any event, the cabinet agreed that this was a case for commutation to life in prison.

Over the course of the following four years further reports about Dolan's health were produced but her moral fitness, more than her physical and emotional condition, became the focus. Although Power's memorandum and the cabinet's merciful decision seemed to end the story, it opened up the possibilities for new stories to emerge. Throughout the period when the death penalty was still applied, commuted life sentences were more symbolic than literal because executive decisions are always subject to subsequent executive review. Friendless, poverty-stricken prisoners, and people who spoke neither French nor English tended to languish the longest; in contrast, imprisoned murderers who were supported by tireless advocates rarely spent more than ten years behind bars. Evidence of serious illness often prompted favourable reviews of commuted sentences.[28] In Dolan's case, medical reports of her epilepsy and lady prison visitors' repeated assurances of her penitence convinced the ministry that three years' detention would suffice. In support of a bid to secure her early release, the prison chaplain at the Kingston Penitentiary lent an archetypal Christian gloss to her tale of sin and redemption: 'a very Magdalen and like her prototype, [she] has long since fallen on her knees at the Divine Master's feet.'[29] On Christmas Eve, 1913, three years after having her death sentence commuted to life in prison, Dolan received an early Christmas present: she was granted an unconditional release on a ticket of leave.[30]

Villain or Victim?

Where did that leave the heartless McNulty? The alleged mastermind of the infanticide plot was tried directly after Dolan in the same courtroom by the same jury. Robinette's assistant in the Dolan trial, Melville B. Tudhope, pitched in – not for the defence this time, but for the Crown! Having reluctantly prosecuted the young woman, Blackstock warmed to his task of hauling in the bigger catch. Once again, Dolan was the star witness, only this time her testimony damned her former lover. Rather than trying to pretend that McNulty and Dolan had not been intimate, McNulty's defence lawyer, A.E.H. Creswicke, suggested she had doled out sexual favours to half the male population of Orillia. Under dogged cross-examination Dolan feebly demurred, claiming that she had loved only this one man. With this statement, she fainted again and required medical attention.

Unlike Dolan, McNulty did not testify on his own behalf; instead, his case hinged on branding Dolan as a liar and a harlot, willing to drag her paramour down with her. Besides, Dolan had admitted that she, not McNulty, had strangled the baby. Unfortunately for McNulty, the jury had listened intently when Judge Britton charged them that counselling to murder is legally the equivalent of committing murder: they convicted him, adding a recommendation for mercy.[31] Britton's earlier sympathy toward Dolan, the woman he had reluctantly sentenced to death, evaporated when he came to sentence McNulty. 'I advise you to hold out no hope of a reprieve,' he grimly counselled the condemned man.

Power's Remissions Branch memorandum regarding McNulty's death sentence, written the same day as his memorandum regarding Dolan's report, was legalistic rather than sentimental. Had he maintained the script he recounted in

Dolan's report, with McNulty cast as the primary player, recommending him to mercy would have seemed anomalous. Yet Power did recommend that McNulty be spared. '[H]owever abhorrent the prisoner's conduct appears to be,' he confided to the minister of justice, 'I confess that I should have the utmost hesitation in recommending that the extreme penalty be allowed to be inflicted on the unsupported evidence of the girl.'[32] During the trial, Power argued, emotions had been heated and McNulty had been convicted by men overcome with sympathy toward Dolan. Her fainting spells, her tales of confinement in an unheated barn, McNulty's betrayal of his wife and children – each of these factors tugged on the jurymen's heartstrings, drowning out the judge's warning about convicting without corroboration. Cued by Power's report, the executive could deliberate with cooler heads and commute his sentence, as they did one week before his scheduled execution. Power redrafted a highly charged melodrama, featuring a duped maiden and an evil villain, into a dry argument about trial procedure and rules of evidence. McNulty's story had been rewritten from a tale of moral fall into a straightforward legal text.

Although McNulty's trial was marred by irregularities, it was a tightly scripted event rather than a forum for improvisation. Trials close off possibilities: only certain actors (lawyers, witnesses, the foreman of the jury, and the judge) are allowed to speak, and they are bound to speak in predetermined, even arcane, ways. Jurors are instructed that they must choose between a limited number of options in rendering their verdicts, and if they fail to agree they are warned against improvising alternative verdicts. Finally, capital statutes in this period required judges to pass the death sentence against those found guilty. As Lawrence Douglas puts it, Western legal discourse has been intolerant of 'moral ambiguity and situational complexity.'[33] In marked contrast to the reliance of trials on rational-legal adjudication, post-commutation deliberation allowed new narrative possibilities. Anyone, no matter how humble, could scratch an 'X' on a petition. Petitioners who supplied their signatures wrote with greater confidence, and people who wrote on fancy letterhead, or who comfortably addressed the minister of justice as 'my dear Allen' were even better positioned to influence case outcomes. Dolan had charitable women, medical doctors, and prison chaplains on her side. But McNulty had his supporters too.

Once commutations were granted, narrative coherence, temporarily anchored in Remissions Branch reports, could break down under the influence of petitioners' protests. McNulty, whose adultery and entanglement in a premeditated murder had stirred his neighbours into moral outrage, was to benefit from the circulation of new truth claims. The McNulty family managed to secure a lawyer who offered a version of the crime that had not fully flowered in court. McNulty, in Thomas Mulcahy's words, was 'more *led* than *leading*, the evidence to the contrary notwithstanding.'[34] To advance his client's interests, he recognized that he first had to erase Dolan's sketch as a woman 'more sinned against than sinning.'

Petitioners' assertions, unlike courtroom arguments, required no substantiating evidence; instead, they produced new stories. At the mitigation stage of case disposition, narratives are spun to stress subjective truths. In Robyn West's words, 'stories expand our knowledge not only of objective history, but also of what is inaccessible, the subjective life of the other.'[35] Thus, petitioning storytellers reinterpreted evidence in an effort to substitute happier conclusions for otherwise sombre endings.

As an 'oppositional storyteller,' McNulty's lawyer, Thomas Mulcahy, petitioned for his client's release in the fall of 1914. Casting his request as a plea for Christian mercy, Mulcahy wrote the new minister of justice, Charles Doherty, a revised version of McNulty's story, complete with new cast members. He dismissed Dolan as a 'bad woman,' contrasting her with the new tragic star: the noble and self-sacrificing Mrs McNulty, the loving wife who yearned for her husband's release. Mulcahy implied that she would 'die of a broken heart' if the prisoner were not released by Christmas. The trial and three years' imprisonment had taught McNulty his lesson, but he could only prove his redemption if he were released and restored to his natural role as husband, father, and provider. In other words, Mulcahy tried to rescript the case as a story of a happy family torn asunder by a 'bad woman.' The illegitimate baby and his murder all but disappeared from the narrative frame of reference.

Mulcahy had already laid the groundwork for this redrafting a year earlier. His aim at that stage had been to demonstrate that sentiment among respectable folk had swung decidedly toward the man and away from the woman. As other historians of justice and mercy have observed, the condemned and the incarcerated have always been best served by elite advocates or people, at the very least, with claims to respectability.[36] Mulcahy followed this ancient tradition and chose his petitioners carefully, gathering signatures from 87 of Orillia's approximately 120 businessmen. 'None of them,' Mulcahy emphasized, 'are engaged in business other than as principals. No clerks or subordinates appear thereon. To put it clearly, the men whose names are there are the thinking business element of our community.'

Gentlemen of discernment were selected to lend an air of credibility to McNulty's revamped story, but the ploy initially failed to sway the executive, who in 1912 were still preoccupied with Dolan's ailments. Once they released her in 1913, however, the injustice of McNulty's continued imprisonment became a local cause in Orillia (and a matter of interest to Stephen Leacock, who lobbied on behalf of 'that unhappy man').[37] Other 'thinking men' in the district were deeply offended that Dolan had returned to the locality, 'disport[ing] herself as if she had no remorse for the past or trouble about its consequences.' As former Orillian Judge Gunn surmised in 1914, 'public opinion is fast turning towards McNulty.'[38]

These supplementary accounts, sent by lawyers, judges, and 'thinking business elements,' as well as by the bereaved wife and her relatives, were not officially recognized until November 1914. Once again, a report prepared by the Remissions Branch spurred the executive into action. In four brief paragraphs, the new chief officer, Pierre M. Coté, reconceived the case as one meriting mercy. Beginning with a reminder that McNulty's accomplice had been released a year earlier, he set the tone for a straightforward call for equal justice. In his first draft to the Justice Minister he wrote: 'McNulty did not actually commit murder.' In the second, he decided to be more explicit: 'McNulty did not by his own hand commit murder.' From his role as the heartless villain in Power's first report on Dolan, McNulty now appeared as the 'alleged father' of the child and the man who had been sent away for life 'upon the sole evidence of Mary Dolan.' Recycling Mulcahy's sentimental appeal on behalf of the prisoner's family, Coté cast Mrs McNulty as the wounded woman 'who, with her little children, are reported to be in distressing circumstances.' For these reasons, Coté argued that 'the ends of justice' would be met if the minister were to commute the sentence to ten years, and to release McNulty on ticket of leave. Five official signatures of approval – Coté's, Charles Doherty's (minister of justice), Arthur Meighen's (solicitor-general), Louis Coderre's (secretary of state), and the Duke of Connaught and Strathearn's (governor-general) – conferred authority on this final version of the crime and the characters.

Conclusion

At this point in their stories we reach the final pages of McNulty's and Dolan's case files. The story that had opened with the discovery of a dead infant had unfolded into a sordid tale of illicit love, betrayal, and murder. Trial and punishment were the next chapters, followed by mercy and redemption. Both convicted murderers seem to have drifted back into the currents of small-town life after their release. Since neither of them faced the glare of publicity in a capital trial again, their stint as criminals was notorious but brief.

But are we any closer to the truth? In actual fact, we are no closer *after* reading the files than when we began. What, for instance, was Mary Dolan's motive? Shame? Spite? Fear? Malice? Was she a designing prostitute who callously implicated one of her lovers in a cold-blooded murder? Or was she the cowed and gullible plaything of an adulterous man? The answers to these questions do not lie in the case files. Rather, what we find is a miscellany of truth claims, some vested with the authority of letterhead that proclaimed 'Judge's Chambers,' and others, shakily penned on newsprint, cloaked in moral conviction, if not the niceties of spelling and grammar. Narratives of crime, guilt, innocence, and mitigation circulated at various points, but only some were deemed *the* truth at any one time. Authorities in the Remissions Branch and the executive adopted some versions of the truth and discarded others, constituting and reconstituting the official version of the story.

There is no greater illustration of the 'power/knowledge' nexus than the textual production of truth in capital case files.[39] In the post-Confederation federal bureaucracy it was no longer considered adequate to leave the fate of the capitally convicted to a sovereign's hunch. Indeed, both the sovereign and her or his representatives were far removed from the process by the late nineteenth century. Mrs McNulty's petition to King George and her assurance that she would 'never cease to pray for our King and Queen' (if only her husband were released) never reached the king's eyes. Instead, her petition and the other items that found their way into capital case files were subjected to bureaucrats' narrative reworkings. The production of knowledge was routinized in the form of the remissions officer's memorandum, an amalgam of information reconstituted into a format that facilitated life-and-death decision making.[40]

Analysing capital case files as texts is not meant to deny that every file documented the tragedy of at least one death, or that hundreds of people were executed or incarcerated for long periods of time as a result of the information contained therein. Instead, this methodology focuses on the textual processes that fed to and flowed from material practices and events. Not only does it expose the justice bureaucracy's informal, deductive means of arriving at the truth about the condemned person's appropriate fate, but it suggests how we might speak more broadly about the cultural construction of culpability. In the Dolan-McNulty case, tropes of gender informed not one, but two divergent readings of the principals' characters. The range of possible readings in capital cases was not unlimited, however.[41] Remission Branch officials, like local worthies and common folk, interpreted capital cases through culturally informed calculations of criminal culpability. Neither true nor false, case file texts represented various players' strategic attempts to order disturbing events into credible narratives of justice. Whether we link fragments in hundreds of case files to profile many people's fates, or zero in on a single case to make broader observations, historians inevitably invent new narratives without ever bringing the stories of the condemned to a close.

Notes

1 For important discussions of post-structuralist theory and history, see Joan Scott, *Gender and the Politics of History* (New York 1988), and Derek Attridge, Geoff Bennington, and Robert Young, eds, *Post-Structuralism and the Question of History* (Cambridge, Eng., 1987).

2 Jeffrey Weeks defines discourse as 'a linguistic unity or group of statements which constitutes and delimits a specific area of concern, governed by its own rules of formation with its own modes of distinguishing truth from falsity.' 'Foucault for Historians,' *History Workshop Journal* 14 (Autumn 1982), 106–20, 111.

3 The following works (with the exception of Mitchell's article) are based on capital case files: Neil Boyd, *The Last Dance: Murder in Canada* (Scarborough 1986); Alan Hustak, *They Were Hanged* (Toronto 1987); Martin Friedland, *The Case of Valentine Shortiss: A True Story of Crime and Politics in Canada* (Toronto 1985); Tom Mitchell, '"Blood with the Taint of Cain": Immigrant Labouring Children, Manitoba Politics, and the Execution of Emily Hilda Blake,' *Journal of Canadian Studies* (Winter 1993/4), 47–71; Franca Iacovetta and Karen Dubinsky, 'Murder, Womanly Virtue, and Motherhood: The Case of Angelina Napolitano, 1911–1922,' *Canadian Historical Review* 72:4 (1991), 505–31; Desmond Morton, ed., *The Queen v Louis Riel* (Toronto 1974); and Thomas Flanagan, *Louis 'David' Riel: Prophet of the New World* (Toronto 1979). Blake's file is one of the few missing from the RG13 holdings at the National Archives of Canada (hereafter NAC). For a comprehensive listing of files, see Loraine Gadoury and Antonio Lechasseur, *Persons Sentenced to Death in Canada, 1867–1976: An Inventory of Case Files in the Records of the Department of Justice (RG 13)* (Ottawa 1992).

4 Kenneth Avio, 'The Quality of Mercy: Exercise of the Royal Prerogative in Canada,' *Canadian Public Policy* 13 (1987), 366–79. For further statistical studies, see Avio, 'Capital Punishment: Statistical Evidence and Constitutional Issues,' *Canadian Journal of Criminology* 30:3 (October 1988), 331–49; David Chandler, *Capital Punishment in Canada* (Toronto 1976); and C.H.S. Jayewardene, *The Penalty of Death: The Canadian Experiment* (Lexington, Mass., 1977).

5 See, for instance, Lynn Hunt, ed., *The New Cultural History* (Berkeley 1989); Domenick LaCapra, *History and Criticism* (Berkeley 1985); Attridge et al., *Poststructuralism*; and Scott, *Gender*. For an informed critique of Canadian historians' failings in applying this methodology, see Lorna Weir, 'The Wanderings of the Linguistic Turn in Anglophone Historical Writing,' *Historical Sociology* 6:2 (June 1993), 227–45.

6 On the question of language *as* power see Pierre Bourdieu, *Language and Symbolic Power* (Cambridge, Mass., 1991).

7 The classic study of a case file, or 'dossier,' is Michel Foucault, ed. (trans. Frank

Jellinek), *I, Pierre Riviere, having slaughtered my sister, and my brother ...: A Case of Parricide in the 19th Century* (New York 1975). See also Patrizia Guarnieri (trans. Claudia Mieville), *A Case of Child Murder: Law and Science in Nineteenth-Century Tuscany* (Cambridge 1993 [1988]). Both of these books analyse the emergent discourse of psychiatry. Natalie Zemon Davis discusses narrative traditions deployed in letters of remission in *Fiction in the Archives: Pardon Tales and Their Tellers in Sixteenth-Century France* (Cambridge, Eng., 1988 [1987]).

8 As the Children's Aid Society assumed responsibility for adoptions in the 1890s, the practice of infanticide gradually declined in large cities such as Toronto. Carolyn Strange, *Toronto's Girl Problem: The Perils and Pleasures of the City, 1880–1930* (Toronto 1995), 72–6, 112–13. On the frequency of infanticide before that period see Constance Backhouse, 'Desperate Women and Compassionate Courts: Infanticide in Nineteenth-Century Canada,' *University of Toronto Law Journal* 31 (1984), 447–78.

9 In spite of infanticide's frequency, or, perhaps, because of it, conviction rates have historically been very low on the full charge of murder. As historians have recognized, jurors were reluctant to convict single mothers who killed their infants out of desperation and shame. See Rachel Fuchs, *Poor and Pregnant in Paris: Strategies for Survival in the Nineteenth Century* (New Brunswick, NJ, 1992), 203.

10 The NAC guide to capital case files covers the post-Confederation period. Before that period each colony disposed of cases through its own colonial bureaucracy. The only women executed after Confederation were those who had killed adults (in most cases their husbands or other men).

11 Foucault observed that scientific discourses, like the religious and 'superstitious' discourses they supplanted, constructed new ways of distinguishing truth from falsity. Professions like psychiatry and criminology did not 'discover' previously hidden truths; rather, they produced new means of constituting truths. Foucault elaborates this point in 'Scientia Sexualis,' *The History of Sexuality*, vol. 1, *An Introduction* (New York 1978), 53–73.

12 For an excellent analysis of counter-hegemonic storytelling strategies, see Patricia Ewick and Susan S. Silbey, 'Subversive Stories and Hegemonic Tales: Toward a Sociology of Narrative,' *Law and Society Review* 29:2 (1995): 197–226.

13 Judges were required by law to pronounce the death sentence when defendants were convicted of capital crimes. In the case of rape (after 1873), they had the option of sentencing convicted men to imprisonment, but in murder cases they had no choice. Judges did have the option to 'record' rather than pronounce a sentence of death in order to cue the cabinet that the accused might deserve mercy. Similarly, juries could recommend mercy, but judges were not obliged to convey their sentiments to the cabinet.

14 There are, as one would expect, missing files and missing values. The data set is nonetheless remarkably complete.

15 Avio, 'The Quality of Mercy,' 366. Avio has devised the 'statistically representative' case for the period he covers (1926–57): the offender was most likely to be a low-status Anglo male in his early thirties with no dependants; the typical victim was a white male or, if female, a person related in some way to the killer. The circumstances were typically that of a premeditated murder, without provocation, and for which neither jury nor judge had recommended mercy. Persons who ran higher risks of being executed had different characteristics and backgrounds: offenders with prior criminal records; labourers; Aboriginals, ethnic minorities or French Canadians; murderers of policemen or high-status persons; those whose crimes were particularly brutal, or who committed murder in the course of another felony. Avio, 'The Quality of Mercy,' 368–9

16 François Ewald, 'Norms, Discipline, and the Law,' *Representations* 30 (Spring 1990), 144. I am grateful to Lorna Weir and Mariana Valverde for bringing Ewald's work to my attention.

17 Eric Monkkonen notes that official homicide data are remarkably inconsistent over time. 'New York City Homicides: A Research Note,' *Social Science History* 19:2 (Summer 1995), 201–15

18 Multivariate analysis determines the importance of more than one variable (such as age or sex) simultaneously. Multivariate regression analysis ranks variables in order of their importance in a given set of relationships.

19 NAC, RG13, Capital Case Files, v. 1489, f. 600A; v. 1499, f. 619A; v. 1529, f. 723A; v. 1479, f. 521A (hereafter Capital Case Files)

20 For a review of semiotics and hermeneutics as methods of textual analysis, see Bernard S. Jackson, 'Narrative, History, and Truth,' in *Law, Fact, and Narrative Coherence* (Merseyside, Eng., 1988), 155–74.

21 Capital Case Files, v. 1461, f. 459A, Power to Minister of Justice, 7 Dec. 1910 (hereafter 'Dolan')

22 Transcript of Evidence, *R. v Dolan*, 26–29 Sept. 1910, in Dolan

23 Thomas Cowper Robinette was arguably the finest defence lawyer of his day, and one of the first to specialize as a defender (appearing frequently without pay). On his success in defending accused rapists, see Carolyn Strange, 'Patriarchy Modified: The Criminal Prosecution of Rape in Toronto, 1880–1930,' in Susan Lewthwaite, Tina Loo, and Jim Phillips, eds, *Essays in the History of Canadian Law*, vol. 5, *Crime and Criminal Justice* (Toronto 1994), 207–51, 248 n.59.

24 Dr Bruce Smith, the Ontario inspector of prisons and public charities and a medical authority often called upon by the province to determine the mental state of offenders, later diagnosed Dolan as 'an absolute and confirmed epileptic.' This mitigating factor was not emphasized in the trial because the defence could not afford to hire the expert. Melville B. Tudhope to Power, 6 Dec. 1910, in Dolan

25 The second time proved more notorious. Seven months after the Dolan trial Britton

was the judge assigned to the case of Angelina Napolitano. His enthusiasm to see Napolitano convicted suggests that he had managed to overcome his squeamishness about convicting women on capital charges. On his courtroom demeanour in the Napolitano case, see Iacovetta and Dubinsky, 'Womanly Virtue.'

26 From 1899, when Emily Hilda Blake was hanged in Brandon for the shooting death of her mistress, to 1923, when Florence Lassandro was hanged in Fort Saskatchewan, Alberta, for her involvement in the death of a constable, every woman sentenced to death was spared. Gadoury and Lechasseur, *Persons Sentenced*, 323.

27 Johnson to Minister of Justice, 15 Oct. 1910; shingle manufacturer to Minister of Justice, 4 Nov. 1910, in Dolan

28 On broader patterns of commutation, see Carolyn Strange, 'The Lottery of Death: Capital Punishment in Canada, 1867–1976,' *Manitoba Law Journal* 23:3 (January 1996), 594–619.

29 M. McDonald to Minister of Justice, 3 Dec. 1913, in Dolan

30 Her sentence was officially amended to ten years, meaning that if she committed any other offence in that period her life sentence would be reinstated and she would be returned to prison. As a rule, women were not required to report to authorities while released on a ticket of leave.

31 McNulty's conviction hinged on Dolan's uncorroborated evidence. This was note-worthy, since the judge had cautioned the jury, as he was required to do in cases without direct evidence, that the defendant *could* be so convicted, but that the law did not *require* a conviction.

32 NAC, Capital Case Files, RG13, v. 1462, f. 460A, Power to Minister of Justice, 7 Dec. 1910 (hereafter 'McNulty')

33 Lawrence Douglas, 'Discursive Limits: Narrative and Judgement in *Billy Budd*,' *Mosaic* 27:4 (December 1994), 141–61, 142

34 Mulcahy to Minister of Justice, 13 Dec. 1913, in McNulty

35 Robyn West, 'Narrative, Responsibility, and Death,' in *Narrative, Authority, and the Law* (Ann Arbor 1993), 419–39, 425. The use of narrative strategies in pursuit of racial justice is considered in Richard Delgado, 'Storytelling for Oppositionists and Others,' *Michigan Law Review* 87 (1989), 2411–41.

36 The definitive work in this area remains Douglas Hay, 'Property, Authority, and the Criminal Law,' in Douglas Hay, Peter Linebaugh, and E.P. Thompson, eds, *Albion's Fatal Tree: Crime and Society in Eighteenth-Century England* (London 1975), 17–63. For interpretations that place less emphasis on class, see John M. Beattie, 'The Royal Pardon and Criminal Procedure in Early Modern England,' Canadian Histori-cal Associaiton, *Historical Papers*, 1987, 9–22; and Peter King, 'Decision-makers and Decision-making in the English Criminal Law, 1750–1800,' *Historical Journal* 27 (1984), 25–58.

37 Leacock to Minister of Justice, 11 Jan. 1914, in McNulty. Leacock avidly supported the Conservative party and was a personal friend of Charles Doherty. In this letter he mentioned that he had previously met with Doherty about the case in 1913.

38 Gunn to Pierre M. Coté, 9 Dec. 1914, in McNulty. Coté replaced Power after his retirement. This was not the first allegation that Dolan was immoral. In 1911, Mrs McNulty petitioned 'His Royal Highness King George V' for her 'dear husband's' release, claiming that he had been convicted on the word of 'a common proscute [sic].' Mrs McNulty, 9 June 1911, in McNulty

39 This Foucauldian concept, that knowledge *is* power and that power is constituted through and conferred by knowledge, is elaborated in Colin Gordon, ed., *Power/ Knowledge – Selected Interviews and Other Writings, 1972–1977* (Brighton, Eng., 1980).

40 On the deadliness of law, see Robert Cover, 'Violence and the Word,' *Yale Law Journal* 95 (July 1986), 1601–29. For further interpretations of Cover's work, particularly in relation to his criticism of capital punishment, see Austin Sarat and Thomas R. Kearns, eds, *Law's Violence* (Ann Arbor 1993).

41 For this reason, some scholars question whether discretionary decision making is as arbitrary as is commonly assumed. See Keith Hawkins, ed., *The Uses of Discretion* (Oxford 1992), and Carolyn Strange, ed., *Qualities of Mercy: Justice, Punishment, and Discretion* (Vancouver 1996).

2

Employment Contracts in Merchant Shipping: An Argument for Social Science History

ERIC W. SAGER

My argument is an old one applied in a new context. The old argument is that social historians have much to learn from the methods of social scientists. The new context is that of the 1990s, when many historians in Canada and elsewhere, often influenced by impressive developments in gender history and cultural history, are making extensive use of 'case files.' I suggest that historians who use such files necessarily confront a common problem: how do we deal with the bias inherent in documents that describe certain people in words and categories that serve the official purposes of other people? The problem arises because most collections of individual case records that historians encounter in the archives were generated in an institutional context: an officer of an institution recorded information about persons or subjects of interest to the institution. My argument begins with this problem, and suggests an approach that derives from my work with crew agreements – employment contracts that sailors signed when they joined the crews of ocean-going ships of Britain or the British colonies. The conclusion is that, different as crew agreements may be from many case files, nevertheless the methods of social science, and especially the use of social statistics and computing, are powerful tools for the unpacking of meaning in case files and for resolving the problem of bias in institutional records.[1]

The problem of bias in institutional records is hardly a new one. Many years ago Charles Tilly was calling for 'a new form of historiography,' one concerned with the nature and properties of historical sources, especially sources generated by administrative systems.[2] Decades ago archivists began the systematic study of the provenance of historical records (by provenance I mean the nature, structure, and intent of the records in the context of their creation).[3] The need to attend carefully to the provenance of official records has also been demonstrated by historians who use census records. So deep is our awareness of the problem of official bias that some would argue that censuses are useful primarily for what they reveal about the construction of administrative knowledge, administrative systems, and the relations of knowledge/power underlying the development of nation-states.[4] Certainly no historian can read official or institutional records as though they were transparent windows into social reality or lived experience. If the records are to reflect anything of the people who were institutional subjects, the first duty of the historian is to attend to the provenance of the records.

The Provenance of Crew Agreements

Generations of historians interested in shipping and seafaring have confronted the problems presented by official records. Understanding provenance is merely one problem that we share with historians who use case files. Another problem, shared with many if not all, is that of a superabundance of records – 'the dilemma of plenitude' to which Carolyn Strange refers in this volume. Consider the documents entitled 'Agreement and Account of Crew' in a foreign-going ship, more commonly referred to as crew agreements or crew articles. Most of the British crew agreements from the early 1860s to the mid-twentieth century have survived. By themselves, they constitute the largest archive of maritime records in the English-speaking world. If there is a larger single archive of employment contracts anywhere, I do not know of it. The crew agreements at Memorial University of Newfoundland (probably 75 to 80 per cent of all extant British agreements) occupy six and a half *kilometres* of linear shelf space.[5]

The sheer volume of these records is itself a historical fact requiring explanation. The explanation takes us directly to the understanding of provenance that the historian must acquire before trying to see the sailors through the documents. The archive of crew agreements is testimony to a vast obsession for information, an obsession demanding rigorous administrative control and the labour of thousands of individuals scattered across the planet. Why do these records exist in such number? Ultimately, they are the product of state intervention in the private enterprise of capitalist employers. They are the work of both state and capital at a particular moment in the history of British and colonial shipping and trade. Although there had been earlier voluntary versions, crew agreements as official records date from the repeal of the Navigation Acts in the mid-nineteenth century. The repeal of the Navigation Acts meant opening British shipping and trade to wider competition from foreign ships and seamen. To ensure that the British industry remained both competitive and dominant, the state intervened with new forms of regulation and protection. The crew agreement did not stand alone: it was one pillar in a new structure of state support

Eng. 1.

*** Any Erasure, Interlineation, or Alteration in this Agreement will be void unless attested by some Superintendent of a Mercantile Marine Office, Officer of Customs, Consul, or Vice-Consul, to be made with the consent of the persons interested.

Executed in Twenty Pages.

AGREEMENT AND ACCOUNT OF CREW.
FOREIGN-GOING SHIP.

The form "Foreign-going Ship" means every Ship employed in trading or going between some place or places in the United Kingdom and some place or places situate beyond the Coasts of the United Kingdom, the Islands of Guernsey, Jersey, Sark, Alderney, and Man, and the Continent of Europe, between the River Elbe and Brest inclusive.

Name of Ship	Official No.	Port of Registry.	Port No. and Date of Register.	Registered Tonnage.		Nominal Horse Power of Engines (if any).
				Gross.	Net.	
"Africa"	100734	Windsor N.S.	28 July 1893	—	679	

REGISTERED MANAGING OWNER.

Name.	Address. (State No. of House, Street, and Town.)	No. of Seamen for whom accommodation is certified (30 & 31 Vict. c. 124.)	FOR PARTICULARS AS TO LOAD LINE, SEE LAST PAGE.
E. Churchill & Sons	Hantsport N.S.		

The several Persons whose names are hereto subscribed, and whose descriptions are contained on the other side or sides, and of whom are engaged as Sailors, hereby agree to serve on board the said Ship in the several capacities expressed against their respective Names, on a voyage from

Hantsport to Tarraboro thence to U.K. or Continent of Europe, thence to any ports or places within the limits of 75 degrees north and 60 degrees south Latitude, to and fro for a period Not to exceed twelve Calendar Months final port of discharge to be in the United States or Dominion of Canada

SUBSTITUTES at the masters option

And the Crew agree to conduct themselves in an orderly, faithful, honest and sober manner, and to be at all times diligent in their respective Duties, and to be obedient to the lawful commands of the said Master, or of any Person who shall lawfully succeed him, and of their Superior Officers, in everything relating to the said Ship and the Stores and Cargo thereof, whether on board, in boats, or on shore; in consideration of which Services to be duly performed, the said Master hereby agrees to pay to the said Crew as Wages the sums against their names respectively expressed, and to supply them with provisions according to the above Scale. And it is hereby agreed, That any Embezzlement or wilful or negligent Destruction of any part of the Ship's Cargo or Stores shall be made good to the Owner out of the Wages of the Person guilty of the same: And if any Person enters himself as qualified for a duty which he proves incompetent to perform, his Wages shall be reduced in proportion to his incompetency: And it is also agreed, That the Regulations authorised by the Board of Trade, which are printed herein and numbered

— are adopted by the parties hereto, and shall be considered as embodied in this Agreement: And it is also agreed, That if any Member of the Crew considers himself to be aggrieved by any breach of the Agreement or otherwise, he shall represent the same to the Master or Officer in charge of the Ship in a quiet and orderly manner, who shall thereupon take such steps as the case may require; And it is also stipulated that the Seamen shall receive the advances of wages entered herein against their names: And it is also agreed, That

The Ship to be considered fully manned with nine hands all told, all over that number Considered Extra, No Cash advanced abroad I or liberty allowed but at the masters option

4 The authority of the Owner or Agent for the allotments mentioned within is in my possession.

In Witness whereof the said Parties have subscribed their Names on the other Side or Sides hereof, on the days against their respective Signatures mentioned.

Signed by H. Harrison, Master,

on the 13 day of July 1893.

Date of Commencement of Voyage.	Port at which Voyage commenced.	Date of Termination of Voyage.	Port at which Voyage terminated.	Date of Delivery of List to Superintendent.	I hereby declare to the truth of the Entries in this Agreement and Account of Crew, &c.
13 July 1893	Hantsport N.S.	14/6/94		71/6/94	H. Harrison, Master.

N.B.—This Form must not be unstitched. No leaves may be taken out of it, and none may be added or substituted. Care should be taken at the time of Engagement that a sufficiently large Form is used. If more men are engaged during the voyage than the number for whom signatures are provided in this Form, an additional Form Eng. 1 should be obtained and used.

The first page of a Crew Agreement, an employment contract that sailors signed when they joined the crews of ocean-going ships of Britain or the British colonies. (Crew Agreement of the *Africa*, Windsor, Nova Scotia, 1874, official number 100734. Maritime History Archive, Memorial University of Newfoundland) implemented through a succession of merchant-marine acts, beginning with those of 1850 and 1854.

Crew agreements emerged from two decades of debate over the condition of the British merchant marine. Three select committees of Parliament (1836, 1839, and 1843) had examined the astonishing losses of British and colonial merchant ships and their crews. By the 1830s several hundred ships were lost at sea each year; on average about nine hundred lives were lost each year.[6] In certain years, and in specific trades, the loss rate was exceptionally high: eight hundred merchant ships lost in all trades in 1833; eighteen vessels and seven hundred lives lost (both passengers and emigrants) en route to Quebec in the spring of 1834.[7] The timber trade was especially dangerous, and prompted the government to set up a select committee in 1839 to study shipwrecks in that trade.

The select committee reports attributed shipwrecks to structural and design problems in the ships, to the practice of carrying heavy deckloads, and to shipowners' neglect of safety considerations.[8] The reports also put the question of work discipline firmly on the parliamentary agenda: 'The instances of disastrous consequences resulting from incompetency, sometimes from ignorance of seamanship, sometimes from ignorance of navigation, sometimes from extreme youth and inexperience, and very often from intoxication and the total absence of discipline would fill a long and melancholy catalogue.'[9] The 'melancholy catalogue' continued in the 1840s, when the Foreign Office undertook two investigations of the condition of the merchant marine. The Foreign Office official who began these investigations, James Murray, made a highly tendentious request for information on the 'incompetency' of British shipmasters and on the 'deficiency of knowledge ... or of moral character' in the labour force at sea. He addressed his request to those who had to deal with the consequences of problems in the merchant marine in foreign ports – the British consuls. Little wonder that the reports, when made public in 1848, led to extensive discussion in the press, in Parliament, and among shipowners. British masters and sailors were described as incompetent, ill-trained, undisciplined, and more often drunk than sober.

By themselves these reports could not have led to the array of legislation that followed. Taken together with the continuing evidence of losses at sea and with the repeal of the Navigation Acts, the reports had an effect, namely, to turn the merchant-marine problem into a problem of management and supervision. Management was the province of the shipowner and the shipmaster, of course, and shipowners, especially through the General Shipowners Society, resisted legislative intrusion into their decisions over the management of ships and crews. They confronted politicians and civil servants who were sceptical about the shipowners' claims that individual responsibility and self-interest would guarantee safety and productivity. As James Murray put it: 'The condition of the sailor, and the necessity of improving our system of navigation and management now observable in our merchant vessels, so as to ensure their not losing ground, as compared with foreigners, would alone appear to require the exclusive attention of a competent department; for it is clear that individuals, however much their personal interests may be concerned, cannot, or will not, make inquiries, or take the necessary steps.'[10] Management was still the responsibility of the shipowner, but supervision was the duty of the state. The 1850 Act established a Marine Department within the Board of Trade to 'undertake the general superintendence of matters relating to the British Mercantile Marine.' The words 'superintendence' and 'supervision' are used in the full force of their dual meaning: the state or its appointed agents would have the right to view every transaction relating to the management of labour in ships; the state would oversee for the purpose of directing such transactions.

Henry Labouchere's Panopticon

Michel Foucault has argued that 'the exercise of discipline presupposes a mechanism that coerces by means of observation; an apparatus in which the techniques that make it possible to see induce effects of power and in which, conversely, the means of coercion make those on whom they are applied clearly visible.'[11] The apparatus of observation in merchant shipping would be complex and telescopic. The 1850 act – 'An Act for Improving the Condition of Masters, Mates, and Seamen, and Maintaining Discipline in the Merchant Service' – was a lengthy one of 124 clauses. The great consolidation of merchant-shipping laws that followed in 1854 contained 548 clauses. Shipowners recognized the coercive intent behind supervision and won the right to share supervisory control: the local marine boards would include elected representatives of local shipowners' associations. These local boards would appoint shipping masters in each port, and sailors being hired by foreign-going vessels would sign crew agreements in the presence of these shipping masters.

Legal regulation of employment contracts was not new, of course: the laws of master and servant were reconstituted by repeated legislation from early modern times into the nineteenth century.[12] Industrial workplaces on land prompted new legislation and new supervisory methods, and in the mid-19th century many employers were giving supervisory powers to a new level of the employee hierarchy – the foreman. Supervision in merchant shipping presented unusual challenges, however: in shipping, capital was dispersed in mobile units that spent productive time far beyond the immediate purview of owners and managers.[13] How was observation to be maintained across the world's oceans? The first step was to delegate new powers of observation and control, not to a new occupation of foreman, but to the existing elite of surrogate managers at sea: the shipmaster and the mates. In full understanding of the connection between knowledge and power, the state would ensure, through schooling, compulsory examination and certification, that masters and mates held appropriate knowledge of navigation, shiphandling, law, and labour management. Such knowledge would prepare them 'to be intrusted with the discipline and superintendence of a ship.'[14] Examinations 'would promote that kind of knowledge which was of deepest interest to the mercantile marine – they would elevate both captains and mates in the scale of their profession, arm them with proper power over their crews, and confer many important benefits upon all concerned in the navigation of the seas.'[15] Knowledge was a greater power than mere physical coercion, and in introducing his bill Henry Labouchere made it clear that the old method of flogging, still practised in the American merchant marine, was inadequate.[16] His new disciplinary apparatus was the nineteenth-century alternative to flogging, answering the needs of both humanitarians and shipping capital.

It was not enough to secure the knowledge of masters and mates. 'To put a stop to evils of alarming magnitude' would require observation of every worker, at every moment of their working time, and throughout the life course of their employment in the industry. The crew agreement was such a means of observation; it was a documentary panopticon, akin to Jeremy Bentham's Panopticon, the model prison in which inmates could be seen at all times from a central observatory. The categories of information in the crew agreement follow from the state's attempt to regulate workplace relationships, and from politicians' understanding of those relationships. The agreement names the ship and the managing owner; in so doing it identifies those who held managerial responsibility. The scale of provisions, or victualling scale, was intended to reduce disputes over food, since 'one half the quarrels and disputes that arose between sailors and their employers turned upon the question of diet.'[17] The general description of the voyage and of its intended length was merely one attempt to limit desertion: 'as many as 14,000 sailors had deserted from British merchant vessels in the course of one year,' said Labouchere.[18] The sailor undertook a binding obligation to serve for the period of time specified, the shipping master explained the obligation, and the sailor signed in the presence of the ship's captain and the shipping master.

The sailor must be identified by name, by age, by place of birth, and by his previous ship. The crew agreement was a census of the seafaring labour force, to be held by the Board of Trade, and it was a record of the performance of every worker in a foreign-going vessel. In establishing this performance record the state was replacing a previous system of registration – registry tickets that named the sailor and gave details of previous experience at sea. The problem with registry tickets was that they were carried by sailors rather than the state. To prevent 'extensive frauds' and the trade in 'forged registry tickets' the state took control of the identification of sailors and the document that named them.[19] Birthplace information was also required so that governments would know how far the merchant marine under free trade depended on foreign labour: the nation required a large seafaring labour force, and the disciplinary benefits of seafaring should be reserved for British workers rather than foreigners.

Rank or 'capacity' in the ship was essential, for rank identified the range of tasks for which the worker had responsibility. The amount of wages was also essential, since the state was attempting to end complaints over the non-payment of wages. In particular, the state was attempting to undercut the role of the crimp in the hiring process (the crimp was the private recruiting agent, often a boarding-house keeper). The crimp was a convenient scapegoat: sailors were not underpaid but 'the high wages they obtained fell into the hands of the crimps and slopsellers.'[20] The state was also attempting to improve the disciplinary power of the wage. Any advances would have to be specified and should be limited, and the balance paid on discharge: the state was reminding both masters and crew that the ship would be in debt to the sailor, and that full payment with no deductions required lawful performance of duty. The date, place, and cause of discharge from the ship were key parts of a performance record: all honourable discharges, dishonourable discharges, and desertions would henceforth be known to the Board of Trade.

We are not at the end of Henry Labouchere's apparatus of supervision. 'A ship at sea is in herself a little kingdom,' said W.S. Lindsay, and the master, as head of state in his little kingdom, exercized civil and criminal authority there.[21] The crew agreement was his census and his statutes; he also possessed a court record – the official logbook. 'In future every merchant vessel would be required to keep a regular logbook according to the form furnished by the Government officer.'[22] Here was the master's record of anything that impeded the progress of the voyage, and of his legal transactions, including fines and imprisonment. Long lists of offences and punishments appeared in the acts of 1850 and 1854, and the Board of Trade also issued supplementary 'Regulations for Maintaining Discipline.' At the discretion of the master, an array of offences could be specified on the crew agreement. Some related to the contractual obligation to provide labour (failure to be on board at the agreed time, sleeping while on look-out, not returning on board promptly at the expiry of shore leave). Other offences buttressed the master's control over time, leisure, and even language: smoking below, neglecting to air one's bedding, failing to attend divine service, failing to be washed and shaved on Sunday, swearing, carrying a sheath knife – these and many other offences, provided that they were specified in advance, could result in deductions from pay. The logbook was a court record, but it also extended and completed the performance record begun in the crew agreement.

To appreciate the extent to which information was hereby structured by the needs of its framers, one may simply try to imagine the shape of the document had it been written by its targets, the workers themselves. Of course there might have been no crew agreement at all, and certainly no government agent, as the protests of sailors against this system in 1850 and 1851 made clear.[23] Had they set the agenda, sailors would have sought to control the hiring process through agents of their choice, either crimps or (much later) union representatives. Essential information, available to all prospective employees, would have included the performance and safety records of both ship and master. The crew agreement might have specified the actual quantities and quality of food provided, rather than the intended quantity. The agreement might have noted departures from the intended voyage pattern and duration. Much more of the agreement would have been completed at the end of the voyage than the beginning, and it would have noted overtime hours – those hours when both watches were on deck. Instead of being the record of the one voice, at once both prosecutor and judge, the logbook might have recorded the case for the defence. I could go on, but the point is made. I recommend such a counter-factual exercise to other historians who use case files. The alternative document, by its very improbability, serves to remind the historian of the extent to which the existing document results from predetermined categories and the radical exclusion of alternative understandings.

The creation of Henry Labouchere's panopticon is a revealing moment in the history of the modern British state and its administrative systems. It is also a lesson in the provenance of state-sponsored statistics, because the supervisory apparatus described here fuelled the volumes of data appearing in parliamentary papers: '[S]tatistics in the service of the state epitomised the political process in which decentralised local enquiry – to supply knowledge as the basis for action – was the necessary route for the reinforcement of central authority.'[24]

Sailors' Voices and Quantitative Methods

Does the voice of the state drown out the voice of the sailor? Is the information in this archive merely or primarily a record of official understandings? To answer affirmatively would be to misunderstand the provenance of these documents. They are better understood as a record of multiple voices, as the product of a dialectic of power and resistance. The document assumed its particular structure precisely because ships were wrecked, because sailors deserted, and because there was a black market in registry tickets. Sailors died at sea, and survivors protested; sailors refused to join unseaworthy or undermanned ships; sailors resisted the authority of masters. In their creation and their use, crew agreements and logbooks are fragments of a long conversation between sailors, their employers, and representatives of the state. Employers and the state framed the conversation by their questions, but the questions themselves were responses to prior actions by sailors.

The voice of the sailor is often muffled or distorted by the interrogator. Only if we hear the interrogator clearly may we hear the sailor. Much has to be discounted. I would not attempt to trace the career paths of a subset of sailors, by linking names from one crew agreement to another, because the system of supervision encouraged the use of aliases, and because the documents are too voluminous to allow such an exercise. I accept the age and birthplace information, because the sailor risked more by lying than by stating the truth.[25] I do not believe that the logbook entries on 'refusals to work' permit the historian to estimate strike frequencies: masters might well have minimized the frequency of disturbances in their ships by effecting extralegal and unrecorded solutions. I would not describe a typology of sailors or their behaviours on the basis of these documents or of court records: the language of the official and the moral reformer intervenes.[26] It is not clear that every honourable discharge meant employer satisfaction; yet the master had no incentive to exaggerate the numbers of those who deserted his ships.

It is not enough to rely on the occasional verbatim quotations of sailors recorded in logbooks. The historian who relied mainly on such voices would be left with fragments and instances. More often than they allow us to hear sailors' voices, the documents allow us to perceive actions and outcomes. The conclusions that follow relate not to individuals but to collectivities: the labour force in an industry, and the industry itself. From the core of two books that completed my work for the Atlantic Canada Shipping Project, I draw a few of these conclusions. In Canadian sailing ships desertion rates increased over time. The crew agreements tell us where sailors were likely to desert, and that desertion was related to specific wage differentials: the wage differentials between ranks within a ship, and the difference between wages in a ship and the prevailing wage level in the port in which a ship arrived. The documents tell us that desertion was a form of wage bargaining, in the absence of formal organization, and that this bargaining achieved a small success: where a ship's destination was a high-desertion port, the sailor earned a higher wage.[27] Desertion is no longer simply the action of individuals; the analysis has revealed a form of collective resistance. This resistance increased as rates of return on capital fell and as owners tried to cut wage costs while demanding more from ships and crews.

The complaints about the quality of the labour force in shipping, repeated by masters and shipowners and many politicians, can now be understood as responses to falling profits and to the resistance of sailors themselves. The rhetoric tells us little about the labour force, except insofar as it suggests a motive for the pressure of owners on masters. Fewer workers sailed the same ships as time passed; between the 1860s and the 1890s they learned to sail the same ships more quickly across the same oceans. The labour force aged, and inexperienced workers all but disappeared from the industry. Wage costs declined as a proportion of all costs. The collapse of the industry in the Maritime provinces had little to do with labour productivity, and little to do with technological obsolescence. Falling rates of return in wooden sailing ships were only one condition of declining investment. The decline of the shipping industry was the result of investment choices by merchant capitalists in the Maritime provinces. Their choices were influenced by the integration of their provinces into a national economy that offered limited support for deep-sea shipping and shipbuilding.[28]

I cite these conclusions in order to make two points. The first is an obvious one: historians must use the official panopticon. Only by looking in both directions through its lenses – by looking from the official observer to the observed, and back from the observed to the observer – may we perceive either side, as they existed in their relationship to the other. The second point may be less obvious: every conclusion in the previous two paragraphs is either a simple quantitative statement or a relational statement (a statement about the relationship between one variable and another). Seeing and hearing beyond the official voice could not have been achieved in the absence of specific statistical methods. There was no other way to arrive at the conclusions about desertion, for instance, without analysing the differences in mean monthly wages among different ports, years, trade routes, and other variables. The only way to study these wage differences, in this context, is by using analysis of variance and associated tests of significance. Of course the historian might look for statements by shipowners and masters about why they paid certain wages at certain times. Even if one found such statements, one would do no more than accumulate instances, and one has thereby no way to know whether the instances were representative of wider trends. A few sailors may tell you where and why they deserted. Using statistical methods, I can tell you where, and in what conditions, desertion occurred in the shipping industry.

I sometimes hear the suggestion that statistical methods necessarily result in 'abstracted empiricism' (the phrase is C. Wright Mills's), or the 'dehumaniza-tion inherent in the process of aggregation.'[29] It has always seemed to me a puz-zling notion that the experience or actions of one may be more authentically human than the experience or actions of many.[30] The notion is sometimes an unfortunate or mistaken by-product of the popular historian's attempt to uncover some authentic 'experience,' uncontaminated by the manipulation of officials or even historians.[31] At other times, the equation of statistical methods with dehumanization is related to what Charles Tilly calls 'softcore solipsism': the privileging of individual or self inherent in the view that action is the result of conscious deliberation or motive.[32] The individual, and his or her motive, become the central unit of analysis, on the assumption that the cultural rules or social relationships that limit individual choice and action are ultimately unknowable.[33] Within such an epistemological position social science methods are redundant, or they are 'merely figures of speech.'[34] There is no need to reit-erate the many objections to this epistemology, from which 'the objective of academic effort reduces to the provision of multiple perspectives on ultimately indeterminate events.'[35] At worst, the position entails a scepticism about all past experiences and events; the powerless have no more claim to truth than the powerful; history brings no lessons from the past into the present.

Quantitative methods are not the only methods available to us, and for certain questions they may offer little assistance; nevertheless it seems to me that case files research will often require appropriate statistical procedures. The historian who uses case files is usually interested in going beyond the presentation of sto-ries illustrating individual character and circumstance, and instead wants to specify the conditions and characteristics of many of those who entered the institutional record. The user of case files is also interested in perceiving rela-tionships between the institution or its officers and those whom the institution sought to serve, control, or influence. Such purposes resolve themselves into a search for patterns, trends, and repetitions. Without careful attention to one's method, the search incurs the risk of implicit or unsubstantiated quantification: 'many' cases seem to confirm a trend, whereas 'a few' suggest occurrences of lesser frequency and 'rarely' signifies the exception. The historian using case files usually wishes to transcend a temporally limited focus and to make state-ments about change over time. Where the dynamics of change are the target, and where the historian is seeking the conditions of change affecting large num-bers of cases, quantitative measures and statements are almost inescapable. The careful historian will want to carry the appropriate tools and to be fully con-scious of their uses and their limits.

It is no answer to say that the methods involve difficulties and pitfalls, or to conclude that other methods are more appropriate given the non-routine and messy nature of many case files and the questions being asked. The toolbox of methods that we bring to the archives sets prior limits to the questions asked and the results obtained. One of the most common problems of case files researchers, for instance, is that of sampling: given the 'dilemma of plenitude,' what sample size is required to make statements about the population as a whole? Historians, because of the preoccupation of our discipline with individuality and with the oppositional 'free rider' who departs from a cultural norm, are often reluctant to take seemingly small samples from a large population. Yet failure to take a sample can itself be very costly. First, the historian who can study *all* cases in the available files is fortunate, but probably rare; furthermore, it may simply be unnecessary to analyse all cases.

Second, the exceptional or oppositional case cannot be discerned until a norm or trend is specified. As Daniel Scott Smith states, in the context of a discussion of wills and inheritance patterns among early American women: 'Individual practice varies considerably, and meaning does not emerge until averages are calculated. Although individuals provide the data ..., the actual subjects to be elucidated and explained are variations in the average value of these indicators and the reasons individuals diverge from the mean pattern.'[36] Smith proceeds to question the frequent use of anecdotes or vignettes about individuals when the target of the analysis is social relationships. In his view anecdotes add flavour rather than analytical point, and may help to persuade 'naive readers.' Anecdotes add little in the way of substantive evidence, since counter-examples can nearly always be found. My own view is that anecdotes may be used for analytical purpose, but rarely are so used. Most often they are merely illustrations of a trend or condition, or they are pure non sequiturs. If an anecdote is meant to be illustrative, the historian should first confirm by other evidence and method the existence of the pattern or norm that is being illustrated. The anecdote or narrative of an individual experience may be used to establish the motive underlying an action, but it is not clear that motive can ever be fully understood, and in any case it is not clear what historical knowledge would be gained if an individual motive were fully knowable, since the motive might be purely individual and idiosyncratic. Effective analytical or illustrative use of the anecdote or vignette also requires careful sampling, and prior decisions about sampling are necessary in order to avoid the fallacy of instancing: starting research with certain assumptions, culling instances or stories from the files that confirm those assumptions, and then reasserting the assumption as though it were proved.

The historian who confronts a collection of thousands of case files may reject random sampling in favour of a focus on specific years or groups within the files (such as women appearing in a court of law). The procedure may be appropriate, but it may also be self-limiting. Sampling will allow the historian to extend the temporal range of cases studied, without sacrificing the ability to generalize; appropriate sampling may allow the historian to transcend a single-sex study and to discern more sharply the workings of gender in the justice system.

Case files are likely to be the product of multiple voices and multiple actions. Statistical methods and representations are a pre-eminent means by which the human sciences present multiple voices and actions. The most common procedure for showing whether and how two or more variables are interrelated is regression analysis. Today regression techniques are very flexible in their application to category variables (such as sex, rank in a ship, occupation, and the like). Carolyn Strange (in this volume) offers a very good example of a multivariate problem for which regression analysis is appropriate: what conditions or characteristics are associated with the decisions to commute or not to commute death sentences in capital cases? A persuasive answer does not need to be definitive in all instances. It is impossible to provide a model or theory that predicts the outcome in all cases. A persuasive answer is one that offers the most parsimonious list of conditions or variables that are significantly related to the dependent variable (whether the sentence was commuted or not).[37] The historian will proceed to examine other sources relating to the commutation decisions, but in Strange's example the regression procedure is an obvious and probably essential first step.

Much of the information in case files is textual in form and highly unsystematic. The information may be quite unlike the routinely generated information in crew agreements or nominal census returns, for instance. Cultural historians, and especially those who follow the deconstructive and linguistic turns in historical thought, may prefer to interrogate the case files as texts. If so, I see no need to discard the tools of the social scientist. Information in the text may not be standardized or numeric in form, but word clusters, verbal associations, and euphemisms may appear and recur. If language is an internal system rather than an organization of referents to an outside world, then the analysis of that system as it appears in case files is likely to proceed furthest when the text is systematically deconstructed and its recurring patterns specified. The patterns may be presented systematically, and even quantitatively, using the rapidly growing range of software available for precisely such purposes.[38]

Conclusion

Making full and creative use of case files requires an open-minded acceptance of a variety of methods. The resistance to quantitative methods and social-scientific approaches remains deep-rooted among some historians, but the remarkable increase in the use of quantitative methods in Canadian history that Kris Inwood has documented is one indication of the healthy eclecticism and methodological breadth that characterize our profession.[39] The methods are sometimes daunting, and historians should never be reluctant to seek out the assistance of scholars or technical consultants more experienced than we may be in the application of sampling methods, statistics, and computing software. In seeking out such assistance we may in turn influence the available expertise so that it is better able to serve the particular needs of historians. Between the historian interested in context, provenance, and the dynamics of change over time, and the social scientist who also studies the complex traces of human actions and social relationships, there remains no necessary opposition but a continuing scholarly exchange of great mutual benefit.

Notes

1 Of course historians borrow or adapt methods and approaches from other social scientists, such as cultural anthropologists. I focus here on specific parts of the social science tradition. A good introduction is Loren Haskins and Kirk Jeffrey, *Understanding Quantitative History* (Cambridge, Mass.: MIT Press, 1990).

2 Jerome Clubb was quoting an earlier statement by Tilly in J.M. Clubb, 'The "New" Quantitative History: Social Science or Old Wine in New Bottles?' in Jerome M.Clubb and Erwin K. Scheuch, eds, *Historical Social Research: The Use of Historical and Process-Produced Data* (Stuttgart: Klett-Cotta, 1980), 22.

3 George Bolotenko, 'Archivists and Historians: Keepers of the Well,' *Archivaria* 16 (1983), 5–25; Chad Gaffield and Peter Baskerville, 'The Automated Archivist: Interdisciplinarity and the Process of Historical Research,' *Social Science History* 9:2 (Spring 1985), 178–9

4 Bruce Curtis, 'On the Local Construction of Statistical Knowledge: Making Up the 1861 Census of the Canadas,' *Journal of Historical Sociology* 7 (1994), 416–34

5 For this information I am indebted to Heather Wareham, Archivist, Maritime History Archive, Memorial University of Newfoundland.

6 Jane H. Wilde, 'The Creation of the Marine Department of the Board of Trade,' *Journal of Transport History* 2:4 (November 1956), 194

7 Clifford Jeans, 'The First Statutory Qualifications for Seafarers,' *Transport History* 6:3 (November 1973), 251

8 David M.Williams, 'State Regulation of Merchant Shipping, 1839–1914: The Bulk Carrying Trades,' in Sarah Palmer and Glyndwr Williams, eds, *Charted and Uncharted Waters* (London: National Maritime Museum, 1981), 56–9

9   James S. Buckingham, who chaired the 1836 select committee, in Hansard, House of Commons *Debates*, 3rd series, XXXVII (1837), 174. See also Report of the Select Committee on the Causes of Shipwrecks, *Parliamentary Papers*, 1836, XVII.

10 James Murray in *Parliamentary Papers*, 1847–8, LIX, 142, cited in Wilde, 'Creation of the Marine Department,' 201

11 Michel Foucault, *Discipline and Punish: The Birth of the Prison* (trans. A. Sheridan, 1977), in Paul Rabinow, ed., *The Foucault Reader* (New York: Pantheon, 1984), 189

12 Douglas Hay and Paul Craven, 'Master and Servant in England and the Empire: A Comparative Study,' *Labour/Le Travail* 31 (Spring 1993), 175–84

13 Politicians understood the problem posed by distance. Sailors were 'a heedless, ignorant, audacious, but most useful class of men' who, by the nature of their employment, 'are necessarily excluded, in a great degree, from the benefits of civilization.' Labouchere, quoting Chancellor Kent, in Hansard, House of Commons *Debates*, 1849, CVII, 225

14 Henry Labouchere, Hansard, 12 July 1849, CVII, 229

15 Labouchere, Hansard, 11 Feb. 1850, CVIII, 671

16 Labouchere, Hansard, 12 July 1849, CVII, 232

17 Ibid., 231

18 Ibid., 225

19 Ibid., 233. The problem of desertion was not solved, and in 1900 the British government introduced the continuous Certificate of Discharge, which sailors were supposed to carry with them and to produce on being hired. Conrad Dixon, 'Legislation and the Sailor's Lot,' in Paul Adam, ed., *Seamen in Society: Proceedings of the International Commission on Maritime History* (Bucharest: Commission internationale d'histoire maritime, 1980), 3: 96–103

20 Ibid., 230. On crimps see Judith Fingard, '"Those Crimps of Hell and Goblins Damned": The Image and Reality of Quebec's Sailortown Bosses,' in Rosemary Ommer and Gerald Panting, eds, *Working Men Who Got Wet* (St John's: Maritime History Group, 1980), 323–33.

21 W.S. Lindsay, *History of Merchant Shipping and Ancient Commerce* (New York: AMS Press, 1965), 3: 497

22 Labouchere, Hansard, 12 July 1849, CVII, 231

23 Wilde, 'Creation of the Marine Department,' 204–5; Sarah Palmer, *Politics, Shipping, and the Repeal of the Navigation Laws* (Manchester: Manchester University Press, 1990), 174

24 Stuart Woolf, 'Statistics and the Modern State,' *Comparative Study of Society and History* 31 (1989), 599

25 Analysis of age distributions yields the expected bunching at decennial intervals, and age distributions are consistent with more impressionistic information from other contemporary sources.

26 I refer to Judith Fingard's typology in her *Jack in Port: Sailortowns of Eastern Canada* (Toronto: University of Toronto Press, 1982), chap. 2; Richard Rice, 'Sailortown: Theory and Method in Ordinary People's History,' *Acadiensis* 13:1 (Autumn 1983), 154–68.

27 Eric W. Sager, *Seafaring Labour: The Merchant Marine of Atlantic Canada, 1820–1914* (Montreal and Kingston: McGill-Queen's University Press, 1989), 186–99

28 Eric W. Sager, with Gerald E. Panting, *Maritime Capital: The Shipping Industry in Atlantic Canada, 1820–1914* (Montreal and Kingston: McGill-Queen's University Press, 1990), esp. chaps 6, 7, and 8

29 Mary Poovey, 'Figures of Arithmetic, Figures of Speech: The Discourse of Statistics in the 1830s,' *Critical Inquiry* 19:2 (Winter 1993), repr. in James Chandler, A.I. Davidson, and Harry Harootunian, eds, *Questions of Evidence: Proof, Practice and Persuasion across the Disciplines* (Chicago: University of Chicago Press, 1994), 415

30 It is worth remembering that historians of the Annales school found the older narrative history to be dehumanizing – 'facts but no humanity.' The new methods of the human sciences, which included statistics, would take history beyond the focus on 'exceptional destinies' to a wider humanity. Fernand Braudel, 'The Situation of History in 1950,' in Braudel, *On History*, trans. S. Matthews (Chicago: University of Chicago Press, 1980), 11

31 Roderick Floud, 'Quantitative History and People's History: Two Methods in Conflict?' *Social Science History* 8:2 (Spring 1984), 151–68

32 Charles Tilly, 'Softcore Solipsism,' *Labour/Le Travail* 34 (Fall 1994), 261

33 Daniel Scott Smith, 'Inheritance and the Social History of Early American Women,' in Ronald Hoffman and Peter J. Albert, eds, *Women in the Age of the American Revolution* (Charlottesville: University Press of Virginia, 1989), 46. I am indebted to Peter Baskerville for this reference.

34 Poovey, 'Figures of Arithmetic,' 421

35 Tilley, 'Softcore Solipsism,' 262

36 Smith, 'Inheritance,' 50

37 Cf. Daniel Scott Smith, 'A Mean and Random Past: The Implications of Variance for History,' *Historical Methods* 17:3 (Summer 1984), 142

38 An example is TACT, from the University of Toronto's Centre for Computing in the Humanities; see Ian Lancashire, 'Computing Creativity,' *Books in Canada*, March 1995, 15–18.

39 Of 359 articles in Canadian history published between 1989 and 1992, 48 per cent used quantitative data 'in a visible and significant manner.' See Kris Inwood, 'The Promise and Problems of Quantitative Evidence in Canadian History,' *Histoire sociale/Social History* 27:53 (May 1994), 139–46.

3

On the Case of the Case: The Emergence of the Homosexual as a Case History in Early-Twentieth-Century Ontario

STEVEN MAYNARD

In February 1911, Walter F., a butcher from Toronto's St Lawrence Market, appeared in Police Court on several charges of gross indecency. The judge presiding over the preliminary hearing decided there was sufficient evidence to send the case on to a higher court. As Walter was remanded to jail, Magistrate Denison ordered: 'Let the doctors see that man before he goes up.' After several weeks awaiting trial in jail, Walter finally received a visit from the doctor. Beginning with Walter's name and age, the doctor proceeded to conduct a mental examination. Walter's answers to the doctor's many questions were recorded by the doctor in a case history: 'Walter F. – age 43 – born 1868 – July 15th – London, England – lived there first twenty years of life – went to school until 16 – afterwards went to learn the trade of butcher – been at it all my life – came to Canada four years ago – came to Toronto – went to Harris abattoirs – worked there three months – then went to St Lawrence Market – married 21 years of age – 5 living children – 3 children dead – Father died age 46 – alcoholic – Mother died age 25 – childbirth – have always indulged freely in stimulants – 20 drinks – has lead irregular life.' Aside perhaps from the taint of an alcoholic father and an intemperate, irregular life, the doctor was unable to find symptoms of mental disease and pronounced Walter fit to stand trial. Walter was found guilty. Although the doctor had discovered no evidence of mental illness in Walter's case, in passing sentence Judge Denton averred that Walter's behaviour was 'evidently due to some disease of the mind.'[1]

It was Foucault who famously remarked that sometime beginning in the nineteenth century the homosexual became, among other things, a 'case history.'[2] It is a mark of Foucault's brilliance that he was so often theoretically right when, as we historians are wont to remind everyone, he actually read very few case histories. But the psychiatric examinations performed by doctors on men like Walter – men charged with homosexual offences in early-twentieth-century

Ontario courts – confirm Foucault's speculations on the way the law and medicine worked together to transform men and their homosexual activities into case histories.[3] Of course, what Foucault meant was not so much that the homosexual became a case history, but that the case history helped to bring the homosexual into existence. In this way, the case history was closely related to what Foucault identified as one of the linchpins of disciplinary power – the examination. 'The examination, surrounded by all its documentary techniques, makes each individual a "case": a case which at one and the same time constitutes an object for a branch of knowledge and a hold for a branch of power.' In terms of the homosexual, Foucault singled out the 'psychiatrization of perverse pleasure,' or the mental examinations and case histories of homosexuals performed by psychiatrists and other medical professionals.[4]

Gay historians, especially those grounded in social history with its traditional emphases on human agency and the material, have been reluctant to wholly embrace Foucault's insistence on the discursive invention of the homosexual. George Chauncey, for one, has convincingly argued that 'medical discourse did not "invent" the homosexual ... [Doctors] were investigating a subculture rather than creating one.' Against those who would privilege discourse in the formation of homosexual identities and subcultures, Chauncey has offered a powerful reconceptualization, one that stresses the role of homosexual men in the making of their own cultural worlds.[5]

The debates within gay history over the relative roles played by discourse and the material in shaping identities and experience have parallels in many other subfields of social history. They have in common a concern with the nature and status of historical evidence, a concern provoked by the post-structuralist critique of historical practice.[6] Case files have emerged as one particularly fractious site in the debates over evidence. Think back to the exchange between Joan Scott and Linda Gordon over the interpretation of the case files of social-welfare agencies. These debates also share a similar structure, one often marked by dichotomous, either/or positions. In the Scott–Gordon exchange, Scott argued that the historian should train his or her analytic gaze on the way the case files constructed the categories and subject positions of domestic abuse; Gordon maintained that the historian could use the case files to recover women's historical experience and resistance of abuse. Neither Scott nor Gordon really allowed any of the other's position. This unproductive stance, one that casts the relationship between the discursive and the material as mutually exclusive, has unfortunately characterized much of the discussion among historians.[7]

In what follows, I want to make a modest contribution to efforts currently under way to think through the material/discursive impasse in the writing of social history through a brief consideration of the psychiatric case histories from the legal case files of men charged with homosexual offences in early-twentieth-century Ontario.[8] If Chauncey is right, and I think he is, that doctors and medical discourse did not invent the homosexual, the question remains, What did they do? During mental examinations, doctors translated men's sexual experiences with other men into cases of 'insanity,' 'perversion,' and 'homosexuality.' Key to this process – and what I want to trace here – were the textual practices of the case history. I also want to look at the discursive linkages between case histories and the broader medical discourse. Worked up into articles in medical journals and texts, doctors' case histories became the basis for an emerging psychiatric discourse in Canada, one that linked homosexual behaviour with mental disease.

The Ontario case also allows us to explore what may be some interesting divergences between Canada and the United States vis-à-vis state formation and sexual regulation. Chauncey has suggested for the United States that medical professionals 'did not play a major role in the state regulation of homosexuality until World War II.'[9] That Ontario courts sent men charged with homosexual offences for psychiatric examination beginning around 1910 – the earliest examination I discovered dates from 1905 – suggests that the Canadian state, at least at the local level, began to draw on the power of medical professionals and medical discourse sooner than in the United States. Chauncey further argues that until the mid-twentieth century, doctors and medical discourse had little impact on the lives and self-understandings of most homosexually active men. What influence doctors had specifically over men's sense of their sexual identities remains an elusive historical question, but it is clear that doctors *did* have an impact on the lives of homosexually active men, at least upon many of those hauled before the courts in Ontario. Thinking of Walter's case, doctors had the power to help determine whether a man stood trial or not. Doctors' expert testimony also had the power to influence the outcome of a man's trial and, if found guilty, whether he was sent to jail, committed to a hospital, or in some cases released on suspended sentence. Thinking of the judges involved in Walter's trials, it is clear that their understanding of sexual relations between men was shaped in part by the emerging medical/psychiatric conceptualization of homosexual behaviour as a 'disease of the mind.' Indeed, I would suggest that links established among criminality, insanity, and homosexuality in the early-twentieth-century Ontario court cases, doctors' case histories, and psychiatric discourse laid some of the groundwork for the intensification of medico-legal regulation during and after the Second World War, most notably in the creation of sexual psychopath laws and their particularly devastating effects on gay men.

Before attending to the discursive operations of the case history, I want to foreground what Judith Walkowitz has termed 'the material context of discursive struggle.'[10] I will do this by tracing the historical and material context of the emergence of the psychiatric case history.

The History of the Case History

Ironically, historians who often rely on case histories as primary sources have paid little attention to the historical emergence of the case history. But the case history does have a history. The medical case history, for instance, has a long genealogy, one stretching back to Hippocrates and the cases in his *Epidemics*. As Julia Epstein has noted, a renewed interest in Hippocratic medicine in the seventeenth century produced a flurry of treatises on case-taking. But, as Epstein demonstrates, 'not until the nineteenth century were these ... translated into particular techniques of notation and data organization in patient histories ... Case-taking did not become a formalized or systematic procedure until it became connected with clinical schools and institutions and their need to produce and codify a professional discourse.'[11] We need, then, to skip ahead to the nineteenth century, in which a changing material context established the preconditions for the emergence of the case history as we know it. Two processes were crucial here. First, rapid urbanization in the nineteenth century demanded the development of new devices, including statistics, social surveys, criminal identification methods, and, of course, case histories, in order to know and regulate increasingly large populations of urban dwellers. As Dorothy Smith explains: 'Case histories and case records evolved ... when government welfare agencies or charitable organizations were confronted with the numbers and anonymities of the late nineteenth-century city, when the particularized knowledge of people and their histories characterizing smaller communities no longer served.'[12] Second, the historical emergence of case histories was also intimately linked with the efforts of experts to professionalize their fields. In her work on the history of single mothers and social work, for instance, Regina Kunzel demonstrates how casework − 'key to the professionalizing project of social workers' − 'used a step-by-step procedure of collecting information about a person's experiences and background, followed by "diagnosis" and "treatment" of their problem.'[13]

Case histories, of course, also proved to be particularly integral to the nineteenth-century emergence of the professions of psychiatry and sexology. One of the pioneers of the sexological case history was Richard von Krafft-Ebing. His classic text *Psychopathia Sexualis*, published in 1886, was originally based on forty-five case histories. As Jeffrey Weeks has noted, Krafft-Ebing's 'case studies were a model of what was to follow, the analyses were a rehearsal for a century of theorizing.' From the beginning, the psychiatric case history was tied to the legal realm. Krafft-Ebing, who described *Psychopathia Sexualis* as a 'medico-forensic study,' was a professor of psychiatry whose 'earliest concern was with finding proofs of morbidity for those sexual offenders dragged before the courts.'[14] Over the next several decades, the case history became central to the practice and professionalization of psychiatry. Elizabeth Lunbeck, for example, in her fine history of psychiatry based on the case records of the Boston Psychopathic Hospital (established in 1912), has drawn attention to the significance of 'the examination and the constitution of the case.'[15]

The reciprocal relationship between the law and medicine was forged in Ontario beginning in the late nineteenth century through the courts' referral of men charged with homosexual offences to doctors for examination. Medical examination took two different forms. Some men were sent to doctors for a regular physical exam to obtain medical evidence of sexual activity. Doctors probed what they preferred to call men's 'anal apertures' on the lookout for the tell-tale traces of penetration: semen, a 'dilated aperture,' and the like. But by the opening decade of the twentieth century, some men were sent by the courts specifically for mental examinations. The issue of an accused's mental condition was an extremely important matter in the courtroom. Lawyers defending men charged with a homosexual offence sometimes argued their clients were not guilty by reason of insanity. The prosecution might also claim an accused man was insane in order to secure a conviction, suggesting that an insane man posed a danger to himself and others. Either way it was necessary to have medical proof. The law required that at least two doctors concur that the accused was insane, and further stipulated that the doctors spell out their diagnoses in a 'Province of Ontario Physician's Certificate.' The physician's certificate was a rudimentary case history recording the doctor's examination of the accused along with a determination of whether the accused was sane or insane.[16] Certificates were entered as exhibits in the trial and sometimes accompanied by a doctor's testimony in court. The significance of the certificate and how to conduct a mental examination constituted a part of medical instruction in late-nineteenth-century Ontario. In his lectures to graduating medical students, published in 1895, Daniel Clark, the superintendent of the Toronto Insane Asylum, explained that the physician's certificate was 'a record of observed facts' and he stressed that the 'medical certificates are important documents, hence great care should be exercised in filling them up properly.'[17]

As one way to bolster the modern, scientific status of the emerging profession, psychiatrists devoted much energy to refining and making more complex the case history, both the mental examination and its corresponding documentary forms. In his annual report for 1906, S.A. Armstrong, the provincial inspector of prisons and public charities, announced that 'a new system of casebook or clinical records, together with a filing system, has now been completed and will be installed in all the Asylums of the province at the beginning of the new year.' Armstrong noted that 'the system will be uniform throughout and will be in keeping with the most modern practice of recording the history and clinical records pertaining to a patient.' The following year, Armstrong was pleased to report that 'the new system of recording clinical notes of cases ... has proved most satisfactory ... In compiling the data necessary for completion of the history of a patient, greater attention will be paid to the case by the attending physician than has been possible heretofore.'[18] The introduction of the new case-history forms and procedures was greeted with enthusiasm by psychiatrists. In October 1907, the *Bulletin of the Ontario Hospitals for the Insane* noted with approval the introduction of the new 'history form.' Two years later, Dr Charles K. Clarke, one of the country's leading psychiatrists and the superintendent of the Toronto Hospital for the Insane after Daniel Clark's retirement in 1905, wrote in an article on 'The Relationship of Psychiatry to General Medicine' that 'in any study of mental disease you must scan closely: the family history, the whole life history of the patient, the history of the disease, and the present condition.' 'No wonder,' Clarke concluded, 'even a poor form of application is elaborate.' Clarke's was one of many similar articles pressing for the acceptance of psychiatry among general practitioners, and key to psychiatry's campaign for professional legitimacy was the case history.[19]

The case history assumed an increasingly central position in psychiatric practice in the opening decades of the twentieth century. This was evident at the Psychiatric Clinic of the Toronto General Hospital. Opened in 1909, the Psychiatric Out-Patient Clinic was the first of C.K. Clarke's efforts to establish a psychiatric practice separate from the asylum system. As Jennifer Stephen has demonstrated, central to the Clinic's work was 'a textual, clinical approach that was rooted in the identification of individual pathology: in other words, an emphasis on the psychiatric case study.' A good number of the Clinic's patients were those referred to it by the courts. As Stephen notes, Clarke became 'a significant contributor to the development of forensic psychiatry in Canada. His sphere of influence extended well beyond the Toronto Psychiatric Clinic into the criminal justice system; he was called upon frequently as an expert witness in notable trials during the period.'[20]

Homosexuality and Ontario Doctors

Before looking at a few examples of the case history, it will be helpful to situate them within the context of Ontario doctors' understandings of sexual relations between men in the late nineteenth and early twentieth centuries. For some Ontario doctors the ample evidence of sexual relations between men supplied by the courts was a sign of the degeneration of civilization in Ontario. Degeneration theory held that sexual and other perversions were manifestations of a physical process of decline in which some people reverted to earlier moments in the evolution of the species. In 1898, Ezra Hurlburt Stafford, first assistant physician at the Toronto Asylum for the Insane, delivered an address on the subject of 'Perversion' before the Toronto Medical Society, subsequently published in the *Canadian Journal of Medicine and Surgery*. Drawing on Krafft-Ebing and Lombroso, Stafford was concerned mainly with prostitution and 'forms of perversion long familiar to readers of the later classical writers.' Stafford explained that these were 'indications of the insidious process of degeneration' and that 'many cases of sexual perversion may be set down as a reversion or a miscarriage in the chain of evolution.'[21]

Degeneration theory coexisted alongside other explanations for homosexual behaviour, theories that stressed homosexuality as a disease of the mind rather than as a reversion in the evolution of civilization. Even Stafford, who held firm to degeneration theory, allowed that some sexual perversion was 'not so often of the nature of a physical defect as of a mental aberration, and therefore a form of insanity.' Referring more specifically to sex between men, Stafford noted that 'in origin it is usually rather psychic than physical, and properly speaking comes under the study of the alienist rather than the surgeon or the physician.'[22] But there were different opinions among alienists as to the root of homosexuality. Under the influence of Freud, some believed that homosexuality, and mental illness more generally, resided in the subconscious. In Ontario, psychoanalytic theories were introduced by Ernest Jones, Freud's biographer and 'the man who almost singlehandedly forced a hearing for Freud's theories, first in North America, and later in England.' On the invitation of C.K. Clarke, Jones came to Toronto from London, England, in 1908 to be the first director of the Psychiatric Clinic. In addition, Jones worked as a pathologist at the Toronto asylum and as an associate professor of psychiatry at the University of Toronto.[23] He published numerous articles in Canadian medical journals, introducing physicians to the principles of psychoanalysis. In 'Psycho-Analysis in Psycho-Therapy,' published in 1909 in the *Bulletin of the Ontario Hospitals for the Insane*, Jones informed his readers that the psychoanalytic method had been used successfully in treating 'practically all forms of psycho-neuroses, the different types of hysteria, the phobias, obsessions, anxiety neuroses, and even certain kinds of sexual perversions.'[24]

But most Ontario doctors remained unpersuaded by psychoanalysis, in large part because it challenged the 'somatic interpretation of nervous and mental diseases that was established orthodoxy among Canadian neurologists and psychiatrists.' Somatic theories held that mental diseases had a physical basis, that they were manifestations of organic brain disease. While numerous factors were believed to give rise to insanity, most doctors agreed that heredity was the primary cause.[25] In arguing for the somatic, hereditary basis of mental disease, doctors went further, claiming that as outgrowths of insanity, immorality and criminality were also inherited. Not surprisingly, then, much of the medical commentary on insanity and perversion overlapped with the medical pathologization of the working class, especially working-class immigrants. Psychiatrists, many of whom were involved in the Canadian eugenics and mental-hygiene movements, never tired of providing statistics to demonstrate the disproportionate number of 'foreign born' among Ontario's insane and perverted. In his 1906 report, Inspector Armstrong claimed that, of fifty-four male patients admitted to the Toronto Asylum, thirty-seven were of foreign birth, one of whom was 'a sexual pervert of the worst possible type.' A 1907 article on 'The Importation of Defective Classes' noted that, of the thirty-four men admitted to the Toronto insane asylum between December 1906 and February 1907, two were 'sexual perverts.' Referring to the 'hordes of immigrants' entering the country, C.K. Clarke used his 1907 annual report on the Toronto Hospital for the Insane to propound, '[I]t is all very well to talk about pumping in the population, but surely the streams tapped should not be those reeking with degeneracy, crime and insanity.' 'One sexual pervert hailing from the London Slums,' Clarke warned, 'has induced others of his family to come here.' Finally, an article entitled 'The Defective and Insane Immigrant,' published in 1908, summed up the connections among immigrants, insanity, and perversion. The author began by noting 'how startling is the preponderance of the foreign born among the insane of the country' and claimed that an analysis of the characteristics of immigrants admitted to Canadian asylums was 'an interesting study in degeneracy of a type we rarely see among Canadians,' including 'sexual perverts of the most revolting kind.'[26] All of the different understandings of perversion can be found in doctors' case histories.

Doing a Case History

Numerous articles in Canadian medical journals provided step-by-step instructions on how to perform a mental examination. As Dr H.C. Steeve wrote in a typical article that appeared in the *Canadian Journal of Medicine and Surgery* in 1922, 'the question of how to examine a patient for insanity is one which often arises.' Key to the answer was the case-history approach. Noting the 'overwhelming importance of the history,' Steeve explained that 'the keynote

THIS MAN IS A PSYCHIATRIST! INTO HIS QUIET, SUBDUED, TASTEFULLY DECORATED CONSULTATION ROOM COME THE *EMOTIONALLY DISTURBED*...THE *MENTALLY TROUBLED*...SEEKING *RELIEF* AND *SELF-UNDERSTANDING*. WITH HIS HELP, THESE PEOPLE ARE ABLE TO *PROBE* INTO THEIR OWN *SUBCONSCIOUS MINDS* AND FIND THE *ROOTS* AND *CAUSES* OF THEIR PROBLEMS. WITH HIS SKILLFUL GUIDANCE, THESE PEOPLE ARE ABLE TO *UNCOVER FORGOTTEN INCIDENTS*...*SUPPRESSED FEELINGS*...*BURIED RESENTMENTS AND HOSTILITIES*, WHICH, ONCE BROUGHT TO *LIGHT*, ARE *RE-EXAMINED*, *RE-EVALUATED*, AND *RESOLVED* IN A MUCH *HEALTHIER* AND *SATISFYING* WAY THAN HAD BEEN DONE IN THEIR DISTANT, DARK PAST. ONCE THE DOOR TO THE PAST IS *OPENED*, AND THE *LIGHT OF UNDERSTANDING* IS *PLUNGED* INTO THE *SUBCONSCIOUS GLOOM*, *HEALTH*, *HAPPINESS*, AND *PEACE OF MIND* ARE THE RESULTS. AND THIS *PROBING*, THIS *OPENING OF DOORS*, THIS *CASTING OF LIGHT*, THIS *UNEARTHING* AND *RE-EXAMINING* AND *RE-EVALUATING* IS *ACCOMPLISHED* BY THE *SCIENTIFIC METHOD* KNOWN AS...

PSYCHOANALYSIS

IN EACH ISSUE OF *"PSYCHOANALYSIS,"* WE WILL E͟XA͟MINE THE *CASE HISTORY FILES* OF *THREE PEOPLE* WHO *COME* TO THE PSYCHIATRIST FOR *HELP*. RIGHT NOW, HE DOCTOR IS PULLING THE FOLDER OF THE *FIRST* PATIENT. *READY?* THEN LET'S SIT IN ON THE *SECOND SESSI͟*ON OF...

Front cover of *Psychoanalysis* 1:2 (May-June 1955). (Tiny Tot Comics Inc.)

of all successful examinations ... is thoroughness and system, bringing out each phase and feature of the case.' The bulk of Steeve's article was given over to the questions to be asked by the examiner. Once the examiner had 'brought out' the answers or the symptoms, they needed 'to be sorted out and classified' and Steeve provided the categories in which to classify and label the 'subjective and objective symptoms' of insanity. 'It is by such a process,' Steeve concluded, 'that the soundness or otherwise of the mind must be judged and I feel quite sure that any physician, whether experienced in psychiatry or not, who will follow out the examinations as suggested here will make very few errors.'

The place to begin the psychiatric case history according to Steeve was with the patient's family history, reflecting the importance attached to heredity in the etiology of mental diseases. Beginning with family history 'not only supplies the examiner with information of inestimable value, but serves to gain the confidence of the patient, to put him at ease, and to make the intricate paths of his mind much more readily accessible to the examiner.' 'Begin with the father,' the article continued, 'learn whether he is alive or dead ... If he is dead, at what age did he die, of what cause.' Crucial in this part of the investigation was the question of whether the father or other family members died at home. 'In answer to this question one will quite occasionally learn that the father or some other member of the family died in a mental hospital when the patient never had any intention of admitting that there ever was such a thing as insanity in the family.'[27] Dr Bruce Smith pursued this line of questioning during his mental examination of Carlo C., an Italian immigrant. Carlo's troubles began after Toronto police discovered his sexual involvement with several different young men over the summer of 1909. Smith learned that Carlo's 'father had died of apoplexy, his mother of epilepsy and a brother had died in the asylum.' Carlo's was diagnosed as a case of 'chronic progressive paranoia, inciting to the most abominable practices.' Smith's diagnosis was corroborated in court by three other doctors, including C.K. Clarke.[28]

Another key element of the diagnostic procedure of the case history zeroed in on the patient's sexual past. As Steeve wrote, 'When the [case] history has brought the patient to the age of fourteen or fifteen the question of sexual development is inquired into with the idea of learning of unusual sexual irritations or excitements; of masturbation or other practices frequently developed at this period of life which may indicate a neurotic or nervous temperament which is so frequently the fertile soil for the later development of mental disease.' The doctor who examined Thomas M., a labourer from Sault Ste Marie charged in 1926 with indecently assaulting a boy to whom he had offered a ride, noted that Thomas 'admits practising masturbation ... Says he has wet dreams nearly every night.' Although Thomas told the doctor that he had not masturbated 'since he was circumcised about two year ago,' the doctor – likely convinced that Thomas's solitary vices were linked to his more public perversions – recorded in the case history that Thomas 'is a great liar. You cannot believe him at all.' This, along with other 'facts indicating insanity,' including a 'dull' appearance and the fact that Thomas 'will not stay at work,' were enough for the doctor to 'certify that the said Thomas M. is insane.'[29]

Other facts indicating insanity were numerous indeed. According to Steeve, insanity might be revealed by a patient's answers to questions as simple as 'Does he recognize the proper season of the year, day of the week, month, etc.?' One doctor had his own 'small test,' which he believed 'very often revealed serious mental weakness.' In 1905, Tennyson W., a married, thirty-six-year-old gardener, was caught having sex with three youths just off Toronto's Yonge Street. Tennyson's lawyer suggested he visit a doctor. As Dr James Richardson wrote in a letter to Tennyson's defence lawyer, 'Mrs W. called upon me last evening along with her husband and told me that you ... wished me to examine him as to his mental condition. I had a long interview with him ... I gave him to multiply four figures by four others ... He soon put down the first, but pondered some time over every succeeding one.' The doctor included the math test along with the case history; Tennyson failed the test. The doctor admitted that 'this may be merely the result of want of eduction, but his writing ... is not that of an ignorant man, and his figures were made correctly and clearly.' Therefore, the doctor concluded, 'I have no hesitation in giving the opinion that' Tennyson 'shows symptoms of incipient lunacy.' But perhaps more germane to the doctor's diagnosis of incipient lunacy was his belief, indicated in the concluding observations of his case history, that 'a married man, whose conduct had always been proper should have acted in the indecent, dirty, foul way he did on a public street in open day light would itself lead one to suspect that there was some mental defect.'[30]

In cases where doctors had a difficult time certifying a man as insane, there existed a whole range of other mental illnesses with which to explain men's homosexual behaviour. Based on intelligence tests that measured 'mental age' and were developed in the eugenics and mental-hygiene movements, the 'mentally defective' were divided into increasingly numerous and discrete categories of mental disorder, including 'idiots,' 'imbeciles,' and the 'feeble-minded.' In Toronto in 1920, Daniel L., a single, twenty-two-year-old tailor, was caught having sex with a labourer in a laneway off Ontario Street. Dr G. Boyer wrote to the court that Daniel had a mental development 'not more than that of a boy of eight or ten years of age' and concluded that 'he is mentally defective.' In another case, two exhibition-goers reported James C. and his friend Charles W. to the police after spying the two young men having sex at the 1913 Canadian

National Exhibition. Awaiting trial in jail, James, a nineteen-year-old labourer, was examined by the assistant superintendent of the Ontario Hospital for the Insane. James had a 'mentality' of 'a child of four years of age.' 'In my opinion,' the doctor wrote, 'he is an idiot.' The assistant superintendent also noted about James that 'physically he is undeveloped, and shows many marks of degeneration such as asymmetry of the face, high palate, asymmetry of his legs and he is also unable to talk plainly.' The physical exam reflected the persistence of somatic theories in which the signs of perversity were read directly off the surface of the body.[31]

The doctors who examined David J., a seventy-one-year-old minister charged in 1925 with committing an act of gross indecency with a younger draughtsman, believed he was suffering from mental impairment and nervous exhaustion. Dr W.T. Parry, the surgeon at the Toronto jail, concluded that 'his mentality shows marked signs of deterioration and yet while he is not insane ... neither do I think that he is entirely responsible for his acts on account of his impaired mentality.' Another doctor, this one from the Ontario Hospital for the Insane at Mimico, noted that David, some thirty years prior to his offence, had suffered a spinal injury that for two years left him unable to work. 'At times during these two years he experienced discreditable impulses ... and sexual improprieties, but they were always of short duration.' At the time of his offence, David had travelled to Toronto and 'was greatly prostrated by the hot weather and the fatigue of the journey ... In his exhausted condition the old impulses re-appeared.' David's condition was also partly to be explained by historical circumstance, in particular, the great Methodist/Presbyterian church union crisis of 1925. David had come to Toronto to attend the General Assembly and was suffering 'disappointment and worry over the action of his congregation in church union and his own future status.' The third doctor, one less historically, more psychoanalytically, minded, believed that David's problem was not so much a spiritual crisis as it was a case of repressed sexual desire for men. 'In my opinion,' the third doctor stated, David was 'suffering from a Psycho-neurosis.' His examination of David revealed 'a short and unhappy married life' leaving him 'without anyone to confide in and rely on intimately and for many years there has been continual repression of emotions and impulses.' Perhaps the opportunity afforded by the psychoanalytic encounter to finally confide and be intimate was therapeutic for David, for as the doctor noted, David 'seemed perfectly frank with me and admitted having had to fight against sex impulses ... These impulses have been associated with men.' Even though one of the other doctors had discovered 'sexual improprieties' earlier in David's life, this doctor concluded that David's was 'probably not a long-standing or deeply rooted perversion.'[32]

The Homosexual Talks Back

In the cases of some men, doctors were unable to find any symptoms of insanity or other mental illness. Even Dr Bruce Smith, who endorsed 'asexualization' for 'perverts,' testified in court in 1909 that men who had sex with other men 'may appear perfectly normal in other respects and may display a fair amount of mental culture.'[33] Unable to find symptoms of mental pathology in their patients, some doctors (though certainly not Dr Bruce Smith) concluded that a man's sexual desire for another man was not a mental disease. This belief originated with the work of sexologists such as Havelock Ellis. Ellis first introduced his ideas in *Sexual Inversion*, a volume in his *Studies in the Psychology of Sex*, published in 1897. Like Krafft-Ebing's *Psychopathia Sexualis*, Ellis's *Sexual Inversion* employed the case-history approach. Ellis wrote that 'when the sexual impulse is directed towards persons of the same sex we are in the presence of an aberration variously known as "sexual inversion" ... or, more generally, "homosexuality."' Ellis argued that homosexuality or sexual inversion was a congenital or inborn characteristic, not an acquired vice nor the product of a diseased, degenerate mind. 'Congenital sexual inversion,' Ellis wrote, is 'akin to a biological variation ... often having no traceable connection with any morbid condition.'[34] While still insisting on its biological basis, the move away from degeneration and disease toward the more neutral concept of 'variation' represented a major medical reconceptualization of homosexuality. While many Ontario doctors persisted in viewing sex between men as a vice or a disease of the mind, a letter written in 1907 suggests that at least one Ontario doctor was familiar with the emerging sexological concept of homosexuality. On 18 October 1907, Dr R.J. Dwyer wrote to His Honour Judge Winchester about the results of his examination of Thomas C., a manual warehouse labourer from Toronto. Beginning with the results of his physical examination of Thomas, Dr Dwyer noted that aside from 'marked atrophy of the sexual organs' and 'a diseased condition of one testicle ... physically he is generally well developed.' Moving on to the results of the 'mental examination,' Dwyer explained to Judge Winchester that while Thomas's 'mental capacity' might be 'below the normal average,' 'he impresses one as being gentle and refined, even aesthetic, having no bad habits and quite far from coarseness or brutality.' Dwyer continued: 'He is evidently the victim of an unnatural and perverted sexual instinct – that form in which the natural attraction towards the opposite sex is replaced by an unnatural attraction for the same sex (Homosexuality).' 'It is further of importance to note,' Dwyer wrote, 'that this condition is one which has existed from birth and is not an acquired condition the result of vice and dissipation.' While Dwyer continued to use the language of the 'unnatural' and the 'perverted,' he used these terms in a very different way than many Ontario doctors. Rather than conclude that Thomas suffered from mental disease, Dwyer preferred to explain Thomas's behaviour as the product of an inborn 'sexual instinct,' his 'homosexuality.'

Sexologists like Ellis believed their theories were politically progressive; insisting on the congenital basis of homosexuality rather than on homosexuals as wilful criminals or perverts with an acquired vice was one way to argue that homosexuals should be removed from the purview of the law. Indeed, Ellis and like-minded doctors supported the late-nineteenth- and early-twentieth-century reform movements to repeal anti-homosexual laws. Some doctors worked toward similar ends on a more case-by-case basis. Often the intent behind the insanity defence in homosexual trials was to save an accused from prison. As Dr Dwyer wrote to the judge, Thomas's homosexuality made him, if anything, 'mentally deficient ... rather than criminal ... I am of the opinion that to commit him to prison would be futile so far as curing him of his condition as he could not be kept there long enough to eradicate his perverted instinct, while on the other hand the factors upon which we depend most to suppress the manifestations of this instinct – his mental and moral faculties, would suffer disastrously by such an experience leaving him worse after than before. The ideal would be to have him placed in charge of some one or some institution which while he was kept actively employed, he could have medical treatment and at the same time have no opportunity or temptation to yield to his instinct. Moreover, it would be a matter of keeping such supervision over him for years as this is not an acquired habit but a congenital condition.'[35]

While claiming homosexuals were simply born that way or were insane did save some men from prison, it simultaneously delivered them into the hands of doctors. Those men sent by the courts to be examined before or during a trial and those later sentenced to be incarcerated in asylums and psychiatric wards of reformatories became case histories not only for the courts but also for psychiatrists. Psychiatrists used the case histories they conducted for the courts to write articles for medical journals and texts. This was another step in the professionalization of psychiatry, for 'as professions and professional discourses have been established, case histories and case records have become part of the knowledge basis of the professional discourse.' To give but one example, during the period January 1929 to September 1933, 150 people charged with sex offences were sent by the court to the Toronto Psychiatric Hospital for examination. Of the 150 case histories conducted at the hospital, 100 went on to form the basis of an article written by Dr A.J. Kilgour published in 1933 in the *Ontario Journal of Neuropsychiatry*, entitled 'Sex Delinquency – A Review of 100 Court Cases Referred to the Toronto Psychiatric Hospital.' Kilgour began

PSYCHIATRIC HOSPITAL, TORONTO

A building that looms large in the history of Canadian psychiatry. Toronto Psychiatric Hospital, 1924–65. (Archives of the History of Canadian Psychiatry and Mental Health Services, Griffin-Greenland slides, V1-2)

his article by classifying the 'types of sex acts' committed by the sex offenders. Here, using the terms in a strictly descriptive manner, Kilgour classified the sex acts as 'homosexual' and 'heterosexual.' When he turned to a discussion of selected case histories, however, those involving homosexual acts were transformed into cases of what he called 'homosexuality,' while the discussion of the case histories involving heterosexual acts remained cases of 'sexual acts with female minors,' 'rape,' 'incest,' and so on, rather than cases of 'heterosexuality,' a term never used in the study.[36]

The introduction of the case-history approach aroused much debate among medical professionals. Doctors were suspicious of the case history because it challenged traditional medical techniques based on physical examination, but even more so because doctors believed it lacked scientific objectivity, relying as it did on the word of the patient. This very characteristic of the case history – the way it allowed the patient to speak – opened up possibilities for patients to resist doctors' efforts to pathologize them.[37] In her analysis of *Sex Variants: A Study of Homosexual Patterns*, a medico-scientific inquiry into homosexuality in New York City in the late 1930s, Jennifer Terry analyses the process 'by which a position or identity space is constructed discursively by sexology and medicine and strategically seized upon by its objects of study.' Terry traces how 'deviant subjects ... have spoken back against the terms of a pathologizing discourse.' A similar process can be detected at work in the psychiatric case histories of Ontario men. In his study of sex delinquency, for example, Kilgour concluded about the homosexual cases that 'the sex life was unsatisfactory in all cases.' But the individual case histories told a different story. 'Case 1,' for example, a forty-year-old, single caretaker, told Kilgour that 'he enjoyed this form of sex act.' Similarly, about 'Case 2,' a thirty-six-year-old, single salesman, Kilgour recorded that 'he said he enjoyed this form of sex activity better than the normal heterosexual variety.' Kilgour was particularly surprised by 'Case 3.' The married labourer 'admitted the acts but did not feel that they were wrong and had no particular feeling of guilt or shame. He said "God said in the Bible if a man wants to be filthy, let him be filthy and He would judge him. The law that says it is wrong is only a man-made law, not God's law, and therefore it was all right for me to do as I did."'[38]

Conclusion

I want to return to the issue of the status of the case histories as historical evidence. It is tempting to read in the psychiatric case histories the doctors' diagnoses of 'homosexuality' and 'sexual perversion' and on that basis argue that the case histories constitute the evidence of homosexual experience in the past. But it is unlikely that all or even many of the men sent for mental examinations thought of themselves as insane, as sexual perverts, or even as homosexuals. In the larger project from which this chapter is drawn I show, following Chauncey, that for some men in early-twentieth-century Ontario sexual relations with other men were an outgrowth of or gave rise to unconventional sexual/gender identities, while many other men who engaged in homosexual behaviour did not adopt such identities and remained within the bounds of what at the time was considered 'normal manhood.'[39] To read the case histories in a way that accepts the doctors' diagnoses at face value would be to assign to many men sexual identities they may never have embraced. It would also be to ignore the complicity of the case history in producing the categories and identities of insanity and homosexuality, and it is here that I find post-structuralist insights into the discursive operations of texts most helpful.

During their examinations, doctors did not objectively record symptoms of illness or simply note down a patient's own sense of identity; doctors actively constructed illnesses and identities for the men who appeared before them. The textual practices of the psychiatric case history – as set out, for example, in the article by Dr Steeve – organized doctors' examinations and diagnoses by providing them with 'standardized methods of observation and investigation, categories, interpretive schemata and practices.' As Jennifer Stephen has wryly observed about the case history in the work of the Psychiatric Clinic, '[T]he forms designed for use at the [Clinic] could hardly remain blank. The point was to locate and identify the abnormal.'[40] In identifying the abnormal, the textual practices of the case history abstracted men and their sexual experiences from their local, lived contexts. Men, some of whom were known in the street as 'pansies,' 'sissies,' and 'fairies,' were labelled by doctors during psychiatric examinations as 'insane,' 'perverts,' and 'homosexuals.' The resulting rupture or disjuncture between experience and text at the centre of the case history informs its status as historical evidence: rather than as the unmediated evidence of a pre-existing homosexual or homosexuality, the case histories and the broader psychiatric discourse of which they were a part are better viewed as constructed 'representations of the object of their knowledge.'[41]

That case histories were representations of men's sexual behaviours and identities, often distorted and inaccurate ones, does not mean they were without repercussions on men's lives. Chauncey has argued that early-twentieth-century medical professionals and discourse had only limited influence on homosexually active men, especially working-class men, because it is unlikely they read elite, obscure medical journals and texts.[42] While I concur with Chauncey that most men did not learn about their sexual identities by reading such literature, a broader range of doctors' impacts on men, especially on the predominantly working-class and immigrant men hauled before the courts, comes into view if we expand our notion of what constitutes 'medical discourse' beyond periodicals and textbooks. That the psychiatric examination/case history of an accused man took place in a jail cell, a doctor's office, a clinic, or even an accused's home, reminds us that medical discourse was a series of concrete practices generating relations of power and knowledge in local settings. In court, doctors and their case histories had the power to influence both judges' understandings of sexual relations between men and the outcome of a man's trial. Thinking of discourses as practices rather than solely as texts – or, to put it another way, thinking of discourses as texts that *work* – is one way to capture something of the materiality of discourse.[43]

As case histories were linked to broader psychiatric and legal discourses, the net of their power relations was cast further afield. To give just one example, in 1948 the Canadian Penal Association, in cooperation with the Canadian Bar Association, the Canadian Medical Association, the National Committee for Mental Hygiene, the Canadian Welfare Council and the federal Department of Justice, established a committee on the 'Problem of the Sex Offender.' Part of the movement that would culminate in the 1954 Royal Commission on the Criminal Law Relating to Criminal Sexual Psychopaths, the committee chose to open its preliminary report with a long, detailed 'case history' with commentary by a penitentiary psychiatrist. In relating the case of a twenty-year-old man, the psychiatrist noted there was no history of neuropathic traits, except that 'at the age of thirteen he developed a nervous state of mind ... responsible for queer behaviour such as chewing on handkerchiefs and shirt collars.' More significant was the fact that he 'was initiated, early in life, in sexual activities along homo-sexual lines. Persisted in that form of activity and has become a confirmed sex-ual invert ... He has been in trouble with the law since about the age of fourteen years over his abnormal sex life.' On the basis on this case history and others like it, the committee rested its conclusion that the problem of the sex offender was 'large in size' and required immediate changes in the law, increased resources for psychiatric treatment, and a public campaign of sex education.[44] The case history – first introduced into Ontario psychiatric/legal practice in the early twentieth century – was one of the principal forms of knowledge and power undergirding the intensified medico-legal regulation of homosexual rela-tions in the post-war period.

While post-structuralism draws our attention to historical sources as active texts, there are also silences in much post-structuralist work. Post-structuralist critics urge historians to historicize all their foundational categories, such as experience and agency, but these same critics rarely bother to historicize dis-course itself, often leaving it as a foundational category in their work.[45] Jenni-fer Terry, for example, makes no reference in her article to the historical or material context in which the *Sex Variants* study was produced. She does admit that 'the deviants' clash with medicine is not entirely dependent on the medical discourse for its enunciation. Much of this conflict comes from lesbian and gay subcultural practices which may overlap with the pathologizing discourse but whose origins, implications, and effects are locatable partially outside the hegemonic formations of science and medicine in a homosexual "under-world."' In an article that aims to suggest new historiographic practices, this crucial point is relegated to a footnote.[46] But to step outside the text (or, more accurately, to read a text not in isolation but against other texts), whether to trace subcultural practices or to set out material contexts, is essential if only because it underlines the fundamental point that discursive forms are histori-cally specific. Historicizing discourse helps us to explain how, why, and when the identities that discursive forms construct (as well as the identities they fail to register) emerge when they do. As I've tried to show briefly, the emergence of the homosexual as a case history was wrapped up in broader historical developments during the late nineteenth and early twentieth centuries, most notably the professionalization of psychiatry. Recognizing that discursive forms have a history, that is, analysing the material context of their emergence, is one interpretive move that makes the sharp differentiation between discourse and the material begin to fade from view. This, in turn, moves us beyond unhelpful, dichotomous positions, opening up a space in which to theorize the 'discursive construction of social experience' in a way that 'can enrich rather than erase our sense ... of material life.'[47]

Notes

1 Archives of Ontario (AO), Crown Attorney Prosecution Case Files, York County, 1911, case 8. *Toronto Evening Telegram*, 20 February 1911, 7, and 22 May 1911, 6

2 Michel Foucault, *The History of Sexuality: An Introduction*, trans. Robert Hurley (New York 1978), 43

3 It is important to remember that the psychiatric case history was only one of many different types of documents that made up the homosexual's legal case file. Despite the array of textual material to be found in the legal case file, historians often treat it as a monolithic whole, pulling pieces of information willy-nilly from the different documents of the file as it suits the demands of their narrative. But many of the documents that make up the case file have their own distinct provenance and textual form, and there are important interpretive reasons for disaggregating the case file. At the very least, we need to distinguish between the *case file* and the *case history*. The legal case file is not itself a case history or, at least, it is unlike the many case histories it may contain, including those produced by medical, social-welfare, parole, and other agencies. Each of these case histories is rooted in the distinct history of its originating agency. If we are to attain a comprehensive theorization of the legal case file, each distinct textual element of the file will require its own discursive genealogy similar to the one I am attempting here for the psychiatric case history. As for the legal case file itself, part of what makes it unique is its discursive practice of centralizing a number of disparate case histories into one textual site, linking them all to the powerful truth effects of the law.

4 Michel Foucault, *Discipline and Punish: The Birth of the Prison*, trans. Alan Sheridan (New York 1979), 189–91; *History of Sexuality*, 105

5 George Chauncey, 'From Sexual Inversion to Homosexuality: The Changing Medical Conceptualization of Female "Deviance,"' in Kathy Peiss and Christina Simmons, eds, *Passion and Power: Sexuality in History* (Philadelphia 1989), 109 and 106. See also Chauncey, *Gay New York: Gender, Urban Culture, and the Making of the Gay Male World, 1890–1940* (New York 1994), 125.

6 See James Chandler, Arnold I. Davidson, and Harry Harootunian, eds, *Questions of*

Evidence: Proof, Practice, and Persuasion across the Disciplines (Chicago 1994) and the special issue of *PMLA* on 'The Status of Evidence,' *PMLA* 111 (January 1996).

7 For the Gordon–Scott exchange see *Signs* 15 (Summer 1990), 848–60.

8 My search through court records housed at the Archives of Ontario turned up 313 case files involving sexual offences between men for the period 1890–1935. The cases employed here come from Archives of Ontario, Criminal Court Records, RG 22, Crown Attorney Prosecution Case Files, various series (hereafter AO, Crown Attorney Prosecution Case Files, county/district name, year, case number). In order to be granted research access to the crown attorney's files, I was required to enter into a research agreement with the Archives. In accordance with that agreement, all names have been anonymized and all case file numbers used here refer to my own numbering scheme and do not correspond to any numbers that may appear on the original case files.

9 Chauncey, *Gay New York*, 125. My thanks to George Chauncey for first drawing my attention to these national differences.

10 Judith Walkowitz, *City of Dreadful Delight: Narratives of Sexual Danger in Late-Victorian London* (Chicago 1992), 9. In addition to Walkowitz, I have found the following particularly helpful in thinking about the relationship between discourse and the material: Regina Kunzel, 'Pulp Fictions and Problem Girls: Reading and Rewriting Single Pregnancy in the Postwar United States,' *American Historical Review* 100 (December 1995), 1465–87; Kunzel, *Fallen Women, Problem Girls: Unmarried Mothers and the Professionalization of Social Work, 1890–1945* (New Haven 1993); Kathleen Canning, 'Feminist History after the Linguistic Turn: Historicizing Discourse and Experience,' *Signs* 19 (Winter 1994), 368–404; Lisa Duggan, 'The Trials of Alice Mitchell: Sensationalism, Sexology, and the Lesbian Subject in Turn-of-the-Century America,' *Signs* 18 (Summer 1993), 791–814; Mary Poovey, *Uneven Developments: The Ideological Work of Gender in Mid-Victorian England* (Chicago 1988), 17.

11 Julia Epstein, *Altered Conditions: Disease, Medicine, and Storytelling* (New York 1995), 36 and 38. See also 'The Art of the Case History,' a special issue of *Literature and Medicine* 11(Spring 1992) and Harriet Nowell-Smith, 'Nineteenth-Century Narrative Case Histories: An Inquiry into Stylistics and History,' *Canadian Bulletin of Medical History* 12 (1995), 47–67.

12 Dorothy E. Smith, 'Cases and Case Histories,' in *The Conceptual Practices of Power: A Feminist Sociology of Knowledge* (Toronto 1990), 89

13 Kunzel, 'Pulp Fictions and Problem Girls,' 1468, and *Fallen Women, Problem Girls*, esp. chapter 4

14 Jeffrey Weeks, *Sexuality and Its Discontents: Meanings, Myths and Modern Sexualities* (London 1985), 67

15 Elizabeth Lunbeck, *The Psychiatric Persuasion: Knowledge, Gender, and Power in Modern America* (Princeton, NJ, 1994)

16 On the medical certificate as case history and the process of committal to an insane asylum, see Wendy Mitchinson, 'Reasons for Committal to a Mid-Nineteenth Century Ontario Insane Asylum: The Case of Toronto,' in Wendy Mitchinson and Janice Dickin McGinnis, eds, *Essays in the History of Canadian Medicine* (Toronto 1988), 88–109, and S.E.D. Shortt, *Victorian Lunacy: Richard M. Bucke and the Practice of Late-Nineteenth-Century Psychiatry* (New York 1986), 50–1.

17 Daniel Clark, *Mental Diseases: A Synopsis of Twelve Lectures Delivered at the Hospital for the Insane, Toronto, to the Graduating Medical Classes* (Toronto 1895), 323–34

18 'Thirty-ninth Annual Report of the Inspectors of Prisons and Public Charities upon the Lunatic and Idiot Asylums ... of the Province of Ontario ... 1906,' Ontario *Sessional Papers*, 1907, ix; 'Annual Report of the Inspectors of Prisons and Public Charities ... 1907,' Ontario *Sessional Papers*, 1908, x

19 *Bulletin of the Ontario Hospitals for the Insane* 1 (October 1907) and C.K. Clarke, 'The Relationship of Psychiatry to General Medicine,' *Bulletin of the Ontario Hospitals for the Insane* 2 (November 1909), 9–10

20 Jennifer Stephen, 'The "Incorrigible," the "Bad," and the "Immoral": Toronto's "Factory Girls" and the Work of the Toronto Psychiatric Clinic,' in Louis A. Knafla and Susan W.S. Binnie, eds, *Law, Society, and the State: Essays in Modern Legal History* (Toronto 1995), 406–7

21 Ezra Hurlburt Stafford, 'Perversion,' *Canadian Journal of Medicine and Surgery* 3 (April 1898), 181–4. I first learned of Stafford's article reading Gary Kinsman, *The Regulation of Desire: Sexuality in Canada* (Montreal 1987), 91–2.

22 Stafford, 'Perversion,' 181–2, 183

23 Thomas E. Brown, 'Dr Ernest Jones, Psychoanalysis, and the Canadian Medical Profession, 1908–1913,' in S.E.D. Shortt, ed., *Medicine in Canadian Society: Historical Perspectives* (Montreal 1981), 315

24 Ernest Jones, 'Psycho-Analysis in Psycho-Therapy,' *Bulletin of the Ontario Hospitals for the Insane* 2 (November 1909), 32–43

25 Brown, 'Dr Ernest Jones,' 339

26 'Annual Report of the Inspectors of Prisons and Public Charities Upon the Lunatic and Idiot Asylums ... 1906,' Ontario *Sessional Papers*, 1907, ix; 'The Importation of Defective Classes,' *Bulletin of the Ontario Hospitals for the Insane* 1 (1907), 3–6; Hospital for Insane, Toronto, 'Annual Report of the Medical Superintendent for the Year Ending December 31st, 1907,' Ontario *Sessional Papers*, 1908, 4; 'The Defective and Insane Immigrant,' *Bulletin of the Ontario Hospitals for the Insane* 2 (July 1908), 10, 8

27 H.C. Steeve, 'The Physician's Responsibility in Connection with Insane and Their

Committal to Hospital, Together with Suggestion for Examination of a Patient,'
Canadian Journal of Medicine and Surgery 51 (May 1922), 199

28 AO, Crown Attorney Prosecution Case Files, York County, 1909, case 93

29 Ibid., Algoma District, 1926, case 203

30 Ibid., York County, 1905, case 87

31 On intelligence tests and the categories of mental illness see Stephen, 'The "Incorrigible," the "Bad," and the "Immoral,"' 421–2. AO, Crown Attorney Prosecution
Case Files, York County, 1920, case 53; 1913, case 11

32 AO, Crown Attorney Prosecution Case Files, York County, 1925, case 73

33 *Toronto Evening Telegram*, 20 Sept. 1909, 6. For Smith's thoughts on the 'asexualization' of 'perverts' see Smith, 'Mental Sanitation,' *Canada Lancet* 40 (1906–7),
976, cited in McLaren, *Our Own Master Race: Eugenics in Canada, 1885–1945*
(Toronto 1990), 42, 182.

34 Havelock Ellis, *Psychology of Sex: A Manual for Students* (New York, 1935), 218,
229. This is a condensed version of *Studies in the Psychology of Sex.*

35 AO, Crown Attorney Prosecution Case Files, York County, 1907, case 89

36 Smith, 'Cases and Case Histories,' 89; A.J. Kilgour, 'Sex Delinquency – A Review
of 100 Court Cases Referred to the Toronto Psychiatric Hospital,' *Ontario Journal of
Neuropsychiatry*, September 1933, 34–50

37 On the historical controversy surrounding the case history and the 'speaking pervert,' see Siobhan Somerville, 'Scientific Racism and the Emergence of the Homosexual Body,' *Journal of the History of Sexuality* 5 (October 1994), 263–4.

38 Jennifer Terry, 'Theorizing Deviant Historiography,' in the 'Queer Theory: Lesbian
and Gay Sexualities' issue of *differences*, vol. 3 (Summer 1991), 59–60. Kilgour,
'Sex Delinquency,' 37–9

39 Chauncey, *Gay New York*, esp. part I, 33–99

40 Smith, 'Cases and Case Histories,' 90; Stephen, 'The "Incorrigible," the "Bad," and
the "Immoral,"' 409

41 Smith, 'Cases and Case Histories,' 89

42 Chauncey, *Gay New York*, 125

43 Mariana Valverde makes a similar point when she argues that discursive practices are
'much broader than relations among words. Insofar as material objects such as
badges or clothes or church buildings function as signs, then the old dichotomy
between idealism and materialism recedes from view.' See Valverde, *The Age of
Light, Soap, and Water: Moral Reform in English Canada, 1885–1925* (Toronto
1991), 10. The idea that discourse is made up of textual and non-textual practices
was Foucault's; he was particularly interested in architecture and space as discourse.
It should be noted that there is some debate over whether Foucault meant there to be
an analytical distinction between 'discourses' and 'practices.' Some argue that 'practices' represent a domain intimately connected to but distinct from 'discourse,' while

others argue that Foucault intended no such analytical separation. With his repeated references to discourse versus 'concrete arrangements' and his insistence on the 'local centres' of power/knowledge, I believe Foucault did mean something unique by practices. The view that discourses are not free-floating but rooted and expressed in concrete practices is perhaps the view most amenable to social historians with a materialist bent. On these debates, see Jan Goldstein, ed., *Foucault and the Writing of History* (Oxford, UK, and Cambridge, Mass., 1994).

44 Canadian Penal Association, 'Interim Report: Committee on the Sex Offender,' June 1948. My thanks to Robert Champagne for passing on to me a copy of this report that he discovered in his research in the papers of the royal commission on the criminal sexual psychopath housed at the Public Archives of Canada. For historical background on the committee and the royal commission see Robert Champagne, 'Psychopaths and Perverts: The Canadian Royal Commission on the Criminal Law Relating to Criminal Sexual Psychopaths, 1954–58,' *Canadian Lesbian and Gay History Newsletter* 2 (September 1986), 7–9, and Kinsman, *The Regulation of Desire*, 125–9.

45 This point is made by Kathleen Canning in 'Feminist History after the Linguistic Turn.'

46 Terry, 'Theorizing Deviant Historiography,' 72

47 Kunzel, 'Pulp Fictions and Problem Girls,' 1473

4

Filing and Defiling: The Organization of the State Security Archives in the Interwar Years

GREGORY S. KEALEY

'George, you won,' said Guillam as they walked slowly towards the car.
'Did I?' said Smiley. 'Yes. Yes, well I suppose I did.'

John le Carré, *Smiley's People*

Le Carré, or rather his protagonist, George Smiley, won his Cold War a decade and a half before the actual demise of the Communist party of the Soviet Union and the United States of Soviet Russia, but for both George and his creator, the former MI5 agent David Cornwell, the moral ambiguities of that victory, and especially of the methods by which it was achieved, were overwhelming. The Smiley novels and the subsequent works of le Carré are moral tales for our time. Le Carré's fiction derives its power not only from riveting plots with detailed depictions of trade craft but also from careful characterization. No character is more important than Smiley, and at his core is an ever-increasing ambivalence about the Cold War. Indeed his doubts appear all the more profound because they develop from his uncertainties about the West itself, not from any delusions about the nature of the Eastern bloc – a point made even more clearly in le Carré's more recent novel *Our Game* (1995).

In sharp contrast to le Carré's focus on ambivalence and ambiguity, however, is the role played in the Smiley novels by the Central Registry, the immense national state security archives, which figures so centrally in the undeclared war fought by proxy by Western and Eastern intelligence services. Among the intriguing cast of characters that surrounds Smiley, none is more curious than the faithful Connie Sachs, 'Mother Russia,' 'the don woman from Oxford,' 'a don's daughter, a don's sister, herself some sort of academic,' whose dismissal from the Service was as crucial to Soviet mole Bill Haydon's survival as her return was to Smiley's eventual 'victory' over Karla, the Soviet spymaster. Connie Sachs's character colourfully embodies the Registry itself – the sacred and secret files in which lay the tortured hints, the implicit truths, the deep secrets, that may reveal the mole's burrow and hence the key to the maze that eventually will lead to Karla, and to 'victory.' Archival research has seldom received such literary celebration as it does in the work of John le Carré.

The purpose of this paper is rather more mundane than that of le Carré's novels. Here I trace the contours of Canada's secret service and examine its Central Registry and the files it contained. Unfortunately, I have found no Connie Sachs to open its secrets to me, and only the often frustrating, always tedious, and sometimes expensive use of the Access to Information Act (ATI) has allowed me some glimpses of the organizational structure of the Central Registry and its contents. Yet, it bears noting that the paper could not have been written without this 'access' legislation, which allows all Canadians to request government information subject to certain exemptions. Cumbersome and expensive though it may be, the ATI of 1983, especially when combined with the National Archives Act of 1986, has helped to create a renewed interest in the study of Canada's secret service.[1] Nevertheless, researchers who wish to pursue such topics should be forewarned that they will have to battle the Canadian Security Intelligence Service (CSIS) every step of the way to access materials even from the 1920s.

I shall begin with an outline of the Registry, proceed to discuss some of its file series, and then briefly consider the makers of the files themselves. Without a clear understanding of the provenance of these files, which played such a central role in the activities of Canada's secret political police, the historian would be in danger of grave misinterpretation. While this is true of all historical data, police reports and especially material compiled by agents and informants must be used with the greatest care.

The Royal Canadian Mounted Police (RCMP) Central Registry and Its Intelligence Section, 1920–1939

'The key to any successful intelligence system is its memory bank, its records, it filing system,' argue S.W. Horrall and Carl Betke in their until recently secret *Canada's Security Service*.[2] And their employer, the RCMP, followed that line from its inception in February 1920. From the outset, the Central Registry received considerable attention. The various Royal North-West Mounted Police (RNWMP) subversive files, carefully created by Commissioner A.B. Perry in 1919 at the height of the Canadian labour revolt, were transferred from Regina to the new Ottawa headquarters of the RCMP early the next year, although some had been centralized in Ottawa from their inception in 1919.[3] Within weeks Perry issued instructions to all branches regarding the new Registry.[4] From its inception the Registry had a separate Intelligence Section, initially headed by Constable John Hart and later by Corporal E.F. Inglis, who also served as secretary to Liaison and Intelligence Officer C.F. Hamilton.[5] A translator, generally a special constable (that is, not a member of the RCMP), also served in the Intelligence Section of the Registry. In 1926 this position was filled by Staff Constable Deighton, who was 'prepared to make authoritative translations' in no fewer than eleven foreign languages, and after a brief vacancy he was replaced in 1927 by Miss M. Babuka.[6] By 1930, when the Civil Service Commission prepared organizational charts for what it termed the 'Bureau of Records,' the Intelligence Section still consisted of a principal clerk from the force and a civilian translator. They were charged, in civil-service bureaucratese, with the 'correlation and classification of intelligence material; supervision of cross-referencing and selection of excerpts; decision as to action re: completeness; allocation; conformity with requirements; custody of records.'[7] The RCMP, however, continued to describe the file system as the Central Registry and did not want it confused with a normal departmental Central Registry, for 'the difference and importance of the RCMP Central Registry lies in the fact that it prepares and presents material to the executive officers and other Branches at Headquarters ready for action; that it anticipates the needs and demands of executive action for further information, precedents, etc., that it *previews everything coming in and reviews everything going out and after action has been taken.*'[8] The Intelligence Section, one of seven components of the Registry by 1930, was responsible for 'the Secret Service work of the Department,' namely 'investigations into the activities of revolutionary organizations and individuals, and covers every imaginable phase of such activities.'[9] The Intelligence Section Head, in addition to the classification and review function of the other section heads, also 'analyses, associates, compares, and tabulates in special records certain aspects of the information contained in the material he handles' before passing it on 'in person' to the Liaison and Intelligence Officer.[10]

The arrival of General J.H. MacBrien as the RCMP's third commissioner in 1931 led to numerous changes in the Force. A senior translator was added to the Intelligence Section to provide English versions of 'Russian, German, Polish, Czechoslovakian and Hungarian revolutionary and communistic propaganda.'[11] A Mr Arnoni received the job, which went unadvertised because of its 'very confidential' and 'highly secret nature.'[12] In 1934 Alexander Goodman, who had been in the Central Registry since its inception in 1920, succeeded V.J. LaChance as the head of the Registry.[13] Two years later, under the direction of

Commissioner MacBrien, Superintendent Vernon Kemp totally revamped the system of handling 'secret' files. The precipitant of these significant changes remains unknown, but in general the new system heightened security provisions. The term 'secret' was now 'only to be applied to correspondence dealing with Revolutionary and Radical Activities.' The Intelligence Branch, 'the Secret Service of Canada,' was to receive separate office space to enhance security, and access to 'Red Files,' 'Personal History Files,' and the 'Weekly Summary of Radical Activities' (*RCMP Security Bulletins*) was to be far more restricted.

Heightened security measures and ever-increasing intelligence and security activities contributed to a rapid expansion in the Registry, which had reached thirty-seven employees by early 1937, an increase of fifteen from 1930.[14] The Intelligence Section had grown from two to five, with an assistant joining the section head, and the addition of a second translator and a stenographer. The new job description indicated that the Intelligence Section Head continued to have the responsibility of 'searching, classifying, and registering all correspondence, reports, cypher and code messages, and literature relating to the Intelligence and Security Service work of the RCMP.' In addition, he personally distributed such material to the few officials entitled to see it, insured its accuracy and completeness, prepared material for the Liaison and Intelligence Officer 'for immediate action,' and generally took physical charge of all 'secret files and documents.' His assistant generally acted under his direction but had specific responsibility for the 'Literature Ledgers.' 'Translator No. 1' reviewed and provided summaries of imported literature in 'some fifteen languages' for decisions concerning exclusion from Canada (that is, censorship), provided translations of confidential police documents, and reviewed and summarized the Canadian radical press. 'Translator No. 2' dealt with all French-language materials. A December 1939 organizational chart of the Registry shows an even greater expansion, no doubt owing to the outbreak of the Second World War. The Intelligence Section, now under Lieutenant-Colonel E.C. Bisson, had grown to four constables, three sub-constables, a stenographer, and an unknown number of translators.[15]

The 'Bolshevik' Files

The files that filled the Intelligence Section of the Central Registry were of three primary types – 175 Subversion, 175P Subversives, 177 Subversive Publications – and all originated in 1919 when the Force became the major bureaucratic beneficiary of Canada's labour revolt.[16] In the spring of 1918 the union government led by Robert Borden became increasingly concerned about the rising militancy of the Canadian working class. By the end of the year the RNWMP, which had declined in size to only about three hundred members, and had had, at best, an uncertain future, suddenly found itself with an expanded mandate to provide federal policing for the nation west of the Lakehead. In the following months leading up the Winnipeg General Strike, the RNWMP put in place an extensive network of undercover detectives and secret agents. From the outset the major target was labour and the Left, and Commissioner Perry recognized that the Force's new lease on life depended on its effectiveness in this area. The structures developed in the first months of 1919 for recruiting and handling secret agents and for collecting and organizing their intelligence reports were carried over into the new RCMP the following year. For our purposes, the crucial innovations were the creation of three file series focused on 'Bolshevik subversion' – 175, 175P, and 177. The 175 series covers subject files dealing with so-called Bolshevism, 175P is the series of Personal History Files, and 177 is the series on 'subversive publications.' Each block began in January 1919 and was continued into the 1930s. While the system was modified in that decade, these file blocks still constitute major groupings in the new National Archives of Canada (NAC) Record Group 146, the records of the Canadian Security Intelligence Service (CSIS).

In early 1919 Commissioner A.B. Perry, Comptroller A.A. Maclean, and even the responsible minister Newton Rowell, a former Liberal, spent considerable time and energy setting up the Security Service side of the newly expanded RNWMP. On 6 January Perry circulated to his commanding officers two crucial memos that set the tone for the Force's focus over its sixty-five years of responsibility for Canada's secret police. Perry warned his men of 'the pernicious doctrines of Bolshevism which are spreading over the world, traces of which are found in many parts of Canada.' In Western Canada, the area of the RNWMP's jurisdiction in 1919, 'the main centres from which the doctrine emanates are Winnipeg, Edmonton, and Vancouver,' Perry noted, but he also drew their attention to 'the various foreign settlements ... which are very susceptible to Bolshevism [sic] teachings and propaganda.' As 'the sole Federal Police Force in Western Canada ... it is therefore our duty to actively enquire into and take such steps as may be legally possible to prevent the efforts of misguided persons to subvert and undermine the settled Government of Canada.' After reiterating the list of banned organizations under PC 2384, the Order in Council of 27 November 1918, he mandated his officers 'to take steps to select some good trustworthy men whom you consider could be employed effectively as Secret Agents.' Perry then drew their attention to the prohibited list of publications and the need to collect others that might fall foul of Criminal Code sections dealing with 'treasonable and seditious offenses.' (Here, then, is the basis for the 177 file block.) Word of mouth did not escape his attention, however, and 'very careful action is to be given to public speeches and addresses' and also to the 'street speeches more or less prevalent in large centres.' Where such speeches were anticipated to be seditious, short-hand accounts should be recorded. All such investigations 'must be conducted in such manner as not in any way to arouse suspicion or cause antagonism on the part of such associations or organizations.' Finally, Perry exhorted them 'to be alert' to furnish the government with 'any information' that would 'keep it early advised of any developments towards social unrest' to prevent such 'to develop into a menace to good order and public safety.'[17]

On the same day, Perry sent his commanding officers a second circular memo, providing more detail on their secret-service work. Under the head, 'Detectives and Bolshevism,' the Commissioner explained that 'Detectives and Secret Agents should make themselves fully acquainted with all labour and other organizations in their respective districts.' 'Each' were to be 'carefully investigated' to determine:

(A) The purpose and object of the Organization.
(B) If the Organization is one which could possibly be influenced by Bolsheviki propaganda in order to gain its ends.
(C) Has the Organization Bolsheviki tendencies at the present time.
(D) Is it a Bolsheviki organization.

Not surprisingly, (B), (C), and (D) 'must receive careful and constant attention.' Such ongoing investigations would feed the 175 file block, but, in addition, Perry also demanded that 'the officials and leaders of these organizations must be carefully investigated and as much as possible studied regarding their ways, habits, and antecedents.' Such study should be recorded in separate, confidential reports to the commanding officers, who in turn were to keep 'a file for each leader or official.' 'By such means,' the Commissioner explained, 'a complete history of these men and their doings to date will be available at any time.' After this seeming nod to the historian, Perry explained his operational purpose: 'It might be found that the officials of one organization take a minor part in the activities of some other organization. If this was carefully recorded on the man's file, it might prove of value at a later date.' Thus, in embryo, the 175P file block.[18]

The actual 175P block was created at the end of February when Assistant Commissioner W.H. Routledge, the head of the RCMP's Criminal Investigation Branch (CIB), centralized in Ottawa the personal files earlier envisioned by Perry. In a CIB memo to all commanding officers regarding personal-history files, Routledge explained: 'For the purpose of having at Headquarters a comprehensive and detailed history of all principal agitators, it has been decided to gather all possible information with regard to these men at the various points where they have been known to have been active at any time during their resident [sic] in Canada.' To highlight the importance of these files, the commanding officers were to 'give their personal supervision to their preparation.' Routledge made a series of modifications as the months passed regarding the data to be collected, but key points included date of arrival in Canada, naturalization, police record, 'degree of intelligence and education and all other possible information which would assist in compiling [sic] a complete record of the man.'[19] Two weeks later, he added 'influence and standing' in associations, 'ability and influence as an agitator,' 'intimate associations,' languages spoken, and 'habits' (smokes, drinks, gambles, etc.).[20]

While this data gathering may have appeared straightforward in Ottawa, it proved rather less so in the field. In mid-April, for example, Cortlandt Starnes, who was later to succeed Perry as commissioner, forwarded the complaints of his chief detective, Sergeant Albert Reames, to Perry. Reames explained that Secret Agent 32 could not get photographs for the personal-history files without arousing undue suspicion 'as on this game our customers are too wise.' Reames cautioned patience and care, while Starnes noted that 'members of the SPC [Socialist Party of Canada] are getting very suspicious of strangers and suspect almost everyone of them to be Secret Service agents of the Government.' Starnes also pointed out to Perry that '[e]nquiries regarding the Personal History of any member of their party, immediately arouses suspicion and the difficulties encountered by our men in obtaining the data required are considerably enhanced by their being strangers in the city.' As a result, Starnes instructed Secret Agent 32 to leave his biographical inquiries until he was 'thoroughly initiated into the different Socialist Parties in the city.'[21]

Thus, from its origins the RNWMP targeted labour as its primary focus. As the Perry memo cited above suggests, the Commissioner attached considerable importance to the development of personal-history files. The National Archives of Canada holds the first register of these files, which consists of a file number, an individual's name and place of residence, and an occasional additional comment. The files themselves are filled with all information gathered by the Force by any means concerning the individual. Many of the files themselves have recently been transferred to the Archives by CSIS and are present in RG146. The first register, covering the years 1919 to 1924, is in the Archives, and subsequent partial lists have been acquired by access requests to CSIS. These lists have been published recently.[22] In those six years 2590 files were opened. These files concerned 2525 individuals once duplicates were removed. A subsequent access request to CSIS for the later registers to the end of 1929 succeeded in gaining a heavily exempted list which indicated that in the following five years another 2216 individual files were opened. In other words, on average, 437 Canadians had files opened on them annually from 1919 to 1929.[23]

The lists lend themselves to relatively limited analysis, but table 4.1 shows the geographical breakdown for the first 2590 files.[24] As can be seen, British Columbia and Alberta are significantly over-represented, Saskatchewan and Manitoba somewhat, and the rest of the country badly under-represented. To some degree at least, this is a statistical artefact, because the RNWMP only had jurisdiction in western Canada in 1919. For example, the first Toronto file is number 1225 and the first Montreal file 1254, which suggests that almost half of the total files were generated before 1 February 1920 when the new RCMP took over national jurisdiction. Other scattered information that can be gleaned from the list is the presence of sixty-eight women, one of whom, Alli Koivisto is quaintly described as 'an agitatress.' In addition, the list includes twenty-three clergy (the Reverends William Ivens, William Irvine, A.E. Smith, J.S. Woodsworth, and Salem Bland are the most prominent), fourteen doctors, six military figures, and five elected officials (John Queen of Winnipeg and Mayor Joseph Clarke of Edmonton, for example). The unfortunately rather random marginalia also identify nine Industrial Workers of the World (IWW) and six One Big Union (OBU) members, as well as an array of less predictable entries such as 'English harvester,' 'Jewish lecturer,' 'Esperanto teacher,' 'Hindu wrestler,' and, perhaps most intriguing, 'ex-RCMP.'[25]

The rapidity with which the files on radicalism and radicals grew created its own internal difficulties for the RNWMP. In late May Routledge wrote the commanding officers concerning the problem of the paper work: 'Considerable difficulty appears to be arising in having easily accessible files ... the present files and especially those dealing with Bolshevism etc., in many cases overlap one another making it necessary to hunt through three or four files before one can find the particular piece of information required. Files are also becoming bulky.' He advised, as partial solutions, supplying clearer and more concise headings, limiting reports to only one subject, and keeping separate personal files for each individual mentioned. The last point especially applied to Bolshevism files; personal-history files were to be 'submitted at the same time or as soon after the fact as possible.' To ensure standard responses he provided a sample form. (See illustration for an example of a completed report.) Finally, because of the explosion of files on the OBU ('It is very evident that this is going to be a very large subject in our work') he attached a current list of OBU file numbers and names as a guide for further subject-file creation.[26]

The subject files do not lend themselves easily to quantitative analysis, espe-

TABLE 4.1
'Agitators' by location, 1919–1924

Number on list	2590
Number of names (after adjustments)	2525
Number of places listed	2287

A. Geographic breakdown of locations (1921)	No. of agitators	% of agitators	% of Canadian population
British Columbia	775	33.9	6.0
Alberta	477	20.9	6.7
Saskatchewan	286	12.5	8.6
Ontario	276	12.1	33.4
Manitoba	253	11.1	6.9
Quebec	158	6.9	26.9
Nova Scotia	15	1.0	6.0
Prince Edward Island	1	–	1.0
Yukon	1	–	
New Brunswick	0		4.4
USA	24	1.0	
Other foreign	5	0.2	
Unknown	16	0.7	
Total	2287	100.3	

B. Geographic breakdown by city with 50+ agitators	No. of agitators	% of total agitators
Vancouver	427	18.7
Winnipeg	194	8.5
Montreal	156	6.8
Edmonton	118	5.2
Toronto	80	3.5
Calgary	74	3.2
Regina	73	3.2
Fort William	65	2.8
Saskatoon	54	2.4
Total	1240	54.3

Source: RG18, v. 2448, Register of Bolsheviks. For list see G.S. Kealey and Whitaker, eds, *RCMP Security Bulletins: The Early Years, 1919–29* (St John's 1994), 383–451.
Note: N = 2287

cially because of the heavy exemptions that CSIS invoked when preparing the documents for release under the Access to Information legislation. Nevertheless, an examination of table 4.2 shows a heavy concentration of file opening in the first few years of RNWMP/RCMP operation, as one would expect with a

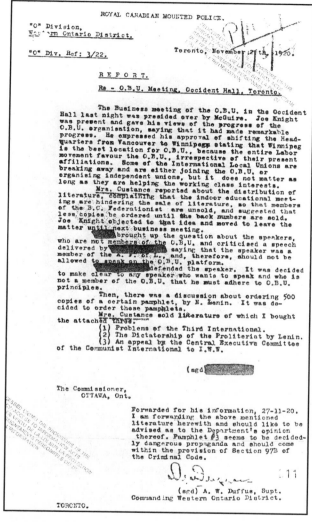

ROYAL CANADIAN MOUNTED POLICE.

"O" Division,
Western Ontario District.

"O" Div. Ref: 3/22.   Toronto, November 26th, 1920.

R E P O R T.

Re - O.B.U. Meeting, Occident Hall, Toronto.

The Business meeting of the O.B.U. in the Occident Hall last night was presided over by McGuire. Joe Knight was present and gave his views of the progress of the O.B.U. organisation, saying that it had made remarkable progress. He expressed his approval of shifting the Head-quarters from Vancouver to Winnipeg stating that Winnipeg is the best location for O.B.U., because the entire Labor movement favour the O.B.U., irrespective of their present affiliations. Some of the International Local Unions are breaking away and are either joining the O.B.U. or organising independent unions, but it does not matter as long as they are helping the working class interests.

Mrs. Custance reported about the distribution of literature, complaining that the indoor educational meet-ings are hindering the sale of literature, so that members of the B.C. Federationist are unsold, and suggested that less copies be ordered until the back numbers are sold. Joe Knight objected to that idea and moved to leave the matter until next business meeting.

███ brought up the question about the speakers, who are not members of the O.B.U. and criticised a speech delivered by ███ saying that the speaker was a member of the A. F. of L., and, therefore, should not be allowed to speak on the O.B.U. platform.

███ defended the speaker. It was decided to make clear to any speaker who wants to speak and who is not a member of the O.B.U. that he must adhere to O.B.U. principles.

Then, there was a discussion about ordering 500 copies of a certain pamphlet, by N. Lenin. It was de-cided to order these pamphlets.

Mrs. Custance sold literature of which I bought the attached three:

(1) Problems of the Third International.
(2) The Dictatorship of the Proletariat by Lenin.
(3) An appeal by the Central Executive Committee of the Communist International to I.W.W.

(sgd ███)

The Commissioner,
OTTAWA, Ont.

Forwarded for his information, 27-11-20. I am forwarding the above mentioned literature herewith and should like to be advised as to the Department's opinion thereof. Pamphlet #3 seems to be decided-ly dangerous propaganda and should come within the provision of Section 97B of the Criminal Code.

(sgd) A. W. Duffus, Supt.
Commanding Western Ontario District.

TORONTO.

This document, dated 26 November 1920, is from the Personal History File of Florence Custance, an important leader of the Communist Party of Canada in the 1920s. It is a report on a One Big Union meeting in Toronto, written by an RCMP undercover agent whose name (along with the names of other individuals) has been blacked out at the bottom by the Canadian Security Intelligence Service. (Canadian Security Intelligence Service, RG 146)

TABLE 4.2
Number of subject files opened, 1919–1930

Year	No. of files	File numbers	% of total	Cumulative %
1919	3459	1–3459	50.4	50.4
1920	300	3460–3759	4.4	54.8
1921	690	3760–4449	10.1	64.9
1922	790	4450–5239	11.5	76.4
1923	434	5240–5673	6.3	82.7
1924	347	5674–6020	5.1	87.8
1925	269	6021–6289	3.9	91.7
1926	179	6290–6468	2.6	94.3
1927	90	6469–6558	1.3	95.6
1928	127	6559–6685	1.9	97.5
1929	82	6686–6767	1.2	98.7
1930	92	6768–6859	1.3	100.0
Total	6859		100.0	

Source: This table is derived from the data in Kealey and Whitaker, eds, *RCMP Security Bulletins*. Please note that it substantially corrects table 2 (p. 18) of that volume. The list is on pp. 452–651.

new file series. Thus, in its first four years of activity, the RCMP opened over 76 per cent of the files opened in the twelve-year period from 1919 to 1930. New files opened fell dramatically after 1922, as, of course, did the combined fortunes of the Canadian Left and the RCMP. The Depression years would bring a new vigour to both.

A perusal of the file register for the mid and late 1920s also suggests a considerable narrowing of focus as the RCMP concentrated ever more specifically on the Communist Party of Canada (CPC), its foreign-language affiliates, and its other related organizations. From its inception the CPC received massive RCMP attention. In early February 1921, Superintendent Albert Cawdron, former head of the Dominion Police and for a brief time RCMP Director of Criminal Investigation, wrote to his commanding officer: 'We are desirous of obtaining at the earliest possible date a complete list of the names of those in your District who are active or in any way connected with the Communist Party of Canada.' All such individuals were to be added to the Ottawa data bank of personal-history files. Such individuals might face 'deportation for being connected with a party affiliated with and adopting the principals [*sic*] of the Third International which is opposed to all forms of Government with the exception of that of a Soviet.'[27] The successful penetration of the CPC from its earliest days, especially by RCMP undercover constable John Leopold (alias J.W. Esselwein) in Regina from 1919 to 1928, has historically been the one, highly promoted success story of the RCMP's Secret Service. Certainly the CPC received extraordinary attention, as can easily be seen in the thousands of pages of CPC subject files I have received through use of the access legislation.[28]

The third file block was 177, the classification for subversive publications, or 'Prohibited or Objectionable Literatures.' This list also originated in 1919, when press censorship was still in force under the War Measures Act, but the list continued throughout the decade. The list for the first three years was obtained from the holdings of the National Archives and thus is not exempted, but the subsequent list for the rest of the decade was obtained from CSIS and has been subjected to many exemptions under the access legislation. Table 4.3 shows the annual rate of file opening, which suggests a slowing in the mid and late 1920s, with a significant increase in activity in 1929.

An analysis of the first three years of activity, where the data remains unexempted, shows that of the 281 files opened 46.3 per cent concerned individuals in possession of such literature or geographic locations where such literature had been discovered. The next largest category of files was the 31 per cent concerning individual newspapers or magazines. Another 14.2 per cent concerned individual pamphlets or books, and 2.1 per cent related to bookshops, publishers, or libraries. A surprising 8.2 per cent of the files covered the publications and activities of the International Bible Students Association, an early version of the Jehovah's Witnesses.[29] While some additional material was suppressed becuase of its pacifist or anti-conscription message, the bulk of the banned literature was published by labour and socialist groups.

The Makers of the Files

In analysing the files, we must continually remind ourselves not only of the overt purposes of their compilation – a matter about which RCMP commissioners were quite forthcoming – but also about the file makers at each stage of the complex process. Files were made up of covert data gathered in the field by paid secret agents, undercover RCMP detectives, and unpaid informants. Overt material, such as flyers, pamphlets, newspapers, and books, was also collected and submitted either to the officer in the district in charge of the Criminal Investigation Branch or to the commanding officer. He (as far as I am aware there were no women agents and certainly no women Mounties in these years) would then comment on the material and pass it on to the Registry in Ottawa. There it was read and sometimes analysed by the Intelligence Officer, who in turn often sent it to the Commissioner. Occasionally such material would then be routed to

TABLE 4.3
RCMP prohibited/objectionable literature files, 1919–1929

Year	No. of files	File numbers	Per cent of total
1919–20	194	1–194	31.8
1921	87	195–281	14.3
1922	56	282–337	9.2
1923	31	338–368	5.1
1924	33	369–401	5.4
1925	35	402–436	5.7
1926	48	437–484	7.9
1927	25	485–509	4.1
1928	35	510–544	5.7
1929	66	545–610	10.9
Total	610		100.1

Source: NAC, RG18, 2433 and CSIS, Access Request. For list see Kealey and Whitaker, *Early Years*, 652–68.

other government departments for their use. Such raw data also provided the material for the Security Bulletins, which were distributed to cabinet and to top-ranking civil servants.[30]

The 'makers' of the files came from rather different socio-economic places. Agents, to be effective, needed to blend into the Canadian working class, and hence were often drawn from Canada's variegated ethnic mosaic. Similarly, RCMP undercover detectives needed to immerse themselves totally in the working class, especially those who stayed underground for long periods of time, such as the famous Sergeant Leopold who acted as an agent in the CPC for almost ten years before being exposed. While information on 'human sources,' both agents and regular Mounties, is among the most difficult to gain from CSIS, a preliminary analysis of some thirty secret agents and fifteen RCMP undercover operatives suggests the obvious – a heavy dependence on European immigrants with foreign-language skills. Among the Mounties this was true of Leopold and of Frank Zaneth, another prominent undercover Mountie who testified in the Winnipeg trials of the General Strike leaders. Among the secret agents were Chmichlewski, Daskaluk, Dourasoff, Eberhardt, Koburagi, Kuzyk, Reithdorf, and Veloskie.[31] On the other hand, there were a few agents from Anglo-Celtic backgrounds, but they tended to have even more exotic backgrounds. For example, there were former Wobbly (IWW member) Robert Gosden, who was exposed as a police agent at the Calgary Western Labour Convention in 1919, and the Petrograd-born Mervyn Black, who had managed cotton mills in Russia and the Soviet Union before migrating to Saskatchewan, where he failed as a farmer, and joined the RCMP.[32] It was men, then, with foreign or exotic backgrounds who provided the Force with its 'human sources.' The men to whom they reported, however, came from further up in the Canadian social order.

The first four commissioners who led the RNWMP and the RCMP from 1900 until 1950 were all born in Canada and all had military backgrounds. A.B. Perry (1860–1956) was born in Napanee of United Empire Loyalist stock, graduated in the Royal Military College's first class, and joined the RNWMP in 1883 after a brief military career in the Royal Engineers. He served in the North-West Rebellion and became Commissioner of the RNWMP (1900–20) and of the new RCMP (1920–23). His successor, Cortlandt Starnes (1864–1934) was born in Montreal, also of Loyalist stock, served with the 65th Montreal Regiment in the North-West Rebellion, joined the RNWMP in 1886, and served as Commissioner from 1923 to 1931. General J.H. MacBrien (1878–1938) hailed from Myrtle, Ontario, served briefly as a Mountie at the turn of the century, fought in the Boer War, served six years in the South African Constabulary, and then returned to Canada and the military. He rose to the rank of brigadier general in the First World War, and served as Chief of the General Staff from 1920 to 1928, before heading the RCMP from 1931 until his death in 1938. The last commissioner of the first half of the twentieth century was S.T. Wood (1889–1961), whose father, Zachary, had been Assistant Commissioner of the RNWMP. The Ottawa-born Wood graduated from Upper Canada College and Royal Military College, joined the RNWMP in 1912, and served as Commissioner from 1938 until his retirement in 1950. To round out this picture, we can add the first Intelligence Officer, C.F. Hamilton (1869–1933), to the list. A journalist and military historian born in Roslin, Ontario, he covered the Boer War for the *Globe*, which made him famous for his scoop in the battle of Paardeburg. He was also very active in the militia and authored many volumes of military history. He joined the RNWMP in 1913, served as Deputy Chief Press Censor and Director of Cable Censorship during the First World War, and joined the new RCMP in 1920 as Secretary and became Intelligence Officer in 1922.[33] Hamilton's successors in intelligence, however, slightly changed the pattern. Arthur Patteson (1887–1934), who had been Hamilton's assistant briefly, was an English immigrant who had been educated at Marlborough. He joined the Force in 1914 and worked his way up through the ranks until his appointment as Hamilton's assistant in 1931. His immediate successors were also British immigrants. Robson Armitage, who also served for only one year, and Charles Rivett-Carnac (1935–9, 1944–5), who was born in Eastbourne, Sussex, in 1901. His father was a police officer in India, where he grew up until returning to England for public school. He later worked in India for a brief period in the 1920s after serving in France during the First World War as an ambulance driver. He immigrated to Canada and joined the Force in the early 1920s.[34]

The pattern then is clear: the 'human sources' and their handlers came from different worlds. Largely immigrant Canadians reported to a Central Canadian–born military elite with, starting in the 1930s, British immigrants of public-school backgrounds as go-betweens. Any precise understanding of this dynamic awaits further work, but it was a relationship fraught with tension. Leopold's career after his exposure as a spy included a series of conflicts with his Anglo-Canadian superiors, and other agents' personnel files contain poignant reminders that life underground was not easy. The physician of under-cover Mountie T.E. Ryan, for example, attributed Ryan's ill health to 'the many years as a plain clothesman with all the temptations that go when there is no uniform.'[35]

Conclusion

As early as April 1922 J.S. Woodsworth, a Winnipeg General Strike defendant and later founding leader of the Co-operative Commonwealth Federation, reflected on the RCMP in the pages of *The Worker*, the major newspaper of the Communist Party of Canada: 'It is strange, indeed, that we should have permitted a system of espionage to be developed here in Canada.'[36] Some seventy-five years later the elaborate secret-service system erected primarily to fight labour and the Left remains as much an enigma for us in its current post–Cold War CSIS guise as the RCMP Secret Service was for Woodsworth in the aftermath of the Winnipeg General Strike. Perceptions of threats from the domestic left have come and gone but our secret service survives, indeed even thrives – or, at least, did so until the most recent budget cuts. For the historian, using these files is fraught with difficulties – indeed, the complexity of acquiring the material is, in and of itself, a major impediment to such research. Analysing the files can be difficult, a process not aided by the ever-present, annoying exemptions that all too often come at what are – not surprisingly – the key points in the documentary record. While this may appear to be only one historian's whining, the point, of course, is that it is absolutely crucial in a liberal-democratic society that citizens have access to sufficient information to allow us to judge the behaviour and impact of our secret police. While some argument is possible about the necessity of limiting this access in the present, its successful implementation increases our necessity to have full and complete access to the secret police's role in the past.

Notes

My thanks to Fiona Capp, *Writers Defiled: Security Surveillance of Australian Authors and Intellectuals, 1920–1960* (Ringwood 1993), for the idea for the title of this article.

1 For a full discussion of these issues, see my article 'In the Canadian Archives on Security and Intelligence,' *Dalhousie Review* 75 (1995), 26–38, and Reg Whitaker, 'Access to Information and Research on Canadian Security and Intelligence,' in Peter Hanks and John D. McManus, eds, *National Security: Surveillance and Accountability in a Democratic Society* (Cowansville, PQ, 1989), 183–95.

2 S.W. Horrall and Carl Betke, *Canada's Security Service: An Historical Outline, 1864–1966* (Ottawa 1978), 387–8, released by the Canadian Security Intelligence Service (CSIS) in response to my ATI request 117-90-107, but with exemptions. For a discussion of this *Historical Outline*'s history, see Larry Hannant, 'Access to the Inside: An Assessment of "Canada's Security Service": A History,' *Intelligence and National Security* 8:3 (1993), 149–59.

3 The RCMP was created in February 1920 by a merger of the Dominion Police and the Royal North-West Mounted Police. The Force largely owed its existence to the perceived need to combat labour radicalism and socialism.

4 Commissioner A. Bowen Perry to All Officers in Charge of Branches, Ottawa, 20 Feb. 1920, in RCMP, G15–26, 91-ATIP-1015

5 V.J. LaChance to S/Const. Deighton, Ottawa, 8 Feb. 1926, in ibid.

6 V.J. LaChance, Memorandum, Ottawa, 3 May 1927, in ibid.

7 Civil Service Commission to Commissioner Cortlandt Starnes, 22 July 1930, in ibid.

8 RCMP, Central Registry Branch, 1930, in ibid., emphasis in original

9 Ibid.

10 Ibid. This title was rendered interchangeably as LIO and ILO, and sometimes only as Intelligence Officer. C.F. Hamilton was replaced in 1933 by Arthur Patteson, his assistant since 1931.

11 J.H. MacBrien to Minister, 23 Nov. 1932, in RCMP, G15-26, 91-ATIP-1015

12 J.H. MacBrien to Secretary, Civil Service Commission, 20 Jan. 1933, in ibid.

13 A. Goodman, 'General Instructions,' 27 March 1934, in ibid.

14 Insp. A. Goodman to Commissioner, 18 Jan. 1938, ibid.

15 Chart of Organization, Central Registry, RCMP, 7 Dec. 1939, in ibid.

16 For general background see my articles '1919: The Canadian Labour Revolt,' *Labour/Le Travail* 13 (1984), 11–44; 'The Surveillance State: The Origins of Domestic Intelligence and Counter-Subversion in Canada, 1914–21,' *Intelligence and National Security* 7:3 (1992), 179–210; and 'State Repression of Labour and the Left in Canada, 1914–1920: The Impact of World War I,' *Canadian Historical Review* 73:3 (1992), 281–314. See also S.W. Horrall, 'The Royal North-West

Mounted Police and Labour Unrest in Western Canada, 1919,' *Canadian Historical Review* 61:2 (1980), 169–90, and Horrall and Betke, *Canada's Security Service.*

17 Perry to Officer Commanding, Regina, 6 Jan. 1919, Circular memo no. 807, RG13, v. 231, f. 113/19; also in RG18, v. 599, f. 1328

18 Perry to OC, Regina, 6 Jan. 1919, Circular memo no. 807A, in RG13 and RG18 sources, n. 17. Interestingly, there is a circular memo no. 807B, which was sent by Perry almost one month later, on 5 Feb. 1919. In it Perry, perhaps after receiving political criticism from his minister, Newton Rowell, or Minister of Labour Gideon Robertson (this is highly speculative), felt it necessary to modify his views to emphasize the existence of 'responsible leaders of organized labour who are opposed to real Bolshevist propaganda and are battling against it wherever they find it in their own labour organizations.' These he contrasted with Bolshevik sympathizers and 'a very small minority, and those principally of foreign birth, who have imbibed the real Bolshevist Doctrine of a class war, and they believe in revolution as a means to obtain their ends.' RG18, v. 599, f. 1328

19 Routledge to OC, Regina, 28 Feb. 1919, CIB memo, no. 10, RG18, v. 2380

20 Ibid., 14 March 1919, CIB memo no. 10A

21 Reames to Starnes, Starnes to Perry, Winnipeg, 15 Apr. 1919, RG18, v. 2170, f. 18-7

22 Gregory S. Kealey and Reg Whitaker, eds, *R.C.M.P. Security Bulletins: The Early Years, 1919–1929* (St John's 1994), 383–451

23 RG18, v. 2448, Register of Bolsheviks, 1919–24. My access request to CSIS was 87-A-41. The rate in the two periods was almost identical, 432 versus 443; however, given that the opening of files should be heavier initially, this suggests some intensification over the period.

24 The subsequent CSIS list had no geographical information for the 54 individuals whose names had not been deleted or could be identified by cross-referencing with subject files.

25 The IWW was originally an American syndicalist organization that grew out of the Western Federation of Miners before the First World War. It enjoyed considerable success among itinerant workers and in the resource sector. Its syndicalist politics made it the major target of American and Canadian state repression. The OBU was a Canadian labour organization founded in 1919 that stood for the organization of the entire working class. It was blamed by the Canadian state for the Winnipeg General Strike and for the generalized labour revolt of 1917 to 1920. It too suffered from extensive state repression.

26 W.H. Routledge to OC, 26 May 1919, CIB memo no. 50, Re: Files, Diary Dates, etc., RG18, v. 2380

27 Cawdron to OC, Ottawa, 2 Feb. 1921, CIB Circular memo no. 306, Re: Communist Party of Canada, RG13, v. 2381. On the political use of deportation, see Barbara

Roberts, *Whence They Came: Deportation from Canada, 1900–1935* (Ottawa 1988), esp. chaps. 5, 7

28 Also, see my article 'The RCMP, the Special Branch, and the Early Days of the Communist Party of Canada: A Documentary Article,' *Labour/Le Travail* 30 (1992), 169–204.

29 For the subsequent story, see William Kaplan, *State and Salvation: The Jehovah's Witnesses and Their Fight for Civil Rights* (Toronto 1989).

30 See Gregory S. Kealey and Reg Whitaker, eds, *The RCMP Security Bulletins* (St John's 1989–97). To date eight volumes have appeared covering 1919–29, 1933–4, 1935, 1936, 1937, 1938–9, 1939–41, and 1942–5.

31 On Leopold, see Reg Whitaker and Gary Marcuse, *Cold War Canada: The Making of a National Insecurity State, 1945–1957* (Toronto 1995), chap. 8; Kealey, 'The Early Years of State Surveillance of Labour and the Left in Canada: The Institutional Framework of the RCMP Security and Intelligence Apparatus, 1918–1926,' *Intelligence and National Security* 8:3 (1993), 129–48; and his RCMP personnel file, obtained by me, 88HR-2533. On Zaneth, see James Dubro and Robin Rowland, *Undercover: Cases of the RCMP's Most Secretive Operative* (Markham 1991), and his RCMP personnel file, 88HR-2533. On other secret agents, see Kealey, 'The Surveillance State.'

32 On Gosden see the unpublished paper by Mark Leier forthcoming in *Labour/Le Travail*. On Black see his RCMP personnel file, obtained by me, 91-ATIP-0459

33 Biographies of Starnes, MacBrien, and Hamilton from W. Stewart Wallace, ed., *Macmillan Dictionary of Canadian Biography* (Toronto 1963); of Perry and Hamilton from Henry James Morgan, comp., *Canadian Men and Women of Their Time* (Toronto 1912); and of Wood from *Canadian Who's Who*.

34 Biographical details from Horrall and Betke, *Canada's Security Service*

35 Kealey, 'The Early Years'; Leopold, RCMP personnel file; and Dr A.R. Landry to Commissioner MacBrien, Moncton, 26 Jan. 1934, in T.E. Ryan, RCMP personnel file, 90-ATIP-158

36 J.S. Woodsworth, 'Royal Canadian Mounted Police,' *The Worker* (Toronto), 15 Apr. 1922

PART TWO
BEFORE THE 'MODERN' CASE FILE:
CHURCH RECORDS AND REGULATING LIVES
AND COMMUNITY

5

Christian Harmony: Family, Neighbours, and Community in Upper Canadian Church Discipline Records

LYNNE MARKS

The church records of Woodstock's Baptist church note that in September of 1825 the entire church was harmonious 'except for Brother P. and Sister H. who were somewhat at variance, Sister H. having reported some unfavourable stories respecting Brother P. which are not so.' The records note that the church members 'humbly trust and pray that matters may be arranged so as not to wound the feelings of the body of the Church.' Harmony between the two members was restored to the satisfaction of church members when 'Sister H. ... confessed to Brother P. and acknowledged her faults publicly.'[1]

In May of 1835 Mrs Francis W. requested the right to take communion at Peterborough's Presbyterian church. This church, like others of the time, sought to maintain family unity and harmony, and as a result the elders were initially unwilling to grant Mrs W.'s request, 'on the ground of the impropriety of her living separate from her husband.' When they called her before them to explain why she had left her husband, Mrs W. explained that she had done so only because her husband had tried to stop her from bringing up her children as Christians. She told the elders that he had 'forbidden the reading of the bible in his house and endeavoured by precept and example to induce their children to violate the Sabbath.' After deliberation the Session conceded that the 'the spiritual good of her family' had required Mrs W. to leave her husband. At the same time, however, as the elders granted her the right to receive communion while remaining separate from her husband, they remained concerned over sanctioning any shirking of wifely responsibilities. The Session thus 'recommended to Mrs W. to do all in her power to provide the comfort of her unfortunate husband.'[2]

In early Ontario three major denominations, the Methodists, Baptists, and Presbyterians, all regulated spheres of life that today we would consider far beyond the purview of religious control. Family life, leisure activities, business practices, sexuality, slander, and private quarrels could all come under church scrutiny. Those who violated Christian standards in these matters were called to account by other members of their church community. Behaviour that was considered too heinous, or too frequently repeated, could result in either temporary suspension or permanent expulsion from the church, although in most cases confession of sin and other evidence of sincere contrition allowed members to be retained in or restored to full membership.

While the Methodists did not keep records of cases of church discipline, both Baptist and Presbyterian congregations did so.[3] Within these denominations existing records of discipline cases are mixed in with the recording of other church events in church minute books. Depending on the diligence of church clerks and the interest of the local congregations, the recording of these cases ranges from very brief notations to detailed description of the issues involved, the testimony of participants and witnesses, and the outcome of the case. When I first became interested in these records, I was struck by their apparent similarity to the 'case file' type of records that historians were beginning to use to illuminate the private lives of ordinary people that would otherwise remain hidden. I thought that, like court records and social-work case files, these records would provide insights into the experience of sexuality, leisure, and family violence. And these sources were for a period for which few other records of personal life exist. The possibilities for opening up the history of Upper Canadian private life seemed exciting indeed. However, I soon realized that given the very limited historiographical context in which to place these cases, they could only tell us so much about the 'real experience' of family violence, sexuality, or leisure in Upper Canada. We need to know a great deal more about Upper Canadian gender relations and social, family, and community life in order to know whether the cases that came before the churches reflected larger patterns, or whether the kind of records found in the church minutes reveal only the particular preoccupations and approaches of certain churches.[4]

Indeed, as I read more of these records it became increasingly clear that while the subjects dealt with in church discipline records have some parallels with those in legal or social-agency documents, the world-view of these churches was far removed from that of either nineteenth-century law courts or twentieth-century social agencies. The very idea that the church discipline records could provide insights into personal, private life would have been quite foreign to members of these churches. The churches readily intervened to regulate the sexual, family, and business behaviour of its members in part because they did not make clear distinctions between the concepts of public and private. These concepts were only beginning to gain currency in the larger society at that time, as the development of new ideological frameworks saw home and family increasingly defined as part of a private sphere, separate from the 'public' world of business and politics.[5] While the lack of public/private distinctions are important here, the way evangelical churches defined the sacred and the secular was even more central to their approach to church discipline. Today we define church attendance and belief as part of the 'sacred,' while all other facets of life, whether defined as private (such as the family and sexuality) or public (such as business), are part of the secular world. Early-nineteenth-century evangelicals divided up the sacred and the secular quite differently. The unconverted, the 'ungodly,' were part of the secular world, while the converted were not. All aspects of their lives were subject to church scrutiny, because after conversion all aspects of their lives were, as Susan Juster has argued, 'a public testimonial to the power of the Spirit.'[6]

This distinction between the sacred and the secular existed not just at the level of the individual, but perhaps more importantly, between the church community and the 'world.' Once individuals experienced conversion they entered into a community of believers, whose members saw themselves as united with each other in fraternal, Christian bonds, and as very much separate from the outside secular world. This conception of evangelical churches as distinct communities, or as American historian Curtis Johnson has put it, 'islands of holiness' in a surrounding world of sin, has major implications for our understanding of the meaning of church discipline.[7] At the same time, an exploration of church discipline can further illuminate the meaning that community had for these churches.

This paper does not examine all forms of church discipline, but instead explores two areas of discipline that can tell us much about the Baptist and Presbyterian understanding of community: the regulation of family life and of quarrels and other disagreements among non-related members of the church. These forms of church regulation are examined through the study of church discipline records for forty Presbyterian and twenty-six Baptist churches from various regions of what is now southern Ontario.[8] Records of churches in large communities, small towns, and rural areas were examined for the period from 1798 to 1860. In examining the regulation of family and extra-familial conflict in these records I found some similarities between church regulation and secular legal regulation, particularly within the realm of the family. At the same time, however, the way in which the churches regulated these various forms of disharmony reveals a concern with and an understanding of the meaning of community that was particular to the churches. A comparison of the regulation of family and extra-family conflict is also instructive in that it points out that even within the community of believers the concept of 'the private' was not completely absent: the boundaries between family and community were certainly not as firm as they were later to become, but they did exist. Other contradictions also emerge around church regulation of families. Most notably, the ideal of the community of fraternal believers, of souls who are equal in the sight of God, did not always mesh easily with the hierarchical gender roles of the ideal Christian family.

While both Baptists and Presbyterians regulated the behaviour of their members, the process of church discipline differed between the two denominations, reflecting in turn some basic theological and organizational differences between them. While some branches of Presbyterianism were more evangelical than others, focusing more on the experience of being 'reborn' in Christ, Presbyterians generally were less evangelical than Baptists, having less of a sense of themselves as a separate community of believers within a world of sin. The legacy of having been the state church in Scotland reduced this sense of separation from the world, while explaining their relatively hierachical system of church governance.[9] Among Presbyterians, the behaviour of members was overseen exclusively by the minister and church elders (the Session), who had the power to demand public confession or to excommunicate erring members. Ministers were male, as were the elders, who were nominated by male church members. Among the more evangelical Baptists the centrality of the 'community of believers,' whose souls were all equal in the sight of God, provided for some degree of equality among all church members, including a shared responsibility to oversee each other's behaviour. While Baptist deacons and ministers (all male) had particular power in enforcing discipline, Baptist discipline cases were discussed at monthly covenant meetings attended by the entire congregation. In many congregations women spoke at these meetings, and had a vote on such cases. They were also among those appointed to visit erring church members.[10]

Before turning to explore further the meaning of community within the churches, it is helpful to gain some understanding of the nature of community and the meanings of public and private in Upper Canadian society as a whole. While the rudimentary nature of Upper Canadian historiography limits us here, in Upper Canada there appears to have been more acceptance of informal community regulation and less of a clear sense of public/private distinctions than later in the century. Over the first half of the nineteenth century the colony gradually moved from the phase of pioneer subsistence farming to a more settled and established society. This process occurred at an uneven pace across the colony, and while towns certainly grew in size over the period, Upper Canadian society remained predominantly rural. The structures of a formal legal system were in place over the first half of the century, but this system had not yet acquired the legitimacy and power it was later to command. Susan Lewthwaite has recently shown that, particularly in rural areas, local magistrates had only limited authority. This authority was readily challenged by local 'gangs,' or even by determined individuals.[11]

The weakness of formal legal authority left considerable space for alternative forms of community control. Certainly church discipline was one such form. Charivaris represented another type of informal community regulation. These events provided local inhabitants with a means of expressing their disapproval of certain behaviour, particularly behaviour related to what we now define as the 'private' sphere of the family. For example, an old widower who married a much younger woman could expect to be 'charivaried' by members of the community, who would surround the house of the unlucky couple after the wedding, making a huge din until they received some payment. Men who beat their wives beyond the limit of community toleration could on occasion also face charivaris or other active community censure.[12]

The churches' emphasis on the power of the community to regulate 'private' behaviour was therefore not an entirely foreign concept within Upper Canadian society. However, the meaning of church regulation was not identical to the more informal types of regulation within the larger society because of the distinct nature of church communities. Those conducting a charivari may have felt that as members of the local community they had the right to protest against the behaviour of particular inhabitants, but these inhabitants often did not agree. Defiance of community interference was not uncommon, although it could certainly be dangerous, with some charivaris ending in violence and death.[13] While certain church members also defied church disciplinary efforts, the situation here was rather different. Such defiance almost always involved an explicit recognition that those who defied the church would be leaving the church community, either voluntarily or involuntarily. Those who remained recognized that church discipline was part of what it meant to be a member of the church. By joining the church and declaring their faith in Jesus, individuals agreed to live according to what their denomination defined as biblically ordained Christian behaviour and, if they strayed from such behaviour, to submit to church discipline. Church discipline records are thus rather different from secular legal records, or social-work case files, in that those being disciplined within the churches are voluntary members of the community, in a much more direct way than is true of citizens of nation states.

Of course, nothing is ever completely voluntary. Presbyterians were closely associated with two ethnic groups – the Scots and the Irish. They often lived in towns and villages where they were the dominant ethnic/religious group. The resulting intersection of ethnic, religious, and family ties within these communities certainly meant that church membership was not simply a matter of voluntary choice. In Upper Canada the Kirk Sessions had no state sanction, but the fact that they had once had such sanction in Scotland may have further reinforced the more coercive meaning of church discipline among Presbyterians. The Baptists were not closely associated with a particular ethnic group, had no previous state ties, and in fact boasted a pround voluntarist tradition.[14] They were also a small minority in Upper Canadian society. Unlike Presbyterians, then, Upper Canadian Baptists did not find themselves in small towns where almost all inhabitants shared their ethnic/religious background. Thus, for Baptists acceptance of church membership, and of church supervision of personal behaviour, can more clearly be characterized as voluntary. This denominational distinction is underlined by the fact that far more Baptists defied the rulings of church discipline than was the case among Presbyterians.[15] Baptists more clearly remained within the church as long as they kept their faith and thus their willingness to have their behaviour overseen. For Presbyterians, a decision to defy church rulings was not so simple.

Nonetheless, while decisions to remain within many of these church communities were not entirely freely made, on some level at least membership was voluntary, and based on an active faith decision. The implications of this for the nature of church regulation was profound. Since all members had actively accepted the same Christian moral code, the churches could much more proactively regulate and discipline those who broke the churches' moral prescriptions than was possible for the state. While the Upper Canadian state was explicitly Christian, it was not theocratic, and had to balance a variety of competing Christian beliefs. It could not as actively regulate behaviour as was possible for the churches.[16] The churches, for example, could, if they heard rumours of wrongdoing, call individuals before them for sins such as 'antenuptial fornication.' Such proactive policing of sexual behaviour was far beyond the purview of the secular legal system. The more proactive approach of the churches is also evident in their regulation of disharmony within families and between unrelated members of the community. The secular legal system usually stepped in to regulate family life and private quarrels only if a particular individual, such as a battered wife, or someone who felt wronged in a business deal, stepped forward to press charges. While the churches did respond to individual complaints, if they heard rumours of conflict they were also more than willing to summon both parties before them. As in cases of sexual misconduct, the churches could be more proactive, since they were dealing with individuals who all ostensibly adhered to a common Christian value system. In cases of conflict, however, the churches were not just regulating misbehaviour more actively than the secular courts. A close reading of church discipline records reveals that the meaning and purpose of such regulation differed from that of the state in dealing with

ostensibly similar cases. Most cases reflect an emphasis on the central importance of community harmony. This contrasts with the more individualistic and
property-centred focus of the secular legal system that was gaining authority
and legitimacy in Upper Canada over the first half of the nineteenth century.[17]

Communities of Christians were expected to live together in brotherhood and
peace. If conflict did occur between two individuals they were expected to follow scriptural authority in dealing with the issue (Matthew 18:15–17). Those in
conflict were to try and work it out amongst themselves and, if this did not succeed, were to bring in one or two others to mediate. Failing that, the church was
to step in and resolve the conflict. Using secular courts to resolve conflict
between church members was forbidden. All conflict between church members
was to be resolved within the church community. While all Presbyterian and
Baptist churches dealt with cases of disharmony through the regular church discipline process, some churches set up specific structures to deal with such
issues. For example, in November 1844 the Port Burwell Baptist church voted
that 'a standing committee of three persons be appointed in each Church whose
duty it shall be to promote peace and harmony. If any member ... shall be found
stirring up strife they shall be dealt with as offenders.'[18]

Church members could be seen to be 'stirring up strife' on a number of
issues. Many conflicts, particularly among Baptists, were church-related. Conflicts could erupt over doctrinal differences, the behaviour or preaching of a
minister or elder, or issues associated with the building of a church. For example, in February 1850 Park Street Baptist church in Hamilton brought several
charges against a Brother H., who had apparently been speaking out against the
pastor in various ways, which included stating that 'the continuance of the Pastor in the Church hindered respectable parties from joining.'[19] Conflict over
church-related issues was much more common among Baptists than Presbyterians, with such conflict making up 32 per cent of all church discipline charges in
the Baptist records examined, as compared to only 6 per cent of Presbyterian
charges (see table 5.1). Among Presbyterians a more hierarchical church polity
may have left less space for doctrinal dissent or challenges to ministers. While
the nature of church governance may explain part of the difference here, attitudes towards community are also relevant. The Baptists' strong evangelicalism
drew them apart from the world into a separate community of believers. While
the notion of community was particularly important to Baptists, it was also particularly fragile – being held together by belief alone, with no common ethnic
or family bonds and no state-church tradition to buttress it, as was the case
among Presbyterians. It is not surprising, then, that the Baptists were particularly concerned to regulate conflict within their church communities to help
prevent their disintegration.[20]

TABLE 5.1
Church discipline charges brought before selected Baptist and Presbyterian churches,
Ontario, 1789–1860

	Baptist churches		Presbyterian churches	
	No.	%	No.	%
Quarrels on church-related issues	158	32.1	20	6
Private quarrels (personal and business)	91	18.5	30	10
Domestic conflicts	27	5.5	12	4
Other charges (sexuality, drink, fraud, violence, 'immoral, unChristian and disorderly conduct')	216	43.9	255	80
Total charges	492	100	317	100

Sources: Records of 26 Baptist and 40 Presbyterian churches, for selected years within
the period 1798–1860 (depending on years for which church records still exist)
Note: Speech-related charges are not included above, since they tend to overlap with
other categories listed.

Quarrels over church matters were not the only source of discord. Quarrels
among members on a variety of personal and business issues also created considerable conflict within church communities. Again, such cases are much more
common within Baptist church records than among Presbyterians (see table
5.1), suggesting the greater emphasis placed on preserving community harmony
among Baptists.[21]

Within both denominations the nature of non-church-related conflicts that
came before the churches varied widely. Some of these cases closely resembled
those regulated by the secular courts. This was particularly true of quarrels over
business dealings. However, while the churches were very much concerned
with the question of individual wrong-doing in such cases, even here the question of community harmony was usually not far from the surface. Such cases
were usually brought before the churches by one party, who was seeking resti-
tution for the wrong done him or her. The Presbyterian Session or relevant Baptist committee investigated such complaints, calling on witnesses if necessary
before coming to a decision. Complaints ranged from charges of fraud to selling
bad meat, stealing a pig, or not paying someone for buying cloth.[22] Not supris-
ingly in a largely rural colony, a significant number involved disputes over
fences. A particularly contentious case of this kind was heard by the Streetsville
Presbyterian Session in 1839. A Mrs K. complained to the Session against John

M. for 'giving her abusive language and for cursing and swearing.' Mr M. in return laid a complaint against Mrs K. for 'laying down his fence and driving his cattle out of his fields into his grain.' After calling various witnesses the Session found that, while 'Mrs K.'s fences were in bad condition,' that she was not guilty as charged – but they found M. guilty of cursing and swearing at Mrs K. Clearly the Session took the charge that M. had given way to 'unChristian-like,' unharmonious conduct towards a fellow church member as seriously as they took his charge against her for more concrete wrongdoing in damaging his property.[23] Concerns about community harmony are also evident in a case brought before the Essa Presbyterian Session in June of 1846. The case involved James S. and John M. quarrelling over the fact that S. felt that M. had not paid him money owed him. After investigating the issue, the Session found that there had been wrong done on both sides, and the two men apologized to each other. A central concern of the Session is reflected in the final notations concerning the case: '[B]oth parties ... consented henceforth to be reconciled with each other.'[24]

Some cases of particularly serious business wrongdoing reflect not just a concern with harmony within the community, but with the reputation of the entire church community in the larger world. For example, when the Picton Presbyterian Church charged John D. with forging a signature on a contract and a bank note, the church decided that 'having received no refutation of the charges against John D., and no appearance having been made by the defendant before this court ... and whereas it would bring scandal on the cause of religion and of the standards and discipline of this church in particular were the said John D. to remain in communion ... we do now declare the said John D. to be no longer a member of this church.'[25] Once again, the issue is not simply individual wrongdoing, but the well-being of the community.

This emphasis on community is also evident in the many cases involving slander, gossip, and other unacceptable forms of speech. In such cases, damage to the individual being slandered or gossiped about was not the only issue. Community harmony is again a central concern. Some such charges were brought forward by individual complainants. For example, in January 1824 the Woodstock Baptist Church minutes note that 'a difficulty was brought by Sister T. and Brother T. against Sister H. for saying that Sister T. was friendly to Mary L. to her face and behind her back spoke evil of her.' While the church found that Sister H. was at fault and required her to 'make confession,' they also censured the Ts for not trying to resolve the issue privately with Sister H.[26] Defamation of individual character was to be avoided, but even the wronged parties were expected to make efforts at reconciliation. In another case involving Sister H.'s propensity to slander other church members, described at the beginning of this paper, the church was very clear about what was at stake. They sought to resolve this conflict 'so as not to wound the feelings of the body of the church.'[27] Many cases of gossip and slander were not brought before the church by individual complainants. Instead, upon hearing reports of such behaviour the church often summoned those involved to appear before them, in order to limit the damage done not only to the individuals, but also to church harmony. For example, when the Brantford Baptist Church heard reports that Sister R. and Brother H. had been speaking out against each other, the church resolved to allow the two 'one week to bury their old grievances and the party that is unwilling to do so we shall consider it our duty to withdraw fellowship from them.' Both parties proved unwilling to be reconciled and so a month later the church 'resolved that we withdraw our fellowship from Brother H. and Sister R. for neglect of duty and the spirit of tattling.'[28] Other such cases ended more happily. In September 1852 a committee of the Hamilton Baptist Church visited W. W. to investigate rumours that he had been accusing Sister E. N. 'of lying respecting his lateness of meals and in despising the discipline of the church.' By November the church had decided that Brother W. was wrong to make such accusations, and in December he 'acknowledged his faults.' By February of 1853 'all parties [were] reconciled with the Church.'[29]

The churches did not only call members before them if they were concerned that church harmony had been damaged through slander and gossip. Any disagreements between church members could lead to a summons to appear before the church. For example, in March 1860 the Delhi Baptist Church resolved that 'there be a committee sent to visit Sister C. and Sister W. ... and to affect a reconciliation between them if no reconciliation then to sight [sic] them to the next church meeting.'[30] In November 1839 the Port Burwell Baptist Church noted that 'in regard to the difficulty between Benjamin M. and Elder M. we consider it to be a misunderstanding for which a few conciliating words from either party might have removed all difficulties existing between them for which they are both liable for public confession.'[31] The churches could lose patience in their efforts to keep the peace between members. In September 1855 the Session of Amherstburg's Presbyterian church conducted an exhaustive investigation into a conflict between James G. and Alex C. Mr G. refused to take communion because 'the conduct of Mr Alex C. had been such towards him that he felt he could not cherish towards him those brotherly feelings which one member ought to exercise towards another.' After investigating Mr G.'s various concerns, the Session decided that Mr G. did not have adequate grounds for his animosity towards Mr C., and was not justified in staying away from communion. The Session's frustration with both parties is evident in the concluding records of the case, as they 'earnestly admonish these Brethren to consider the evil wherein such unseemly variances inflicts upon the Church of Christ, and counsel them to cultivate a spirit of brotherly love and Christian forebearance in all their intercourse.'[32]

Conflicts between unrelated individuals were closely regulated, to maintain the harmony of the community. What about conflicts within families? Surely such conflicts also challenged community peace. The churches recognized this, and attempted to mediate family conflict. However, cases of family conflict appear in both Baptist and Presbyterian records much less often than do cases of conflict between unrelated individuals. The records contain almost three hundred charges regarding conflict between unrelated individuals, but less than forty charges related to various kinds of family conflict (see table 5.1).[33] How can this apparent reluctance to intervene within the family be explained? Certainly such treatment of the family seems to point to a contradiction in the churches' understanding of community. In their willingness to regulate business disagreements, personal quarrels, and sexual and leisure misconduct, the churches do not appear to recognize the existence of the concept of 'private' behaviour. In the sacred/secular distinction as defined by the evangelical churches, all behaviour of the converted was subject to Christian regulation, as the churches policed the boundary between the community of believers and 'the world.' The churches' apparent reluctance to regulate family behaviour does suggest, however, that while the family was not exempt from church intervention, it was something of a special case. Certainly not the private sacrosant sphere it was later to become, even in this period the family was not fully open to community control.[34]

While the Baptist and Presbyterian churches were less likely to regulate family conflict than conflict between unrelated individuals, some cases of family conflict did appear in the church records. What did such cases look like? Some were treated in much the same way as conflict between unrelated individuals. In several cases the church heard rumours of conflict between husband and wife and chose to intervene to restore harmony. For example, in December 1810 the Beamsville Baptist Church minutes note that 'the church has been informed of a difficulty between Bro. R. and his wife.' Church members appointed a committee to investigate the matter and report back.[35] Between May and October 1850 members of the Wicklow Baptist Church attempted to mediate a major disagreement between 'Brother D. K. and his wife Sister H. K.' over whether or not she had lied about visiting another town the previous Christmas.[36] The mediation of these family disputes differed little from the treatment of other disputes. As in other cases, the church sought to determine the nature of the conflict and attempted to restore harmony, since such harmony was considered essential within both the family and the larger community. The majority of cases of family conflict are not, however, treated in such a straightforward manner. Most cases of church involvement in family conflict reveal the churches' imposition of a very specific, and hierarchical, set of gendered expectations on both husband and wife.

The imposition of hierarchical gendered expectations in the mediation of family conflicts points to a further contradiction the family created in the churches' understanding of community. As Susan Juster has noted, in their most revivalist phases the evangelical churches' concept of community, with its emphasis on the spiritual equality of all of the saved, existed in sharp contradistinction to both the hierarchical ideal of the traditional family and a more hierarchical, familial, church structure.[37] This issue was particularly relevant to the Baptists, who saw themselves as joined together in the fraternal bonds of egalitarian Christian fellowship. While among Presbyterians the souls of all of the converted were equal in the sight of God, the Presbyterians, as we have seen, had a much more hierarchical 'familial' church polity.

Not surprisingly, then, while both churches accepted and indeed reinforced relations of inequality within the family that contrasted with the ideal of equality embedded in the concept of the community of believers, the Presbyterians enforced a more deeply patriarchal vision of the family than the Baptists. Both churches believed that men should rule their households and that women should obey them. For example, in 1826 Jerseyville's Baptist church excommunicated Isaac V. for various sins, including 'not ruling his own house as becometh a Christian.'[38] While concepts of Christian equality had little impact even among Baptists, their discipline records point to a greater sense of the reciprocal rights and responsibilities of men and women within the family. Presbyterians were more likely to uphold male power and authority regardless of circumstances. There were only a few cases of wife abuse found in either the Presbyterian or Baptist church records, reflecting the general reluctance to intervene within the family. However, existing cases were treated differently in each denomination. In three out of the four cases found in the Baptist records, the women's stories were believed, and the men censured. In November 1822 the Woodstock Baptist Church stated that 'for the sake of the cause of their own conscience' they would 'withdraw the hand of fellowship' from a member accused of excessive drinking and wife abuse.[39] The records of Norwich Baptist Church include a lengthy discussion of the case of William G., who was accused of treating his wife very badly. Both his wife and two witnesses testified that he had spoken very abusively to her. Mrs H., who lived in the same house as the Gs, stated that 'when she went into their room Mr G. would appear to be very pleasant to his wife, but witness saith that Mr G. did nights after he had got to bed scold his wife and threaten her, saying he could break her bones and he should be justified in so doing.' As a result of G.'s 'hard threats and tyrannical behaviour to [his] wife,' as well as his refusal to support her any longer, and his further refusal to come before the church to answer charges on these matters, the Norwich church 'withdrew [their] Christian hand of fellowship' from him.[40] Other abusers were more conciliatory. A Brother C., of Delhi Baptist Church, who was accused of whipping his wife, 'when he made a satisfactory acknowledgement of the wrong to his wife and to the church ... was restored in fellowship with the church.' The Baptists did not, however, simply see wife abuse as an issue of male sin. They also defined the issue as a more general loss of familial harmony, which also weakened church harmony, for which both partners had to take responsibility. In the above case, therefore, Brother C. was not the only one censured. Because of the conflict in her family, Sister C. was required to 'make a satisfactory acknowledgement of the wrong she had done to the church and [be] willing to make a reconciliation with her husband' before she was 'restored in fellowship with the church.'[41]

Not all churches were willing to believe charges of wife abuse. In Vittoria, when Baptist church member Daniel B., accused of 'whipping his wife and abusing his child,' denied that he had hit his wife and claimed that he had 'only chastized his child,' others agreed with him that the child was bad and had only been chastized, not abused. In this case it was the female church member who brought the charge who was excommunicated.[42] While this could happen within Baptist churches, a refusal to take charges of wife abuse seriously was the normal pattern for cases brought before Presbyterian Sessions. When Widow M. attacked Robert M., saying that 'unless he were a poison he should not so treat his own wife,' her allegations were not even investigated by the Embro Presbyterian Church. Instead she was accused of slander, and was temporarily denied the right to take communion. As well, the minister 'exhorted her to make a proper and Christian use of the unhappy situation in which she was placed.'[43] When William S. 'raised a disturbance abusing one of his children and so terrifying his wife that she fled in her night clothes to William M.'s,' the Session of Essa Presbyterian Church was only willing to censure him for intemperance. His treatment of his wife and child were not considered an issue.[44] St Elmo's Presbyterian Church were willing to censure one husband, David M., for being jealous of his wife, and as a result 'in alledging to her charge deeds of immorality when in his heart he believed her innocent,' as well for 'making use of unbecoming language towards his wife.' However, the church seemed more concerned about his wife's behaviour, charging her with imprudence, disobedience to her husband, as well as having 'been guilty of a violation of her marriage vows inasmuch that she left her husband and her family without such a reason as the truth of God justifies.' Ultimately, the Session wanted to restore family harmony, and recorded with satisfaction that both Mr and Mrs M. 'man-ifested deep penitence and declared their willingness of either side to forget and forgive all past injuries and to return to the Lord.'[45]

The fact that Presbyterian Session members were all male, while in most Baptist churches both male and female church members decided on discipline cases, no doubt helps to explain the relatively greater willingness among Bap-tists to censure men for not fulfilling their appropriate Christian family roles. Certainly the Baptists did not see ideal gender roles in anything like egalitarian terms. However, in requiring men to live up to the Christian ideal of the male provider, who ruled his household without recourse to excessive violence or abuse, the churches could provide at least minimal support for women. This was true of cases of non-support as well as cases of wife abuse. The all-male Presbyterian Sessions do not appear to have censured men who abandoned or otherwise failed to support their families, while the Baptists were much more willing to do so. For example, Brother S. of Boston Baptist Church was told by the church that he had to 'make a confession to his wife and the public for his wrong in leaving her and become reconciled with her in order to retain his membership and that he shall have a month to do it in.'[46] Men who ran away from their families were routinely excommunicated.[47]

Baptist church discipline provided somewhat more protection for women than that available through the all-male Presbyterian Sessions, although the reluctance of both churches to intervene in family matters limited such support. This reluctance appears to mirror that of the secular courts of this period, although further research is needed before we can determine whether the Pres-byterian or Baptist model was closer to the secular courts' treatment of issues such as wife abuse and non-support. Like the secular courts, when intervening within the family, both Baptists and Presbyterians upheld a clearly hierarchical model of family life and gender relations.[48] The values they were upholding here were not, however, identical to those of the secular courts. Within the churches maintaining harmony was a central focus. But while harmony in the larger church community was based on some assumption of equality among members of a Christian fellowship, no such assumption entered into the regula-tion of family relations.

One issue could overcome expectations of wifely obedience and male power within the evangelical churches. If the choice had to be made between obedi-ence to God and to husbands, God came first. Individual spiritual redemption could not be sacrificed to mere earthly authority. When the churches had a con-flict with a married man, there is some evidence to suggest that if they were aware that his wife did not share her husband's views, they would try to ensure that she was dealt with separately. When the Jerseyville Baptist Church excommunicated John C. for 'the failure of his promise to come to the church,' they also 'thought it proper to enquire after Sister C.,' to determine if she wished to continue with the church. In several other cases it was made clear that a husband's excommunication did not apply to his wife, who remained a member in good standing.[49] Women who left the church for their husband's denomination were not excused on the grounds of wifely obedience, but were perceived as erring sinners.[50] While obedience to husbands was generally expected, women were viewed as independent and responsible beings in the spiritual realm. As the example cited at the beginning of the paper reveals, even among the more patriarchal Presbyterians, marriage to an unbeliever could justify a woman in rupturing family unity. While the Session of Peterborough's Presbyterian church were reluctant to sanction Mrs W. in leaving her husband, his unwillingness to allow his children to be brought up as Christians appears to have left them no alternative. Decisions to put God ahead of earthly patriarchies were certainly not unique to Upper Canadian Baptists and Presbyterians, but were common among evangelical Christians. For example, Cecilia Morgan has found that, while Upper Canadian Methodists upheld a patriarchal family structure, the unbelief of husbands and fathers could justify the disobedience of wives and children. Of course, when the head of household was converted, he returned to his rightful position of authority.[51]

Church discipline records can be viewed as an early form of case files. Like other such records, these early 'case files' tell us as much about the assumptions of those who created these records as about the lives and behaviour of those recorded in them. What makes these records particularly valuable is that while the assumptions recorded in late-nineteenth- and twentieth-century legal records and social-agency case files are not that foreign to us, the assumptions embedded in these church records reflect a very different world-view and structure of meaning from our own.

In this world the division between sacred and secular was very different – with the sacred associated with the community of converted Christians, and the secular with 'the world' beyond. This clear division between sacred and secular left little room for a sense of private behaviour within the community of believers, since a primary imperative within this community was to keep its members separate from the world of sin around them. All behaviour could thus be subject to church regulation. When behaviour we might define as 'private' was regulated, the central concerns at work were often quite different from those that we might see on first reading, given our liberal individualist tendency to 'read' cases of wrongdoing as wrong done to individuals and property. Such issues were not irrelevant, especially if a particular wrong, such as stealing or adultery, was prohibited by Scripture. However, there was a further concern in most such cases with the wrong done not just to the individual, or his or her property, but to the church community itself. The particularly evangelical focus of the Baptists, as well as their relative lack of other forms of community cohesion, meant that they focused far more than did the Presbyterians on cases of interpersonal conflict, sins that could threaten the harmony, and indeed the very existence, of community.

The way in which family conflict was dealt with in the discipline records of both denominations points to several contradictions in the churches' understanding of community. Families were 'semi-private' spheres; they were not exempt from church regulation, but conflict among family members was much less likely to come before the churches than similar conflict among non-related church members. The assumption of egalitarianism within the Christian community of believers did not extend to the churches' understanding of the family. The hierarchical Christian gender roles enforced by these churches could provide some protection to women, particularly among Baptists, but the ideal family remained patriarchal. The emphasis on the spiritual equality of all members of the Christian community could, however, negate the enforcement of patriarchal gender roles, if the two came into direct conflict. At this point, Baptists and Presbyterians alike placed obedience to God ahead of any earthly hierarchies. Again, we have here a set of assumptions and priorities very different from the dominant values of our own world.

After mid-century a major part of the evangelical world-view – the firm distinction made between the church community and 'the world' – rapidly faded away. As the churches became more integrated into the world, the sacred and secular came to be distinguished in ways much more familiar to us today. Only questions of church attendance and belief remained within the realm of the sacred, and only they remained legitimate areas of church regulation. The fact that within the larger society the distinction between public and private was gaining increasing currency helps to explain the churches' move away from the regulation of what was now seen as personal, 'private' behaviour, as does the integrally related shift towards a greater emphasis on individualism.[52] As forms of community regulation, such as church discipline, lost legitimacy in the face of such ideological shifts, many behaviours once policed by the churches were not left uncontrolled. An increasingly hegemonic legal system regulated many of the business practices that had formerly concerned the churches. A range of non-marital sexualities came under the purview not only of the legal system but also of a powerful medical profession. While the churches abandoned the regulation of the leisure practices of their members, they campaigned – with at least some success – to have the state step in to regulate the leisure of all Canadians. Some behaviours that had been of central concern to church discipline committees did, however, fade from regulators' view. While the state was willing to intervene in violent confrontations between its citizens (particularly those occurring outside the family), more minor interpersonal conflicts were rarely subject to external control. The concerns motivating the regulation of such conflicts – the preservation of harmony within a community of Christian believers – were no longer part of how most Canadians understood their world.

Notes

I would like to thank Chris Dorigo, Carol Chamberlain, Lisa Codd, Karen Duder, and Natania East for the excellent research work they did for this project. I would also like to acknowledge the financial support of a University of Victoria Internal SSHRC grant and work-study positions in funding this research. I am grateful to Duff Crerar for his generosity in sharing his research findings on Eastern Ontario Presbyterian church discipline cases with me. I would also like to thank John Blakely and the participants in the 'On the Case' conference, particularly Annalee Golz, Franca Iacovetta, and Wendy Mitchinson, for their comments on an earlier draft of this paper.

1 24 Sept. 1825, Church minutes, Woodstock Baptist Church, Canadian Baptist Archives (hereafter CBA). To protect anonymity only initials are used for individuals, rather than full last names.
2 19 and 31 May 1835, Session minutes, Peterborough Presbyterian Church, microfilm, National Archives of Canada (hereafter NAC)
3 Together the Baptists and Presbyterians made up about a quarter of all Upper Canadians in the first half of the century. Each denomination was divided into various sub-denominations that further divided and reunited over the period.
4 There is beginning to be an increasing amount of important work on the social and gender history of Upper Canada. See, for example, Janice Potter-Mackinnon, *While the Women Only Wept: Loyalist Refugee Women in Eastern Ontario* (Montreal and Kingston 1993); Susan Lewthwaite, 'Violence, Law and Community in Rural Upper Canada,' in Jim Phillips, Tina Loo, and Susan Lewthwaite, eds, *Essays in the History of Canadian Law*, vol. 5, *Crime and Criminal Justice* (Toronto 1994); Jane Errington, *Wives and Mothers, Schoolmistresses and Scullery Maids: Working Women in Upper Canada, 1790–1840* (Montreal 1995); Katherine McKenna, *A Life of Propriety: Anne Murray Powell and Her Family, 1755–1849* (Montreal 1994); and Cecilia Morgan, *Public Men and Virtuous Women: The Gendered Languages of Religion and Politics in Upper Canada, 1791–1850* (Toronto 1996).

5 See, for example, Morgan, *Public Men and Virtuous Women,* and Leonore Davidoff and Catherine Hall, *Family Fortunes: Men and Women of the English Middle Class, 1780–1850* (London 1987).

6 Susan Juster, *Disorderly Women: Sexual Politics and Evangelicalism in Revolutionary New England* (Ithaca and London 1994), 82

7 Curtis D. Johnson, *Island of Holiness: Rural Religion in Upstate New York, 1790–1860* (Ithaca and London 1989). Also see Randolph A. Roth, *The Democratic Dilemma: Religion, Reform and the Social Order in the Connecticut River Valley of Vermont, 1791–1850* (Cambridge 1987), and in the Upper Canadian context, William Westfall, *Two Worlds: The Protestant Culture of Nineteenth-Century Ontario* (Montreal and Kingston 1989).

8 Among Baptists church discipline cases are to be found in the congregational minutes. Presbyterian discipline cases are found in the minutes of the Kirk sessions.

9 The 'Old Kirk' Presbyterians were the least evangelical, being the most directly linked with the Scottish tradition of the state church, while Presbyterians from the United States and the 'Free Church' Presbyterians had a more evangelical and voluntarist focus. For further discussion of such differences see John Webster Grant, *A Profusion of Spires: Religion in Nineteenth-Century Ontario* (Toronto 1988), 78–9, 123–5.

10 This may not have been true in all churches, but it was certainly the case in many smaller communities. See Judith Colwell, 'The Role of Women in the Nineteenth Century Church of Ontario' (unpublished paper 1985, CBA), 8–9.

11 Lewthwaite, 'Violence, Law and Community in Rural Upper Canada'

12 Bryan Palmer, 'Discordant Music: Charivaris and Whitecapping in Nineteenth-Century North America,' *Labour/Le Travailleur* 3 (1978)

13 Palmer, 'Discordant Music'

14 It is true, however, that the majority of Baptists were of American origin.

15 See Lynne Marks, 'No Double Standard?: Leisure, Sexuality and Sin in Upper Canadian Church Discipline Records,' *Gender in Canada* manuscript, ed. Kathryn McPherson, Cecilia Morgan, and Nancy Forestell.

16 For a valuable discussion of these themes see, for example, Mariana Valverde and Lorna Weir, 'The Struggles of the Immoral: Preliminary Remarks on Moral Regulation,' *Resources for Feminist Research* 17:3.

17 See Margaret Banks, 'The Evolution of the Ontario Courts, 1788–1981,' in David Flaherty, ed., *Essays in the History of Canadian Law,* vol. 2 (Toronto 1983), and John Weaver, 'Crime, Public Order, and Repression: The Gore District in Upheaval, 1832–1851,' in R.C. Macleod, ed., *Lawful Authority: Readings on the History of Criminal Justice in Canada* (Toronto 1988). For a discussion of assumptions behind the secular legal system in a different part of British North

America see Tina Loo, *Making Law, Order and Authority in British Columbia, 1821–1871* (Toronto 1994).

18 1 Nov. 1844, Minutes of Port Burwell Baptist Church, CBA

19 5 Feb. 1850, Minutes of Park St Hamilton Baptist church

20 For a discussion of a similar concern to regulate conflict in pre-Revolutionary American Baptist church communities see Juster, *Disorderly Women*, 73–83.

21 Part of the explanation for the higher proportion of cases of interpersonal conflict among Baptists may lie in the fact that among Presbyterians many cases of discord among church members appear to have been settled privately, with only the more serious cases coming before the Session. However, efforts at private reconciliation were also made among Baptists.

22 See, for example, August 1821 and April 1822, Church minutes of Oxford Baptist Church, CBA; 24 Apr. 1844, Church minutes of Norwich Baptist Church, Family History Archives, Victoria (hereafter FHA).

23 12 Dec. 1839, Session minutes, Streetsville Presbyterian Church

24 27 June 1846, Session minutes, Essa Presbyterian Church

25 28 Dec. 1845, Session minutes, Picton Presbyterian Church. Similar reasons were sometimes given for excommunicating church members who were habitually seen drunk. It was assumed that they also would hurt the reputation of the church.

26 3 Jan. 1824, Church minutes, Woodstock Baptist Church, CBA

27 24 Sept. 1825, Church minutes, Woodstock Baptist Church, CBA

28 12 May and 23 June 1838, Church minutes, Brantford Baptist Church, CBA

29 Sept. 1852–Feb. 1853, Church minutes, Hamilton Baptist Church, CBA

30 4 Mar. 1860, Delhi Baptist Church minutes, FHA

31 23 Nov. 1839, Church minutes, Port Burwell Baptist Church, CBA

32 23 Sept. 1855, Session minutes, Amherstburg Presbyterian Church

33 The churches were also far more likely to regulate issues of sexuality, particularly premarital sexuality, than questions of family conflict, with over 180 cases of sexual 'misconduct' being found in the records examined. This detailed regulation of sexuality, which on first glance may not fit with a reluctance to interfere in the family, served to 'separate out' the family from the larger community. By controlling premarital and extramarital sexuality, the churches saw themselves as supporting and protecting a Christian ideal of the family, with heterosexual monogamous marriage at its centre. The boundaries of such families were policed to ensure they were not undermined by illicit sexual passions. The Presbyterians were particularly concerned with the regulation of sexuality. For further discussion of church regulation of sexuality, see Marks, 'No Double Standard?'

34 This meshes with Cecilia Morgan's exploration of Upper Canadian Methodist discourse regarding the family. Morgan identified a sense of home and family as a private sphere, although this did not seem to preclude at least some religious interfer-

ence within the family. The religious interference discussed by Morgan involves active efforts to convert the unconverted husbands of Christian wives. Morgan, *Public Men and Virtuous Women.*

35 29 Dec. 1810, Beamsville Baptist Church minutes, Murray Meldrum notes (hereafter MM), CBA

36 18 May 1850, Church minutes, Wicklow Baptist Church, CBA

37 Susan Juster, 'Patriarchy Reborn: The Gendering of Authority in the Evangelical Church in Revolutionary New England,' *Gender and History* 6:1 (April 1994)

38 7 Jan. 1826, Church minutes, Jerseyville Baptist Church, FHA

39 Woodstock Baptist Church minutes, November 1822, CBA; also see Duff Willis Crerar, 'Church and Community: The Presbyterian Kirk-Session in the District of Bathurst, Upper Canada' (M.A. thesis, University of Western Ontario, 1979), 70.

40 13 Mar. 1841, Church minutes, Norwich Baptist Church, FHA

41 29 Nov. 1859, Church minutes, Delhi Baptist Church, FHA

42 August 1831, Vittoria Baptist Church minutes, MM, CBA

43 20 June 1842, Session minutes, Embro Presbyterian Church

44 14 Sept. 1856, Session minutes, Essa Presbyterian Church

45 12 Jan. 1854, Session minutes, St Elmo Presbyterian Church

46 18 May 1839, Boston Baptist Church, MM, CBA. For similar examples of men being excommunicated for abandoning their families, see 6 May 1848, Yarmouth Baptist Church minutes, CBA, and April 1848, Oxford Baptist Church minutes, CBA.

47 See, for example, April 1848, Church minutes, Oxford Baptist Church, CBA; 6 May 1848, Church minutes, Yarmouth Baptist Church, CBA.

48 See, for example, Annalee Golz, 'Abusive and Murdering Husbands: The Historical Relationship between Wife Abuse and Wife Murder in Nineteenth and Early Twentieth Century Ontario,' paper presented at the Family History Conference, Ottawa, Ontario, May 1994. For a later period see, for example, Terry Chapman, "''Til Death Do Us Part": Wife Beating in Alberta 1905–1920,' *Alberta History* 36:4 (Autumn 1988) and Katherine Harvey, 'Amazons and Victims: Resisting Wife Abuse in Working-Class Montreal, 1869–1879,' *Journal of the Canadian Historical Association,* new series, 2 (1991).

49 See, for example, Hamilton Baptist Church minutes, 7 Dec. 1849, and Dundas Baptist Church minutes, 8 July 1843, CBA.

50 See, for example, October 1837, St Catharines Baptist Church minutes, CBA.

51 Morgan, *Public Men and Virtuous Women.* Also see George Rawlyk, *Ravished by the Spirit: Religious Revivals, Baptists and Henry Alline* (Kingston and Montreal 1988).

52 This increasing sense of individualism did of course focus primarily on the individualism of men, both as citizens and as economic actors.

6

Elderly Inmates and Caregiving Sisters: Catholic Institutions for the Elderly in Nineteenth-Century Montreal

BETTINA BRADBURY

Chronicles, Registers, Nuns, and the Elderly

'The first was a remarkable day,' wrote the sister responsible for recording what went on in the mother house of the Sisters of Providence of the first of February 1880. That morning, Delphine Thoin, an elderly woman, had died. So had a nun.[1] It was not the deaths, however, that made the day remarkable. For deaths were frequent in this institution dedicated to the care of the elderly and the infirm as well as of orphans and the poor. Rather, explanation and collective reflection were in order because Delphine had died without receiving her final rites in a lucid state from the priest.

A careful look at the events surrounding her death as written in the chronicles, tells us much about the nuns and their work, about their position in the spiritual power structure of the Catholic Church, and about the role of such chronicles within these institutions. The events of that day also offer hints about the relations between nuns and their elderly clients and about why some elderly Montrealers may have chosen to end their lives in an institution run by Catholic nuns.[2] This paper examines these issues in institutions run by the Grey Nuns and the Sisters of Providence in Montreal between the 1830s and the 1890s.

I draw largely on the chronicles and the registers that were recorded by the nuns. These are precursors of sorts to case files. Chronicles were kept in most Catholic institutions of charity and education. In these two orders they were the task of one sister, who was allocated that job by her Mother Superior. Until the mid to late 1870s the chronicles were handwritten. They resembled a diary or perhaps a ship captain's log more than the annual reports of later nineteenth-century Protestant charities or the case reports of twentieth-century social workers. As in many diaries, days sometimes passed without any entries, followed by a flurry of detail. Entries varied, with much detail at times on apparently trivial matters and little detail on events that might seem important to historians today. These were not public documents produced for the wider community. It is even unclear how widely they were read within the community. Like diaries, they often contained a combination of the listing of events with some form of spiritual evaluation, as we shall see in the case of Delphine Thoin.

Yet, the chronicles were not private, individual diaries. They were written to edify the other sisters in the order and to teach future generations of nuns about the challenges faced at particular periods. By the 1870s and 1880s, when both orders had sisters working in schools and missions across North America, the nature of the chronicles changed. They were printed up monthly, or a specified number of times a year, usually by one of the sisters who ran the in-house printing press. In this monthly bulletin format they served the function of news sheets holding together a geographically dispersed religious community through shared knowledge of each other's joys, privations, and challenges. They were private, in the sense that they were written only for members of the order. Yet they were also public because they were made to be read widely throughout the order, and were seen consciously as a way of preserving history and of reaffirming faith. Several of the chronicles have been copied and recopied over time, so that the original wording and content may have changed.[3] All these characteristics make the chronicles a challenge to read.

The chronicles allow us only glimpses of the elderly inmates who are my focus here. They appear through the lens of the spiritual and material concerns of the nuns.[4] The focus is clearest on special occasions or when some event was seen as memorable by the chronicler. The inmates themselves left no records evaluating the material or spiritual care they received. Few verbatim transcriptions of their words of gratefulness or resistance appear in the chronicles, although reports regarding edifying spiritual experiences are more frequent – again as reported by a sister. If the observed – the elderly clients – are hard to know through such records, it is not clear that the observers and their motivations can be more readily known. The reasons for writing the chronicles, combined with the kinds of vows the nuns made and the primacy of their spiritual priorities over individual or material ones, mean that their own subjective assessments are generally submerged in collective and often didactic reconstructions of events. Their ways of viewing their charges and their own daily work were suffused with understandings of the world that they drew largely from their vocation.

Closer to case reports in such institutions were the carefully kept registers detailing who entered, died, or left.[5] When someone arrived the nun in charge wrote down the person's name, their age and sometimes their place of birth, occupation, marital status and spouse or parents' names in a large, leather-bound register. All registers had a column for the date of death or departure from the institution. In addition to this standardized data, occasional comments refer to the inmates' mental or physical state.

As historians, our knowledge about individual inmates is limited to what the nuns recorded in these registers or reported in the chronicles and fragmentary traces in other sources.[6] The nuns, by contrast, clearly knew a great deal more about their charges. The Grey Nuns were instructed to make sure all newcomers were versed in the principal mysteries of the faith and knew the main prayers and the meaning of the various sacraments. Any client deemed a moral or spiritual danger to the others, or likely to cause scandal, was to be discharged.[7] Unfortunately, the registers do not indicate who was dismissed or who left voluntarily. Only occasionally does an entry like 'did not sympathize' indicate a spiritual or moral non-conformity that may have led to departure. Most information remained in the nuns' heads, as did their feelings toward inmates whom they knew intimately from daily contact. In the case of Delphine Thoin, however, we learn more about her character, the nuns' feelings toward her, and her death. Nevertheless, by piecing together the records of events in the chronicles with the sparse standardized data of the registers, it is possible to reconstruct aspects of daily life and death in the institutions for the elderly and sick run by the Grey Nuns and the Sisters of Providence.

The Death of an Inmate

The chronicler was at pains to explain why the nuns had not expected Delphine Thoin to die that February morning in 1880. Delphine had been sick for over a month when she died. She had been a difficult patient. The chronicling sister explained that she was so capricious that the sisters had misjudged how close she was to death and had repeatedly denied her requests to see a priest to take communion and to confess. She, in turn, had refused to get out of bed to go to where the other sick and elderly women had their confessions heard. The community's incumbent priest had finally come to her bedside the day before her death. He heard her confession there, but she could not take communion because she was vomiting too much. The early-morning mass in the chapel of the Sisters of Providence had scarcely finished when the community's chaplain was called upstairs to the dormitory where the sick and elderly women resided. He arrived too late. Delphine Thoin was already unconscious. He delivered the final sacraments to her in this state.[8]

It was unusual for the nuns to describe an inmate's death in so much detail. Delphine's death clearly shook the community for several reasons. First, Delphine had not died what was militantly and ubiquitously proclaimed a 'good death' in the Catholic discourse of the times. 'Nothing more necessary and desirable than a good death, nothing more terrible than a bad one,' proclaimed Montreal's bishop, Ignace Bourget.[9] A good death meant the dying person had prepared for their death, organized their affairs, written a will, and planned what alms they would give to the poor and the infirm so as to receive God's grace at the final judgment. Most important, a good death involved a final confession, repentance, and receiving the final sacraments from a priest. In a pastoral letter published during April 1876, Bishop Bourget emphasized how important it was that the final confession, final sacrament, and annointing of the sick person's hands and forehead with holy oil be performed while the patient was in full consciousness. This, he explained, would avoid 'the illusions of demons aiming to mislead them so as to prevent them from enjoying the necessary benefits and grace.'[10] It was here that the sisters had failed. Delphine had not been conscious.

This failure was particularly poignant to the Sisters of Providence as caring for the sick and elderly and ensuring that they died a good Catholic death was their major and earliest mission. This had been the work to which their founder, Emilie Gamelin, had dedicated herself in the early years following her widowhood in 1827.[11] In the intervening years they had sheltered over five hundred elderly and infirm women with few similar failures. Yet the collective anguish reflected in the chronicles went beyond their failure. It served to expiate their guilt and teach a lesson. The chronicling sister admitted that they had allowed Delphine's difficult character to try their patience and to prevent them from responding as good nuns should. Sisters were expected to treat their charges calmly at all times. Careful preparation for death was one of their most important tasks. It involved sitting with the dying, making sure the religious paraphernalia necessary for the last rites were at hand, and, above all, calling the confessor at the first sign of the possibility of death.[12] They were also to study their own character daily to make sure they were behaving with decorum. In this case they had not. The chronicles thus served as a collective examination of conscience and character, but also as an occasion to reflect on their faith. Why had God let this happen? Why had the nuns failed? asked the sister. Here clearly was a challenge from God, a test of their faith. A lesson could be taught and learned: '[A]ll saw in this event a charitable lesson for us. No doubt the poor sick woman did not need this last grace to be saved. The Community did need a lesson so that they would act with more charity the next time.'[13]

Such exceptional deaths might work to prevent the sisters from being diverted from their mission another time by someone's difficult character. They alert us to the limits to nuns' spiritual power in the Catholic church. In the sexual and spiritual division of labour and hierarchy of the Church, the nuns themselves really had no power to ensure a good death. Their task was to cultivate the spiritual ground. Preparing the sick for death, encouraging them to suffer with patience, even converting them back to Catholicism if necessary, were within their power.[14] The following stages – the final confession, final sacrament, and annointment of the dying – however, had to be performed by ordained members of the Church. Herein lay the problem of the nuns. Although each community had its own priest who came daily, there was no guarantee he would be there when needed for an inmate. The nuns knew they could not always count on a priest agreeing to see a particular patient.[15] The chroniclers discuss such problems, complaining, for example, about one priest who 'hardly felt it was worth the bother' to give a blessing to someone who had 'already lost her judgment.'[16]

Sisters and the Elderly

Delphine Thoin was one of over three thousand adult women and about two thousand adult men who spent some time in the wards for poor and elderly men and women in the Montreal mother houses of the Sisters of Providence and Grey Nuns or in one of the other hospices run by the Grey Nuns between the 1830s and the 1890s (see table 6.1). These two orders were the major Catholic congregations working with the poor and sick of Montreal in their homes as well as in institutions. The registers allow us to determine some of their characteristics. Men and women of all ages were taken into these institutions. Some children entered with their parents. A few men and women in their teens and twenties were admitted. So, these places were not like the nineteenth-century old people's hospices in France, where men and women under seventy had little chance of being admitted, and where the supply of places seems to have always fallen short of demand.[17] Most of those cared for were indeed elderly. Together the resident adults averaged about seventy years of age, somewhat younger than in roughly equivalent institutions in France. The oldest, a black widow named Mary Anne Jackson, was reported to be around 115 years old.

Institutionalization was the experience of a significant number of Montrealers, though many more spent their final days with their families. For example, nearly one out of ten Montreal widows and widowers who were in their seventies was listed as being in an institution when the census was taken in 1861. Among those over eighty, around one in every six widows and one out of every five widowers were residing in some kind of asile, hospice, or general hospital.[18] Many more would have spent some time within such an institution.

The nuns were not consistent about recording marital status. The Sisters of Providence did so more consistently than the Grey Nuns. Among those whose marital status was given, most were men or women whose spouse had died. This is not unexpected given the dominance of widows and widowers among the elderly of the city. What is at first glance more surprising is the high number of women who had never married, especially among the women housed by the Sisters of Providence, where between 25 per cent and 40 per cent of all inmates were single women (see table 6.1). Their numbers are disproportionate to their part in the city population, where the unmarried seldom reached 20 per cent in any cohort.[19] Men and women who had never married faced old age lacking the major nineteenth-century social security-system – children. As they aged, so did their siblings. Lacking other places to turn, single inmates and women in particular were disproportionately represented in the institutionalized population. The challenges faced by such unmarried elderly women merits further attention by historians.[20] Widows and widowers, in contrast, usually had offspring to turn to for support in illness and old age, and it was with their own children or other relatives that the vast majority of Montreal's aged widowed population lived.[21]

The majority of women and men who entered these institutions died there, although the proportion decreased across the century. During the 1840s and 1850s four out of five of the widows with the Grey Nuns and nine out of ten of those with the Sisters of Providence died in the institutions. Between the 1870s and 1890s around two out of three did. Other inmates stayed for periods of four days to seventeen years. For example, among those in the Saint Charles hospice, which was opened by the Grey Nuns in 1877, the average stay between 1877 and 1881 was just over two years for those who died in the institution and between five and six months for those who left.[22]

In the absence of carefully kept case files describing each person's personal and family histories, it is impossible to know exactly what led these men and women, or their kin, to seek refuge with the nuns. Occasionally the registers listing their arrival contain evocative hints about their state of health or mind, their links to other family members, and their background. Cursory notations identifying some women as 'idiots,' epileptics, paralysed, or blind, or as having pulmonary problems, suggest the kinds of physical and mental infirmities that would make it difficult for relatives to care for them. Sometimes family members are specifically identified as placing their elderly or sick relatives. One woman was brought in by her nephew, who paid a pension for her.[23] A widower and his daughter arrived together. He was welcomed among the elderly men, while she joined the orphans and later in life became a nun in another community. Some of those who came had sisters, aunts, even daughters, who were nuns in that order.[24] At least one poor old woman was dumped unceremoniously outside the Asylum of the Sisters of Providence on an early December

TABLE 6.1
The adult clientele of the Sisters of Providence and the Grey Nuns, 1830–1891*

	Marital status not mentioned	Single	Married	Widowed	Total
	A. Asylum of the Sisters of Providence				
Women					
1830–49	29 (22%)	32 (24%)	3 (2%)	70 (52%)	134
1850–69	38 (18%)	78 (36%)	43 (20%)	57 (26%)	216
1870–91	16 (4%)	168 (40%)	63 (15%)	173 (41%)	420
Totals	83 (11%)	278 (36%)	109 (14%)	300 (39%)	770
Men	125		5 (16%)	25 (84%)	30
	B. Institutions run by the Grey Nuns**				
1830–49	68	1 (1%)	4 (3%)	45 (38%)	118
1850–69	487 (71%)	15 (2%)	31 (5%)	154 (22%)	687
1870–90	672 (39%)	138 (8%)	201 (12%)	693 (41%)	1704
Totals	1227 (49%)	154 (6%)	236 (9%)	892 (36%)	2509
Men	658 (39%)	183 (11%)	363 (22%)	484 (29%)	1688

*The registers also list inmates under 20. This analysis is based only on those aged over 21. For sources see note 5.
**Four of their institutions are included here: the poor in the Mother House, the Saint Joseph hospice, the Saint Charles hospice, and the seeing residents of the Nazareth Asylum. The most important missing institution is the Saint Brigitte Refuge. Marriage was such an important social signifier for women that I suspect the majority of those for whom no civil status was mentioned were single. This was standard practice in census taking, for example. The nuns seem to have found the marital status of men much less important to record, so few conclusions should be drawn about them.

night with her name and age pinned to her clothes. After recounting her story, she pleaded successfully to be kept, offering to sleep on the floor when told there was no vacant bed. She died shortly thereafter.[25] In both communities a few relatively wealthy women were taken in as pension-paying residents who had their own separate apartments. They shared intimately in the spiritual and community life of the orders, often contributing their wealth to the decoration of chapels, altars, and churches.[26]

TABLE 6.2
Occupations listed for the husbands of married women and widows
sheltered by the Sisters of Providence, 1855–1889

	Widows	Married	Total	%
Farmer	26	6	32	19
Labourer	36	26	62	36
Carter	6	3	9	5
Carpenter or joiner	15	6	21	12
Skilled worker or artisan	27	10	37	22
Professional or clerical	2	2	4	2
Commerce, bourgeois, rentier	7	0	7	4
	119	53	172	100
No information	59	29		
Totals	178	82		

Source: Archives of the Sisters of Providence, Montreal, 'Registre des femmes
vieilles et infirmes de l'Asile de la Providence, Montréal, depuis 1830'

Such relatively wealthy inmates were exceptions. Most inmates did not pay. Only the Sisters of Providence recorded any details about the occupations of the men they sheltered or of those held by women's husbands or fathers. Between the 1850s and 1880s the women they sheltered were disproportionately the wives or widows of farmers or of the most vulnerable fractions of Montreal's emerging proletariat – labourers, construction workers, or carters[27] (see table 6.2). About half of all the widows reported as residing with these two orders in the 1861 census were listed as illiterate.[28] The Grey Nuns may well have attracted a broader clientele in all their institutions. Certainly some of their hospices catered to elderly of a wider range of class backgrounds. In 1879, in the depths of winter and economic depression, their Saint Charles hospice was described as the pearl of their works. The chronicling sister suggested that 'all the elderly debris of lives of former ease' could be found there mixed together, including elderly merchants, lawyers, teachers, and 'veterans of all professions and trades,' as well the poor, elderly, and infirm women.[29]

The inmates of these institutions came from within the changing, industrializing city of Montreal and the surrounding regions. As the century advanced, growing numbers of farmers and immigrants gravitated to the city seeking wages and work in the expanding factories and construction sites. Some may also have been attracted to the expanding network of charitable institutions, thus swelling the institutionalized population of the city. Since the sisters did not systematically record people's previous place of residence, it is hard to measure the extent of such migration. However, for the period between 1877 and 1883 the nun in charge of the registers of the Saint Charles hospice did note how long entrants had been living in Montreal. Most were Montrealers: two out of five had lived there for over twenty years. More had lived in the city for at least five years. Only a few, about one out of every ten, appear to have migrated to the city specifically to seek refuge. They were recorded as having arrived in Montreal the very day that they entered the hospice.[30] The places of residence recorded for women sheltered by the Sisters of Providence suggest that over the century growing numbers came from Montreal.[31] If these cases are at all representative, then it does look as if the city's institutions for the elderly catered mostly, though never exclusively, to the Montreal population.

To try and understand why some people chose or were sent to spend time or to die in such institutions, it is important to investigate what daily life might have been like in such hospices. The elderly and sick men and women cared for by the Sisters of Providence and the Grey Nuns entered vast, complex, religious institutions run by the nuns and integrated, each in its own way, into the hierarchies, power structures, and power struggles of the Catholic Church. The chronicles demonstrate clearly how the rhythm of their days was set by the regulations of the respective communities. The unfolding of the year was heralded by religious celebrations and holidays and punctuated by visits of Catholic dignitaries. The atmosphere was determined at a general level by the ultramontane practices and romantic Catholicism of the period.[32] Within each institution, however, the ambience was set by the personalities of the nuns and other workers, and by the very different organization, rituals, and hierarchy of each order.[33] While the Grey Nuns and Sisters of Providence both performed similar kinds of social work – visiting the poor, sheltering orphans, the sick, and the elderly, running dispensaries for the sick and soup kitchens for the poor – they were very different kinds of orders, each with their own history, collective personality, and specific challenges.

The Grey Nuns had been providing for Montreal's poor and elderly since the widowed Marguerite de Lajemerais d'Youville began offering shelter in the 1730s. She and her successors had received financial and spiritual assistance from the Sulpicians over the intervening years and had built up their experience and traditions over the century. Emilie Gamelin had also begun her work as a widow during the 1820s. The Sisters of Providence were officially founded only in 1843, with the encouragement and spiritual support of Ignace Bourget, the recently appointed bishop of Montreal.[34] These two orders frequently became puppets in the ongoing power struggle between the powerful Sulpicians, seigneurs of the island of Montreal, and the bishopric.[35] As friction mounted between the Sulpicians and the bishop, the Sisters of Providence received less and less financial support from the Sulpicians and were compelled to devise alternative ways to make and save money.[36] Making a virtue out of their constant state of financial need, they were more explicitly dedicated to a life of poverty and to a reliance on Providence than were the Grey Nuns. Financial difficulties shaped the daily work of the Sisters of Providence and the daily life of their inmates more than those with the Grey Nuns.

In both communities the poor elderly and infirm resided within specific rooms or dormitories.[37] The numbers of women cared for at the Providence Asylum increased steadily from the handful with Mère Gamelin when it became a religious community in 1843 to around one hundred by the 1860s and 1870s and well over one hundred thereafter. Initially they admitted only women, but after 1858 they took a few men each year. It remained much more an institution run by women for women than the General Hospital, where the Grey Nuns cared for both men and women, though always more women than men (table 6.1). They housed over two hundred infirm men and women throughout the 1860s and 1870s. Unlike the Sisters of Providence, the Grey Nuns created several new and separate institutions within the city including the Saint Joseph hospice, which opened in 1854, and the Saint Charles hospice, which opened in 1877.

Each dormitory was in the hands of one sister, helped at times by another sister or a lay person. The Grey Nuns were exhorted to treat their poor with patience, affection, and generosity – as a mother would treat her children.[38] Inmates faced a high turnover of the sisters in charge because of illness, exhaustion, death, and frequent assignment to other responsibilities. The other helpers included men or women who had failed to become nuns and priests but still dedicated their lives to caring for the infirm.

Immobilized inmates could remain within these rooms and have most of their material and spiritual needs covered. There was great joy at the Providence asylum when Bishop Bourget allowed mass to be held inside daily in 1840, for several women had been unable to walk to the church. Over the years small chapels, altars, and sanctuaries were established within the various dormitories of the Grey Nuns where mass was said on occasion.[39] Physically mobile inmates, in contrast, left their rooms to attend mass elsewhere in the buildings and sometimes in churches outside. On important holidays and feast days they participated in celebrations, or their rooms became part of elaborate ritualized processions through the community. And on special occasions, such as the one-hundredth anniversary of the Grey Nuns' hospital work in 1847, the resident poor went walking in the town following numerous masses.[40]

It is hard to assess either the care these elderly and often sick women and men received or their standard of living. For those who had known better days materially and physically, the accommodation and diet may have seemed spartan. Yet more may well have received better material care than they would have in the world outside – some better than ever in their lives. They were assured a bed, meals, clothing, and a wash at least as often as was normal in the society of the time. It is a remarkable testimony to the levels of sanitation and care in both communities that the sisters appear to have succeeded in preventing the spread of contagious diseases to the sick and elderly, even during serious typhus and cholera epidemics, when the nuns were in daily contact with those infected.[41]

We should not imagine that life in such institutions was always tranquil and quiet, or cut off from the events and dangers of nineteenth-century life. The chroniclers graphically described the fires and floods that were just as likely to disrupt daily life in a convent or hospice as in the houses of the city. When the nuns moved the elderly to different quarters or when the Grey Nuns' entire convent was moved to a different part of the city, the chroniclers recorded almost caricature-like sketches of the inmates on the move – men and women leaning on crutches or on each other and grasping their belongings, those old women capable of walking, 'limping or blind,' dragging 'themselves as best they could, some with a chair, a pot or a box, into their new rooms.'[42] In another move, an elderly blind man's greatest joy was reported to be finding his own chair and spittoon in his new dormitory.[43]

Nor was their life one of leisure. Able male inmates were expected to perform physical labour.[44] Women made their own beds and did some light housework each day, as well as helping to make clothing, bedding, covers, and other things needed within the institution.[45] In the early years of the Providence asylum the elderly women helped the sisters do the washing for the priests of the archbishopric of Montreal to raise money for the institution.[46] During the cholera epidemic of 1854 some helped care for the little children at the asylum to free the sisters to work with the sick. They probably also helped fabricate the 'Syrup of Spruce Gum' for which the Grey Nuns were known, along with the wax statues of baby Jesus, soutanes, shoes, and sheets for the dead that were among the major goods the Sisters of Providence produced to raise money.[47] Inmates also contributed their time, and sometimes their money, to religious projects. The nuns reported frequently on inmates' contributions to the religious capital of their institutions. In 1865, for example, the elderly women in the General Hospital of the Grey Nuns offered to take on extra work so that they could contribute to the purchase of religious relics that Bishop Bourget offered to procure in Europe for the mother house. Women paying pensions contributed to decorations for altars and chapels.[48]

The timing of work, prayer, and care were strictly determined in each community. The daily rhythms and monthly rituals of the inmates and the nuns unfolded according to rules set by the communities themselves and their religious superiors. Daily life, like death, was saturated with the beliefs, rituals, rhythms, and goals of the Catholic church. The inmates lived and died surrounded by the symbols and language of an increasingly imperialistic, rigid, romantic, and ultramontane Catholic church. Social and spiritual celebrations merged inextricably, as did prayer and laughter or the smells of incense, incontinence, and disinfectant.

The elderly played a different role in these institutions than did the other main charges of the nuns – the orphans. They, like the orphans and the other people the nuns helped, were one link in the complex, hierarchical network of spiritual and charitable ties that bound the sisters and their clients to the wider Montreal Catholic community. But the elderly and sick, because they were close to death, held a special place in a theology that stressed the importance of a good Catholic death and used the horrors of purgatory and hell to encourage the faithful to conform. More than just the recipients of charity and care, they were also objects and symbols of charity, charged with religious meanings and significance.[49] Powerless materially, and often sick, weak, or senile, they wielded a collective power because their closeness to death made them important both in the work of the nuns and in the discourse of the church.

They were potent symbols of imminent death, of the need for all to be prepared for it, and for the prescription that only priests could ensure a good death. At an 1878 dinner given by the gentlemen of the Saint Vincent de Paul Society for eighty old and infirm residing in the St Charles hospice of the Grey Nuns, the bishop talked explicitly about their being close to their tombs, and how important it was that they could come to the end of their time on earth peacefully after fighting the miseries of life.[50]

The inmates surely did not need to be reminded of their imminent deaths. Dying and death were ever present in their daily rituals and experiences. They and the sisters prayed with dying inmates and sat with them and with their corpses. When Eliza Allard looked as if she would die without receiving the final sacraments in a lucid state, the other women in her room were reported to have prayed successfully together so she might obtain the grace to confess.[51] Inmates also prayed for dying and dead sisters, attended their burials, and were obliged to take their place beside their bodies in church. They attended masses for dead benefactors.[52] The chroniclers invariably describe them as rejoicing along with the sisters when deaths went well and as sharing their conviction that a death well died was an occasion of joy, not sorrow.[53]

We cannot know how many of the inmates believed fully in the teachings of the church, or felt secure that their chances of a good death were greater inside than outside the institution or outside the Catholic Church. It was the job of the nuns to care for their charges' souls and religious practices as well as their bodies. They were to make sure that all those who were able listened to the mass with attention and piety, observed fasting days, and confessed. For devout Catholics this religious framework no doubt offered spiritual security and satisfaction, giving them the feeling of contributing both to the institution and to their own salvation. Praying together for the revival of a colleague so she could confess and take the last sacraments, for rain during a summer drought, or for butter to supplement their spartan diet may have forged personal links of spiritual and social solidarity between the inmates.[54]

Such daily practices, combined with the power of the dominant discourse on death, purgatory, and the final judgment, may have outweighed any personal doubts. For the inmates these cannot have been abstract teachings, words heard occasionally, then forgotten. They infused the lives and deaths of those around them. Most practising Catholics would probably have welcomed the religious rituals and atmosphere that pervaded the institutions and that were inextricably linked to the care, food, and shelter the nuns provided. Non-believers, Protestants, or even moderately fervent Catholics, by contrast, may well have found life in such institutions unbearable.

Those elderly who found their role as objects of charity, their work, or their religious obligations objectionable had several options. They might avoid some responsibilities by accentuating their infirmities. They could conform outwardly and keep their beliefs to themselves. Or they could leave of their own accord. What they chose to do may well have depended less on their beliefs than on their own disabilities and their options outside. When resistance was too overt, however, they were asked to depart.[55]

Over the century growing numbers left. During the 1830s and 1840s only 20 per cent of widows with the Grey Nuns and 10 per cent of those sheltered by the Sisters of Providence departed before their death. Between the 1870s and 1890s well over 30 per cent did so and they were, on the average, men and women who had entered younger than the earlier cohorts of inmates. Those leaving from the 1870s on were more likely to be Montrealers than those who remained. Around four out of ten women who listed their residence as Montreal departed, compared to under a quarter of those from other parts of the region or province.[56] Some returned to family members. One widow seems to have remarried. A few left then came back again, dying shortly after their return. The increase in the proportion who left 'of their own accord' may reflect discontent with the increasing rigidity of institutional Catholic life.[57] Or, more elderly who recovered from bouts of illness may have been able to find shelter with their own families in the city. The expansion of wage labour, and the changing labour needs within households offered healthy elderly relatives, and women in partic-

TABLE 6.3
Proportions of poor dying in General Hospital of the Grey Nuns and Asylum of the Sisters of Providence, 1830–1891 (widows only)

Years	Average age at admission	Number of widows in in registers	Number who died (%)	Number who left (%)
		A. General Hospital of the Grey Nuns		
1830–49	–	46	36 (78%)	10 (22%)
1850–69	–	100	55 (55%)	45 (45%)
1870–90	–	188	108 (57%)	80 (43%)
Total		334	198	135
		B. Providence Asylum		
1830–49	74	70	57 (81%)	13 (18%)
1850–69	68	57	39 (68%)	17 (28%)
1870–91	71	173	121 (69%)	53 (31%)
Total		305	217	83

Sources: ASGM, 'Registre d'admission des pauvres, Vol. II, 1797–1854' (G6\IR3); 'Registre des pauvres et des orphelins, Vol. III, 1854–1890' (G6\IR5); APSP, 'Registre des femmes vieilles et infirmes de l'Asile de la Providence, Montréal, depuis 1830' (1830–1891). Numbers are different here from table 6.1 as only those in the General Hospital are included.

ular, new roles as babysitters while a mother was working or shopping. In families where several adults were earning in skilled trades, revenues might stretch to support a spinster aunt or widowed parent.[58]

Nevertheless, the majority of the elderly inmates who entered these institutions continued to die there (see table 6.3). Except in extremely rare cases, like that of Delphine Thoin, they had the daily religious support of the sisters, backed up by the incumbent priest, visiting priests, and Catholic dignitaries. They could die a good Catholic death.

Links to the Wider City: Visitors, Charity, and Death

Neither inmates nor their caregivers were completely cut off from the people of the city or the wider world. Visitors, charity, and theology forged material and spiritual links that bound inmates, nuns, and Montrealers in a set of complex economic and spiritual ties that transcended the walls of the convents and both bound and set apart citizens of different classes, ages, states of health, economic means, and spiritual resources. Inmates and sisters wove webs of prayer that tied them not just to the living of the city but to the souls of the dead. Threads of these webs emerge in the chronicles.

A hierarchy of visitors gave the nuns and the inmates of these institutions a filtered contact with contemporary events and personalities of the nineteenth century, and especially, but not exclusively, of the Catholic world. Friends and relatives could visit the inmates of the Grey Nuns without the special permission required from the Mother Superior for other visitors.[59] They brought news about families and neighbourhoods. In addition to the priests who came regularly to say mass, hear confessions, and perform the spiritual tasks that sisters could not, a steady stream of other Catholic dignitaries of varying rank, order, and origin passed through both institutions. Some came alone or in small groups and stayed in the convent while in Montreal; others came in large groups for particular religious occasions.[60] Some brought religious news; a few, political information. Secular dignitaries included the governor-general, the Marquis of Lorne and his wife, Princess Louise, in 1879.[61] On such formal visits, the guests either greeted the elderly and sick in their rooms, as the princess did, or the elderly were lined up to greet them. Bishop Bourget was a more regular visitor, especially to the Sisters of Providence, whom he saw as his creation and ruled with a patriarchal rod. On most of his visits he spent some time with the elderly women, sometimes giving them communion in their room.[62]

In this period when the Quebec church became more and more romanized, when the infallibility of the Pope was proclaimed as dogma and a papal cult reigned among many, the visits of men sent to Quebec by the Pope himself must have excited both the sisters and the religious elderly. The apostolic delegates were men who had actually seen and conversed with the Pope and could bring news directly from the Vatican.[63] Mgr Conroy was sent to Canada in 1877 as the Pope's apostolic delegate to sort out dissensions within the Quebec church. He may well may have been relieved to spend time in the relatively tranquil atmosphere of these communities.[64] He visited the Grey Nuns at least twice. Their chronicling sister described his encounters with the elderly. Some inmates, she wrote, were 'leaning on their sticks, others supporting themselves with the assistance of a stronger companion, some blind, others really deformed.' The image is of them eager to talk with him, to kiss the cross around his neck or his ring, or to receive a special benediction. His visit to the Sisters of Providence was similar. Again he payed special attention to the elderly, 'touched by their sorrows ... [H]e talked very kindly to them and seemed genuinely interested in them. Five of these poor unfortunates were bedridden because of their illness. The Delegate went to each one addressing them with some words of consultation, then retired giving the papal benediction.'[65] The visit of the subsequent apostolic delegate, Smeulders, six years later was described in similar terms. 'The visit of Pope Léon XIII himself could not have provoked greater emotion for these dear old women, so much did they feel filled with respect and love toward his designate.'[66]

While frequent visits by dignitaries gave inmates contact with the religious world outside, charity linked them in rather different and often indirect ways to the lay people of Montreal. The elderly and sick were the object of the money-raising schemes of the Sisters of Providence, but they were not directly involved. The Dames de Charité were laywomen who worked with the sisters organizing the bazaars that annually raised around $1000 of much-needed money for the nuns' works.[67] The Sisters of Providence held collections in Montreal churches and sought donations directly from citizens known to be good contributors. They also took to the streets, soliciting money, a task they particularly disliked that brought them into direct contact with citizens who might be sympathetic, apathetic, or antagonistic. The elderly men and women inmates profited from the food and clothing and improvements to their quarters made with money earned in these ways. They also shared the other gifts in kind bequeathed by local tradesmen and merchants, the food left at the door of the Providence asylum, or given annually at Christmas. Such gifts given by sympathetic Montrealers were crucial in this community, founded with greater religious fervour than financial security. When the visiting apostolic delegate Mgr Conroy asked Bishop Bourget how he supported so many people on so few resources, Bourget simply responded that he had placed its fate in the hands of Providence. His answer belied all the hard work of seeking donations of food and money and the other unpaid physical and spiritual labour that the sisters had to put into keeping their community viable. It also completely hid the contributions paid annually by the government of Lower Canada and later Quebec.[68]

Only rarely did the three major players in this charitable relationship – the inmates, the nuns, and Montreal's lay charity workers and givers – come together. This occurred at charitable dinners given at least once a year for the poor in each institution, which were frequently described in the chronicles.[69] A careful look at what was written about several of these dinners reveals how the chroniclers portrayed the social and symbolic relationships involved on such occasions. Over one hundred citizens, all reported as eager to serve the poor, partook of a dinner hosted at the Grey nunnery in January 1867 by the male associates of the Saint Vincent de Paul Society. It began shortly after 5 p.m. with a blessing by Bishop Bourget, who handed plates of turkey to the men who were serving the inmates. He then went from table to table communicating with the inmates. The chronicling sister recorded that 'despite all the preparation done in advance, and the rapid service given by the men, the dinner lasted nearly an hour. This was not too long for the gourmets of last night. For although their advanced age and their infirmities slowed down their movements, their eyes were lively.' She noted that 'the most infirm, encased in huge chairs were not forgotten,' and were treated kindly. 'After dinner, Monseigneur said grace and the men visitors left with the benediction and thanks of the poor. They were introduced to the shrine of our Venerable Foundress. The bishop congratulated them and everyone departed with the peace and good feeling that follows doing good.'[70]

The sister is describing a ceremonial meeting between one group of Montreal's poor and the men of the Saint Vincent de Paul Society. The latter met the city's poor on other occasions when they visited them in their homes and distributed charity. But in these encounters each maintained their social place. Here, in contrast, the laymen served the poor, reversing normal class relations. The sister described with approval 'two gentlemen who took hold of the bowls of two of the most disgusting of our sick and fed them with a spoon with charming politeness and goodness.' She concluded by praising the merits of charity, because 'it triumphs over the most strong repugnances of nature.'[71] In this highly ritualized reversal of class relations, gender roles were also subverted. Not only did the men serve food to the poor – more normally women's work as wives, nurses, or nuns – but they also donned the white apron of a female servant. Furthermore, they were praised for exhibiting 'feminine' qualities, namely patience, politeness, and goodness. The chronicler assumes, probably rightly, that these men left feeling the peace and goodness that such charity bestowed. Did a temporary but simultaneous crossing of the major divides of society, class, and gender intensify the spiritual profit accumulated? Or were these men displaying new middle-class male ideals of tenderness, love, and serving?[72] Such charitable performances do seem to have constituted a wonderful stage upon which to cultivate these citizens' spiritual bank account and display their worthiness to the world.

Dinners given at the Providence asylum for the elderly were smaller, less public, less ritualized, and less likely to involve men.[73] The first one mentioned was in 1850. It was hosted by several of the Charity women who, after serving the dinner, joined the old women in a period of festivity. Other times the sisters themselves hosted the dinner, sometimes with help from their own families. Luce Cuvillier, a benefactress of the order, hosted dinners on at least three occasions between 1869 and 1884 – all but one of these after the death of her lover, the politician George-Étienne Cartier. The description of the dinner she hosted in 1884 highlights the much more informal atmosphere that prevailed. The chronicling sister described Miss Cuvillier as doing the 'honours, helped by seven of the Community's sisters who happened to be there.' After dinner, she sat 'among these good old ladies,' telling them stories while giving them tobacco. This description resonates with Brian Young's depiction of her as an 'unorthodox romantic' who 'smoked, wore trousers' and lived relatively openly with Cartier before his death. What is intriguing is the portrayal of this woman in her sixties, with a distinctly unorthodox reputation as a 'charitable young lady.'[74]

If those participating in such dinners or performing other good works hoped to improve their chances of going quickly to heaven, other gifts were tied more explicitly into shortening the period between death and the afterlife. For devout Montreal Catholics damnation or time in purgatory were real possibilities following death. Like Catholics everywhere, they sought to increase the number of people praying for the souls of their dead loved ones so as to shorten their time in purgatory, if necessary. The church had long counselled those making their wills to order masses and almsgiving for this reason. Some wealthy Montrealers donated their jewels and money, others left legacies, sometimes of considerable amounts, to the sisters in return for prayers for the repose of their own souls or those of their deceased husbands or wives or other relatives. For the Grey Nuns, in particular, this seems at times to have been an extremely profitable business.[75] Anna Devins, the widow of Mr J. Tiffin, and the sister of a Grey Nun, for example, gave around $2500 worth of jewels to the order in the early 1880s after her husband died, offering them for the repose of his soul. On subsequent travels in Europe, she in turn lit candles and prayed for the Grey Nuns and promised more gifts.[76]

Catholic ideas about purgatory and hell, a good death, prayers for the departed, and charitable giving tied together the living, the dying, and the dead of Montreal's Catholic population. Citizens benefited from the prayers of the nuns and the inmates, and from the satisfaction and spiritual reward of giving. The relationship was reciprocal. As the chaplain of the Sisters of Providence explained: 'If the people of the world need the prayers of the community, they in turn could not continue to pray without the support of the alms of the rich.'[77]

Conclusion

The registers in which the nuns carefully inscribed the demographic details of their clients are closer to twentieth-century case files than are the nuns' chronicles. The carefully listed standardized information in the registers shows that most of the men and women who spent some of their final years with the Grey Nuns or Sisters of Providence were elderly, averaging over seventy years, Catholic, and predominantly French Canadian. The majority of inmates were widows and widowers, as fits their proportion in the elderly population. Elderly single women and a smaller number of men, who were more likely to lack family support systems, were disproportionately likely to be residents. Most were from the most vulnerable fractions of the population, poor and frequently illiterate. These systematic records reveal little else about these people. We seldom know why they came to the nuns for care, what they felt about living in Catholic institutions, or why growing numbers chose to leave after a short stay.

The chronicles, like diaries or court records, seem to offer a better understanding of daily life in such institutions. It is tempting to try to read them 'against the grain' to strive to capture the lives of the inmates, the relations between the elderly inmates and the caregiving sisters, or how the nuns felt about their work, or about their charges.[78] Historians have undertaken such readings of court records or case files in part because they have built up theoretical and empirical understandings of the relations of class and power that were at play. Feminist theory offers us fewer guidelines for a nuanced analysis of how religious relations intermeshed with those of class and gender. To read the nuns' chronicles with or against the grain involves taking gender and religion seriously. It also requires acknowledging the nuns' spirituality.[79] Their religious mission cannot be peeled away or discounted. For them religion, work, and even subjectivity were intermeshed, suffusing their lives as workers, nuns, and women. Only by acknowledging the primacy of religion, rather than trying to obscure it, can we begin to sort out the relation between the nuns and their charges, between caring for the elderly and the broader Catholic mission. Only by thinking about how religious impulses and other power relations were inextricably linked can we begin to understand the multidirectional social and spiritual relations that constituted charity and the different rewards the diverse participants secured.

For the hierarchy of Quebec's Catholic Church the care the nuns provided for women like Delphine Thoin was an important part of the overall project of gaining greater social, religious, and political control in a secularizing society. In Montreal, where Protestant churches and secular diversions abounded, this was particularly important. The bishop and the Sulpicians struggled constantly about how the Catholic project should be managed. The nuns of these two orders were repeatedly caught in the religious and financial crossfire. Church leaders did, however, agree that it was crucial that the Grey Nuns and the Sisters of Providence, along with lay visiting groups like the Saint Vincent de Paul Society or the Dames de la Charité, visited the poor, identified the dying, and offered shelter to those requiring care.

The chronicles suggest that the institutionalized elderly played a special role within this broader social-work system. Senile, simple, sometimes loathsome, and always dependent, they participated in public religious celebrations, important visits, and dinners within these communities. They appear as part of the choreography of such public occasions – lined up in the corridors, living parts of the decoration that included incense, fragrant flowers, greenery, and welcome signs.[80] Living evidence of the Church's charity work among the poor, they were also potent symbols of the imminence of death, often in explicit opposition to the nuns' other charges, the youthful orphans.[81] On such occasions, the elderly step bodily into the church's discourse on death, confirming by their presence in a Catholic institution the crucial importance of a good Catholic death and legitimating the broader role of the Church in the religious and political economy of Montreal. In turn, the promise to help save people from eternal damnation was a powerful tool of spiritual control that extended beyond the elderly to the city's entire Catholic population.[82]

The work and dedication of the nuns was crucial to the church's broader mission. Their success, both as promoters of Catholicism and as managers of complex social-work institutions, depended on building up links between their works, their poor, and the wider spiritual and economic community of Montreal. They sought material, religious, and moral support for their work and used what they raised or were given to care for hundreds of elderly and sick men and women during the final years of their lives. The elderly, sick, and dying were as important to their work, and to their satisfaction, as they were to the male church hierarchy or the members of the Montreal community who took part in the dinners for the poor or gave money to ensure that the poor were fed. In the nuns' work with their charges, physical and spiritual care, spiritual guidance and spiritual coercion were inextricably linked. Their own satisfaction in the work they did caring for the poor would have been inseparable from their success in ensuring their charges were ready to die a good Catholic death. Hence the anguish expressed in the chronicles when this was not done for Delphine Thoin.

Nuns had chosen their life of religious service over marriage. Feminist scholars have demonstrated that some were able to exercise considerable power and develop talents and skills that laywomen could not.[83] Not enough attention has been paid, however, to the limits placed on their authority over religious matters within the structure of power in the Catholic Church. Delphine Thoin's death highlights nuns' inability to perform the final rites. Other accounts in the chronicles reveal their irritation at priests who could not always be counted on to arrive in time to perform them.

For many Catholic clients such institutions must have seemed a safe and spiritual haven. Others may have put up with the religious life there in order to receive the physical care they needed. This would have been easiest for those elderly who were bedridden or deaf, and thus able to avoid some of the timetables and rituals. Growing numbers of the elderly left as the century progressed, perhaps because religious institutional life became more regimented, or perhaps because more Montreal families could shelter elderly dependents. Those who remained knew they would not face death alone, that they would be cared for materially, and that their chances of receiving their final rites from a priest while still lucid were probably better inside than out.

The chronicles appear to lead us to a world behind convent walls, peopled by nuns in their habits, priests in their robes, and Dickensian elderly men and women, some bedridden, others leaning on crutches or lined up on public occasions. We see them in prayer and sometimes eating, laughing, smoking, and dancing. Yet, even in the chronicles, this is not a religious world set apart from the secular, industrializing city outside. Nor is it a world without relations of power based on class, gender, or even race. The ties that bound the elderly inmates, the wider Catholic community, the secular city, and the sisters together were religious, economic, and political, and as often fraught with the tensions of those relations as with Christian love.

Notes

This chapter could not have been written without help from the archivists of the Sisters of Providence and the Grey Nuns, financial aid from SSHRC and FCAR and research assistance from Nathalie Picard and Sylvie Perrier. I am more than grateful for all this support. The chapter is an adaptation of 'Mourir chrétiennement: La Vie et la mort dans les établissements catholiques pour personnes âgées à Montréal au XIXe siècle,' which appeared in the *Revue d'histoire de l'Amérique française* 46:1 (Summer 1992). My thanks to the editors for permission to reuse it.

1 Archives Providence des Soeurs de la Providence (hereafter APSP), 'Chroniques de la Maison Mère [hereafter 'Chroniques'], III (1876–1881),' février 1880, 367–8. Similar regrets were expressed when an inmate of the Asile St Jean run by the Grey Nuns died in 1884; Archives des Soeurs Grises de Montréal (hereafter ASGM), 'Circulaire Mensuelle [hereafter 'CM'], III, 1884–1887,' 58.
2 In this paper I attempt to bridge family history and more institutional histories by including those living outside families as recommended by Katherine Lynch in 'The Family and the History of Public Life,' *Journal of Interdisciplinary History* 24:4 (Spring 1994), 678, 683. See also my chapter 'Widowhood and Canadian Family History,' in Margaret Conrad, ed., *Intimate Relations: Family and Community in Planter Nova Scotia, 1759–1800* (Fredericton: Acadiensis Press, 1995).
3 I draw in particular on the following chronicles. ASGM, 'Ancien Journal [hereafter 'AJ'], I (1688–1857)'; 'AJ II (1857–1867)'; 'AJ III (1867–1877)'; 'CM I

(1877–1880)'; 'CM II (1881–1883)'; 'CM III (1884–1887)'; 'CM IV (1888–1892)'; 'Chroniques de l'Institut Nazareth (1861–1892)' (hereafter 'Chroniques Nazareth'; 'Chroniques Hospice Saint Joseph (1854–1892)' (hereafter 'Chroniques Saint Joseph') (L10\H4). APSP, 'Chroniques (1828–1864),' (not paginated) typewritten ms; 'Chroniques (non terminé) (1864–1872),' (not paginated) typewritten; 'Chroniques II (1864–1872)'; 'Chroniques III (1876–1881)' (handwritten); 'Chroniques IV (1881–1886).'

4 On the problems of using such sources, see the introduction to this volume and especially Joy Parr, 'Introduction,' *Labouring Children: British Immigrant Apprentices to Canada, 1869–1924* (Toronto: University of Toronto Press, 1994), xii, and Joan W. Scott, 'Review of Linda Gordon, *Heroes of Their Own Lives*,' *Signs*, Summer 1990, 850; and Linda Gordon, 'Response to Scott,' *Signs*, Summer 1990, 852.

5 All men and women over the age of twenty present between 1828 and 1891 were transcribed from the following registers: ASGM, 'Registre d'admission des pauvres [hereafter 'Registre des pauvres'], II (1797–1854)' (G6\IR3); 'Registre d'admission des pauvres et des orphelins, 1854–1907, Hospice Saint Joseph' (L10\T6); 'Registre des pauvres et des orphelins,' III, 1854–90 (G6IR5); 'Registre d'admission des pauvres et des enfants trouvés, 1834–1945' (G6\IR9 and L2\IR9); 'Registre no 1, Hospice Saint Charles à Montréal (ouvert le 1 mai 1877), (1877–1894)' (hereafter 'Registre Hospice Saint Charles'), (L35\R1); 'Index du registre d'admission, 1861–1974 (Institut Nazareth)'; APSP, Montréal, 'Registre des femmes vieilles et infirmes de l'Asile de la Providence, Montréal, depuis 1830' (hereafter 'Registre des femmes depuis 1830'); ibid., 'Registre des vieillards et infirmes de L'Asile de la Providence, Montréal, depuis 1849' (M2.43).

6 In the larger project of which this is part, I have traced some inmates to parish registers and to the censuses of 1861, 1871, and 1881, for example, to reveal more about their demographic characteristics.

7 ASGM, Table de la 2ème partie du Coutumier, 'Petites règles' (F103-26/3), 131–3, 137

8 APSP, 'Chroniques III (1876–1881),' 367–8

9 'Lettre Pastorale de Mgr. L'Évêque de Montréal, concernant les catholiques qui, dans leurs maladies, vont se faire soigner à l'hôpital-général protestant,' 26 Apr. 1876, *Mandements, lettres pastorales, circulaires et autres documents publiés dans la diocèse de Montréal*, vol. 7, 1887, 321, 318

10 Ibid. On the emergence of this idea of a good death see, especially, Philippe Aries, *L'Homme devant la mort* (Paris: Seuil, 1977), 299, 405–42. On Quebec see Serge Gagnon, *Mourir hier et aujourd'hui* (Quebec: PUL, 1987); Brigitte Caulier, 'Les Confréries de dévotion à Montréal au 19e siècle,' Doctorat, Université de Montréal, 1986; Brigitte Caulier, 'Bâtir l'Amérique des dévots: Les Confréries de dévotion montréalaises depuis le Régime français,' *RHAF* 46:1 (Summer 1992) and Philippe

Sylvain and Nive Voisine, *Histoire du catholicisme Québécois: Réveil et consolidation*, Tome 2, *1840–1898* (Montreal: Boréal Express, 1991), 340–1. Marie-Aimée Cliche argues that church teaching on preparing for death changed little between the Council of Trent and Vatican II; 'L'Évolution des clauses religieuses traditionnelles dans les testaments de la région de Québec au XIXe siècle,' in Benoît Lacroix et Jean Simard, *Religion Populaire. Religion de clercs?* (Quebec: IQRC, 1984), 367. On the fascination with demons and spirits during this period, and the reaction of the church, see Sylvain and Voisine, *Histoire du catholicisme*, 85.

11 Denise Robillard, *Émilie Tavernier-Gamelin* (Montreal: Méridien, 1988), 93–171
12 ASGM, 'Table de la 2ème partie du Coutumier. Petites règles' (F103-26\3), 138
13 APSP, 'Chroniques III,' February 1880, 368–9
14 *Mandements*, vol. 7, 1876, 318
15 Sylvain et Voisine report that priests' neglect of their duties to the dying was one of the major causes of complaints against the clergy during this period. *L'Histoire du catholicisme: II*, 342
16 APSP, 'Chroniques (1864–1872),' n.p., December, 1871
17 Maurice Garden, 'Les Hospices de vieillards: Du Comité de mendicité à la loi d'assistance obligatoire (1790–1905),' in A.-E. Imhof, J.-P. Goubert, A. Bideau, and M. Garden, eds, *Le Vieillissement: Implications et conséquences de l'allongement de la vie humaine depuis le XVIIIe siècle* (Lyon: Presses universitaires de Lyon, 1979), 103–6; Olivier Faure, 'Les Classes populaires face à l'hôpital,' *Cahiers d'Histoire* 26:3 (1981), 267
18 Ms census, Montreal, 1861. The numbers of widows and widowers in institutions is given as a proportion of the total number enumerated in the city. The greater institutionalization of men than women, and of widowers in particular, is not unique to Montreal. See Peter Laslett, *Family Life and Illicit Love in Earlier Generations* (Cambridge: Cambridge University Press, 1977), 200, and Margaret Tenant, *Paupers and Providers: Charitable Aid in New Zealand* (Allen and Unwin: Historical Branch, Wellington, 1989).
19 Or more if, as I suspect, a majority of those for whom no marital status was listed were indeed single.
20 Exceptions include Tamara Hareven, 'Life Course Transitions and Kin Assistance in Old Age: A Cohort Comparison,' in David Van Tassel and Peter N. Stearns, eds, *Old Age in a Bureaucratic Society: The Elderly, The Experts, and the State in American History* (New York: Greenwood Press, 1986), 119–20; Elizabeth Jane Errington, *Wives and Mothers, Schoolmistresses and Scullery Maids: Working Women in Upper Canada, 1790–1840* (Montreal and Kingston: McGill-Queen's University Press, 1995); Michèle Stairs, '"An Independent and Incomplete Existence"? Spinsters in Late Nineteenth-Century Prince Edward Island,' unpublished M.A. thesis, University of New Brunswick, 1995; and Catherine Renaud, 'Une place à soi? Aspects du

célibat féminin laïc à Montréal à la fin du 19e siècle,' unpublished M.A. thesis, histoire, Université de Montréal, 1994.

21 See graph I, Bradbury, 'Mourir chrétiennement.' Compare with David Thomson's
argument that in nineteenth century England the community was much more impor-
tant as a provider for the elderly than were families; in Margaret Pelling and Richard
M. Smith, eds, *Life, Death, and the Elderly: Historical Perspectives* (London and
New York: Routledge, 1991), 194–217. On Canada in a later period see James G.
Snell, *The Citizen's Wage: The State and the Elderly in Canada, 1900–1951*
(Toronto: University of Toronto Press, 1995).

22 ASGM, 'Registre Hospice Saint Charles' (1877–94)

23 ASGM, 'Registre des pauvres,' 1845

24 ASGM, CM I, 1877–80, 337; CM II, 1881–83, 118, 391

25 APSP, 'Chroniques, IV (1881–1886),' 165–6

26 Ibid., 27. Note the similarity here with the role of Protestant women in church deco-
rating. See Lynne Sorel Marks, *Revivals and Roller Rinks: Religion, Leisure, and
Identity in Late-Nineteenth-Century Small-Town Ontario* (Toronto: University of
Toronto Press, 1996).

27 Bettina Bradbury, *Working Families: Age, Gender and Daily Survival in Industrializing Montreal* (Toronto: McClelland and Stewart, 1993)

28 The proportions were 40 per cent of those with the Grey Nuns and 57 per cent of
those with the Sisters of Providence in the ms census of institutions, 1861.

29 ASGM, CM I, April 1879, no. 14

30 ASGM, 'Registre Hospice Saint Charles'

31 APSP, 'Registre des femmes depuis 1830'

32 Lucien Lemieux, *Histoire du catholicisme québécois. Les XVIIIe et XIXe siécles: Les
Années difficiles (1760–1839)*, vol. 1 (Montreal: Boréal, 1989), 10

33 Claude Langlois, remarks on the very different personality of each order in his *Le
Catholicisme au féminin: Les Congrégations françaises à supérieure générale au
XIXe siècle* (Paris: Éditions du Cerf, 1984), 71

34 Robillard, *Emilie Tavernier-Gamelin*

35 Brian Young, *In Its Corporate Capacity: The Seminary of Montreal as a Business
Institution, 1816–1876* (Montreal: McGill-Queen's Press, 1986)

36 APSP, 'Chroniques.' Huguette Lapointe-Roy reports that the Grey Nuns received
nearly twenty times the amount of aid from the Sulpicians that the Sisters of Providence did; *Charité bien ordonnée: Le Premier réseau de lutte contre la pauvrété à
Montreal au 19e siècle* (Montréal: Boréal, 1987), 36. The friction was not only financial. It arose repeatedly in questions about the territory covered by each order and
when retreats should be held.

37 ASGM, CM I, February 1880, no. 24, 485–6

38 ASGM, 'Petites reglements, Chap. IX. Règle des Hospitalières'

39 ASGM, 'AJ III (1867–1877),' 242; 305

40 ASGM, 'AJ I, (1688–1857),' 519

41 ASGM 'AJ I, 1847,' 507; APSP, 'Chroniques, 1847'

42 APSP, 'Chroniques,' 1846; ASGM, 'AJ, III,' 1870, 197–220

43 ASGM, CM I, 438

44 ASGM, 'Petites Règlements,' article II

45 Lapointe-Roy, *Charité*, 190–1

46 APSP, 'Chroniques (1824–1864)'

47 APSP, 'Chroniques (1828–1884)'

48 ASGM, 'Chroniques II,' 1867, 16; 1865, 253

49 The representations of the elderly that dominate in the chronicles fit two aspects of the portrayals of old age that, Carole Haber and Brian Gratton argue, began to prevail in the United States from the early nineteenth century. First, the stress is on their physical infirmities, in contrast to earlier representations of old age as a gift from God for a life well led. Second, Haber and Gratton argue, as death rates in younger groups began to diminish, ministers began to emphasize 'the inherent and inescapable connection between old age and mortality.' *Old Age and the Search for Security: An American Social History* (Bloomington and Indianapolis: Indiana University Press, 1994), 152–3

50 ASGM, 'CM I,' March 1878, 92–3

51 APSP, 'Chroniques III,' April 1845

52 APSP, 'Chroniques II,' 1872.

53 Stories of good deaths abound in the chronicles and they are frequently about the deaths of young nuns. Witness the story of one twenty-one-year-old, torn as she weakened between her desire to die and the feeling that she was causing her mother pain by remaining in the convent. When a series of visits relieved her anxieties, she is reported to have died exclaiming, 'Oh!, you see how good it is to die as a Grey Nun.' ASGM, CM II, November 1881, no. 7, 211

54 APSP, 'Chroniques,' 1845; December 1871

55 ASGM, Table de la 2ème partie du Coutumier, 'Petits règlements,' 131, 137

56 APSP, 'Registre des femmes depuis 1830'

57 See Marta Danylewycz, *Taking the Veil: An Alternative to Marriage, Motherhood, and Spinsterhood in Quebec, 1840–1920* (Toronto: McClelland and Stewart, 1987), 29–49. After 1844 the Grey Nuns stopped serving wine three times a day on holidays and festival days; the number of periods of silence increased after 1849. Bishop Bourget urged stricter controls on Sisters of Providence in the 1860s, and even their singing was criticized by Bishop Laflèche in the 1880s as too profane. ASGM, 'AJ I,' 107–10; 113; APSP, 'Chroniques II, 1864–1872,' April 1864; APSP, 'Chroniques III,' 402

58 Widows living at home with their children appear to have benefited from the expan-

sion of job-earning possibilities that accompanied industrialization as their offspring were more likely to report jobs than those in two-parent families. See Bettina Bradbury, 'Surviving as a Widow in Nineteenth Century Montreal,' *Urban History Review* 17:3 (February 1989), 152–3, and *Working Families*, 203–6; and Lorna R. McLean, 'Single Again: Widow's Work in the Urban Family Economy, Ottawa, 1871,' *Ontario History*, 83:2 (June 1991): 134–7.

59 'Petits règlements,' 31, and the chroniques of each institution
60 This occurred largely with the Sisters of Providence.
61 ASGM, CMI, June 1879, no. 16, 352–3
62 APSP, 'Chroniques,' 1843, January 1869, June 1871, April 1868; ASGM, 'AJ II,' 105–6, 'AJ III,' 143
63 Sylvain et Voisine, *Histoire du catholicisme*, 2, 41, 73, 203
64 Roberto Perrin, *Rome in Canada: The Vatican and Canadian Affairs in the Late Victorian Age* (Toronto: University of Toronto Press, 1990), 73–7, 223–5
65 APSP, 'Chroniques III,' 1877, 133; my translation.
66 APSP, 'Chroniques IV,' 1883, 175
67 On lay women and charity work see Jan Noel, '"Femmes Fortes" and the Montreal Poor in the Early Nineteenth Century,' in Wendy Mitchinson et al., *Canadian Women: A Reader* (Toronto: Harcourt Brace, 1996).
68 APSP, 'Chroniques III,' 1877, 136; Quebec, *Sessional Papers*, no. 1, 'Statement of the Public Accounts, 1877–8,' $600 paid to Revd. Sister Thomas at the Sisters of Providence, and $4000 to Andrew Robertson for the Grey Nuns.
69 ASGM, 'AJ III,' 1, 120, 225, 340, 447
70 Ibid., 1–3; my translation.
71 Ibid.
72 On evangelical Protestants and these new ideals of masculinity see especially Leonore Davidoff and Catherine Hall, *Family Fortunes: Men and Women of the English Middle Class, 1780–1850* (Chicago: University of Chicago Press, 1987), 110.
73 Dinners are mentioned in the following chroniques: APSP, 'Chroniques,' 1850, 1856, 1858, December 1869; 1876, 21; 1881, 14; 1883, 86; 1884, 184, 258.
74 On Luce Cuvillier see Brian Young, *George-Étienne Cartier: Montreal Bourgeois* (Montreal: McGill-Queen's University Press, 1981), 34–8. She was president of the Dames de Charité de L'Asile de la Providence in the early 1860s. APSP, 'Chroniques,' October 1862, November 1864. Quote from 'Chroniques IV, 1884,' 184
75 Sylvain et Voisine, *Histoire du catholicism*, 21, 307; Louis Rousseau, *La Prédication à Montréal de 1800 à 1830: Approche religiolique* (Montreal: Fides, 1976), 161–3; and, on the sisters being asked to pray for family members, see ASGM, 'CM I,' 254, 258; II: 312, 382, 426; and Marie-Aimée Cliche, 'L'Évolution des clauses traditionelles dans les testaments,' 367.
76 ASGM, CM, January 1882, no. 8, 311

77 APSP, 'Chroniques III,' 1876, 24
78 Karen Dubinsky explains how she does this with court records in the introduction to *Improper Advances: Rape and Heterosexual Conflict in Ontario, 1880–1929* (Chicago and London: University of Chicago Press, 1993), 6–7.
79 Until recently women's historians have tended to evade the issue of spirituality by focusing on women's work within the church. Ruth Compton Brouwer's argument, that 'personal spirituality and transcendent concerns have largely been overlooked, along with forms of religious activism that did not necessarily bear fruit in a larger sphere for women,' is still timely. 'Transcending the "Unacknowledged Quarantine"': Putting Religion into English-Canadian Women's History,' *Journal of Canadian Studies* 27:3 (Fall 1992), 48. Admirable steps in this direction include Marks, *Revivals and Roller Rinks*; Marguerite Van Die, '"A Woman's Awakening": Evangelical Belief and Female Spirituality in Mid-Nineteenth-Century Canada,' in Mitchinson et al., *Canadian Women: A Reader*, and Christine Hudon, 'Des Dames chrétiennes: La Spiritualité des catholiques Québécoises au XIXe siécle,' *RHAF* 49:2 (Fall 1995), 169–94.
80 ASGM, CM, July 1878, no. 7, 170–2
81 Their descriptions of orphans as beautiful like angels reminds us that in Montreal in this period the very young were as likely to die as the elderly.
82 Sharon Cook argues that Protestant old-age homes for women and men in Ottawa offered a quiet place to die, but stresses that they aimed also at social control. The concept of social control of the elderly does not seem to me to capture the dynamics at work in these Catholic homes, where spiritual aspects seem to have been so important, and where it is unclear what use internalizing control would have served for those close to death. '"A Quiet Place ... to Die": Ottawa's First Protestant Old Age Homes for Women and Men,' *Ontario History* 81:1 (March 1989)
83 Marta Danylewycz, *Taking the Veil*; Nicole Laurin, Danielle Juteau, and Lorraine Duchesne, *A la recherche d'un monde oublié: Les Communautés religieuses de femmes au Québec de 1900 à 1970* (Montreal: Le Jour, 1991)

PART THREE
MAKING 'GOOD' MEN, PUNISHING 'BAD' MEN:
'COMMUNITY' STANDARDS AND THE STATE

7

Males, Migrants, and Murder in British Columbia, 1900–1923[1]

ANGUS McLAREN

Only in the past few years have historians begun the investigation of the gendered nature of masculinity.[2] Researchers who have plotted the evolution of definitions of manliness tell us that in the late nineteenth and early twentieth centuries there was a perceptible shift away from the cult of rugged masculinity towards a new model of 'masculine domesticity.' These findings, though suggestive, are based primarily on the prescriptive literature that laid out the duties of the middle-class, urban male. Did the new middle-class ideal filter down to the working class? And is one talking about real changes in behaviour or only in cultural stereotypes? A convincing account of the shifting boundaries of appropriate masculine behaviour is unlikely to be attained as long as research is restricted to traditional literary sources.

Sources that have as yet gone largely untapped but that promise to contribute to our understanding of popular notions of masculinity, dealing as they so often did with men's use of violence against other men, are the records generated by the criminal-justice system. Forcefulness continued to be hailed by contemporaries in the late nineteenth and early twentieth centuries as a crucial aspect of male gender identity, while its counterpart, acquiescence or passivity, was attributed to the female. But at what point did the forceful man become the violent brute? When could a lack of forcefulness brand one an effeminate coward? One way of answering such questions is by using court records that chronicled recourse to the most extreme form of violence – murder. Judges and juries faced with such acts had to say, on the behalf of the community, how far legitimate force could be pushed.[3]

In addition to revealing how degrees of tolerable violence were carefully calibrated by communities in the past, the documentation generated by murder trials provides unusually intimate portrayals of male interactions.[4] According to an old maxim, men, unlike women, 'do not like to talk,' but the most taciturn, when put on trial for their lives, became loquacious.[5] Such material, though obviously having to be used with caution – often the thoughts and actions of working-class immigrants being interpreted for and by middle-class Anglo-Saxon lawmen – nevertheless provides a priceless source for the investigation of the meanings given manhood.

Gender preoccupations obviously coloured such deliberations, yet the fact that every jury decision did not win public approbation serves as a forceful reminder that the criminal-justice system did not stand in for society in an unproblematized fashion. All court verdicts involving men were obviously not based solely on the community's interpretation of masculinity. Moreover, those who served the courts had their own agendas; their chief preoccupation was to oppose threats to the rule of law. Proof that the accused had resorted to vigilantism could accordingly counter any sympathy he might have garnered by demonstrations of manly assertiveness. Legal practitioners were naturally intent on demonstrating that cases were decided, not on the basis of simple public prejudice, but on the evidence presented. That having been said, the investigator of such sources is repeatedly struck by the inclusion in the 'evidence' of both hard facts and vague gender expectations. At a 1910 British Columbian murder trial, one defence witness stated that the accused had 'always treated him like a man,' a second testified that at the time of the killing the accused had asserted that 'a man has to defend his home,' and the accused himself recollected that when served with a warrant he had asked the special constable 'why he had not produced it like a man.'[6] This essay accordingly seeks to tease out the various meanings of the assertion, so frequently crucial to a court's deliberations, that the accused had or had not acted 'like a man.'

Common Murder

Let us begin with a not untypical male killing. On 15 September 1915 Hugh McGill, a Cranbrook Canadian Pacific Railway shop employee, beat to death Samuel Watson, a former CPR brakeman. The inquest jury found that Watson 'met his death from a fractured skull caused by falling against a verandah post through a blow struck by accused, McGill.'[7] The chief of police attributed McGill's attack to the fact that the twenty-five-year-old Watson 'had been paying too much attention to his [McGill's] wife.' Apparently a number of people in Cranbrook knew that Watson and Nellie McGill either had or were having an affair. They had exchanged letters. One read at the inquest, addressed to Sam and signed 'Your devoted lover Nellie,' referred to a past sexual relationship.[8] McGill, knowing that Watson was coming to visit, lay in wait on the verandah and lashed out at his rival as soon as he knocked on the door. If there was a fight it was very much one-sided. The accused was left with marks on his knuckles, but none on his face. The verandah post and the ground on which the victim lay were covered in blood. How had Watson died? A medical witness testified at the preliminary hearing that though the victim had been drinking, falling from the verandah and hitting his head on a post could not alone have caused death. An examination of the deceased suggested that he had been hit about the head with a blunt object three or four times. Once Watson was down in a pool of blood McGill's first thought was not to summon medical aid, but to fetch his friend, Percy Adams, the chief of police. McGill, though excited, was clear-headed enough to be already framing his defence. 'You remember the man I told you about last year? ... Well I got him. Come and see where he is. I will show you where he is.' Adams on being shown the body called for a doctor and arrested McGill. Told by the police that his victim had died and warned to watch what he was saying, McGill replied: 'It was coming to him. It was in self defence.'

The Cranbrook court house where McGill's preliminary proceedings in September and his trial in October took place was packed with his friends.[9] The crown counsel informed the attorney-general's office that the accused enjoyed 'a great deal of public sympathy.'[10] Nevertheless, the prosecution proceeded with the case, arguing that McGill had to pay a price for being the aggressor in a fight that ended in death. The defence countered that Watson – though warned – had refused to stay away from the McGill house, made threats, and on the fatal night struck first with a riding crop. McGill now claimed that he simply defended himself and in the ensuing mêlée Watson accidentally fell backward and hit his head. The spectators, by their applause for the defence summation, made their loyalties known. The jury was out no more than thirty minutes before returning with a verdict of not guilty. Why had McGill been acquitted? The short answer is because he acted in a way that the community considered appropriate for a man. Murder was a desperate act, but it was understood that in a given situation a man had the right to have recourse to it.

By analysing British Columbian trial and inquest reports for the years 1900 to 1923 this paper sets out to provide a fuller answer to the questions of how, where, and why men killed other men. The first part will deal with the 'how' and the 'where,' that is, account for the number, location, and means of killings. The second part will focus on the trickier issue of 'why.' There can be little doubt that because of the way gender concerns patterned the use of violence it was more 'normal' for men than for women to resort to deadly force. Beginning with the premise that certain forms of male violence were sanctioned by juries, the purpose of this portion of the paper is to see what murder trials tell us about the social construction of masculinity. Were there 'manly' ways of killing?

What in short – according to judges, policemen, jurymen, lawmen, and news-papermen – did it mean to be a man?

Men and Murder

The overwhelming majority of British Columbian killers were, as in the McGill case, men. In western Canada as elsewhere, then as now, men were far more likely than women to have recourse to violence.[11] Moreover, in the early decades of this century British Columbia, like other pioneering communities, experienced a serious sex-ratio imbalance, men far outnumbering women.[12] Between 1900 and 1923, 270 men and only 18 women were cited in murder cases. Males also dominated as victims: 221 men were killed, but only 35 women. This disparity between male and female murder rates is confirmed by the figures drawn from inquest records on unsolved and untried murders. Of the 205 victims who died in suspicious circumstances, 164 were men and 41 were women. The sex of the majority of the assailants (149) was unknown, but of the known assailants (who usually had avoided trial by escaping, dying in jail, or committing suicide), 51 were men and only four were women.[13] In the years we have examined, 214 were the victims of male murderers. As in the McGill case, men 'normally' killed other men of the same class and ethnicity. The 'typical murder' involved a male (likely drunk) killing an acquaintance, friend, or work mate. Murders were endogenous: to kill outside of one's class, gender, or ethnic group was highly unusual. What follows is an attempt to understand the meanings given masculinity in early-twentieth-century British Columbia by examining the murders carried out by white working-class males (many of them immigrants from Europe and the United States), the justifications they provided for their acts, and the responses made to them in the courts and in the press. As will be seen in what follows, though various ethnic groups no doubt differed in their notions of appropriate gender roles, most men fell back on common notions of masculinity in defending their recourse to violence. The murders carried out by Aboriginal and Asian men will be treated elsewhere, because the prejudicial treatment the courts accorded members of visible minorities deserves more extensive analysis. Killings of and by women will, for similar reasons, also be set to one side.

Where were men killed? Both McGill and his victim worked for the railway. A grand jury noted in 1904 that murder 'may, perhaps, be attributed to the floating population following railway construction.'[14] A commonplace, often repeated by the press, was that a mobile, male culture served as a natural breeding ground for violence. The point usually missed by contemporary observers was that such communities were more stable than they often appeared to outsiders. Killers were rarely strangers; men were mainly murdered by those whom they knew – men with whom they lived, worked, and played. Setting aside the cases in which women were the victims and the murders committed by Native peoples and Asians, the reports reveal that in 130 cases the relationship of the white male murderer to the male victim was as follows:

Acquaintance	38.5%
Friend, neighbour, boarder	27.7%
Stranger	18.5%
Workmate, employee, employer	12.3%
Relative	3.0%

Most men worked together in what were largely single-sex industries. The peaceful workplace could suddenly become a murder site. Guns and knives – the most common instruments of death – were readily at hand in the bush, on homesteads, and on ranches, but fists, boots, and ordinary tools sufficed as weapons. Miners were bludgeoned to death, fishermen knifed or drowned, loggers' skulls split by axes, soldiers shot. A typical scenario saw a Greek fisherman meet his fate in a boat in Plumper's Pass off Vancouver Island. According to the accused, 'I told him to get out and not come into my boat but just the same he jumps in the boat all right and grabbed me by the throat from behind. I bent forward and I was drunk myself and he had me down; I had a knife in my hand; the knife I had was one we had for cutting bread, cleaning fish or anything, one we used on the boat, the knife was about as long as this sheet of paper ... I don't know how he got the cut; I was lying down and he was on top of me; I think he must have stept [sic] on it himself in the row.'[15] Murders at the workplace usually saw labourers turning on each other, but firing an employee could provoke similar violence. A storehouseman at the Esquimalt Naval Yard, dismissed in 1903 for negligence, retaliated by emptying his pistol at his supervisor.[16] In 1912 it was the Canadian Northern Railway gang foreman, Barney Mulligan, who killed an irate worker who made the mistake of screaming at him in the camp kitchen, 'You old bull shitter, you are no good, you come outside and I'll fix you up for what you did yesterday, you Irish son of a bitch.'[17] Mulligan, who had dismissed the worker the day before, then struck him.

Men not only worked together, many lived together.[18] Criminologists often draw a distinction between 'domestic' murders involving men and their families and 'public' murders involving mainly men. But in British Columbia in the early decades of the century such clear-cut distinctions could not always be made. Murder-trial accounts of a squad of soldiers eating together day after day in the same canteen in Victoria, of six Italian labourers baching together in a house in Vancouver, and of three drunken prospectors holed up in a cabin at Summit Camp capture the suffocating atmosphere of men piled up together both day and night, getting on each others' nerves, enjoying little privacy, and having nowhere to escape. Men were crammed together on fish boats and railway bunk cars and in isolated cabins and shacks, forced to endure either each others' company in the shared accommodations of thin-walled rooming houses or the inquisitiveness of the suspicious families with whom they boarded. Large numbers slept in the barracks provided for soldiers and sappers and the bunkhouses for loggers, railwaymen, and road gangs.[19] Privacy was not even found in bed. In 1915 two Ruthenian labourers working on the CNR tunnel at Mile 127, having opposite shifts but sharing the same bunk, eventually came to blows.[20]

Some sense of how the day-to-day tensions of such claustrophobic situations could escalate into violence was conveyed in the diary of Frederick Trumper, who in 1907 shared a tiny cabin at Pouce Coupe with an increasingly cantankerous sixty-year-old trapper.

Oct. 15th Had talk with Coleman on his grouchiness.
Oct. 27th Coleman is on one of his cranky spells again.
Nov. 10th Coleman is on a tear again.
Nov. 18th Coleman is now talking of moving out.

Unfortunately for Trumper, Coleman did not leave; instead, on 25 November Coleman came at him with a rifle and, in warding him off with a mallet, Trumper delivered a fatal blow.[21]

Labourers may not have had the same desires as the middle class for privacy, but some single men would have liked at the least the option of living on their own; given the lack of public facilities, it was rarely possible. The irony was that the vast expanses of 'frontier' wilderness often offered newcomers less privacy or anonymity than the larger cities of the east coast and Europe. And men not only worked and lived together; their leisure-time activities, especially drinking and gambling, were largely shared with other men.[22] For many men – be they British, American, or European newcomers to British Columbia – to be a man was to drink. 'The deceased was a pretty good man,' said an Italian of a compatriot, 'he drank just enough to keep him in grand shape.'[23] Alcohol played a precipitating role in about half of the murders.

Where did murders – usually of friends and acquaintances – occur? If not at the workplace, shack, or campsite, then the likelihood was wherever liquor was available. The hotel bar or saloon was usually the village or town's most important all-male institution. Murders frequently followed drinking bouts – at the

Victoria Hotel in Vernon (1901 and 1908), at the bar room of Starke's Hotel, Peterborough (1901), outside the Germania Saloon in Victoria (1902), at the St Elmo's Hotel at Trail (1907), Kirby's Hotel in Keremeos (1907), the Palace Hotel in Vancouver (1908), the Manhattan Saloon in Nelson (1911), the Queen's Hotel in Kamloops (1913), the New Telkwa Hotel in Telkwa (1913, 1915), and the Empress Hotel in Prince George (1921). Bartenders, often the only sober bystanders at such encounters, consequently found themselves being called as witnesses at inquests and trials.

The court records describe the extensive popular vocabulary employed to describe drinking to excess. One man's dying declaration began with the line, 'I am dying. I got full the day after pay day and Ed Morella threw a rock at my head and no one saw him throw it.'[24] Victims and murderers were said to be 'full,' 'on a spree,' 'wobbly,' 'under the influence,' 'quarrelsome in his cups,' 'mad drunk,' 'fighting drunk,' and 'absolutely inebriated, good and drunk.' Participants in such drinking sessions could not always be sure that what began as parties or celebrations, and degenerated into quarrels, 'friendly scuffles,' and brawls, might not end in murder. One prospector recalled that seven or eight bottles of whiskey were consumed by half a dozen men at a Cariboo country get-together. 'I left and that was the last I know of it, except the howling and screeching and shooting all night long as there was lots of noise.'[25] Despite the commotion he was genuinely surprised to discover the next morning that his friends and partners' party had culminated in bloodshed. So too was the acquaintance of two trappers who exchanged shots in 1911: 'they were good friends except when they were drinking.'[26]

Although A.W. Vowell, superintendent of Indian Affairs in British Columbia, placed the blame for the high number of native murders on the presence of liquor, no group seemed to be immune.[27] The importance of drink was possibly exaggerated. Claiming to have been drunk and not remembering what had happened was a convenient excuse for those who could think of no other. But the repeated making of such pleas suggests a real expectation that a male culture would take them seriously. James Dale blamed drink for his 1906 shooting up of the town of Carmi that resulted in two deaths.[28] Likewise Charles Egan claimed, 'The first time I knew a man had been killed was the next day Tuesday. Prisoner told me I had killed a man. When I first heard it I got sick.'[29] 'I got full,' claimed a third murderer, 'and can't remember anything after.'[30] 'I was full at the time,' lamented Albert McDougal, who had killed his brother. 'I don't remember how this thing happened.'[31] Such lame defences could be successful inasmuch as the accused would occasionally be found guilty of manslaughter as opposed to murder, and they were accordingly trotted out again and again. Drug stupefaction was rarely mentioned, though a witness said of a gunner who in 1910 killed his captain at Victoria's Work Point barracks, 'It is the dope that does it.'[32] In 1908 the manufacture and sale of opium was banned in Canada but at least as late as 1914 it was still freely available even in jail.[33]

The most common type of murder was that which resulted from friends' or workmates' arguments escalating, under the influence of drink, into a trading of insults and finally to violence. Something as trivial as a rivalry in banjo playing led Frederick Collins in 1901 to kill Arthur Dando, better known as the 'Banjo Kid.'[34] Sometimes the tension between friends rose over the course of months if not years; on other occasions it flared up after a drink or two. Such killings were rarely premeditated. The day of 7 January 1914 began with Serre Coval and Andrew Charnot, two Russians working on railway construction near Thompson's Crossing, celebrating Russian Orthodox Christmas; it ended with Coval shooting Charnot.[35] John Doherty's last words, said of a fellow hospital orderly in 1919, were, 'It is all right, he is afraid to press the trigger.'[36] John Casey, a soldier in the Forestry Battalion, when told in 1917 that he had killed a comrade, drunkenly retorted, 'Oh, he's all right, he's only fooling.'[37] But he was not. 'Get up Ernie, you son of a bitch,' bellowed Charles Neff at his best friend whom he floored on 11 August 1913 with a welding hammer, 'You are not dead.'[38] But he was. Such brawls were a sort of lottery; who murdered whom depended largely on chance. Such was not the case with the one or two 'psychopaths' who killed more than once. Rocco Farrante, an obviously insane Italian BC Electric Railway labourer, the month after being found not guilty of the shooting death of a friend in November 1915, decapitated his room-mate.[39] In 1918 John Walsh, who had previously served seven years in prison for manslaughter in his native New Brunswick, was sentenced to death for the murder of a fellow logger.[40]

When strangers were murdered it was often the unintended consequence of planned, but bungled robberies. In 1911 the owner of the Manhattan Saloon in Nelson and in 1912 the owner of a Vancouver liquor store were murdered during robbery attempts.[41] Mike Popovich's sudden prosperity in 1914 linked him to the robbery and murder of a Russian labourer near Endako.[42] In Vancouver three Scots' attempt to stick up a bootlegger ended in the latter's death in 1919,[43] two Irishmen killed a logger for his money in 1920,[44] and a deaf man's failure to understand two thieves' order to 'stick 'em up' led to his death in 1921.[45] Finally, two teenage muggers' 'warning shot' killed a Victoria bank clerk in 1923.[46]

The police killed, of course, but as their deeds were not treated as murder they will not be examined here. But lawmen were also numbered among those killed. At two in the morning of 29 August 1914 a dishevelled Mickey McKillarney told a friend that 'he had a shooting scrape and he thought he had croaked a bull.' Lawmen stood out as the usual victims of the handful of murders carried out by professional criminals. William Haney, an American bank and train robber, in 1909 shot to death a special constable outside of Ashcroft and successfully got away.[47] In 1912 Walter James killed a police guard on board the steamer *Okanagan* while attempting to escape custody, and constable Lewis J. Byers died in a shoot-out in Vancouver. The same year at the New Westminster penitentiary two convicts, in the course of a jail break, murdered a prison guard.[48] In 1913 Henry Wagner and William Julian (Americans who were purportedly old members of Butch Cassidy's gang) shot to death a special constable who had surprised them during a robbery at Union Bay.[49] In May of 1913 a constable was the victim of two Vancouver robbers evading a police search.[50] One of the most famous murders of a lawman occurred in 1914 in Vancouver, when, following the Komagata Maru affair, Mewa Singh gunned down immigration officer William Hopkinson in the city court house.[51] The second police killing of 1914 in Vancouver took place when Mickey McKillarney, the ex-convict noted above, shot a detective.[52] In June 1914 a police constable was killed in Kamloops by a person or persons unknown.[53] In 1917 Malcolm McLennan, Vancouver's chief of police died in a shoot-out with Bob Tait, a small-time African-American drug dealer.[54] Fred Deal, another black man, in 1922 killed a Vancouver police officer while resisting arrest.[55]

Murders resulting from run-ins with the police and bungled robberies represented only a small fraction of all cases. Most killings were precipitated, as we have seen, by quarrels and arguments. A threat to one's livelihood – which jeopardized both a man's property and honour – could also result in a death. Such struggles might involve the control of scarce resources. In 1908 Vernon farmers fatally fought over irrigation water.[56] Long feuds between Cariboo ranchers over gates and grazing rights ended in bloodshed in 1920 and 1923.[57] Conflicts over property that led to violence were usually over the ownership of such things as guns, watches, bottles of liquor, sacks of potatoes, and sides of beef, in which the struggle between men was as much if not more over power, honour, and self-respect as for the apparently paltry goods in question.

Men in Court

We have seen where men killed each other and have some notion of the circumstances. Once arrested, what arguments did they employ as justifications for their acts? What responses were made to them by juries and newspaper reporters? At the trial what had often been private confrontations were suddenly made public. Those who had murdered in the course of a robbery or in a fight with a lawman received short shrift. The six white men who between 1900 and 1923 were tried for the murder of a law-enforcement officer were each found guilty and sentenced to death.[58] When it came to more typical murders, questions of intent and provocation were of crucial legal importance; it was understood that in struggles over honour and in defence of one's family a good man might be forced to kill. Had the accused, the public wanted to know, been sufficiently provoked? This was a life-and-death question. If the accused did not know what 'he had to say,' he was no doubt soon informed by his counsel. Generally agreed-on notions of masculinity played a key role in the community determining whether or not the accused had acted like 'a man' or like an effeminate sneak, whether he should go free or be punished, and, if punished, whether lightly or severely. Such gender concerns were especially evident in sex-related murders, but played a part in the presentation of every conflict that pitted one man against another. Judges and juries, aware of the dangers frontier life posed for men, were not unsympathetic even to such venerable gambits as that essayed by a Dutch pre-emptor (or homesteader) who shot his partner in 1915: 'I did not know the gun was loaded.'[59] Since the murderer and his victim were in the vast majority of cases members of the same class and ethnic group, the accused's guilt or innocence largely depended on what the court thought of a man's character, the situation in which he claimed he had to defend himself, the fairness of the fight, and his respect for the law.

   Juries carefully scrutinized the character of both the accused and the victim. How was a man's character determined? Though testimony that the accused was truthful, temperate, and law-abiding was diligently recorded, lawmakers seemed particularly taken by the notion that a man's morality could be judged by his attitude towards work. A bad worker, it was assumed, was a bad man. Such aspersions were often cast on the dead, who were not there to defend themselves. Arthur Dando, shot to death in 1901, was disparagingly described by the chief constable of Peterborough as 'formerly a bugler in the N.W.M.P., a young man of inferior character disliking work.'[60] Another murder victim was reported to have been 'a heavy, powerful fellow, who did no work, but lived by card playing and "bootlegging" and was constantly looking for trouble.'[61] An Italian labourer charged with murder in 1910 shrewdly claimed that he was provoked into fighting by a man who, lazily dropping his tools, had bragged, 'We don't give a damn for the job and I don't care to work.'[62] To be work-shy, it was understood, was unworthy of a real man.

   A good worker was assumed to be a good man. Witnesses were constantly asked to comment on the work ethic of the accused. A policeman was quizzed regarding a prisoner charged with a 1901 Victoria murder:

Q. You found him a quiet orderly man? *A.* Yes.
Q. A hardworking fellow? *A.* Yes.

In 1915 a judge recommended that a bridgeworker, whose single punch had caused the death of a drinking partner, be given a suspended sentence. Despite the fact that the accused had been previously fined for fighting, the judge concluded that 'character evidence shows [he is a] good workman.'[63] A constable at a 1917 inquest who began his testimony with the assertion that the accused was 'a hard worker' appeared to regret having to add 'but [he] has a crazy streak in him.'[64] To be able to present oneself as 'steady and industrious' was vitally important for any man on trial. The press's description of the accused in a 1921 trial as 'a young man of frank and clean cut features ... hardworking and honest' was a clear signal of the community's belief in his innocence.[65]

The hardworking individual presumably would have neither the time nor the inclination to go about picking fights. Nevertheless, the notion that a reasonable man could not simply walk away from every provocation with full self-respect provided the basis for the argument of self-defence. 'I shot Frank Martin,' declared the accused in a 1919 trial, 'first because I was afraid of him for he was twice my size. Secondly, because he was a bully. Thirdly, because he had threatened me, and fourthly, because he was a pro-German, unscrupulous, and a menace to the crown and government.'[66] The protestations of nationalist concern, presumably tacked on because the Great War had just ended, today ring jarringly false. A more believable presentation was made on behalf of Murdock Campbell, who beat to death a fellow Scots miner. Campbell, so his friends claimed, in leaving a drinking establishment, had tried his best to avoid a confrontation with a bully. 'The abuse was enough to make some men get up and fight. The prisoner in getting up and going out was subjecting himself to the taunt of being a coward.'[67] A reasonable man could only take so much; the victim in pursuing Campbell was at fault. Campbell was found not guilty. Charles Egan's supporters likewise testified that he had been goaded into attacking his friend William Shiells: 'Shiells was using bad language calling him a son of a bitch and a cock sucker. He was trying to provoke Charlie to fight.'[68]

If things came to blows, it was expected that you would 'take your medicine like a man.' But a 'fair fight' was one in which the odds were judged to be even. Frank Nicolas, who stabbed a fellow Greek fisherman, protested, 'If I hadn't killed him, he would have killed me.'[69] Guiseppe Bianca, a stonemason who knifed a bricklayer, similarly argued that he had only defended himself.[70] But in each case the accused had a knife and his victim did not. Nicolas was sentenced to five years in prison and Bianca to seven.[71] The community often made clear its views of such murderous encounters. When James McGill des Rivières for

no apparent reason in a drunken quarrel stabbed to death his friend Harry Row-
and, his argument of self-defence was accepted. The Greenwood *Weekly Times*
explained, 'Public opinion here is strongly in favour of the prisoner.'[72] These
things – in the eyes of the male community – happened. But when a sixty-
six-year-old man shot a sixty-year-old Vernon friend for making fun of him, a
witness noted that the accused 'showed more anger and excitement than the
matter would warrant, more than I have ever known in him.'[73] Similar negative
community sentiment was expressed in 1913 in the small Cariboo village of
Freeport. The cigar-store keeper reported that Mulvihill 'said he heard I accused
him of shooting Kelly. I told him I had not expressed my opinion ... but all the
boys thought so.'[74] The jury responded to the community's condemnation and
found the accused guilty.

There was little judicial sympathy for the man who, claiming he had nowhere
else to turn, actually launched a premeditated attack. Such was the case of Frederick Collins, whose house having been broken into and believing he knew who
did it, declared, 'I want to see a magistrate as I want some satisfaction. If I cannot get satisfaction from a magistrate, I have got means of satisfying myself.'[75]
He then killed the purported intruder. Similarly, a Vernon farmer who shot
down a neighbour who was digging a ditch on the accused's property claimed
he had no choice. 'He said that the law did not protect him and he would have to
protect himself.'[76] Judges made clear by imposing heavy punishments that they
did not approve of such pre-emptive forms of self-defence. But the accused,
who measured up to the model of the hard-working individual who tried to
avoid violence and fought fairly when he had no other recourse, even if he had
caused a death, stood a good chance of walking away from court a free man.
His chances were further improved if it could be argued successfully that his
adversary's actions had threatened the accused's very 'manhood.'

Fear of physical violence was used to justify murder; so too was men's fear
of sexual violence. Early-twentieth-century British Columbia was very much a
male world, for some a 'homosocial' world. Even in bed a man could be
attacked. An Italian worker asleep in a bunkhouse who found himself 'picked
up blanket and all' from his cot, in a rage shot to death the camp bully and went
free.[77] This particular case had no obvious sexual overtones, but it is not surprising that references to homosexual acts should occasionally emerge from the
murder records.[78] The way in which they were treated tells us a good deal about
how far one could go in defending one's masculinity.

On 13 October 1901, in the canteen of the Work Point Barracks just outside
Victoria, Harold Gill, a twenty-year-old English sapper in the Royal Engineers,
shot and killed Garland Clinnick, a gunner in the Royal Garrison Artillery. It
was an accident; Gill, a poor shot, had meant to kill gunner Mahoney, who was

sitting next to the unfortunate Clinnick. Gill's defence was that he had been 'goaded into desperation' by rumours spread by his fellow soldiers of a homosexual relationship he had had with Mahoney. Gill and Mahoney, both being members of the garrison band, had participated the week before in celebrating the leaving for England of the Royal Horse Artillery. After an all-night drunken party at the St George's Inn they had been seen asleep together on a couch with only their shirts on. Gill was thereafter unmercifully teased. 'Look out, this man belongs to the band' and 'Look out, here's Mahoney's pal' greeted the blushing Gill wherever he went. A comrade who admitted participating in the gossiping and teasing later protested, '[N]othing I told him would lead him to believe that an unnatural offense had been committed against him.' Nevertheless, Gill broke down under his tormentors' relentless hazing and apparently believed that he had been sodomized. How do you prove that you are a heterosexual? Gill, in order to reassert his manhood, sought to kill – not the persecuting troublemakers, but the fellow victim of this gossip, his purported homosexual seducer, Mahoney. Gill, by attacking Mahoney (following the advice of one or two friends who clearly put him up to it), thought he could thereby demonstrate beyond doubt that he was not a pervert.

This incident says something about how seriously the charge of being a homosexual could be taken in an all-male environment.[79] Some in the garrison no doubt thought it was a joking matter, but others believed it could justify murder. Gill described immediately after the shooting as 'excited and hysterical,' cried that he would 'rather be dead than dishonoured.' He bitterly regretted killing Clinnick and had no qualms about making it abundantly clear that when he raised his carbine his intention had been to murder Mahoney. At the ensuing trial Gill's defence attorney pursued the argument that Gill's tragic act was understandable, if not entirely forgivable, because 'he had been or believed himself to be, the victim of a monstrous indignity at Mahoney's hands.' Indeed, the defence argued, Mahoney was the real culprit, a man who lied about the events at the St George's Inn and sought 'to conceal his guilt.' Gill, who had suffered an 'outrage to his manhood' had, his lawyer argued, simply acted in 'a blind instant of passion.' This brazen attempt to argue that a homosexual act was worse than murder did not work for the simple reason that there was no proof that such an act had ever taken place. Gill, found guilty of the manslaughter death of the 'innocent' Clinnick, was sentenced to fifteen years' imprisonment.[80]

The verdict did not mean that the seriousness of the 'disgraceful acts' committed by perverts was in any way diminished in the eyes of the court. Sodomy, it should be recalled, was still a crime and even some heterosexual acts were regarded by the bar as perverse. The judge at a 1906 murder trial refused to allow evidence to be admitted of the accused's 'peculiar sexual desires' (for cunnilingus). Such evidence, his lordship said, would 'tend to indicate insanity.'[81] In the Gill case one suspects that if the accused had, as he intended, killed Mahoney a much lighter punishment would have been imposed. With Mahoney not in court to defend himself, a skilled counsel might well have succeeded, given the taunts and sneers that the subject of same-sex acts elicited, in blaming the victim for his own murder.

Just such a defence was called into play on 22 October 1907, when Edward Bowen, a young English labourer, shot and killed Paratreap Singh at the Spokane Rooming House in Vancouver. The two men had only met that day at the bar of the Alexander Hotel. After drinks the new-found friends returned to Singh's room, a shot was heard, and a white man was seen running away. A policeman tracked Bowen down a few streets over from Singh's rooming house. 'And the boy said he shot the Hindoo. ... And he said "Will I show you the place where the Hindoo was?" ... And he told me that he had shot the Hindoo, and that the Hindoo had tried to commit an indecent act.'[82] A friend of the accused corroborated the story that the Hindoo 'tried to bugger him [Bowen].' Was this the case or had Bowen attempted to rob Singh of the two hundred dollars he was reputed to have? The press laid out the options in a headline reading, 'Bowen's Honour or Hindu's Purse.'

Ironically, for a trial that focused on masculine honour, the defence asserted that 'a man has the same right as a woman and was justified in taking a life to protect his honour.'[83] Bowen and his counsel hoped that the community's revulsion against homosexuality was such that the claim of having been sexually attacked held out to the accused the best hope of getting away with murder.[84] But once again, as in the Gill case, the prosecution succeeded in showing that there was no evidence of a homosexual attack; indeed, there was much to suggest that Bowen's story had been contrived to cover his crime. Nevertheless, he was found guilty of manslaughter rather than murder and sentenced to ten years in prison. As in the Gill case, Bowen's conviction did not signify a downplaying of the dangers posed by homosexuality. The public was left to understand that a homosexual advance might justify recourse to murder; the problem was that the attorneys in both trials had failed to convince the juries of the reality of such attacks on their clients' honour.

Such questions of loss of 'honour' more commonly figured in men's struggles over women. Some men tried to seize other men's property; some men tried to carry off those who in common parlance were referred to as other men's women. Latter-day notions of chivalry which held that if a man had a right to defend himself he had a duty to defend his woman were repeatedly and successfully used to justify murder. Leo English, found not guilty of murder in 1901, employed just such a defence when charged with the shooting death of his brother-in-law. English claimed to be protecting his sister from her husband who was treating her badly. The victim, disliked in Vernon as a dangerous drunk, attacked English with a stick and English shot him. A witness, although accidentally wounded in the mêlée, backed up the accused with the claim, 'If ever a man had justification English had, to shoot.'[85]

More typical was the case of a husband asserting that he had been forced to kill to protect his wife. In 1904 Louis Gillier was found not guilty of the murder of a logger whom the Frenchman had shot twice with a shotgun. Gillier's story was that the gun had gone off accidentally while he was attempting to free his wife from the drunken embraces of the victim.[86] In 1905 Ole Oleson's shotgun killing of George Holcroft led to a not-guilty verdict after Oleson's wife testified that Holcroft 'pulled my clothes to pieces and hit me in the breast.'[87] In 1921 the same verdict was rendered for a similar case on Moresby Island in which a man forced his attentions on a friend's spouse. Such actions were, declared the press, 'ample provocation for the desperate deed.'[88] The inquest jury was so impressed by the testimony of a Vancouver man who shot to death his wife's ex-pimp that he was not even indicted. The fact that the victim was an African-American who had broken into the accused's home and attacked him no doubt played a role in the mercy shown.[89]

What if, as in the case of adultery, the wife did not want to be protected from the other man?[90] If a love triangle led to murder, the husband was usually the murderer and the lover or wife the victim, but on occasion the male roles were reversed. Louis Paquette killed Alfred Legère in order to obtain his wife. Paquette, Olive Legère testified, 'was telling me that he loved me. He has been telling me that for nearly three years. He told me he was going to shoot me the next time I went to Notch Hill.' Paquette's story was that 'his passion became unbearable and he made up his mind to kill the husband and wife and then kill himself.'[91] This violation of the family resulted in a death sentence. Similarly, in 1913 Bruno Cutri, who while attempting to run off with Maria Diatella, killed her brother-in-law, was sentenced to death.[92] But on occasion there were special circumstances in which 'the other man' was not convicted. In 1910 Harriet Carlson's abusive husband was strangled by someone who broke into their house. The evidence pointed to an ex-lodger with whom she was friendly, but the prosecution could not produce enough evidence to convince the jury.[93] In 1912 twenty-year-old Harold McNaughton successfully avoided going to jail for the accidental beating death of his woman friend's husband. McNaughton apparently had acted in self-defence, but was unwise enough to pay the young woman to leave town. Given such suspicious behaviour, why was he treated so leniently? The fact that he was the son of a leading Vancouver socialite and one of the few members of British Columbia's middle class to face a murder charge probably had an effect.[94] One might also assume that his age had something to do with it since McNaughton was described in the press as 'a West End youth.' But class and age were linked. A middle-class twenty-year-old male was referred to as a 'boy' or 'youth'; a working-class twenty-year-old as a 'man.' McNaughton's sixteen-year-old woman friend, the wife of an iron worker, was never referred to as a 'girl.'

As was demonstrated in the Hugh McGill case described at the beginning of this essay, men knew that when adultery led to murder the courts were far more likely to sympathize with an accused husband than with an accused lover. In 1906 Charles Johnson was found near the dead body of his lodger yelling, so a witness recalled that, 'he would learn somebody to come around to try to fuck his wife.' Hilda Johnson testified that her husband had been drinking all night: 'My husband came into the front room and then he come and sit on the edge of the bed and I was laying in the bed and then he said "somebody will be killed tonight." Then he said for me to get up in the middle of the floor and then he'll kill me and then I jumped over the foot of the bed. When he was sitting on the edge of the bed he had a gun and put two cartridges into it ... I called "John bring the revolver, he'll kill us" ... In a minute or very quickly after John came into the room the shot went off.' Johnson did not deny the fact that his gun caused the lodger's death but he claimed that he had been having 'trouble' with his wife – she said she had been sleeping with John – and that it was her who, in trying to grab his gun, caused it to discharge and kill the lodger.[95] The defence was successful.

An even more dramatic example of the lenient treatment accorded to an enraged husband was provided in a 1919 Prince George trial. The accused's statement was clear enough. 'I said to Mast I understand you are going to take my wife away and break up my family. He said it is none of your damned business if I am, and started to abuse me and call me names and came towards me with his fists clenched and said he would make me eat smoke before he had done with me. I knew there was a rifle in the blacksmith shop so I stepped inside and took up the gun, which was standing in the corner. When he saw me with the gun he ran towards the sleigh, as soon as I saw him running I threw up the rifle and shot at him. When I fired he dropped to the sleigh and started pulling at the blankets in the sleigh and, as I thought he was getting at his gun I fired again and then a third time; at the third shot he fell to the ground.'[96] Although he fired three bullets into his rival's back, the fact that the farmer immediately gave himself up was enough to convince the jury of his good intentions; he was found not guilty. In such cases the wife would often be the star witness, but on at least one occasion the defence was successful in arguing that she could not, because of her status under the Canada Evidence Act, testify against her husband. He accordingly went free.[97] All the evidence suggests that a husband who murdered to keep his woman stood a very good chance of getting away with it.

In 1922 a Swiss immigrant ranching in the Kootenays, in order to 'redeem one's woman's honor,' shot to death the man bothering his wife. When he was declared not guilty, the local press noted that 'while the letter of the law was lost sight of by the jury their verdict was a just one.' The judge was not so sure and told the accused that it was 'in some ways incomprehensible to me they have found you not guilty.'[98] But why should the judge have been surprised? Although judges on more than one occasion warned that they did not want to see 'southern justice' become common in Canada, in practice judges and juries repeatedly gave credence to the notion that the 'protection of the home' could justify murder.[99] We can conclude, as we began, with the Hugh McGill case. In it the court made explicit its acceptance of a husband's right to use deadly force to ward off sexual competitors. McGill acted like a 'real man' in defending the patriarchal family and his ownership of his wife by murdering the man to whom she was attracted. McGill's sanity was never questioned; his morals were never disparaged. Indeed the judge congratulated McGill on his acquittal and, in case anyone should have misread the jury's findings, reminded the audience that the not-guilty verdict served as 'a salutary warning to any man who in future sets out with the purpose of destroying another man's home.'[100]

Conclusion

This paper has had two goals. The first was to show how murder records can be employed to illuminate male relationships. The trials obviously do reveal much about the little-documented living and working lives of labourers scattered across the province of British Columbia in small towns, farmsteads, mines, and work camps. The paper's second goal was to determine how the criminal-justice system contributed to the social construction of masculinity. The model male who emerges from the trial transcript and press reports was the honour-able, hard-working, fair-fighting individual who was loath to take the law into his own hands. But as law-abiding as he was, the courts warned any interloper that judges and juries would back up his right to employ violence against those who attacked his honour or violated his home. That men should have turned more readily than women to murder is hardly surprising and certainly does not require the assumption of any innate masculine aggressiveness. Men were sup-posed to be forceful; they were repeatedly instructed by the courts and the press that in some situations their recourse to violence would not only be condoned but applauded.

We have found little evidence in early-twentieth-century British Columbia of the purported transition from the cult of rugged masculinity to that of 'masculine domesticity.' A softer image of masculinity might well have been emerging in eastern advice manuals, but in western courtrooms there was more evidence of continuity than of change. That was to be expected, given that the ranks of the accused in British Columbian courts were not filled by middle-class, urban males. Moreover, the erosion of sharp lines of gender differentiation, a development associated with the rise of secondary industry and the growth of the service sector, was unlikely to occur in a region where physical skill and strength were still very much in demand. But one is struck by the fact that even the urban, middle-class judges and journalists of the province, in drawing the moral of what a 'man' might be forced to do, rarely appeared to discriminate along class lines. Was the province, in sustaining traditional notions of manliness, manifesting its 'cultural lag' and out of step with other North American jurisdictions? One suspects – though only further investigations could provide confirmation – that across the continent general societal expectations of how a 'real man' should behave when he felt himself seriously threatened had in fact changed very little.

Notes

1 This study could not have been written had it not been for the extraordinarily painstaking work of my research assistant Susan Johnston. A version of this article first appeared as a chapter in *The Trials of Masculinity: Policing Sexual Boundaries, 1870–1930* (Chicago 1997). I wish to thank University of Chicago Press for permission to reprint this material.

2 Peter N. Stearns, *Be a Man: Males in Modern Society* (New York 1984); Mark C. Carnes and Clyde Griffen, eds, *Meanings for Manhood: Constructions of Masculinity in Victorian America* (Chicago 1990); J.A. Mangan and James Walvin, eds, *Manliness and Morality: Middle-Class Masculinity in Britain and America, 1800–1940* (Manchester 1987); Michael S. Kimmel, 'The Contemporary "Crisis" of Masculinity,' in Harry Brod, ed., *The Making of Masculinities* (Boston 1987), 122–55; Marilyn Lake, 'The Politics of Respectability: Identifying the Masculinist Context,' *Historical Studies* 22 (1986), 116–31; Jock Phillips, *A Man's Country? The Image of the Pakeha Male* (Aukland 1987)

3 Such community norms were as much created as defended by the courts. See Julia Epstein and Kristina Staub, eds, *Body Guards: The Cultural Politics of Gender Ambiguity* (London 1991), 1–4.

4 Such sources, dealing as they do with deadly conflicts, are unlikely to reveal the working-class male's penchant for 'cooperation, fraternity, and equality' found by others. See Bryan Palmer, *A Culture in Conflict: Skilled Workers and Industrial Capitalism in Hamilton, Ontario, 1860–1914* (Kingston 1979), 40.

5 On men's greater reluctance to talk when accused of killing women, see the paper by Annalee Golz in this collection.

6 *Nanaimo Free Press*, 12 Oct. 1910, 1–2

7 Papers of the Attorney-General of British Columbia [hereafter BC] GR 419, vol. 198, file 1915/50

8 Letter dated 24 Apr. 1915 in BC GR 419, vol. 198, file 1915/50

9 Cranbrook *Herald*, 22 Sept. 1915, 1; 21 Oct. 1915, 1

10 Sherwood Herchmer to J.P. McLeod, 23 Oct. 1923, BC GR 1323, reel 2121, file 7049-4-15

11 On low female rates elsewhere, see Judith A. Allen, *Sex and Secrets: Crimes Involving Australian Women Since 1880* (Melbourne 1990), 28–30.

12 Population of British Columbia

	1901	1921
Males	114,160	293,400
Females	64,497	231,173
Total	178,657	524,582

Source: Census of Canada, 1931, table 16

13 Perhaps the most notorious escapee was William McLaughan, who in 1912 killed two men and a woman. Vancouver *Daily Province*, 14 Oct. 1912, 1

14 BC GR 429, box 11, file 5, #3142/04

15 BC GR 419, vol. 135, file 1909/73

16 BC GR 419, vol. 97, file 1903/54

17 BC GR 419, vol. 160, file 1912/134

18 Compare to Miles Fairburn and Stephen Haslett, 'Violent Crime in Old and New Societies – A Case Study Based on New Zealand, 1853–1940,' *Journal of Social History* 20 (1986), 89–126. For a classic account of living conditions, see Edwin Bradwin, *The Bunkhouse Man: A Study of the Work and Pay in the Camps of Canada, 1903–1914* (New York 1928).

19 On a fight between German prisoners of war at the Vernon internment camp leading to murder, see BC GR 419, vol. 229, file 1919/127.

20 BC GR 419, vol. 198, file 1915/42

21 BC GR 419, vol. 125, file 1908/27a

22 In October 1907 a poker game at Kirby's Hotel, Keremeos, led to a shooting death. BC GR 419, vol. 127, file 1908/52. This case was unusual in that the accused successfully escaped police custody.

23 BC GR 419, vol. 161, file 1912/151

24 BC GR 419, vol. 101, file 1904/52

25 BC GR 419, vol. 125, file 1908/27b ·

26 BC GR 419, vol. 147, file 1911/27

27 BC GR 429, box 14, file 2 #2181/07

28 BC GR 419, vol. 119, file 1907, 35

29 BC GR 419, vol. 135, file 1909/63

30 BC GR 419, vol. 152, file 1911/104

31 BC GR 419, vol. 162, file 1912/129

32 BC GR 419, vol. 148, file 1911/45

33 BC GR 419, vol. 190, file 1914/155

34 BC GR 419, vol. 87, file 1901/27

35 BC GR 419, vol. 183, file 1914/13

36 BC GR 419, vol. 229, file 1919/120

37 BC GR 419, vol. 210, file 1917/59

38 BC GR 419, vol. 175, 1913/122

39 BC GR 419, vol. 201, file 1915/95; ibid., vol. 203, file 1916/8. For the case of a deranged rancher who in 1922 killed a neighbour he believed was 'murmuring' against him, see BC GR 419, vol. 255, file 1922/73

40 BC GR 419, vol. 218, file 1918/99

41 BC GR 419, vol. 160, file 1912/138; ibid., 419, vol. 157, file 1912/77

42 BC GR 419, vol. 189, file 1914/144

43 BC GR 419, vol. 232, file 1920/25

44 BC GR 419, vol. 236, file 1920/99

45 BC GR 419, vol. 255, file 1922/64

46 BC GR 419, vol. 266, file 1923/29

47 BC GR 1327, B 2384; BC GR 419, vol. 145, file 1910/91

48 BC GR 419, vol. 162, file 1912/170; ibid., vol. 163, file 1912/179; Vancouver *Daily Province*, 26 Mar. 1912, 1, 4

49 BC GR 419, vol. 169, file 1913/46

50 BC GR 419, vol. 184, file 1914/59

51 BC GR 419, vol. 193, file 1914/191

52 BC GR 419, vol. 197, file 1915/26

53 BC GR 419, vol. 204, file 1916/43

54 BC GR 419, vol. 208, file 1917/15

55 BC GR 419, vol. 258, file 1922/113

56 BC GR 419, vol. 129, file 1908/105

57 BC GR 419, vol. 235, file 1920/69; ibid., vol. 271, file 1923/74

58 In 1910 Donald MacDonald was found not guilty of murdering Frank Savage who, though sworn in as a special constable, was viewed by the community as a bully who used his temporary authority to terrorize an old rival. Nanaimo *Free Press*, 12 Oct. 1910, 1–2

59 BC GR 419, vol. 196, file 1915/9
60 BC GR 419, vol. 89, file 59
61 Kamloops *Inland Sentinel*, 15 May 1913, 1
62 BC GR 419, vol. 144, file 1910/63
63 BC GR 1323, reel B2121, file 6515-4-15
64 BC GR 1327, reel B2399, file 1917/54
65 Prince Rupert *Daily News*, 10 Jan. 1921, 6
66 Prince Rupert *Evening Empire*, 18 Jan. 1919, 2
67 BC GR 419, vol. 101, file 1904/54
68 BC GR 419, vol. 135, file 1909/63
69 BC GR 419, vol. 91, file 1902/6
70 BC GR 419, vol. 147, file 1911/34
71 These were typical prison sentences. Juries had the option of acquitting the accused or finding him guilty of either manslaughter (under provocation or by criminal negligence) or murder. Fifty-eight of 125 men tried for murder went free because they were found not guilty or their cases were dropped or dismissed. Thirty-eight received prison sentences that ranged from one year to life, the average being between five and ten years. Twenty-nine men were sentenced to death.
72 Greenwood *Weekly Times*, 9 May 1901, 1
73 BC GR 419, vol. 125, file 1908/29
74 BC GR 419, vol. 176, file 1913/166
75 BC GR 419, vol. 87, file 1901/27
76 BC GR 419, vol. 129, file 1908/105
77 BC GR 419, vol. 93, file 1902/61
78 On the distinction between homosexual acts and homosexual identity, see Steven Maynard, 'Through a Hole in the Lavatory Wall: Homosexual Subcultures, Police Surveillance, and the Dialectics of Discovery, Toronto, 1890–1930,' *Journal of the History of Sexuality* 5 (1994), 208.
79 For the argument that some homosexual relations were tolerated, see Steven Maynard, 'Rough Work and Rugged Men: The Social Construction of Masculinity in Working-Class History,' *Labour / Le Travail* 23 (1989), 159–70. For the legal context see Terry L. Chapman, '"An Oscar Wilde Type": The Abominable Crime of Buggery in Western Canada, 1890–1920,' *Criminal Justice History* 4 (1983), 97–118.
80 BC GR 419, vol. 89, file 1900/77; Victoria *Daily Colonist*, 29, 30 Oct. 1901
81 BC GR 419, vol. 116, file 1906/79
82 BC GR 419, vol. 124, file 1908/2
83 Vancouver *Daily Province*, 9 May 1908, 1
84 The only murder case in which actual proof of a homosexual act was provided took place in 1913. A simple-minded Clifton ranch hand was sentenced to death for bug-

gering and then killing the four-and-a-half-year-old boy left in his care. BC GR 419, vol. 176, file 1913/164

85 BC GR 419, vol. 87, file 1901/12
86 BC GR 419, vol. 101, file 1904/55; Vancouver *Daily Province*, 21 May 1904, 2
87 BC GR 419, vol. 108, file 1905/58
88 BC GR 419, vol. 246, file 1921/43; Prince Rupert *Daily News*, 10 Jan. 1921, 6
89 BC GR 1327 B3294, #122/14; BC GR 419, vol. 187, file 1914/86
90 The option of the husband killing the wife will be treated in a paper I hope to write on inter-sexual murders.
91 BC GR 419, vol. 92, file 1902/36; Kamloops *Inland Sentinel*, 29 Apr. 1902, 2
92 BC GR 419, vol. 146, file 1913/149. Diatella was the common-law wife of Felice Zappia's brother.
93 BC GR 419, vol. 141, file 1910/28
94 BC GR 419, vol. 167, file 1913/14; Vancouver *Daily Province*, 15 Oct. 1912, 30; 28 Mar. 1913, 22; 29 Mar. 1913, 3. Mary Henrietta McNaughton, the accused's mother, was a leading member of the WCTU and in January 1912 the first woman elected to the Vancouver city council. On class and murder elsewhere, see Carolyn A. Conley, *The Unwritten Law: Criminal Justice in Victorian Kent* (New York 1991), 56–9.
95 BC GR 419, vol. 113, file 1906/27
96 BC GR 419, vol. 230, file 1919/135
97 BC GR 419, vol. 272, file 1923/92
98 *Kootenaian*, 19 Oct. 1922, 1; Nelson *Daily News*, 14 Oct. 1922, 1
99 Prince Rupert *Daily News*, 6 June 1921, 4
100 Fernie *Free Press*, 22 Oct. 1915, 1

8

Work Hard and Be Grateful: Native Soldier Settlers in Ontario after the First World War

ROBIN BROWNLIE

The mythology of the self-sufficient family farm has long held a place of honour in Canadian tradition. The family farm's reputed power to instil habits of sober industry made it a central feature of the Canadian government's plans to assimilate the First Nations. Apart from a few experiments in the 1830s, Native people in Ontario received little material assistance in the move to an agricultural economy.[1] In the years following the First World War, however, Aboriginal war veterans participated in a scheme that provided them with concrete aid. This was the federal soldier settlement program, designed to assist returned soldiers by providing them with loans to establish farms.

The soldier settlement program was designed for all returned soldiers, largely as a measure to prevent wide-scale unemployment following demobilization. This paper will focus on the experience of Aboriginal veterans, whose loans were administered by the Department of Indian Affairs. In its principles and implementation, the program closely resembled the approach of the Department of Indian Affairs: it was profoundly paternalistic, hierarchical, and resistant to input from those whom it was intended to benefit. Accordingly, its implementation was accompanied by conflict between officials and Native veterans over decision-making power, the inflexible repayment schedule, and the goals of the program. The veterans frequently resented the controlling hand of Indian Affairs, as well as its determination to collect on their loans. Moreover, they were plagued by economic hardship: the wartime boom in agricultural prices ended shortly after the armistice, and was succeeded by a collapse in prices. Within a few years, many soldier settlers found themselves facing excessive debt burdens, falling incomes, rising seed and equipment costs, and the prospect of losing their farms.[2]

Based on the case files maintained by the Indian Affairs department, this paper will investigate the shortcomings and frustrations of soldier settlement among Native veterans in Ontario.[3] It will concentrate on two reserves where a substantial number of loans were made: Cape Croker, located on Georgian Bay on the east side of the Bruce peninsula; and the Moravians of the Thames, on the Thames River northeast of Chatham.[4] Most commentators agree that the soldier settlement program as a whole failed, since almost half of its (primarily non-Native) 25,000 participants across Canada had abandoned farming by 1930, and almost two-thirds by 1939.[5] Native veterans fared little better: by 1940 approximately 43 per cent of them had also left or lost their farms.[6]

The program's failure is not difficult to explain. Aboriginal soldier settlers were typically provided with insufficient means to build prosperous farms even in good times. Yet the interwar years were marked by consistently low prices for farm produce. In addition, some settlers rebelled against repayment, believing that eventually the government would be forced to excuse their debts. Aboriginal men had voluntarily risked their lives for a country that had consistently excluded them from the benefits of its prosperity. They perceived their soldier settlement loans as a well-earned reward for their sacrifices. But once on their farms, most found they were doomed to a desperate struggle for subsistence. The result was a legacy of bitterness and disappointment.

Working with the Indian department's case files means attempting to draw conclusions from a biased and incomplete set of records. The Department of Indian Affairs maintained case files to track the loans it made, record the amounts repaid, and monitor the settlers' farming activities. Almost all of the material in the files was produced by Indian Affairs employees, and thus reflects the views of non-Native bureaucrats. The files do contain some letters from the soldier settlers themselves, which have been used as much as possible to explore Aboriginal experiences. Still, most of the information about what happened on soldier settlers' farms has been gleaned from the reports of officials. Two sets of factors operated to favour the officials' exercise of power over Aboriginal people: the structure of the Indian Affairs system and the racist ideas of Canadian society as a whole. Officials perceived Aboriginal people through lenses distorted by stereotypes, their own self-interest, and power imbalance.[7] It has been necessary to analyse this information critically and with due regard for its biases.

Another shortcoming of the records is their large gaps. Most files record basic facts such as the amounts loaned and purchases made. Beyond this the main information takes the form of occasional reports from Indian agents and department inspectors. Files were more extensive for soldier settlers who were not faring well or were judged to be making insufficient effort. The files of the more successful settlers often contain almost no information beyond the first year or so of the loan. In most cases it is not even clear whether or not the loan was finally paid off. The case files, then, offer glimpses of the program's workings. They reveal the principles that animated Indian Affairs employees and the flaws that these men perceived in the system. A few letters from Aboriginal veterans allow some conclusions about their experiences. The case files, which ostensibly document the soldier settlers, in fact provide more information about the documenters themselves.

Re-establishment of Returned Soldiers

Devised during the First World War, the soldier settlement program was part of the federal government's planning for post-war reintegration of war veterans into civilian life. Planners were concerned above all to avoid the 'pension evil' that had befallen the U.S. government after the Civil War – at one point the United States was spending a fifth of its national revenue on veterans.[8] Canada intended, instead, to restore returning soldiers to self-sufficiency as quickly as possible. The soldier settlement scheme was simply an expanded version of a time-honoured and politically popular Canadian endeavour: the colonization of unfarmed lands. The program would be administered strictly from the top down; as military historian Desmond Morton has summarized the government's attitude, 'Veterans were expected to work hard and be grateful.'[9]

One of the central problems of soldier settlement was that veterans and government had conflicting conceptions of its purpose. For the government it was simply a business proposition: the returned soldiers were being assisted so that they would not require further financial support, and they were expected to repay their loans diligently. The veterans, on the other hand, preferred to see the program as an expression of Canada's gratitude toward them. They never forgot the pledge of Prime Minister Robert Borden, made in a 1917 address to Canadian soldiers: '[Y]ou need not fear that the government and the country will fail to show just appreciation of your service to the country and Empire.'[10] The veterans expected soldier settlement to conform to the spirit of this promise, and they lobbied the government doggedly to ease the terms of repayment and refrain from foreclosures.[11]

Market forces worked against the program's success right from the beginning. While prices for farm produce had been at a peak when the program was conceived, in 1920 the grain market collapsed, so that many settlers were unable to make the first payments on their loans. This was the beginning of a prolonged agricultural depression;[12] except for a few years in the mid-1920s, the agricultural slump lasted almost uninterrupted until the next world war. The settlers' farms, stock, and equipment were purchased at the height of the postwar inflation, at rates as high as double their assessed value a few years later. In 1924, the Soldier Settlement Board made an inquiry into the current values of land, stock, and implements and concluded that livestock prices had decreased by over 50 per cent since the program began. It also acknowledged that land deflation had affected many settlers.[13] The veterans were left paying off debts inflated by wartime prices, in a period of plunging farm incomes. As a result of ongoing complaints, the board finally implemented a land revaluation in 1927, which reduced the loans by roughly one-third. This measure eased the situation somewhat, but the economic picture for most remained bleak.

Soldier Settlement and the Indian Department

A Soldier Settlement Board was set up by the federal government to administer the program nationwide, but responsibility for Aboriginal veterans was handed over to the Department of Indian Affairs. Throughout the war the department's annual reports had highlighted the generosity of First Nations in their contributions to the war effort, through patriotic donations and military service.[14] Native men had a high rate of enlistment in the armed forces: one in three of the able-bodied Aboriginal men, of age to serve, enlisted – approximately 4,000 in total.[15] Ontario Natives enlisted in the largest numbers.[16] Aboriginal soldiers were often praised for their courage, endurance, and highly developed hunting skills, which were easily adapted to scouting, raiding, and sniping.[17] Everyone agreed that they merited assistance under the soldier settlement program. Yet as a group they received a good deal less than their non-Native former comrades. Aboriginal soldier settlement loans were typically much smaller than those granted to non-Natives (see below). Similarly, from 1932 to 1936 Native veterans on reserves were treated like other status Indians when it came to depression relief, rather than as veterans. This meant that the maximum monthly rate they could receive was $10, a fraction of the $70 per month granted to a married non-Native veteran.[18]

The goals and administrative methods applied in the federal program paralleled those of the Indian department. Both the Settlement Board and the Indian department exercised close supervision and paternalistic control over their clients. Both envisioned a population of nuclear families working on their own farms, largely without the benefit of automated equipment.[19] Both assumed a European patriarchal model of farming in which a man owned his land individually and farmed it with the help of his wife and children.[20] Although women could theoretically qualify for soldier settlement loans, in practice the screening criteria eliminated women along with most disabled veterans. Federal loans were thus placed in the hands of men only.[21]

A case file was kept for each soldier settler, containing his original application, correspondence about any failure to pay loan instalments, requests for loan extensions or additional assistance, and departmental letters to the individual or to his local agent. The files document the amounts of money loaned, property and equipment bought, land transactions, and the efforts of department officials to ensure that the farms were 'properly' worked. Both local Indian agents and district agricultural representatives regularly visited settlers to inspect their farms and make judgments about their farming practices. These judgments were reported to the department. In addition, some files contain letters from the individual concerned, usually defending himself against charges that his farming efforts were inadequate. These records reveal the tensions between settlers and administrators and a growing disillusionment on both sides as years of agricultural depression turned the returned soldiers into struggling debtors. From partners in an assistance program, the two sides increasingly became antagonists with competing goals: where the settlers wished to see their financial burden eased, the administrators grew more and more concerned with recouping the money loaned.

The program itself was not universally accepted among the First Nations. On the Six Nations reserve, in particular, concern was raised about the expanded powers the Indian department had received. Until this time the power to allot reserve land belonged to the band councils alone, and it was illegal for any outsider to own or hold a mortgage on reserve property. A special section had to be added to the Indian Act to enable the department to buy land for Aboriginal war veterans without band council permission, and to hold a mortgage on these lands.[22] The farms were mortgaged to the Indian department until they were paid off. Some Aboriginal people feared that the department would sell the land to non-Natives if a settler defaulted on payments. Adherents of the traditional Six Nations (longhouse) government waged a fierce battle against the implementation of soldier settlement. The resulting disputes were an important factor in moving the Indian department to impose the elected-band-council system on the Six Nations in 1924.[23] As it turned out, however, the settlement program did not lead to the loss of reserve lands. When loans were cancelled, the department was forced to find band members to buy the farms.

Implementation of the Program

Aboriginal soldier settlers as a group received much smaller loans than non-Natives. Where the average loan for all settlers in Canada (including Natives) stood at $4065, the average for Aboriginal settlers was approximately $1894 – less than half the national figure.[24] In part this may reflect the lower market value of reserve land. But it appears that aboriginal settlers were poorly equipped in almost every respect: many received small farms on poor quality land, insufficient livestock, and an incomplete complement of agricultural equipment. Assumptions about the Aboriginal veterans' prospects for success, based on racist beliefs, were clearly a factor in keeping the loans low. As Duncan C. Scott, Deputy Superintendent General of Indian Affairs, wrote in 1919, 'great care must be exercised in making advances to Indians, [since] due allowance must be made for aboriginal characteristics.'[25]

Although the changes to the Indian Act allowed Aboriginal veterans to settle either on or off reserves, in practice they were all settled on reserves.[26] Good farming soil was generally in limited supply on Ontario's small reserves, so that many settlers found themselves on marginal agricultural land. This applied to most of the veterans at Cape Croker, since the reserve was situated on the sandy, rocky terrain typical of the Georgian Bay shore, and suffered from the area's short growing season. The Moravian reserve offered some fertile land, but not enough for all the soldier settlers. Commenting on this problem in 1927, Moravian Indian agent Nelson Stone noted that settlers in his agency had consistently paid about $30 per acre, but that some had received land worth only a tenth of that price.[27] One farm, for instance, consisted largely of 'very light blow sand,' which was completely useless for agricultural purposes.[28] The properties were also comparatively small, which further reduced the likelihood of success.[29]

With respect to stock and implements the situation was similar. Field officials noted later that the settlers had often been supplied with insufficient equipment, so that at critical seasons of the year they were forced to borrow implements from neighbours. They were supplied with the bare minimum in terms of livestock, which meant that building up a profitable herd would take years. Cape Croker agent A.D. Moore tried repeatedly in the late 1920s to rectify these mistakes. In 1926 and again in 1929 he wrote a number of letters to Ottawa recommending increases for settlers who were becoming discouraged with the low return on their labour.[30] Moore argued for additional funds to buy more livestock and equipment such as cream separators, in order to render the farms profitable.

But the department was unwilling to follow his advice. Although it increased some loans in an arbitrary and piecemeal fashion, it would not make the further investment to establish a sound dairy economy. By 1929, the condition of the Cape Croker settlers remained unchanged and the agent was disgusted with the half-measures that had been taken. He noted that caring for the one or two cows the settlers had received was as much trouble as tending a herd of four or five, but generated almost no revenue. Moore summarized the overall problem in damning terms: 'It is more apparent each year that these Soldier Settlers, when given their loans were only supplied with sufficient stock and equipment to be a burden to them in many ways.'[31] The settlers apparently concurred, for by this time many were dedicating less and less time to their farms.

Experiences of Native Soldier Settlers

Some Aboriginal farmers recorded their frustrations with the program in letters to the department, which were typically written in response to accusatory letters they had received. John C. Jones of Cape Croker was deeply offended by a communication the department sent him in 1922, scolding him for his failure to pay his loan instalment and alleging that he had neglected his stock. He replied promptly that he had had a poor crop the previous year and that the depreciation of his livestock had been very discouraging to him. As for neglecting his animals, he vigorously rejected this charge and asserted that his stock was as good as any in the area, while the crop was well above average.[32]

Jones's letter revealed the damaging delays of the bureaucratic process. He stated that he had found himself short of feed for the winter and informed the agent immediately that he would need four tons of hay. The agent supplied only one ton, and later censured him for buying more without authority. Yet, according to the farmer, his prompt action had been essential to prevent his stock from starving, and the agricultural representative had confirmed this view. Jones concluded pointedly that the department was at fault: 'The difficulty rests between you and your representatives failing to produce sufficient information and we are the victims of this practice.'[33]

Jones was not the only settler who received unsolicited advice. Archie Peters, of the Moravian reserve, was a very active farmer who habitually rented extra land to work. When he began to fall behind in his payments in 1928, he received a letter from departmental secretary J.D. McLean, delivering a lecture on his failings as a farmer. The secretary noted that Peters's crop that year was only 'fair,' which the Indian agent attributed to insufficient attention to the crop. The secretary counselled Peters to cultivate his own land more intensively and provide himself with good seed. His tone was distinctly patronizing: the farmer was advised to 'endeavour to remedy this error of yours.'[34]

Peters responded to this disparagement in tones of indignation, justifying his choice to rent extra land and making his own countercharges against the new agent: 'There is more weeds grown on this reserve since you changed agents; now we never see agent in planting time we never see him when harvest comes, he does not care whether we plant or harvest.'[35] He also provided specific information about his agricultural ventures. Peters had experimented with raising

The Plight of Native Veteran Farmers

In a letter to Indian Affairs Secretary J.D. McLean dated 31 May 1922 (excerpted below), John C. Jones of Cape Croker, Ontario, expresses both the resentment of Native veterans towards Indian Affairs officials who accused them of incompetence, and their determination to succeed in spite of hostile conditions and government parsimony.

In reply to yours of 28th inst. I beg to refer you to my failure in accordance with payment on loan. Last year I suffered severe reverses on crop and also depreciation of the value of stock which to a beginner is sufficient to totally discourage. Also as to my neglecting my stock is entirely and totally a false-hood. I devoted every attention to the maintenance of my stock.

In February of last winter I found to my disappointment my supply of feed would not carry me through the winter. I then immediately applied to our Indian Agent (Capt Garland) for feed. I told him how much would carry me through (4 tons of hay) he gave me an order for (1) one ton. Which I procured in due time. I applied for more long before my limited supply would be exhausted, He (Capt Garland) then warned me to not incur any unnecessary expenses as the Department have already issued sufficient feed and allowances and I wasn't in a position to pay cash for any supply. I then undertook to buy the hay with out his consent with which I was duly justified. He then disapproved of my actions where as if I waited on his authority, likely all my stock should of starved. When your representative Mr Abraham visited here on his rounds he approved of my action and also gave authority to procure another ton of hay which when you look over my account was some where in the neighbourhood of four tons and I have left some 600 lbs of hay. My stock and crop will compare favourably with any farmer in this vicinity but my crop much above the average farm.

As far as my neglecting my stock is prejudice to my training and I resent any such vague statements and remarks. The difficulty rests between you and your representatives failing to produce sufficient information and we are the victims of the practice.

When your representative pays us another visit I shall by all means have an interview with him and take a complete stock of my property and if he finds me unqualified in any way you are at liberty to dispose of my property as I am thoroughly acquainted with the rules pertaining to Indian soldier settlers.

Hoping to avert this undue criticism, I remain Your Obedient Servant, John C. Jones.

Source: NAC, Indian Affairs, RG 10, v.7493, f.25008-21, pt. 1

hogs the previous year, and the gamble had caused a loss of between two and three hundred dollars. The 1928 season had been no better, for he had suffered serious crop failures and was forced to take wage labour to make ends meet. Two years of bad luck had clearly disheartened Peters: 'I shall try only 1 more year to pay up. Then you can close up my business, if [you] want to, last year's gamble on pigs ruined me for this year.'[36]

Three months later Peters wrote again to explain his inability to meet his loan payment. This letter contained a crucial piece of information that probably explains both the farmer's previous defaults in payment and his later agitation against the department. Peters stated that he had expected the land revaluation of 1927 to wipe out his arrears. This conviction was shared by other farmers, and did not disappear with the conclusion of the revaluation process. Naturally, the settlers were disappointed with the process, which fell far short of their expectations and left all of them still deeply in debt. At this point Peters promised to pay at least half of his arrears, or $300, in the coming year. He concluded with a summary of his extra costs the previous season, including his luckless gamble on hogs and this year's costs of buying a horse, reroofing his stable, painting his house, and repairing all his fences.[37] These types of running expenses were common to all farmers and in the 1920s they were rising while farm incomes fell. An economist observed in 1924 that the typical Canadian farmer would have gone bankrupt if he had paid himself the wages of unskilled urban labourers.[38]

One of the most consistent problems of the program was that settlers often needed further capital advances after a few years on the land. These needs clearly stemmed in part from the choices made by the administrators at the outset, which provided settlers with few animals and relatively small farms; livestock replacements and additions to farms were the main reasons for requesting new loan extensions. The department's decisions in these cases were based on the recommendations made by the local Indian agent, and here the cycle of discouragement became obvious. Although the agents often took great interest in the settlers at the beginning, in later years their comments indicated disillusionment and a tendency to blame the settlers for their own difficulties. In the case of John Jones, for instance, agent A.D. Moore appeared to begin with a favourable attitude, but lost his patience when Jones had difficulty fulfilling his plans.

In 1925 Moore recommended an extension of $250 to Jones's loan in order to build a barn. The agent felt that the barn was necessary and noted that the man had already begun the work.[39] A year later Jones had not finished building his barn, but wished to acquire milk cows to help feed his growing family. He therefore proposed that the remaining funds from the $250 loan extension be used to buy two cows. But Moore now took a much more negative tone, criticizing the farmer for failing to increase his stock or finish his barn. It was true that the farmer needed cows for his four small children, but still the agent recommended against the proposal. Moore's words suggest that he intended to discipline the settler by denying his request: 'this Settler should be informed that no loan for cattle will be granted him and that he must erect his barn next Summer or that the amount authorized will be cancelled and no more assistance given him.'[40]

By 1927, two years after the loan extension was approved, both men appeared very dissatisfied and the building remained unfinished. Moore had clearly been pressuring Jones, but the farmer had not found time for the construction. Jones was finding it difficult to make a living and was contemplating turning to wage labour for a few years, since he could not feed his family properly without cattle on his farm. It was clear that the settler was frustrated and felt unfairly treated. The agent, for his part, seemed to blame the difficulty on Jones's duties as a father, quipping that the man was 'more of a nurse maid than farmer as it is at present.'[41] The agent now argued that the loan extension should be withdrawn.

But Jones was one of the lucky ones, for his disfavour was temporary. By the following year this settler had managed to turn his situation around and regain the agent's approval. He had remarried and begun to make regular instalments on his loan, no doubt in part because his new wife took the children's care off his hands.[42] He had also found the time and funds to start building a house, which earned him official support for more assistance. The inspector visited his farm and recommended a further loan of $100 to complete a house as well as a barn. Agent Moore now wrote approvingly that Jones had improved his farming endeavours and paid his instalments regularly since his marriage, which justified the extra loan.[43] Jones had succeeded in making the right impression on the department's officials, which paid off in the form of further financial help. By 1929 he had a completed house and stable, and Moore recommended that he be loaned additional money to buy five head of dairy cattle and a cream separator.[44]

Another man's story demonstrates the arbitrariness of official approval, as well as the kinds of mistakes made under the program. Wellington Elliott, also of Cape Croker, had a disastrous experience as a soldier settler and it appears that the department showed poor judgment in granting and implementing his loan. To begin with, Elliott was afflicted with tuberculosis, a very incapacitating disease that was epidemic among First Nations people at the time. In addition, he was granted a large loan and settled on rocky, uncleared land, far from roads and even farther from markets.[45] The healthiest farmer would have been hard pressed to make good under these conditions. The loan was made in late 1919, and it is possible that Elliott's physical condition was unknown at the time.[46] Just a year later, however, the Indian agent was reporting, 'This man is a T.B. patient and very much bloated and may soon die. He is not making a success farming.'[47]

But Wellington Elliott apparently recovered sufficiently to lose the sympathy of other department officials. In fact, no later report made any mention of his state of health. Instead officials exclaimed about his laziness, lack of progress, and poor farming habits. Agent A.D. Moore disparaged the settler in 1922 for his unwillingness to perform roadwork – a gruelling form of labour for a man with tuberculosis. Elliott had in fact done some roadwork and the agent had garnisheed his wages to pay a small bill he owed the department. Moore ordered the settler to work longer, but Elliott refused. Moore described him as 'very lazy,' and complained that he 'would rather sit around the house all day, than do a little to keep himself from starving.'[48]

An assistant agricultural representative who reported on Elliott in 1923 was similarly unsympathetic. He acknowledged that the farm was poorly located, but claimed that the settler could have cleared more land and planted more crops. In the next breath he noted that 'considerable acreage of this place is nothing but rock and rocky pasture.'[49] Even this description did not capture the full extent of Elliott's obstacles: by the agent's account, his rocky, uncleared land was situated 'in a very isolated district' and could be reached only by rough roads. The roads were in such bad shape that they damaged the binder of the man who cut Elliott's crop in 1922. The next year the man refused to subject his machine to similar punishment, so the settler was forced to cut his entire crop by hand.[50]

Under the circumstances, it is hardly surprising that Wellington Elliott eventually lost interest in farming. He tried for seven years to earn a living, in part by renting other farms to work. This was contrary to the intent of the soldier settlement program, which aimed at providing veterans with their own farms. In 1926 the agent found Elliott's home locked up and learned that the man was away from the reserve. By 1928 he was back, but had apparently lost his enthusiasm for agriculture: Moore reported in June that one of Elliott's horses had died during the previous winter and that he had not planted any crops.[51] Unfortunately, this case file does not record the ultimate outcome of Wellington Elliott's farming endeavours. But the record of the first decade suggests he faced insurmountable barriers as a result of the choices made in implementing the loan.

Conflicts over Loan Repayments

The Indian department was determined to enforce the repayment of loans, but faced a number of hindrances in its attempt to do so. Not only were some settlers unable to pay, others were unwilling. On the Moravian reserve, for instance, a number of settlers formed the conviction that they could not lose their farms because the land could not be resold. Moreover, they clearly felt that the repayment schedule imposed undue hardship on them, and in some cases reacted by resisting the agent's efforts to make collections. In later years, a few engaged in political agitation and sought outside support to secure changes in the program.

In 1922, Moravian agent Edwin Beattie reported that the Moravian settlers had identified the department's dilemma in cases of non-payment: first, the land could not be sold to anyone but other band members; and second, no one in the band could afford to take on the soldier settlers' liabilities. Beattie concluded, 'Consequently several are getting the idea that nothing will happen to them, and they will quite likely be allowed to retain their properties.'[52] This was, in fact, a thorny issue. It was true that the department could not resell the land to outsiders, and that it was difficult to find band members who could afford to take over the original loans. Moreover, because land values had decreased drastically since the establishment of the program, it was impossible to recoup the loans entirely through selling the farms.[53]

The settlers' resistance to making loan payments was heightened by the advice they received from R.H. Abraham, the department's agricultural representative in southern Ontario. Abraham counselled them (inaccurately, as it turned out) that the land revaluation that was being considered in the mid-1920s would erase the arrears they had accumulated. Moravian agent Nelson Stone complained in 1927 that he had heard Abraham state this several times, and that consequently he was having difficulty in collecting from the farmers. Some of them were withholding their payments in the belief that their debts would be forgiven.[54]

The discontent on the Moravian reserve continued into the 1930s. In 1931 Stone claimed that certain individuals on the reserve were urging others not to pay. Archie Peters was one of those named – apparently he had not given up the hope of seeing his debts erased. Peters and Emerson Snake were telling fellow settlers that they would be foolish to make their loan payments, since the government would eventually cancel the debts.[55] The two men also took political action on the issue, attempting to engage outside assistance. Stone informed the department in 1930 that they had been travelling around the region, approaching the Canadian Legion, a lawyer, the department's agricultural representative, and the local MLA of the riding, 'telling how harshly the Settlement Board are dealing with them and all other Settlers of this agency.'[56] No doubt they met a sympathetic hearing at the Legion, which worked tirelessly throughout this period to reduce the indebtedness of soldier settlers.[57] In fact, in this same year it won a 30 per cent reduction in soldier settlement loans.[58] This, however, was as far as the government would be pushed. The only other course available to settlers was to fall behind in payments and hope that the department would refrain from cancelling their loans and seizing their farms.

Loan Cancellations

Despite the difficulties, the department did foreclose the loans of some settlers who consistently failed to meet their instalments. Such a case occurred in the Moravian agency in 1924. Agent Stone reported that one settler, Dan Hill, had abandoned his farm, left the reserve, and moved to Buffalo, New York. He believed that Hill had no intention of returning, but advised that selling his property would recoup little more than half the original loan. The horses that had been bought for over $400 were worth less than $40 now. Stone did not recommend cancellation, but remarked very unfavourably on the state of the program: 'I am willing and intend to aid and assist the Settlers all I can, I think they deserve it, but it grieves me to see the bungle the whole affair is in.'[59]

In spite of Stone's advice, Hill's loan was cancelled and his belongings seized and sold by auction. This decision did not bring a great deal of benefit to the department. The sale of Hill's effects brought little cash, while it proved impossible to sell the land for the price Ottawa wished. In fact, the farm was never sold despite the agent's best efforts. Land prices in the area declined steadily, and Stone's superiors rejected the few offers he received. In 1927 Stone wrote to Ottawa, 'Farm property is not easy to sell these times, 50% of all farms in this district are being offered and at ridiculously low prices.'[60] The best the agent could do was to lease the land, while its value continued to plunge.[61] At the same time, the move had a very negative impact on the other soldier settlers. Stone grumbled that it had brought on him the ill will of all the settlers and of Dan Hill's friends and relations.[62]

Yet the department did not learn its lesson, for it cancelled another loan in this agency in 1928. The individual in question, Reuben Tobias, was a returned soldier who had chosen to 'enfranchise' after the war. Enfranchisement was an act whereby status Indians could voluntarily relinquish Indian status and become full Canadian citizens. This meant that they ceased to be wards of the state and to be bound by the terms of the Indian Act, thus gaining the right to vote and drink alcohol. An enfranchisee also received her or his share of band funds at the time of enfranchisement. On the other hand, the process also stripped one of band membership, of the right to live on a reserve, and of the protections granted by the Indian Act.[63]

Tobias was therefore no longer an 'Indian' and the department technically had no further responsibility for him, but it continued to administer his loan. Tobias received $1700 from band funds when he enfranchised and another $500 through an inheritance, all of which was applied to his loan. This made up the amount of his annual payments until at least 1928. Tobias was also among the settlers who rebelled against the department's terms of repayment, perhaps in part because it had absorbed $2200 that he might have preferred to spend as he chose. Stone claimed that this settler had boasted at the time of Dan Hill's cancellation that the same could not happen to him, and that the Settlement Board would be sorry if it tried to cancel his loan.[64] The agent portrayed Tobias as an agitator who took a 'defiant attitude' and believed that the department could not confiscate his property under any circumstances.[65]

This case illustrates poor communication about the status of the settlers' loan. Although Tobias did not make regular instalments on his loan, it remained up to date because of the $2200 paid in lump sums. In 1926, seemingly unaware of this, Stone wrote that the man was 'piling up arrears of payment' and implied that the reason was excessive spending.[66] Two years later the agent's attitude was more sympathetic, but internal officials were convinced that the loan was in arrears – apparently they had not checked their own records. Accordingly, they decided to cancel Tobias's loan. The agent expressed serious misgivings about evicting the family from the farm when they had 'nothing but debt facing them on every hand.'[67] Nevertheless, the Department sent a notice of cancellation to Tobias on 13 February 1928.[68]

But Reuben Tobias was not going to give up his farm without a fight. According to Stone, the settler boasted that he had employed a lawyer, and if Indian Affairs evicted him, the lawyer 'would have the whole Indian Dept. disqualified and removed from office.'[69] The prescribed thirty-day grace period elapsed, Tobias failed to make a payment, but no further instructions arrived from Ottawa for the agent to sell the land and equipment. Stone pressed for action, stating that he had never recommended cancellation of this loan or any other, but that it must be proceeded with now in order to maintain credibility.[70] Yet the department had by now realized that Tobias was not actually in arrears, and therefore delayed for over a year. In December 1928 it even approved an addition to his loan in order to pay his land taxes.[71]

The impact on attitudes among the rest of the settlers was predictable: Stone reported that several were now refusing to make their payments, having concluded that they had little to fear.[72] But their confidence was to be dashed again, for in the end Tobias's loan was cancelled and his farm sold. In early 1929 the department was considering his proposal to lease the property for five years, but rejected the idea. Shortly thereafter the land was divided into parcels and, since it was no longer reserve land, it was sold to two local non-Native farmers.[73] Ironically, the department had no more luck with these individuals than with Tobias. Two years later it had not received a single payment from either of the buyers, who pleaded lack of funds. By 1937 one of the purchasers had disappeared, without ever paying a cent of the $500 purchase price.[74]

When it came to cancelling loans, the Indian department was slow to adapt its methods to the market conditions of the time. At least until the end of the 1920s it was inclined to take the punitive route of cancellation, even though this seldom increased returns – often the land was left idle because no one could be found to farm it. At the same time, the department was constrained by the guardianship role that made it responsible for the welfare of Aboriginal people. When settlers lost their farms they were frequently left without means of support, which meant that Indian Affairs had to provide them with relief. Discussing the cancellation of John Huff's loan in 1941, Moravian agent Stuart Spence[75] recommended that Huff be allowed to keep one of the three lots that belonged to his farm. He pointed out, '[A]fter all, what are we going to do with him, after his loan has been c[a]ncelled, and perhaps the property sold, we may still be obliged to supply him with a home.'[76] By this time the department was apparently taking a less severe approach, for Huff was left in possession of one lot, and agreed to rent the other two at $1.00 yearly per acre.[77] This more reasonable solution seems to indicate that Indian Affairs had at last recognized the merits of a compromise solution.

Impact on Native Veterans

Taken as a group, Aboriginal war veterans experienced a great deal of embitterment and discouragement as participants in the soldier settlement program. Many of these men had returned from overseas with a strengthened sense of self-worth and a conviction that they had done their duty well, a view that was shared by non-Natives. Seven years after the war's end Nelson Stone wrote feelingly about the part the veterans had played: 'These Indian Settlers ... enlisted voluntarily to fight for their Country, and as far as I know rendered splendid service overseas, and this Reserve gave as large a percentage of her members as any municipality in Canada to this work.'[78] Like many others,

Stone felt that the country owed a debt of gratitude to the soldiers. As the years wore on, however, there was a noticeable alteration in the agents' attitudes. The 'returned men' had become debtors, struggling farmers, and in some cases loan defaulters. Although their status as former soldiers had initially elevated them above the ordinary category of 'Indian,' their position as aid recipients undermined the image of competence and bravery they had earned in wartime.

The soldier settlement program was based on the assumption that agriculture was the 'basic industry' of Canada, a premise that was probably outdated. After the post-war depression, the market for farm produce never recovered its wartime levels, which wrought havoc with efforts to repay the loans. Most important, few Aboriginal veterans were able to purchase good quality agricultural land. They received insufficient equipment in many instances and were burdened with loans inflated by wartime prices. As early as 1926, Nelson Stone had become a vocal critic of the program's implementation, for he felt that officials had shown poor judgment in many cases, and that cancelling the loans was an added injustice. He apparently felt that some of the loans should never have been granted, and stated that the settlers bore less responsibility for defaulting on payments than the officials who had involved them in such an 'ill advised Agreement.' The result, according to Stone, was that many men were 'penalised in place of being assisted.'[79]

By the late 1920s agent Moore testified to flagging enthusiasm among the farmers at Cape Croker. He noted that even some of the 'best' settlers were beginning to neglect their farms, and others had already abandoned them. The agent's exasperated generalizations about the settlers indicate a pattern of initial enthusiasm and dedication on their part, followed by disillusionment and neglect of their farms. He wrote that most of them would be 'model settlers for a number of years and then break up quickly and go bad.'[80] Moore reported in 1928 that a number of Cape Croker settlers were purchasing cars, a luxury he claimed was absorbing much of their income and far too much of their time.[81] This trend suggests a desire to participate in the mass consumerism that was then taking root in Canada. But the small-scale farming that the soldier settlement program was designed to promote consigned the settlers to the margins of the Canadian consumer economy.

Native agricultural endeavours in this period were not entirely unsuccessful. There were certainly those who achieved relative prosperity and were able to meet most of their instalments. A.D. Moore noted in 1929 that six of the settlers at Cape Croker had built up profitable dairy operations that provided them with a comfortable living, so that they did not have to rely on their interest money.[82] A minority chose to give up their farms voluntarily and seek a more reliable means of supporting themselves. Others, such as Archie Peters, doggedly pur-

sued their chosen vocation, but clearly felt cheated and actively sought to modify the program to suit the economic realities of the time. Generally, the records
suggest that some were able to support themselves in relative comfort, while
others could only eke out a poor subsistence. In many cases, especially at Cape
Croker, instalments were covered not by cash earned from the sale of produce,
but by the department's withholding the semi-annual interest payments received
by the members of wealthier bands.[83] This practice was clearly resented, for
these men had been accustomed to using this income supplement in other
ways.[84]

Conclusion

An internal Indian department memo of 1940 summarized the statistics on the
soldier settlement program across Canada. Of 230 loans to Native veterans, 98
were labelled 'inactive,' which meant in most cases that they had been cancelled. The remaining 132 were considered 'active,' but were described as
'barely alive,' since the total collections for the previous year amounted to only
$8698.50. The Soldier Settlement Board had advanced $435,641.11, of which
$239,206 (or 55 per cent) had been repaid by 31 March 1940.[85] The outstanding
balance of $224,855.61 included $158,651.31 in interest charges many years in
arrears.[86] The memo did not record the number of loans that had actually been
paid off, although the Ontario case files show individuals who did succeed in
repaying the full amount. As of 1940, then, approximately 98 soldier settlers
had lost or abandoned their farms, while 132 farms were still under cultivation,
and many of those farmers were far behind in their payments.[87]

Between 1914 and 1918, Canada needed Aboriginal people for the first time
since the War of 1812. Many First Nations rallied to the cause and sent a high
proportion of their men to the armed forces. As military historian Fred Gaffen
concluded in his study of these 'forgotten soldiers,' Canada received political
and economic benefits from the war, but its Native soldiers had little to show
for their sacrifices.[88] Veterans as a group experienced a difficult readjustment
on their return from war, and Aboriginal veterans were no exception. As Desmond Morton wrote mournfully, 'It was given to few men of the CEF [Cana-
dian Expeditionary Force] to find much comfort from the land they had
volunteered to defend.'[89]

The soldier settlement program, which seemed to promise peace and prosperity, ended up involving Native veterans in a fresh series of battles, this time
against two powerful adversaries: an impersonal international economy and
their own government. Market conditions were undoubtedly the critical factor
in dooming the soldier settlers economically. But the government also made

unfortunate choices in implementing the program, providing Aboriginal settlers with poor land and inadequate resources. The settlers' achievements were at least equal to those of their non-Native fellows; in fact they repaid a slightly larger proportion of their loans and were significantly less prone to abandon farming. But their letters reveal a tale of thwarted hopes and confidence betrayed. While many First Nations celebrated their returned fighters, most Canadians quickly forgot them. Soldier settlement was a largely failed project that offered Aboriginal veterans a miserly reward for their wartime service.

Notes

The author wishes to acknowledge the generous support of the Social Sciences and Humanities Research Council of Canada.

1 See R.J. Surtees, 'The Development of an Indian Reserve Policy in Canada,' *Ontario History* 61:2 (June 1969), and Ruth Bleasdale, 'Manitowaning: An Experiment in Indian Settlement,' *Ontario History* 66:3 (September 1974).
2 Jack Jarvie and Diane Swift, *The Royal Canadian Legion, 1926–1986* (Toronto 1985), 28
3 Ontario Natives received the bulk of the loans granted to First Nations veterans: of a total of 230 Aboriginal soldier settlers across Canada, 184 were in Ontario. 'Land Settlement. Annual Report of the Soldier Settlement Board of Canada' (Ottawa 1929), 21. The report shows 11 Aboriginal settlers in all of British Columbia, 2 in Alberta, 18 in Saskatchewan, 4 in Quebec, 5 in Prince Edward Island, and none in Manitoba, Nova Scotia, and New Brunswick.
4 There were approximately 25 settlers at Cape Croker, and at least 13 on the Moravian reserve. Other reserves examined for this study include Alnwick, now the Alderville reserve, on Rice Lake near Peterborough; Caradoc, also known as Muncey, on the Thames River just south of London; and the Mississaugas of the New Credit, who were originally located on the Credit River in what is now the city of Mississauga, and were later moved to a piece of land that had formed part of the Six Nations reserve, on the Grand River near Brantford.
5 Desmond Morton, *When Your Number's Up: The Canadian Soldier in the First World War* (Toronto 1993), 271, 273. See also James Hale, *Branching Out: The Story of the Royal Canadian Legion* (Ottawa 1995).
6 National Archives of Canada, RG 10, v.7485, f.25001-1-2, pt.1, memo from D.J. Allan, Superintendent, Reserves and Trusts, 11 October 1940
7 An exploration of bureaucratic stereotypes about Aboriginal people is beyond the scope of this paper. For a thorough discussion, see Noel Dyck, *What Is the Indian*

'*Problem': Tutelage and Resistance in Canadian Indian Administration* (St John's 1991).

8 Desmond Morton, *When Your Number's Up*, 255

9 Ibid., 264

10 Jarvie and Swift, *The Royal Canadian Legion*, 43

11 See Clifford H. Bowering, *Service: The Story of the Canadian Legion, 1925–1960* (Ottawa 1960), 60–9.

12 Desmond Morton and Glenn Wright, *Winning the Second Battle: Canadian Veterans and the Return to Civilian Life, 1915–1930* (Toronto 1987), 151

13 'Land Settlement. Third Report of the Soldier Settlement Board of Canada' (Ottawa 1925), 8–9. The board was probably understating the case. See below.

14 See annual reports of the Department of Indian Affairs for the years 1914 to 1918, in Canada, *Sessional Papers* (Ottawa). See also Canada, Veterans Affairs, *Native Soldiers, Foreign Battlefields* (Ottawa 1993).

15 Veterans Affairs, *Native Soldiers*, 5

16 Fred Gaffen, *Forgotten Soldiers* (Penticton, BC, 1985), 20

17 Ibid., 21, 28

18 Ibid., 37. In 1936 protest from the Canadian Legion forced the government to reverse this policy and grant Aboriginal veterans the same pensions as other vets. For the Indian department's relief rates in the 1920s and 1930s, see Robin Brownlie, 'A Fatherly Eye: Two Indian Agents on Georgian Bay, 1918–1939,' Ph.D. thesis, University of Toronto, 1996.

19 The Soldier Settlement Board argued that it had insufficient funds to provide loans for this purpose ('Soldier Settlement on the Land. Report of the Soldier Settlement Board of Canada' [Ottawa 1921], 36). The Indian department had pursued a similar policy with Aboriginal farmers for some time. In western Canada, from 1889 to 1897, a policy of 'peasant farming' was enforced, under which Native farmers were actively prevented from employing labour-saving machinery. See Sarah Carter, 'Two Acres and a Cow: "Peasant" Farming for the Indians of the Northwest, 1889–1897,' *Canadian Historical Review* 70:1 (1989), repr. in J.R. Miller, ed., *Sweet Promises: A Reader on Indian–White Relations in Canada* (Toronto 1991), and her monograph, *Lost Harvests: Prairie Indian Reserve Farmers and Government Policy* (Montreal and Kingston 1990). Horse-drawn farming remained the norm on Ontario reserves into the period following the Second World War.

20 The farms purchased under the soldier settlement program were considered the property of the men who received the loans. The interest shares of their wives and children, however, were routinely applied to pay the loan instalments.

21 Morton and Wright, *Winning the Second Battle*, 145. Women who had served as nurses were technically eligible at first, but were encouraged to re-establish themselves in other sectors, and in 1920 they were formally excluded from the program.

Widows of soldiers were supposed to be eligible if they had enough sons to run a farm.

22 The added section was simply the Soldier Settlement Act with 'Department of Indian Affairs' substituted for 'the Settlement Board.' See *Revised Statutes of Canada 1906*, chap. 81, s. 194, 4(d) and 102, in Sharon H. Venne, ed., *Indian Acts and Amendments, 1868–1975. An Indexed Collection* (University of Saskatchewan Law Centre 1981), 210, 240.

23 This move eliminated the official status of this nation's traditional government. See RG 10, v.7504, f.25,032-1-2, pt.1.

24 The overall average for Ontario was higher than the national figure, standing at $4394 'Soldier Settlement,' 48. An internal memo of the Indian Affairs Branch in 1940 showed a total of $435,641.11 disbursed to 230 individuals, an average of approximately $1894 per person. RG 10, v.7485, f.25001-1-2, pt.1, memo from D.J. Allan, Superintendent, Reserves and Trusts, 11 Oct. 1940. Loans typically ranged between about $800 and $2500, exceeding the latter figure only in rare cases.

25 RG 10, v.7489 f.25008-1, pt.1, Duncan C. Scott to A. McLean Moffat, 27 Mar. 1919

26 One veteran from the Maria reserve in Quebec later stated that he had wished to buy a farm off the reserve, but that his application to do so had been refused because local non-Natives objected. He had been forced to accept an inferior farm on his own reserve. RG 10, 7487, f.25007-2, J. Milton Gedeon to Department of Indian Affairs, 1 Oct. 1924

27 RG 10, v.7497, f.25015-8, pt.1, Nelson Stone to DIA, 24 Dec. 1927

28 Ibid.

29 RG 10, v.7496, f.25015-5, pt.1, Stone to DIA, 19 Sept. 1930

30 RG 10, v.7490, f.25008-3, pt.1, A.D. Moore to DIA, 3 July 1926

31 RG 10, v.7489, f.25008-1, pt.1, A.D. Moore to DIA, 6 Feb. 1929

32 RG 10, v.7493, f.25008-21, pt.1, John C. Jones to DIA, 31 May 1922

33 Ibid.

34 RG 10, v.7496, J.D. McLean to Archie Peters, 8 Sept. 1928

35 RG 10, v.7496, f.25015-5, pt.1, Archie Peters to DIA, undated letter, received at department 25 Oct. 1928.

36 RG 10, v.7496, f.25015-5, pt.1, Archie Peters to DIA, undated letter received at department 28 Oct. 1928. In this second letter Peters requested that the department return the first to him and disregard it. The reason was apparently that he had made other allegations about the agent's behaviour and was concerned about possible reprisals.

37 Ibid., Archie Peters to Duncan C. Scott, 30 Jan. 1929

38 Morton and Wright, *Winning the Second Battle*, 151

39 RG 10, v.7493, f.25008-21, pt.1, A.D. Moore to DIA, 3 Nov. 1925

40 Ibid., Moore to DIA, 24 Nov. 1926

41 Ibid., Moore to DIA, 3 Dec. 1927. It would appear from this remark and Jones's later marriage that the farmer was raising his four small children single-handedly at this point. He did not have a house or barn on his farm until 1929. Between child care and working his farm he cannot have had much time to complete his barn.

42 Ibid., Moore to DIA, 11 Sept. 1928

43 Ibid.

44 RG 10, v.7489, f.25008-1, pt.1, Moore to DIA, 14 Mar. 1929

45 Unfortunately, the file does not reveal who chose the land for Elliott. Typically, an agent would select appropriate land in consultation with the settler. In any event, the agent's approval of the property was required before any money was released.

46 Elliott's medical condition was not noted in his application, but lung diseases were common among Aboriginal soldiers, according to their military records. Personal communication with Prof. Mark McGowan

47 RG 10, f.25008-13, pt.1, R.G. Garland to DIA, 27 Oct. 1920

48 Ibid., A.D. Moore to DIA, 29 Sept. 1922

49 Ibid., G.R. Paterson to J.D. McLean, 18 June 1923

50 Ibid., Moore to DIA, 23 Nov. 1923

51 RG 10, v.7489, f.25008-1, pt.1, Moore to DIA, 12 June 1928

52 RG 10, v.7495, f.25015-1, pt.1, E. Beattie to DIA, 12 June 1922

53 Agent Stone noted in 1927 that the farms on the Moravian reserve had originally been purchased at about $30 an acre. RG 10, v.7497, f.25015-8, pt.1, Nelson Stone to DIA, 24 Dec. 1927. Reuben Tobias's farm, when it was sold in 1929, commanded $20 per acre. In 1941 the agent estimated another farm's value at $10 per acre, adding that 'this would be the top price of any Soldier Settler land on the Reserve.' RG 10, v.7496, f.25015-7, pt.2, Stuart Spence to DIA, 2 Apr. 1941

54 RG 10, v.7495, f.25015-1, pt.1, Nelson Stone to DIA, 13 Sept. 1927

55 RG 10, v.7496, f.25015-5, pt.1, Stone to DIA, 21 May 1931.

56 Ibid., Stone to DIA, 28 Mar. 1930

57 See Hale, *Branching Out*, 25–35.

58 Ibid., 35

59 RG 10, v.7497, f.25015-10, pt.1, Stone to DIA, 29 Nov. 1924

60 Ibid., 15 Nov. 1927

61 RG 10, v.7496, f.25015-6, pt.1, Stone to DIA, 12 Feb. 1929. The case file ends at this point, which suggests that the land was never sold, since its sale would have occasioned an entry in the file.

62 RG 10, v.7495, f.25015-2, pt.1, Stone to DIA, 30 Dec. 1926

63 Enfranchisement was introduced into federal Indian policy in 1857. In the time period with which this essay is concerned it was still the department's stated goal for all Aboriginal people, since it relieved the government of any responsibility for the enfranchisee. Before the First World War very few Native people chose this course.

In the 1920s, and again in the 1950s and 1960s, there was a wave of enfranchisements.

64 RG 10, v.7496, f.25015-6, pt1., Stone to DIA, 28 Mar. 1928

65 Ibid., Stone to DIA, 28 Mar. 1928

66 Ibid., Stone to DIA, 18 June 1926

67 Ibid., Stone to DIA, 8 Feb. 1928

68 Ibid., Stone to DIA, 28 Mar. 1928

69 Ibid.

70 Ibid.

71 RG 10, v.7496, f.25015-6, pt.1, Stone to DIA, 19 Dec. 1928

72 RG 10, v.7495, f.25015-1, pt.1, Stone to DIA, 14 Nov. 1928

73 The original purpose of the enfranchisement provision was thus successfully realized. Tobias purchased his farm on reserve land and then enfranchised, removing the land from collective band ownership. When Tobias's loan was cancelled, his farm was sold to non-Natives, and the process was complete.

74 RG 10, v.7496, f.25015-6A, pt.1, H.W. McGill to E.J. Sexsmith, 8 Oct. 1937

75 Nelson Stone retired in 1936 and was succeeded by Stuart Spence.

76 RG 10, v.7496, f.25015-7, pt.2, Stuart Spence to DIA, 2 Apr. 1941

77 Ibid., Stuart Spence to DIA, 23 Apr. 1941. In the 1920s and 1930s the settlers were typically dispossessed of all of their holdings when their loans were cancelled.

78 RG 10, v.7495, f.25015-2, pt.1, Stone to DIA, 30 Dec. 1926

79 Ibid.

80 RG 10, v.7493, f.25008-20, pt.1, A.D. Moore to DIA, 3 Sept. 1928

81 RG 10, v.7489, f.25008-1, pt.1, Moore to DIA, 12 June 1928. In this entertaining letter Moore grumbled about a Cape Croker 'epidemic of buying old and worn out motor cars,' which he claimed was resulting in a total abandonment of farming, for the car owners were 'in them day and night.'

82 RG 10, v.7489, f.25008-1, pt.1, Moore to DIA, 6 Feb. 1929. Moore stated that these settlers were earning about $300 a year, which many Canadians at the time would not have considered a 'comfortable living.' Moore himself was earning $1680 per annum. RG 10, v.9183.

83 At Cape Croker this seems to have been the typical method of covering loan payments. See, for instance, RG 10, v.7491, f.25008-10, pt.1, Moore to DIA, 8 Sept. 1928. Not all First Nations had sufficient capital funds to receive interest payments.

84 John Akiwenzie, for instance, a settler of Cape Croker, complained about the practice in a letter to the department. RG 10, v.7492, f.25008-15, pt.1, John Akiwenzie to A.S. Williams, Assistant Deputy Superintendent General, 27 Jan. 1932

85 In percentage terms, about 55% had been recouped. By comparison, the Soldier Settlement Board had advanced a total of $110,700,818.68 to non-Native settlers, of

which $55,033,643, or about 50%, had been repaid as of 1937. Report of the Soldier Settlement Board, 1937 (Ottawa, 1938).

86 RG 10, v.7485, f.25001-1-2, pt.1, memo from D.J. Allan, Superintendent, Reserves and Trusts, 11 Oct. 1940

87 Not all of these farmers would have been war veterans, since farms were sometimes sold to non-veterans when the original settler could not continue. The new settler assumed the remaining debt.

88 Fred Gaffen, *Forgotten Soldiers*, 33

89 Morton, *When Your Number's Up*, 275

9

A Case for Morality: The Quong Wing Files

JAMES W. St.G. WALKER

On 5 March 1912 the Saskatchewan legislature passed *An Act to Prevent the Employment of Female Labour in Certain Capacities.*[1] The act specified that '[n]o person shall employ in any capacity any white woman or girl ... in ... any restaurant, laundry or other place of business or amusement owned, kept or managed by any ... Chinaman.' Chinese diplomatic pressure, and Chinese-Canadian complaints, led to an amendment in this original wording. A new act was passed in 1919 stating only that '[n]o person shall employ any white woman or girl in ... any restaurant or laundry without a special license from the municipality.'[2] But while the act had contained its explicit Chinese prohibition, a Moose Jaw restaurant owner named Quong Wing had been charged and fined $5 by a local magistrate on the grounds that he employed two white waitresses. He appealed his conviction, eventually to the Supreme Court of Canada in 1914, but the courts decided against Quong Wing and upheld the discriminatory Saskatchewan act.

Exploring Motivations

Why did the Saskatchewan legislature pass such a law, and why did the courts uphold it? The Supreme Court of Canada's own records seemed a useful place to begin looking for an answer, and the appropriate dossier was found in case file no. 3389, *Quong Wing v The King*, now located in the National Archives in Ottawa.[3] This search led next to the records of the Saskatchewan courts, for the Moose Jaw magistrate's conviction and the provincial Supreme Court's concurrence in it, both of which were found in file 3474, 'R v Quong Wing,' in the Saskatchewan Archives in Regina.[4]

According to these case files, the Female Labour Act was passed and upheld as a device to protect white women from the immoral influence of Chinese men. In court Quong Wing argued that the law discriminated against him illegally, introducing as evidence his certificate of naturalization, which declared that he was 'entitled to all political and other rights, powers and privileges, and is subject to all obligations to which a natural-born British subject is entitled or subject within Canada.'[5] But the Saskatchewan Supreme Court found that 'the Act was passed in the interests of morality and for the protection of white women, and not for the exclusion of Chinese ... The sum and object of this legislation is to prevent white women from coming ... under the control or influence of any Chinaman ... It is surely competent for the province to legislate for the protection of any class of its citizens – in this case white women and girls.'[6] When the case was heard on appeal before the Supreme Court of Canada, the Saskatchewan government maintained that 'the regulation of places of business ... kept, owned or managed by Chinese ... may very properly be considered necessary to the welfare of women and girls in Saskatchewan.'[7] The court agreed, finding the act appropriate for 'the protection of white women and girls' and similar in principle to any factory act intended 'not only to safeguard the bodily health, but also the morals of Canadian workers.' Only one justice, John Idington, dissented from the majority judgment. He concluded that the act did conflict with the promise of equality contained in the Naturalization Act, and he brought a different sense of morality to bear on the question: '[I]n a piece of legislation alleged to have been promoted in the interests of morality, it would seem a strange thing to find it founded upon a breach of good faith which lies at the root of nearly all morality worth bothering one's head about.'[8] Even Idington's dissent, however, confirmed that morality was the fundamental force behind the Female Labour Act, and the principal grounds for the court decisions upholding it.

Despite these explicit statements, most scholars have concluded that the moral issue was a euphemism, and that racially restrictive legislation had an economic purpose.[9] The Quong Wing case has not, however, received a great deal of specific attention, and is usually mentioned only in passing during discussions of the more numerous legal restrictions against Chinese in British Columbia.[10] The prevailing interpretation is that the instruments of the state deliberately enforced a 'split labour market' to induce white labour's cooperation with business in maintaining a pool of cheap Chinese labour.[11] So there is a dilemma here: the answer found in the case files contradicts the conventional wisdom of current scholarship based on the economic analysis of a number of comparable cases.

Rather than dismissing the evidence in the case files I decided to explore the explanation contained there. But to take the 'moral' argument for the Female Labour Act at all seriously, even as a credible euphemism, I would have to establish that Chinese were perceived as a threat to white women and, in addition, that white women were regarded as vulnerable and in need of the kind of protection this law offered. This was in fact a quest for the existence of an attitude profound enough to affect the law of the land, a set of beliefs and assumptions fixed in the 'common sense' of those who accepted the validity of a law such as this. After all, laws are an expression of the culture that produces them; in a democracy such as Canada, they are supposed to embody 'community standards.' What standards, then, were encapsulated in the Quong Wing case? To corroborate, or contradict, the case file would require research into contemporary sources such as newspapers and magazines, novels, parliamentary debates and reports, legislation, records of labour, church, women's, and community organizations, the census, and other collections of statistics. The 'Quong Wing file' had to expand beyond the legal dossier.[12]

An early clue to the act's inspiration appeared in the minutes of the 1911 national convention of the Trades and Labour Congress, when a resolution was passed unanimously: 'Whereas ... Orientals employing white girls have used their positions as employers to seduce and destroy all sense of morality by the use of drugs and other means, bringing them down to the lowest depths of humanity; therefore, be it resolved, that this Congress impress on the Federal Government the necessity of passing legislation making it a criminal offense for Orientals to employ white girls in any capacity.'[13] At its annual meeting with the Saskatchewan cabinet in February 1912, the provincial TLC executive included this law in its list of demands.[14] In less than three weeks the attorney-general introduced the Female Labour Bill, explaining that '[i]ts purpose was ... to suppress what had become a menacing feature of the white slave traffic,' and he insisted the bill was necessary 'to prevent a certain state of affairs which frequently results from the employment of white women in establishments conducted by Chinamen.'[15]

Its origin in a trade-union delegation suggested of course that the act could have been intended to protect the economic interests of white labour by excluding Chinese competition. But Saskatchewan's Chinese workers were already 'ghettoized,' primarily in restaurants and laundries, and posed no perceptible threat to white wages. On the contrary, if the Chinese were driven out of their own businesses they would be *more* likely to come into competition with white labour. Nor was there in Saskatchewan a white employers' lobby trying to utilize any Chinese labour that might, conceivably, have been displaced from self-employment by laws attacking restaurants and laundries. Furthermore, as contemporary newspapers revealed, organized labour was not the only constituency demanding restraints on the Chinese community. The Saskatchewan Social and Moral Reform Council, established in 1907 primarily as a temperance organization, was also expressing concern about the potential dangers to white women from Chinese employers. The Reformers were advised by a 'prominent citizen' that '[t]hrough the three prairie Provinces and British Columbia these Oriental almond-eyed anthropoids own a large proportion of our eating houses, and are found working side by side with white women in almost all of our hotels and restaurants. In Western Canada our sisters, even our mothers, are working under these harpies and with them for sixteen and sometimes as many as eighteen hours a day. To my certain knowledge many of them afterwards go down into the underworld to suffer a fate worse than death. You who make a business of combatting social evils must take this one into consideration speedily. Each day's delay means scores of Canadian women lost to decency, and shames our country in the eyes of all moral nations.'[16] The council included representatives from all the major churches, temperance societies, and women's organizations, as well as from retail merchants', medical, and teachers' associations, who combined with organized labour to convince the Saskatchewan government of the necessity for the Female Labour Act.[17]

It was becoming apparent that there was a wide and even representative group of interests combining to demand the Saskatchewan act. Had they been aroused by some incident involving a Chinese man and a white woman? Though the attorney-general announced that this was a 'frequent state of affairs,'[18] there is no published legal record of the conviction of a Chinese person in Saskatchewan on any sex-related charge in the first two and a half decades of the twentieth century. Quong Wing himself was not accused of any particular incident of immorality. At his trial his female employees insisted that he was 'respectable' and the prosecutor volunteered, 'I know he is a very fine gentleman.'[19] If Saskatchewan Chinese were regarded as immoral, it was a general perception, not the product of any specific event that had occurred in the province.

Defining a Chinese Threat

The Chinese community of Moose Jaw did not resemble the city's other ethnic groups. Since the population was almost exclusively male, there were few Chinese families and fewer children in the local schools. In the 1911 census there were 279 Chinese males for every Chinese female in Canada, by far the greatest imbalance for any ethnic group at that time.[20] This was not entirely a matter of choice. The escalating head tax made it unlikely that a poorly paid Chinese worker could afford to bring his family to Canada.[21] The tax was in any case merely symptomatic of Canadian attitudes toward the Chinese. A market gardener told a royal commission in 1902: 'I have been here 12 years ... My wife and two children are in China ... I would like to bring my children here ... The people in this country talk so much against the Chinese that I do not care to bring them here.'[22] In Moose Jaw, as elsewhere, social contact was virtually non-existent, and even economic integration was minimal. Most of the Chinese men were employed in Chinese-owned restaurants and laundries.[23]

As was often the case in different parts of Canada, Moose Jaw's Chinatown was located in one of the least desirable sections of the city. River Street was separated from the main residential areas by the commercial district, giving the street a certain attraction for businesses anxious to avoid public scrutiny. With the cooperation of the city's police force, Moose Jaw's River Street harboured brothels and bootleggers and effectively became the red-light district for Regina, less than forty-five miles away along the CPR.[24] The north side of River Street contained an assortment of gambling dens, drinking joints, and hotels worked by up to 100 prostitutes in the summer season. The south side of the street was occupied by Chinatown.[25] Chinatown's proximity to the city's sin centre gave the Chinese community itself an aura of immorality, and a stereotype was sustained of the 'Chinaman' as an inveterate gambler, drug addict, and procurer of prostitutes.[26] As such the Chinese were an apparent threat to the white men who might become their customers and, more ruinously, to white women who could be corrupted into prostitution.

Thousands of young men, the Trades and Labour Congress lamented, 'can lay their ruin to the Chinese who taught them the terrible habit of opium smoking.'[27] An unsubstantiated but widely disseminated report claimed that most brothels across Canada were operated by Chinese or Japanese.[28] The Woman's Christian Temperance Union and the Women's Institute warned particularly that women would be enticed into Chinese dens, addicted to opium, and held in prostitution. Reports came from Lethbridge and Saskatoon that young girls were becoming addicts and prostitutes under Chinese auspices, recruited right off the streets.[29] The Methodist Church listed Chinese restaurants as 'dangerous places' for white women.[30] In Toronto a Vigilance Committee circulated a broadside urging 'strenuous efforts to break up Chinese dens of infamy, kept for the purpose of ruining young Canadian girls.'[31] 'Entrapment' of white women foolish enough to work in Chinese restaurants or laundries, or even to visit them as customers, became an accepted scenario in the popular imagination.[32] In September 1911 the Toronto magazine *Jack Canuck* located the 'Yellow Peril' in the city's laundries: 'The bland smiling Oriental and his quaint pidgeon English does not *appear* very formidable to the young woman who enters his store for the weekly wash. She does not notice the evil lurking in the almond eyes as she accepts the silk handkerchief or other trifling Oriental knick knack.'[33] One labour official warned that not even home was safe, for Chinese house servants were adulterating their employers' food with drugs, 'thus placing the female members of the household at their disposal and unscrupulous will.'[34]

This Chinese assault upon white womanhood was never supported with actual cases or statistics; it was a 'truth' constructed without evidence. Since the Chinese libido was understood to produce lascivious urges toward white women, 'common sense' insisted that such cases must exist.[35] It was also alleged that the Chinese were deliberately setting out to undermine the superior 'white race' through an attack on its moral fibre.[36] Emily Murphy wrote in 1922 that Chinese were trying to bring about 'the downfall of the white race,' and that the spread of opium and prostitution was motivated by 'their desire to injure the bright-browed races of the world.'[37]

Protecting Female Workers

A parallel 'truth' existed about women, or at least Anglo-Saxon women, casting them as nurturing and sacrificial but, at the same time, dependent and vulnerable. The widespread movement for reform that attracted so many Canadian women at the turn of the century both accepted and perpetuated this 'truth.' The reformers did not seek to change woman's nurturing role but to extend it, so that her maternal instincts would benefit the community at large.[38] They proposed no programs that would have encouraged women's economic independence, for the prevailing ideology of 'separate spheres' assigned the provider role to men.[39] It was acknowledged that some women had to work, but this would be temporary, premarital, or at least pre-maternal, and should not normally become a 'career.' Yet the number of young women working for wages was increasing with urbanization, arousing concerns for their physical and moral safety against threats that might affect their later lives as mothers. Even white-collar work, it was feared, could provoke nervous disorders that might be passed along to future offspring and lead ultimately to 'race degeneration.'[40] Helena Gutteridge, leading BC female activist and women's labour organizer, sought to encourage women's employment opportunities, yet she insisted that 'short hours are far more essential to women than they are to men ... The injurious physical and mental effects of such work are plainly visible ... and the rapid aging of the working women has its injurious effects on the next generation.'[41]

The maternal reformers therefore added protective legislation for female workers to their national agenda,[42] lobbying in particular for factory acts shielding women from hazardous tasks and providing for their special needs as workers.[43] Hours of labour were limited and night work was banned, proper dining and dressing rooms were required, and leaves for pregnant and nursing mothers were established. Women were not permitted to serve alcohol in many provinces, or to work in labour camps.[44] Even shops were required to have seats for female employees, lest a day spent waiting on the public have a detrimental physical effect, and female clerks could not be employed after 6 pm.[45] Minimum wages were introduced for female employees to reduce their vulnerability to exploitation.[46] Moral protection followed a parallel path. The Criminal Code in 1892 created a special offence for an employer or manager to seduce a female employee under his direction. At first specifying only factories, mills, and workshops, the offence category was extended to shops and stores in 1900 and to all places of work in 1920.[47]

This legislative direction was launched and sustained without any specific reference to 'race,' but racial assumptions lent certain implications to its application. Most fundamentally, women were the bearers of the 'white race' and the preservation of the latter required the protection of white women from, inter alia, racial impurities. Contemporary stereotypes made Chinese particularly liable to identification in this regard. Among the images brought back by Western missionaries and travellers in China was one of a wretchedly low condition of women in that civilization. Female infanticide, concubinage, and polygamy attracted the particular distaste of Canadian women who expressed concern that the Chinese example could seduce Canadian males 'away from higher Anglo-Saxon standards.'[48] In Canada, too, Chinese men were alleged to be buying and selling Chinese women, and Chinese house-servants were referred to as 'slave girls' by the reformers.[49] These manifestations were confirmation of the society-wide belief in Chinese moral inferiority, and aroused an interventionist response from Canadian women. For example, in 1909, when Chinese merchants in Victoria hired some white female students as English-language instructors for their children, the Local Council of Women asked city council to pass an emergency by-law to prevent it.[50] The idea of using the state to legislate morality in general, and the protection of white women in particular, was well established by the first decade of the twentieth century.

Convergence

These were the assumptions that permeated the Moose Jaw courtroom on 27 May 1912 when Quong Wing appeared to answer the charge against him. Defence attorney Netson R. Craig did not deny that his client employed Mabel Hopham and Nellie Lane; rather, he attacked the stereotypes – as they related to both 'race' and gender – underlying the Female Labour Act. Mr Craig challenged the very concept of 'race,' forcing witnesses to explain what they meant by the term 'Chinaman' and how a Chinese person was different, or behaved differently, from any other person. The responses he evoked displayed the conventional wisdom that racial categories were both meaningful and obvious. Craig asked Police Chief Johnson:

Q. I suppose you have never been in the Orient, Chief?
A. No ...
Q. You are not a professional Ethnologist.
A. No ...
Q. Do you know the difference between a Chinaman and any other man. Is there any difference between a Chinaman and any other man?
A. I know the difference when I see them.

Second, Netson Craig challenged the vulnerability and dependency of white women and their need for protection against Chinese, and in this he had the wholehearted agreement of the female employees who were called as witnesses. Nellie Lane was asked about her working life with Quong Wing:

Q. You have been working for him for twelve months.
A. Yes, and never worked for a better master, he pays me to the day and has an honest living.
Q. Respectable?
A. Yes, they call him Chinese, he is as good as me.
Q. You have no fault to find with him at all?
A. No fault whatever.[51]

But Netson Craig's fundamental challenge was not answered, was not even considered, by Magistrate Dunn, the Saskatchewan Supreme Court, or the Supreme Court of Canada. 'Common sense' accepted Quong Wing as a threat and employees Hopham and Lane as needing protection. The only question entertained by the courts was whether the Saskatchewan legislature could legitimately pass legislation restricting the rights of a Chinese who had become a naturalized British subject. The answer, at every level, was in the affirmative.

Contextual Considerations

In Saskatchewan there was no apparent urgency to disarm Chinese competition. The immediate economic situation fails to deliver a convincing explanation for the act or the court decisions. They must be understood, first, in the context of a momentum already established, which was producing increasing restrictions upon Chinese because of dangers they seemed to pose to the welfare of white

Canadians. In addition, any trends of which the Quong Wing decision formed a part can only be revealed through the history of subsequent developments relating to the Chinese in Canada. The history to which Quong Wing belongs neither began nor ended in 1912. What happened afterwards is equally essential to any explanation.

In 1913 Manitoba passed an act similar to Saskatchewan's,[52] as did Ontario in 1914.[53] Under pressure from the Chinese consulate, and pending Quong Wing's appeal, both these acts were left unproclaimed.[54] In 1919 British Columbia followed suit,[55] having been assured by a police investigation that '[a]part from its "race bearing" – the employment of Caucasian by Mongolian – there is no doubt white women introduced to Orientals through this medium succumb to both immorality and narcotics.'[56] Submitting in turn to Chinese diplomatic pressure, British Columbia amended its law in 1923 to omit the specific racial reference, but continued to require local police to determine whether each instance of the employment of females by Chinese was 'advisable in the interests of the morals of such women and girls.'[57] The removal of the word 'Chinese' or 'Chinaman' from the restriction made little difference to its enforcement. Whatever euphemisms or generalities might appear in the amended legislation, it soon became clear that the Chinese remained the intended target. In further confirmation of this trend, in 1922 the House of Commons debated the proposition that 'in the opinion of this House, the immigration of oriental aliens and their rapid multiplication is becoming a serious menace to living conditions, particularly on the Pacific coast, and to the future of the country in general, and the Government should take immediate action with a view to securing the effective restriction of future immigration of this type.'[58] The consequence was passage of the Chinese Immigration Act of 1923,[59] which abolished the head tax but which banned all Chinese from entering Canada as permanent immigrants.

The laws prohibiting Chinese from employing white females continued to be refined and enforced after Chinese immigration was ended. In August 1924 Yee Clun applied to the Regina city council for a licence to employ white women in his restaurant and rooming house, claiming that because of the new Chinese Immigration Act there was a shortage of Chinese males available to hire.[60] Opposition to his application was mobilized by the women's reform movement in Regina. About twenty women representing the WCTU, Local Council of Women, and Women's Labor Council attended city-council meetings, arguing that 'it was not in the best interests of the young womanhood of the city to grant the request,'[61] that '[e]mployment of white women by Chinese might lead to mesalliances,' and that Regina's claim to be 'Queen City of the West' could be corrupted to 'queer city of the west.'[62] A lawyer hired by the Local Council of

Protest White Girl Help in Chinese Restaurants

When Yee Clun applied for permission to hire white women in his Regina restaurant, women's organizations rallied to oppose him. Racial 'common sense' of the era depicted Chinese as a moral threat from which white women must be protected.

Objection against Chinese restaurateurs in the city being allowed to employ white female help is being raised by Regina women.

The question has been brought to the front as a result of the decision of the aldermen in special committee Thursday to grant the application of Yee Clun, proprietor of the Exchange Grill on Rose street for permission to hire white women help, the decision being subject to ratification by council at its next meeting.

Opposition of Regina women to the proposal is expected to crystallize at a meeting of the Central, Westend and Northside branches of the W.C.T.U., at the home of Mrs. Robert Sinton, 1810 Albert street, this evening when the question is to be given an airing.

Efforts to call a meeting of the Local Council of Women have proved abortive owing to the absence of the officers from the city on vacation, but it is pointed out that the L.C.W. opposed similar proposals when they came before the city council a year or two ago.

Yee Clun's application to the civic fathers had the support of the license inspector. One of the aldermen present thought no harm would be done by recommending the council to approve the application, as such a decision could easily be reversed if opposition developed sufficiently in the meantime to warrant a reversal. Opponents of the proposal took the view this would place the council in a ridiculous position. The matter will probably be under discussion by the aldermen again Thursday night, when the special committee meets.

Source: *Regina Morning Leader*, 12 August 1924

Women quoted Emily Murphy's *The Black Candle* to illustrate the dangers of opium and entrapment waiting for white women in Chinese restaurants. In the face of such opposition, council ignored the advice of its own solicitor and rejected the application.[63] When Yee Clun appealed to the courts, however, Justice Philip Mackenzie decided that the 1919 amendment to the Female Labour

Act (changing the prohibition from 'no Chinaman' to 'no person ... without a license') was sincere, and since Yee Clun was an honest and respectable businessman he should not be denied a licence on the exclusive complaint that he was Chinese.[64] Immediately afterwards the Saskatchewan legislature amended the act again so that it could remove any licence already granted and so that a city council could refuse a licence at its own discretion without giving any reasons.[65] The legislature's intent, unchanged since 1912, was made quite clear.

British Columbia's Women and Girls' Protection Act, was indifferently enforced until the mid-1930s, when a violent crime involving a Chinese suspect and a white female victim prompted Vancouver city officials to begin warning Chinese restaurants that they must dismiss their white female employees or lose their licences. In September 1937 Vancouver council suspended the licences of three Chinese cafes when it was discovered that they continued to employ white waitresses. The owners, one of whom was president of the Chinese Benevolent Association, threatened to sue, but a compromise was reached whereby the Chinese agreed to fire the waitresses and drop the court action and the city would restore the licences. The former waitresses, whose own jobs had disappeared in the course of these negotiations, appeared before city council on 12 October 1937 to plead for the restoration of their jobs. 'We must live and heaven knows if a girl is inclined to go wrong she can do it just as readily on Granville Street as she can down here [in Chinatown],' they argued. Denying the validity of the threat to their morals, the waitresses alleged that racial discrimination underlay the city's action. Mayor George Miller declared, 'It is ridiculous to suggest that there was racial discrimination,' and the women's plea was rejected.[66] A year later another Chinese restaurant was discovered with a white waitress and its licence was suspended, being restored only after the waitress was fired. Chief Constable W.W. Foster was asked to conduct an investigation into whether employment by Chinese was a verifiable threat to women's morals. In his March 1939 report Chief Foster wrote: 'In view of the conditions under which the girls are expected to work it is almost impossible for them to be so employed without falling victims to some form of immoral life.'[67] Early in 1943 the League of Women Voters asked Vancouver city for a by-law to prohibit Chinese from employing white women. Mayor Cornett replied that a by-law was not necessary because 'there was a gentleman's agreement with the proprietors of Chinese cafes not to hire white girls.'[68]

The most bizarre developments in the same direction occurred in Ontario. The female-labour clause remained unproclaimed and forgotten until in 1927 Ontario consolidated its laws in the *Revised Statutes of Ontario*. Included, apparently inadvertently, was the clause that outlawed the employment of white women by Chinese. Police in Toronto and elsewhere began prosecuting Chinese under the law, and when pressed in different directions by the Chinese consulate and by organized labour, the provincial government decided at first to leave the law in place.[69]

Press reaction was mixed. *Labour* pronounced that its readership 'has long sought this regulation and it expects the Ontario government to enforce the law.'[70] The Toronto *Globe* asserted 'that indiscriminate mixing of different colours and races is criminally unwise,' but on the other hand '[t]o lump all Chinese ... as a class of invariable moral degenerates is ... hideously unjust.'[71] Between these two positions fell an article in the December 1928 *Chatelaine*,[72] offering comments representing different points of view. A report from the National Council of Women outlined the various provincial restrictions and concluded, 'The bar raised by the statute is not for the purpose of discriminating against an Oriental race but inasmuch as Orientals have not Oriental women in this country and as naturally an employee is more or less under the control of her or his employer, this Act protects the white girls and is passed for their protection only.' A missionary to the Toronto Chinese community revealed that the white waitresses whom he had interviewed in Toronto 'feel no need of protection and resent interference with their liberty of action'; Magistrate Helen Gregory MacGill, on the other hand, approved of the protection of women but thought it wrong to single out a particular 'race' as the source of danger. The *Chatelaine* article, too, accepted the premise that Canadian women required 'moral as well as industrial protection,' and did not so much object to the legislation as complain that it did not go far enough. What was needed, according to *Chatelaine*, was a proper national program addressing the 'growing problem' of 'women placed in circumstances prejudicial to their welfare.'

The federal government, to whom the Chinese government appealed, said it could not disallow this particular clause without disallowing the entire *Revised Statutes of Ontario*, which would leave the province without any laws at all. The impasse was finally broken through the interference of London, for Britain was at that time renegotiating the so-called 'Unequal Treaties' with China and wished to give no offence. For the sake of the Empire, Ontario agreed to amend the act to restore the provision that it would come into force only when proclaimed by the lieutenant-governor. So the law went back on the shelf where it had been between 1914 and 1927.[73]

It is apparent that the public, press, courts, legislatures and law-enforcement agencies of Canada continued to perceive the Chinese as a threat, and continued to countenance discriminatory restrictions against them. It may be instructive to examine the impact of these restrictions and popular attitudes upon the Chinese themselves. In the first place, the Chinese population of Saskatchewan continued to grow. The 1921 census showed 2613 Chinese in Saskatchewan (of whom only 39 were female), an increase of almost 200 per cent since 1911. By 1931, the rate of growth slowed by the 1923 immigration act, there were 3221. Especially interesting is the continued Chinese trend toward the hotel, restaurant, and laundry industries. In 1921 50 per cent of Saskatchewan Chinese were employed in restaurants (as owners, cooks, or waiters); in 1931 this had increased to 70 per cent. Most of the remainder were owners or employees of laundries and hotels / rooming houses; 90 per cent of Chinese men and 100 per cent of Chinese women in Saskatchewan were engaged in typical (or stereotypical) service industries in 1931.[74] This was occurring despite the existence of laws and licensing restrictions that prevented Chinese from hiring white women. The restrictions obviously did not discourage Chinese from entering the targeted industries or drive them out of the province.

If the motivation for such restrictions were *purely* economic, then surely the failure of the 'white female' tactic to limit Chinese restaurants and laundries should have prompted a more effective method; yet none was attempted. Instead, laws that clearly did not impede the spread of Chinese laundries and restaurants were more urgently enforced, often at the insistence of white women's organizations with no possible economic benefit to themselves. What the courts of the time described as a 'moral' concern can be understood as an encompassing world-view that interpreted visible biological differences as profoundly meaningful and as justifying legal as well as social distinctions. The origin of 'separate spheres' defined in terms of 'race' has been identified with the establishment of European hegemony and the 'differential incorporation' of marginalized peoples into a Euro-centred global economy.[75] By the time it reached Saskatchewan the sphere assigned Chinese-Canadians both a 'place' and a 'character' with more than economic implications. The franchise, for example, was denied to Saskatchewan Chinese according to an understanding that they were unfit to participate in Canadian democracy.[76] The protection of white women against Chinese seduction was symbolic of an urgency to protect Canadian society against alien intrusion, and to maintain the separation that biology and common sense seemed to demand. The moral choice was clear, for to decide in favour of Quong Wing would have required a questioning of the foundations of Canadian society. On the Supreme Court of Canada bench only John Idington saw a different morality, arguing that racial inequality would in itself undermine Canadian justice and democracy. At the time, he was in the minority.

Conclusions

And so a circle is completed: a range of contemporary sources supports the explanation of the court files that the prosecution of Quong Wing was deemed a moral issue in 1912. The case illustrates the affect surrounding 'race' in the early years of the century, enabling us to regard racism as more than a tool for economic exploitation, more than a political ideology: it was an expression of prevailing mentality. 'Race' was 'common sense,' and it meant that you could read people's mental or moral character simply from their biological category. We learn further from Quong Wing that the stereotypes triggering his trial cannot be traced to specific events, they were not produced by conscious rivalries, they were not generalizations based on limited experience: they could actually precede any direct experience at all. Scholars of 'race relations' in Canada who concentrate on British Columbia may conclude that the 'Oriental menace' was a combination of locally explicable circumstances such as economic competition and cultural conflict.[77] But because the Quong Wing case was launched in Saskatchewan and concluded in Ottawa, where those circumstances had far less purchase, it requires an acknowledgment of global forces beyond site-specific terms of self-interest, fear of being overwhelmed numerically, or industrial relations. This does not deny a role for economics in the formulation of a racial world-view, but it does suggest caution in assigning personal motives to individual actors, whether they were trade unionists, women reformers, legislators, or judges.

Quong Wing's case also demonstrates the role of law in the racialization of Canadian society and the normalization of racial distinctions. It has become conventional to regard 'race' as a social construct, but in Canada we have not generally recognized that 'race' is also a legal artefact. The law made observable (and imagined) physical differences *real* in human lives: people became different as a result of differential treatment. The law took 'common sense' and turned it into something tangible, enforceable, and obeyable. Whatever relationships existed between Quong Wing and his employees before 1912 – and testimony at trial implies a mutual respect – the Saskatchewan law imposed a distinction that overwhelmed everything else. Despite their protests, Nellie Lane and Mabel Hopham were fired in order to protect them from the 'Chinaman.'[78]

For social historians more generally, Quong Wing reveals the utility of the 'singled-out case' approach recommended by Natalie Zemon Davis. In pursuing this method, Davis advises, one singles out a story or dramatic event for analysis, not necessarily because it is 'representative' but because it can provide a 'key' to its historical moment. For this purpose historians must select 'telling' events, ones that 'speak beyond themselves.' 'The significant variables are most likely to be cultural ones,' Davis writes. 'They are not quantified or correlated, but "read," "translated" or "interpreted."' As we engage in this interpretation, she continues, '[o]ld habits of thought are as important as current attitudes, unreflective commitments as important as conscious weighings of interest.'[79] The Quong Wing files offer an eminently suitable candidate for this kind of treatment. One methodological implication would seem to be the necessity for the historian to take the evidence in the files seriously. This does not mean to believe it out of hand, but to approach it with respect and to interpret it in the context of its own times – to test it against other expressions of the same cultural moment. There is sometimes a tendency to judge the past in terms of the present, as if other ages should have had a supra-historical sensitivity that we lack. Sometimes, it's true, we do know certain things about the past that were obscured to contemporaries, but we also carry a 'common sense' of our own that comes between us and the experience of the people we study. Davis's admonition to attend to 'habits of thought' and 'unreflective commitments' can open a case to interpretations that may be more 'telling' than our own conventional wisdom might have predicted. As historians of the past, as well as citizens of the present, most of us could benefit from a greater awareness of how 'common sense' operates on our minds and assumptions. Many of the things we preserve in our own files will seem quaint to future historians.

Notes

1 *Statutes of Saskatchewan* 1912 c. 17. The original wording included Japanese in the prohibition, but Japanese government intervention achieved an amendment just a few months later: SS 1912–13 c. 18.

2 SS 1918–19 c. 85

3 National Archives of Canada (NAC), RG 125, vol. 340, file 3389, *Quong Wing v The King*

4 Saskatchewan Archives Board (SAB), Collection R 1267, file 3474, docket 192/12, 'R v Quong Wing'

5 Ibid., Certificate of Naturalization, dated 7 Dec. 1905

6 Ibid. For the published case report see [1913] 12 *Dominion Law Reports* 656.

7 NAC, *Quong Wing v The King*, Respondent's factum

8 [1914] 39 *Supreme Court Reports* 440. Idington quotation is at 456.

9 For an interesting articulation of this interpretation see Bruce Ryder, 'Racism and the Constitution: The Constitutional Fate of British Columbia Anti-Asian Immigration Legislation, 1884–1909,' *Osgoode Hall Law Journal* 29 (1991), 619–76. The most authoritative survey of Chinese in Canada acknowledges the 'moral concern,' but concludes that 'economic reasons were paramount' and the true legislative aim was to exclude Chinese from the restaurant business. Edgar Wickberg et al., *From China to Canada: A History of the Chinese Communities in Canada* (Toronto 1982), 120

10 One of the few scholarly interpretations directly addressing Saskatchewan's Female Labour Act (Constance Backhouse, 'White Female Help and Chinese-Canadian Employers: Race, Class, Gender and Law in the Case of Yee Clun, 1924,' *Canadian Ethnic Studies* 26:3 [1994], 34–52) accepts that the underlying purpose of the legislation was economic. Backhouse writes, 'Although the legislation did not directly bar Asian entrepreneurs from operating restaurants, laundries or other businesses, it enjoined them from hiring white women, something which was *intended to have significant economic consequences* (p. 35: emphasis added). Backhouse has maintained the same orientation in 'The White Women's Labor Laws: Anti-Chinese Racism in Early Twentieth-Century Canada,' *Law and History Review* 14 (1996), 315–68.

11 The concept of the 'split labour market' originated with Edna Bonacich, who observed that it was most often the white working class, rather than the capitalists or professional middle class, who publicly insisted upon restrictions against minority workers. She concluded that it was in the interest of employers to 'split' the majority white workers from the minority, by offering them certain apparent advantages in pay or in protected job categories, to prevent a unified labour campaign for better wages and conditions. According to Bonacich, the white workers were thus unwittingly furthering the object of their bosses, contrary to their own true interests, when they demanded and received racist legislation from politicians. See Edna Bonacich, 'A Theory of Ethnic Antagonism: The Split Labor Market,' *American Sociological Review* 37 (1972), 547–59.

12 The case and its contextual setting are described at greater length in James W. St.G. Walker, *'Race,' Rights and the Law in the Supreme Court of Canada: Historical Case Studies* (Waterloo 1997), chap. 2.

13 TLC, *Reports of the Proceedings of the Annual Convention*, 1912, 107

14 Regina *Morning Leader*, 7 Feb. 1912

15 Ibid., 27 Feb., 2 and 5 Mar. 1912

16 Ibid., 5 Sept. 1912

17 Moose Jaw *Evening Times*, 6 Sept. 1913, 21 and 24 Feb. 1914

18 Regina *Morning Leader*, 27 Feb. 1912

19 SAB, 'R v Quong Wing,' Examination of witnesses, 27 May 1912

20 *Census of Canada*, 1911, vol. 2; Moose Jaw *Evening Times*, 8 Aug. 1911

21 A head tax of $50 was first imposed in 1885: *Statutes of Canada* 1885 c. 71. This was increased to $100 in 1900, SC 1900 c. 32, and to $500 in 1903, SC 1903 c. 8.

22 Canada, Parliament, Sessional Papers, 1902, vol. 13, no. 54, Royal Commission on Chinese and Japanese Immigration, *Report*, 1902, 65

23 SAB, Project Integrate, 'An Ethnic Study of the Chinese Community of Moose Jaw' (1973)

24 James Gray, *Red Lights on the Prairies* (Toronto 1971), 77. A contemporary

observer quoted by Gray remarked: 'Moose Jaw isn't a city or a municipality or even a geographic location! Moose Jaw is a goddam virus that has permanently afflicted Regina and for which there is no known cure!' (76).

25 Ibid., 75–80; James Gray, *The Roar of the Twenties* (Toronto 1975), 269. There were frequent newspaper accounts of raids and arrests in Chinatown: e.g., Moose Jaw *Evening Times*, 31 Oct. and 18 Dec. 1911, 14 Mar. 1912. An allegation that Police Chief Johnson personally appropriated the gambling stakes during such raids was reported in the *Evening Times*, 11 May 1912.

26 A full discussion of how this kind of stereotype was constructed is found in Kay J. Anderson, *Vancouver's Chinatown: Racial Discourse in Canada, 1875–1980* (Montreal and Kingston 1991).

27 T.L. Chapman, 'The Anti-Drug Crusade in Western Canada, 1885–1925,' in D.J. Bercuson and L.A. Knafla, eds, *Law and Society in Canada in Historical Perspective* (Calgary 1979), 91–109; Paul L. Voisey, 'Two Chinese Communities in Alberta: An Historical Perspective,' *Canadian Ethnic Studies* 2 (1970), 21

28 Mariana Valverde, *The Age of Light, Soap and Water: Moral Reform in English Canada, 1885–1925* (Toronto 1991), 57; Regina *Morning Leader*, 28 May 1912

29 Chapman, 'Anti-Drug Crusade,' esp. 91–4, 97, 98, 101, 109; Voisey, 'Two Chinese Communities,' 21

30 Valverde, *Light, Soap and Water*, 97–8

31 Quoted in *Globe and Mail*, 11 June 1994

32 Emily F. Murphy, *The Black Candle* (Toronto 1922), and Hilda Glynn-Ward, *The Writing on the Wall* (Vancouver 1921; repr. Toronto 1974), each devote an entire chapter to the theme of entrapment.

33 Cited in K. Paupst, 'A Note on Anti-Chinese Sentiment in Toronto before the First World War,' *Canadian Ethnic Studies* 9 (1977), 58.

34 Cited in Robert A. Huttenback, *Racism and Empire: White Settlers and Colored Immigrants in the British Self-Governing Colonies, 1830–1910* (Ithaca and London 1976), 137–8.

35 Pierre Bourdieu has commented that 'common sense speaks the clear and simple language of what is plain for all to see.' It is something that does not need to be proved or even argued, for it is taken for granted. *In Other Words: Essays Towards a Reflexive Sociology* (Stanford 1990), 52

36 Chapman, 'Anti-Drug Crusade,' 103; Shirley J. Cook, 'Canadian Narcotics Legislation, 1908–1923: A Conflict Model Interpretation,' *Canadian Review of Sociology and Anthropology* 6 (1969), 43

37 Murphy, *Black Candle*, 188–9

38 See for example the constitution of the National Council of Women of Canada, founded in 1893, quoted in Veronica J. Strong-Boag, *The Parliament of Women: The National Council of Women of Canada, 1893–1929* (Ottawa 1976), 81. Emily Mur-

phy insisted that it was a husband's responsibility to ensure the effective functioning of his wife's maternal destiny. *Black Candle*, 235

39 Most items on the reform agenda were long-standing domestic concerns applied to a national scale. Others were products of more recent anxieties, such as prostitution, immigration, and alcohol abuse. E.g., see Valverde, *Light, Soap and Water*, chap. 5; Alison Prentice et al., *Canadian Women: A History* (Toronto 1988), 150, 193; Carol Lee Bacchi, *Liberation Deferred? The Ideas of the English-Canadian Suffragists, 1877–1918* (Toronto 1983), 52–3, 104; Strong-Boag, *Parliament*, 247. The National Council of Women convention in London, Ontario, in 1912 passed resolutions on child welfare, prevention of tuberculosis, pure milk, playgrounds, training of women teachers, Chinese and Japanese 'houses of ill-fame,' and the international white slave traffic. Regina *Morning Leader*, 28 May 1912

40 Valverde, *Light, Soap and Water*, 109

41 Quoted in Susan Wade, 'Helena Gutteridge: Votes for Women and Trade Unions,' in Barbara Latham and Cathy Kess, eds, *In Her Own Right: Selected Essays on Women's History in BC* (Victoria 1980), 193.

42 Prentice et al., *Canadian Women*, 227; Ruth Frager, 'No Proper Deal: Women Workers and the Canadian Labour Movement, 1870–1940,' in Linda Briskin and Lynda Yanz, *Union Sisters: Women in the Labour Movement* (Toronto 1983), 46; Janice Acton et al., eds, *Women at Work: Ontario, 1850–1930* (Toronto 1974), 5

43 The Ontario Factories Act, *Statutes of Ontario* 1884 c. 39, for example, set a 10-hour day and 60-hour week for women factory workers, insisted that they be allowed a full hour for lunch in a suitable room away from the machinery, prevented women from being assigned to clean machinery while it was in motion, and stated generally that '[i]t shall not be lawful to employ in a factory any child, young girl or woman, so that the health ... is likely to be permanently injured.'

44 NAC, RG 25, vol. 1524, file 867, 'Canadian Laws Governing the Employment of Women,' enclosed in H.H. Ward, Deputy Minister of Labour, to L. Beaudry, Department of External Affairs, 28 Sept. 1928

45 E.g., Ontario Shops Regulation Act, SO 1888 c. 33

46 NAC, 'Canadian Laws.' This Canadian legislation evolved in a continental context, as American states passed similar laws. See Alan Brinkley, 'For Their Own Good,' *New York Review of Books*, 26 May 1994, 42.

47 James G. Snell, '"The White Life for Two": The Defence of Marriage and Sexual Morality in Canada, 1890–1914,' *Histoire sociale / Social History* 16 (1983), 121

48 Strong-Boag, *Parliament*, 186

49 E.g., Karen Van Dieren, 'The Response of the WMS to the Immigration of Asian Women 1888–1942,' in Barbara K. Latham and Roberta J. Pazdro, eds, *Not Just Pin Money: Selected Essays on the History of Women's Work in British Columbia* (Victoria 1984), 80–9

50 David Chuenyan Lai, *Chinatowns: Cities within Cities in Canada* (Vancouver 1988), 54

51 SAB, 'R v Quong Wing,' Examination of witnesses

52 *Statutes of Manitoba* 1913 c. 19

53 SO 1914 c. 40 s. 2(1)

54 NAC, RG 25, vol. 1142, file 308, Pope to Borden, 28 Feb. 1914; SAB, Scott Papers, Allan to Marten, 5 Dec. 1918

55 *Statutes of British Columbia* 1919 c. 63

56 Provincial Archives of British Columbia (PABC), Attorney General's Papers, file 2060, 1181, copy in NAC, MG 31 E55, Tarnopolsky Papers, vol. 43, file 5, Parsons to Attorney General, 16 Aug. 1922

57 SBC 1923 c. 76

58 *Hansard*, 8 May 1922, 1509

59 SC 1923 c. 38

60 Backhouse, 'White Female Help,' 39–45; Regina *Morning Leader*, 8 Aug. 1924

61 *Morning Leader*, 12 and 13 Aug. 1924

62 Ibid., 20 Aug. 1924

63 Ibid., 8 Oct. 1924

64 [1925] 3 *Western Weekly Reports* 714

65 SS 1925–26 c. 53

66 NAC, Tarnopolsky Papers, vol. 43, file 5

67 Ibid.

68 Ibid.

69 Toronto *Star*, 22 Aug. 1928. Ontario Premier Ferguson was apparently willing to withdraw or amend the act if the federal government would make a formal request to do so, but federal Justice Minister Lapointe demurred. NAC, RG 25, vol. 1525, file 867, Memorandum initialled 'HLK' to O.D. Skelton, 27 Feb. 1929

70 *Labour*, 8 Sept. 1928

71 *Globe*, 2 Oct. 1928

72 Anne Elizabeth Wilson, 'A Pound of Prevention – or an Ounce of Cure? A Plea for National Legislation on a Growing Problem,' *Chatelaine*, December 1928, 12, 13, 55

73 NAC, RG 25, vol. 1524, file 867; SO 1929 c. 72 s. 5

74 *Census of Canada, 1931*. Tables 49 and 69 in vol. 7 give a detailed breakdown for the gainfully employed in 1921 and 1931.

75 On differential incorporation and the theory of 'pluralism' see M.G. Smith, *The Plural Society in the British West Indies* (Berkeley 1965); M.G. Smith and L. Kuper, eds, *Pluralism in Africa* (Berkeley 1969); and Leo Kuper, *Race, Class and Power: Ideology and Revolutionary Change in Plural Societies* (London 1974). A concise statement of the theory can be found in M.G. Smith, 'Pluralism, Race and Ethnicity in

Selected African Countries,' in John Rex and David Mason, eds, *Theories of Race and Ethnic Relations* (Cambridge, Eng., 1986), 187–225.

76 SS 1908 c. 2 s. 11

77 There is a large literature on the history of the Chinese in British Columbia, most of it proposing *in situ* explanations for white fear and hostility directed against Asians. Some of the more sophisticated accounts are offered by W. Peter Ward, *White Canada Forever: Popular Attitudes and Public Policy Toward Orientals in British Columbia* (Montreal 1978), Patricia Roy, *A White Man's Province: British Columbia Politicians and Chinese and Japanese Immigrants, 1858–1914* (Vancouver 1989), and Anderson, *Vancouver's Chinatown.*

78 Female employees of Chinese restaurants in Vancouver and Toronto, as has been noted above, were equally adamant in insisting that they needed no protection.

79 Natalie Zemon Davis, 'The Shapes of Social History,' *Storia della storiografia* 17 (1990), 28–34

PART FOUR
EXPERTS AND CLIENTS:
SITES OF CONTESTATION

10

Ontario Mothers' Allowance Case Files as a Site of Contestation

MARGARET HILLYARD LITTLE

Social scientists have utilized case files to explore, among other things, the production of 'truth.' Influenced by postmodernism, scholars have become increasingly concerned about the fragmentary and incomplete nature of case files as a source to reveal the lives of people, especially those who are the subjects of these files. As subjects, they rarely have an opportunity to submit their own words into the case file; instead, most of their experiences are interpreted by the caseworker, who may have very different interests, opinions, and experiences. The imperfect nature of case file research became ever more apparent to me during 1994/95 when I was a member of the political studies department at University of Manitoba. Over the course of that year I experienced a number of chilly-climate incidences that I dutifully reported to the Sexual Harassment Officer, the Human Rights Officer, and the Dean of Arts. All of these administrative officers created files based on my year's experience at the university. In some instances, I was able to write in my own words and add these notations as evidence in my files. But even when this was possible, I was always conscious of the bureaucratic frameworks within which I wrote. In other cases, the officers wrote their own notes, and made their interpretations and assessments from the experiences I recounted. While all three of these officers were well meaning, they were also in positions of institutional power that required them to be concerned with other university interests than my own well-being. The fact that my life at University of Manitoba became a series of case files made me more aware of both the challenges and pitfalls of case file documentation and interpretation.

Case files become an even greater challenge when they become the only source of information about a social group. While there may be multiple sources of information regarding the lives of working-class and bourgeois women, this is seldom the case when we study the lives of poor women. Empirical data from censuses and employment records reveal important details about the general contours of poor women's daily lives, describing their employment, family size, and income levels. But too often the use of these sources reduces the poor to wooden aggregates devoid of personality and subjectivity. 'It would appear that only the privileged had personalities,' says historian Linda Gordon.[1] It is their diaries, correspondence, and memoirs that tend to have survived while the sentiments, aspirations, and difficulties of the poor have long disappeared.

In an attempt to understand the lives of poor single mothers better, this paper examines Ontario Mothers' Allowance case files, spanning the first decade of the policy's implementation, 1920 to 1929. Ontario Mothers' Allowance (OMA) is one of the first pillars of welfare-state legislation in the country. First enacted in 1920 to support poor widows, it expanded during the decade to include mothers who had been deserted for five years, mothers with permanently disabled husbands, and foster mothers. To be eligible a mother had to be a British subject and be able to prove both financial need and moral fitness.

While there is now an emerging body of literature on the history of mothers' allowance policies in Europe and the United States, none of these scholars make use of case files. In contrast, I was fortunate to locate approximately three cubic feet of 1920s case files from the city of London, Elgin County, Oxford County, and a scattering of problem or sample cases from throughout the province. These case files include minute details of these mothers' lives, following them from the time they wrote out their application, through the schooling of their children, to the tabulation of their accumulating debts. As such, they permit us to examine how this relationship between social worker and client was established and simultaneously contested.[2]

Given that the caseworkers' opinions, comments, and evidence dominated the case files, it is often difficult to hear the muted voices of the single mothers. And yet there is evidence to suggest that clients were less than passive victims of welfare policy. The vast majority of single mothers actively sought out state aid; they argued their case before the welfare worker or investigator and they also appealed for outside support when necessary. Despite their limited resources they used tremendous ingenuity to protect and nurture their children. It is this contestation and co-operation of investigator and client that will be given particular focus here.

The Importance of Case Files

The OMA case records represented a tremendous improvement in record keeping from nineteenth-century charity work. Generally conducted by volunteer and/or untrained labour whose record keeping was haphazard and inconsistent, nineteenth-century records tended to be in the form of ledger books where the barest outlines of the family were handwritten on three or four lines of the ledger. Emphasis tended to be on the number of families aided and the amount or type of help given. In contrast, the 1920s was a period of consolidation for welfare workers, during which the Canadian Association of Social Workers was founded to organize and regulate these new professionals.[3] Social workers expounded on the usefulness of casework to detail carefully and 'objectively' the lives of the less fortunate; the formal OMA application forms and quarterly investigative reports were at least partly a response to this belief.

These case files are rich in details about an individual single mother's situation. The application form marked the first official interaction between the investigator and the single mother. A standard application form of four pages contained information about the date of application, the ages of the mother, father, and children, the number of children, the places of birth and racial origin, the reasons for application, the family financial circumstances (including any employment by family members), and the names of three referees. Pages two and three of the form were generally reserved for financial questions. The mother would be asked to list her sources of income (profits from business; sale of produce; rental property; savings or insurance; pension or annuity; Workmen's Compensation; interest on investments; income from boarders or lodgers; other income; and the total per month) and her expenses (rent; taxes; principal; interest; house insurance; light and water; fuel; cleaning materials; food; recreation; clothing; life insurance; sundries; and the total for the month). The fourth and final page was blank and reserved for the comments of the investigator. Generally, the investigator's personal, subjective opinions rather than 'objective' data characterized this page. It is in this section that the investigator commented freely upon the mother's moral fitness for the allowance. In this initial stage of the process, the mother's voice was almost completely silent. Her sole contribution was to provide her signature at the bottom of the form.

Attached to many application forms were lengthy follow-up notes from the investigator and letters from the community to support or condemn the applicant. The subsequent documentation of the case provided fewer quantitative details and even more room for subjective determinations. Also included in many case files were inter-agency memoranda, letters and queries from the clients, as well as correspondence from neighbours, store owners, clergy, doctors, charity leaders, and other interested people.

For a number of reasons these case files are fragmented and often distorted in the stories they tell. The OMA case records are uneven in the amount of evidence they contained, depending mainly on the thoroughness of the individual investigator. Also bureaucratic errors could result in loss of evidence when information was sent to and from various interested parties. Second, the voices of the investigators dominate the papers. Even when the investigator is attempting to represent the views of the mother, the investigator's opinions shine through. Fortunately, within many case records are letters from the mothers to OMA officials or to community leaders seeking help with their particular case. Generally written in a humble, pleading tone, such correspondence, however, cannot be unquestioningly taken as the mothers' true feelings about their experiences of OMA administration. Not wanting to jeopardize their mothers' allowance cheques, recipients would be careful of complaining too vigorously about their unfair treatment. Letters from these mothers found in the Premier's Office and in the Prime Minister's Office papers support this assumption, for they were generally more assertively written. While neither source of letters can be considered representative of a single mother's experience of the policy, the subject material of the letters can give one some sense of what the mother believed was negotiable, given the discretionary nature of OMA administration generally.

Other difficulties exist in teasing out the voices of single mothers from these welfare files. First, there was little acknowledgment that a single mother knew or understood her 'symptoms' of poverty better than the investigator. In fact, there was a great deal of class arrogance and insensitivity expressed by the investigators toward the specific situations of many single mothers. For example, Elizabeth McIntyre, a mother of six children, lived in a four-room shack with no indoor plumbing, and in order to make ends meet 'worked out' whenever possible. Yet the investigator complained, 'Place was fearfully untidy when I called and Benef. said she was away working. I told her that there was no excuse and *made* her sweep while I was there and in 15 minutes she had it looking different.'[4] In another case the investigator showed no sympathy for the fact that a mother, of Eastern European descent, was ill. 'I visited this home and found it in a most unsanitary condition... The place was most untidy, and looked as though the woman was a very poor manager, and certain required some lessons on cleanliness ... I called the woman's attention to the odour, and asked her to put the place in as decent a shape as possible. She stated that she was not strong and had a young baby, and did the best she could under the circumstances.'[5] This insensitivity meant that there was little attempt to ensure that a mother's experiences were accurately recorded.

Second, seldom was there a frank exchange between welfare administrator and recipient. Even a well-meaning caseworker worked within the constraints of the emerging social-work institution, which was defined by professional standards and procedures. The application form required the investigator to ask personal questions that the client could interpret as irrelevant and/or intrusive. Both the investigator's class position and the structures in which she worked made it extremely difficult for honest communication between investigator and client. Single mothers were asked to provide some quantitative details for the case file (such as number of children, years of their births, and amount of income), but they were not asked to *describe* their daily life in any manner. Generally their experience of poverty was not validated. Given the demeaning comments made by some investigators, there was little to encourage a mother to be forthright about her conditions. In addition, clients often had something to hide. Whether it be male acquaintances, social activities, liquor, luxuries, or children not at school, there was always some aspect of a single mother's life that would be condemned, if discovered, by the investigator. Since condemnation could culminate in the cancellation of the allowance, the barriers to frank discussion and disclosure were both real and potentially life-threatening.

Third, a single mother was not in a position of power or influence. Even if she had been raised in a middle-class or bourgeois environment, she had to prove herself to be totally impoverished before she could apply for the allowance. Although she may have maintained some cultural or social capital, she no longer had the material capital to assert her demands in quite the way she might have wished.

The investigator's words also must be interpreted with caution. Senior administrators often evaluated investigators by assessing the latter's case file reports. Consequently, the investigator usually wrote with an audience in mind. She did not want to be interpreted as being either too sympathetic nor too callous towards her client. Neither did she want to be perceived as too independent-minded, questioning the authority of her superiors. In all, a great deal of the investigator's reports are justifications for actions taken.

As a result, the OMA case file provides a site from which to observe a number of complex and unequal power relationships between investigator and client, investigator and other administrators, the bureaucracy and the community, and the community and the single mother in question. Through these relationships meanings of gender, motherhood, the role of the state, and the role of the community are constantly being challenged and reasserted. It is the case file as a site of contestation that makes this source so rich and yet so difficult to distil.

The Case File: A Site of Contestation and Resistance

The period leading up to the introduction of the OMA was one of tremendous social flux. Rapid industrialization and large-scale immigration greatly altered the social and economic fabric of Canadian society. Industrialization led to dangerous working conditions that resulted in incapacitation or early deaths for many male breadwinners. The dissolution of many families was further exacerbated by the First World War and the 1918 influenza epidemic. Consequently, the number of widows, deserted, and unwed mothers increased, as did the accounts of neglected and delinquent children. Women and children were often forced to work at unhealthy and dangerous jobs. There was a great fear that the family unit was being destroyed. The combined effect of urbanization and industrialization made the poor more visible and, simultaneously, produced the emergence of a middle class who were anxious to solidify their new-found socio-economic position. The middle class were concerned about their declining birth rate in relation to the working class. They believed this could lead to 'degeneration' or a deterioration in the moral fibre of the province's citizens. Concerned, also, that ethnic-minority immigrants had higher fertility rates and would overwhelm the white Anglo-Celtic population, middle-class social reformers demanded state intervention in an effort to bolster that population against potential 'race suicide.'

These changing class and race relations had a particular impact upon women. With industrialization came the separation of home from work and the removal of at least bourgeois women from productive activities. As a result, women's identity increasingly came to be focused on their role as mothers. Some white Anglo-Celtic middle-class women used the increasing social emphasis on motherhood to assert a position for themselves in the public sphere. Welfare reforms such as Mothers' Allowances provided an opportunity for them to establish themselves as maternal experts and promote their version of the ideal family, with husbands as the sole breadwinner and mothers and children in the home. This familial ideology was influential, even though most working-class and immigrant families were not able to adhere to it. Once the OMA was enacted in 1920, certain white Anglo-Celtic middle-class women were able to benefit directly from it as OMA investigators. These investigators were the most visible embodiment of OMA administraton as they 'visited' homes, determining who was and was not worthy of the allowance.

Social work was an emerging profession and the case file was viewed by the investigator as a means not only to define the 'professional' but simultaneously to construct the 'other.' The professional investigator's very purpose and essence stood in opposition to the client's. Consequently, the investigator's financial security and social position were established through this unequal power relationship; the investigator would be adamant to affirm and solidify that imbalance. Hence, the case file was indeed a site of continuous struggle through numerous encounters between worker and client. Some of these encounters would be formal and circumscribed by the newly established bureaucratic rules, such as the initial application procedure. Other encounters would permit more discretionary decision making on the part of the social worker and permit the client to cajole, plead, defy, or otherwise attempt to get her own needs met. These needs or wants could be completely contrary to the goals of the policy.[6]

Most of the investigators were not trained social workers. Initially, more than three hundred people applied for these positions and those chosen were often women with public-health or educational backgrounds but no formal social-work training; usually they owed their appointments to good political connections.[7] For most of these women it was their first opportunity to participate in the paid workforce. During the first decade of the OMA there were between seventeen and nineteen investigators, the majority of whom were unmarried women.[8] Each of the investigators was assigned a large region of the province to cover. According to their letters, they had exhausting schedules, travelling alone by rail, buggy, car, or foot from one home to another. A day in the life of one investigator involved a drive of '120 miles over bad roads on Saturday, 40 on Sunday 45 the following Thursday and 80 on Friday.'[9] Such a life was both exhilarating and exhausting for independent-minded single women. In 1921 each investigator was responsible for an average of 156 cases, and by the end of the decade this figure had risen to approximately 300.[10]

These untrained investigators attempted to draw upon both early charity work and the newer scientific social-work practices. Nineteenth-century charity workers concentrated upon moral issues, believing that economic deprivation was at least partly due to immoral behaviour such as drinking, promiscuity, and unsanitary habits. In order to curb these tendencies, nineteenth-century charity workers would visit, advise, and guide the poor towards a moral and thrifty life-style. In one sense the 'visits' conducted by investigators were a departure from previous welfare practice in that they were carried out by the state, rather than by private organizations. With the exception of Children's Aid Society activities, this was the first time 'an agent of Queen's Park was figuratively parachuted into the fringes of the province to inquire into basic social problems.'[11] Yet at the same time much about these 'visits' was familiar. The word 'investigators' itself connotes the type of detailed, intrusive work associated with earlier philanthropic activities. As in nineteenth-century charity work, moral concerns tended to dominate economic issues. As well as a verbal inquiry, there would be a number of forms to fill and certificates to peruse. Upon the investigator's detailed report, a local board consisting of volunteer community leaders would approve or disapprove of the case. Their recommendation would then be sent to the provincial OMA Commission to make the final pronouncement. If the allowance was granted, the investigators would make visits to the home, whenever possible, to ensure that the regulations were carried out. These visits were, for the most part, unannounced, and if the applicant was out a calling card would be left and a return visit made. In difficult cases, the investigator would visit 'almost daily ... keeping the mother constantly mindful of what was expected of her.'[12] Thus, these investigators had a great deal of power to influence a needy mother's future.

This is not to suggest that this power went unchallenged. An examination of 1920s case files reveals the many different ways clients resisted bureaucratic regulations, yet had their own needs at least partially met. Collective struggle was difficult if not impossible given the isolation and social stigma experienced by the clients. Instead, clients were more apt to resist in an *individual* manner.

Most of the clients initiated the contact with the social worker through the application process. This does not mean that the client controlled this unequal power relationship. But it does mean that the applicant did enter this relationship with some understanding of its difficulties, and yet of its potential to give her some economic security. Consequently, the application process alone does not permit us to see the applicant as a victim of an intrusive and oppressive policy. Using the 'powers of the weak,' these women did everything in their power to obtain the allowance.[13] What they lacked in resources they replaced with creativity and determination. One of the most frequently reported acts of resistance was lying or withholding information. They would hide information from the administrators and enlist the help of community leaders in their struggle.

Mothers often withheld or falsified information about their children or presented illegitimate children as legitimate. Since a mother was no longer eligible for the allowance when the child reached sixteen years, some mothers lied to the social worker about the child's age. The child had to be in regular school attendance in order to be eligible, but a number of mothers ignored this rule. One mother allowed her son to skip school, stating that 'she did not believe in education.'[14] More than one lied and said their children regularly attended school, when the children were doing full-time work.[15]

Any socializing with men was also carefully concealed from the prying eyes of the investigator where possible. Male boarders were a site for contestation. The policy on taking boarders was contradictory at best. Insofar as boarding brought money into the home and did not require the mother to leave the children, this type of work was encouraged. But having one male boarder was positively disallowed. And it only took one Melva Turmin, who ran away with a boarder, to convince the regulators that they had every reason to fear the male boarder. No one would have denied that Melva Turmin had a difficult life, caring for her two children and an ailing husband almost twenty years her senior who was in a sanatorium. But, as her neighbour explained to the local board, 'Mrs. Turmin had no possible excuse for taking in a boarder, let alone running away with him, knowing him to be a married man who had deserted his wife and two small children in the Old Country, and I consider it a direct slap in the face to those friends who provided so liberally for her and family, and to the citizens in general, by her misconduct ... Personally, I don't think this class of people ought to be a burden on the citizens, but should be deported.'[16] Even having a male caller was grounds in itself for dismissal, but occasionally administrators would continue the allowance of a mother who was found socializing with men if they felt it was in the greater interests of society. For example, Velma Austin had defied all regulations by socializing with a number of men. Yet because this mother had contracted venereal disease, the OMA administrators decided to continue the cheques in an effort to control Velma's VD. According to the city clerk, '[The Investigator] says she [Velma] is saucy and impudent: doubtful whether she should be getting the allowance at all, but it is the only way they can insist on her taking the treatments.'[17] Thus the mothers' allowance cheque served as a bribe for mandatory VD treatment.

Occasionally mothers bravely asserted their own needs in the face of OMA regulations. In Mary McLean's case, the investigator said, 'I have found her very abusive in her manner when questioned in regard to any of her affairs and she has been reported to me as living under rather doubtful conditions. She was at one time helped by the Catholic people and now claims that she is a Protestant. I would not think that this woman would be a right person for the Mothers' Allowance.' Mary complained about the unfair administration of the Mothers' Allowance. She wrote, 'When I called ... [the investigator] on the telephone the other day and asked her if she had done any thing for me. Oh no because I am not able to bribe her or [the city clerk] or give them a Bottle when they want it.'[18]

At times a mother assumed the subject position expected of her by the social worker, only to discard it once the worker terminated the visit. I have conducted a series of interviews with single mothers who receive welfare in the late 1990s. These recipients spoke at length about how they 'perform' the expected attitude for the worker, well aware that it is a temporary performance to ensure the monthly welfare cheque.[19] There is reason to believe that welfare clients in the 1920s may have conducted similar performances. It is, however, very difficult to provide evidence of this conduct. How do you locate resistance of this kind? How do you determine what is and is not a performance?

The one possible evidence of performance is revealed in the cases of false repentance. Often a mother would try to get her needs met by proclaiming that she had 'reformed.' Repentance could take the form of the mother attending the local church, refusing to associate with 'questionable' friends, or proclaiming that she was a 'reformed woman.' In Maud Reinhart's case, the mother 'has been in [to see the investigator] and states that she is reforming; she wants Mothers' Allowance. [A local board member] is satisfied and [the City Relief Department officer] is trying to get work for her.'[20] In this case, because the mother repented, the local board agreed to re-consider her case and, as well, attempt to find employment for her. She was later rejected when it was discovered that she had not given up her old ways.

Other mothers clearly resisted the humble, grateful subject position. This was evident in Elizabeth Carpenter's case file: 'Mrs. C immediately greet[ed] the worker with a long list of her needs and felt the assistance from the Welfare Dept. was very inadequate and complained at length ... John [her son] talked a good deal about the family need and was rather demanding in his attitude. Albert [another son] is still at school but already shows evidence of the begging tendency his mother and older brother have.'[21] Race and class did have an impact on a mother's ability to challenge the subservient role expected of her. Generally, those mothers who had previously enjoyed some stature in the community more aggressively pursued the OMA administration. These mothers often had contacts with professional men who lobbied on their behalf. Also they more convincingly demonstrated they were attempting to achieve the middle-class ideal of a full-time mother. After all, many of them had done so before their husband's death or desertion.

Ethnic-minority mothers who similarly tried to appeal to leaders in the community did not meet with the same approval. For instance, Eliza Jones, an Afro-Canadian single mother, was considered suspicious because the investigator noted that her husband, who had recently died, had been a community activist 'in favour of uplifting the colored people.' The investigator concluded, 'I have known these people for along time and they are quite aggressive and able to look after their own affairs.'[22]

The clients were not the only ones to raise objections to the OMA administration. While it was overwhelmingly the case that community members volunteered to scrutinize and condemn OMA recipients, occasionally these people would defend the clients and protest about the administration. Labour representatives and local administrators, in particular, were known to complain about the intrusive role and the 'holier-than-thou' attitude of these provincially appointed investigators.[23] Often the local board administrators raised concerns about the process, as one former member of the Simcoe County local board explained:

As a former secretary on our local board, I had a good chance to observe the workings of this authority. I heard complaints about the domineering attitude of the investigators and was myself the victim of it, if reports were true. Why any fur-coated investigator should be allowed to go into a widow's home and demand that she give an account to her of every cent of her allowance is more than I could ever swallow for justice or sympathy ... Why is all this interference with widows tolerated, and not applied to the rest of us?[24]

Similarly, labour representatives also charged that these OMA investigators were class-biased and insensitive when one needy mother who worked part time as a waitress had her allowance cut off. The investigator had stated publicly that 'waitresses were the lowest types of girls that walked.' The mother was told her allowance was cut because 'a letter had been received by the board stating she was running around with men and had been brought home intoxicated in a taxicab ... The story of her being brought home in a taxi was started when she was carried home [from work] suffering from burns ... [caused] by scalding coffee knocked from her tray.' The commission refused to say who wrote the letter and the mother was given no opportunity to deny the allegations. In outrage, local labour officials declared that this was an 'attack upon the character of the best types of women – those who worked for a living to maintain their families – [and] would not go unchallenged.'[25] Labour officials lobbied the provincial government on behalf of this woman and complained about the intrusive, class-biased investigation by OMA administrators, but the allowance was not reinstated.

In a few isolated cases, businesses came to the rescue of the destitute mothers. For instance, the industrial nurse from Beatty Brothers Manufacturing Company wrote the local board explaining their aid to Sonya Tanovich: 'We visited her in London shortly ago and found her having a very hard time to get along. We purchased food and clothing for her through Beatty Brothers Welfare, but of course will not be able to keep on providing for her. We would appreciate it very much if you could let us know whether Mrs Tanovich will be receiving the Mothers Allowance or not, also if she will be receiving it when could we expect the payments to start.'[26] In another instance, the dentist of the town of Collingwood was known for treating the children of Mothers' Allowance recipients free of charge.[27] Some local proprietors were eager to have an allowance granted to a mother if this meant that she could better afford their products.[28] Very occasionally, a neighbour would come to the aid of a single mother. And in one unique case, a group of ratepayers for the Township of Bayham, Elgin County, signed a petition requesting the local board to 'reconsider the case of Susan Rodette who at one time received aid through the Allowance fund but was refused any more aid. This is a case that should be given some help.'[29]

Even more rarely, investigators themselves would resist administrative pressures and bend the rules. OMA recipients generally viewed the investigators as intrusive, but occasionally a supportive relationship developed between them. Some lonely mothers would write to the investigator, encouraging a friendly correspondence. Because the investigator travelled widely and knew many people, some mothers used them as a source of contacts to find summer jobs or boarding places for their daughters. Such 'constructive and rehabilitative work' was encouraged, although investigators were cautioned not to weaken the beneficiary's feeling of independence or erode the family's own initiative through this intensive guidance.[30] This supportive relationship, however, was an exception to the general rule. As a result of her busy schedule and heavy case load, the investigator was rarely able to develop such a role, even if she was so inclined.

From the evidence presented, it is clear that a variety of people actively challenged or resisted the administrative rules of the OMA policy. Clients, community leaders, and investigators attempted in their own ways to contest regulations with which they did not agree. Much of this help provided was patronizing at best, but their efforts do suggest that the policy was not uniformly endorsed. Instead, the policy was a site for the contestation of class, gender, and race relations.

Conclusion

Case files are among both the most challenging but also the most rewarding sources for those of us who want to retrieve the voices of the less powerful. We are never able to extract the complete story of a client's life, for the story is often fragmentary, partial, or distorted. It is rare that a recipient was able to record her own words on the OMA application form. And even when she wrote letters to the administration, the single mother was always aware that she had to tread carefully. She could not complain too vehemently about her treatment if she wanted to keep her allowance. Given these limitations, it is still possible for the case files to provide us with an opportunity to observe negotiations between administrators and recipients during the first decade. Because both the policy and the profession of social work were new during this era, the relationship between welfare worker and single mother was particularly open to negotiation. With some sensitivity and reading between the lines, we can at least begin to acknowledge how state policies and procedures did not go unchallenged and were, instead, a site of struggle. From the evidence provided in this paper, it is clear that single mothers and their allies contested the definitions of eligibility, the intrusive administrative procedures used, and the authority of the administrators. In doing so they attempted to get their needs met, however unsatisfactorily, within a system that was often insensitive to their hardships.

Notes

I would like to thank the editors of this book for their patience and their helpful suggestions, Lykke de la Cour for our many discussions of the trials and tribulations of case file research, and Rose-Marie Kennedy for encouraging me, despite my initial resistance, to engage in a little postmodern thought.

1 Linda Gordon, *Heroes of Their Own Lives: The Politics and History of Family Violence, Boston, 1880–1960* (New York: Penguin Books 1989), vi

2 In order to protect the anonymity of former OMA applicants and to meet the terms under which I was permitted access to case records, I have used fictitious names and, in recounting case histories, have either eliminated or modified biographical details.

3 Andrew Armitage, *Social Welfare in Canada: Ideals and Realities* (Toronto: McClelland and Stewart 1975), 272

4 Archives of Ontario (AO), RG 29, series 36, box 1, file 1.2

5 D.B. Weldon Library (DBW), Western Regional Collection, London, Ontario, Mothers' Allowance case files, City of London, 1920–40, 'Letter from Inspector to City Clerk, August 19, 1926'

6 Through her examination of the International Institute, a Toronto agency for immigrant families, Franca Iacovetta explores both the multiple encounters between client and worker and the often pragmatic ways that immigrants utilized the agency to meet their own specific needs. See Iacovetta, 'Making "New Canadians": Social Workers, Women, and the Reshaping of Immigrant Families,' in Franca Iacovetta and Mariana Valverde, eds, *Gendered Conflicts: New Essays in Women's History* (Toronto: University of Toronto Press 1992), 261–303.

7 Margaret Kirkpatrick Strong, *Public Welfare Administration in Canada* (Chicago 1930), 135, cited in James Struthers, *The Limits of Affluence: Welfare in Ontario, 1920–1970* (Toronto: University of Toronto Press 1994), 33 n. 40. For a more general discussion regarding the emergence of professional social work, see James Struthers, '"Lord Give Us Men": Women and Social Work in English Canada, 1918–1953,' in Allan Moscovitch and Jim Albert, eds, *The 'Benevolent' State: The Growth of Welfare in Canada* (Toronto: Garamond Press 1987), 126–43.

8 'First Annual Report of the OMA Commission, 1920–21,' 15–16, and 'Seventh Annual Report of the OMA Commission, Fiscal Years 1925–26, 1926–27,' 23

9 'Second Annual Report of the OMA Commission, 1921–22,' 21

10 In 1921 there were 2660 OMA beneficiaries and 17 investigators; therefore the average caseload was 156 families. By 1922 the number of beneficiaries had increased by 33.8 per cent, but the number of investigators remained constant, with a caseload of approximately 209 cases. In 1929 the chairman claimed that the caseload averaged 300 families. The calculations for 1921 and 1922 were made by Carol Cole, 'An Examination of the Mothers' Allowance System in Ontario, 1914–1940,'

unpublished M.A. thesis, History Department, University of Waterloo, 1989, 85; see also 'Ninth Annual Report of the OMA Commission, 1928–1929,' 5.

11 Charles Johnston, *E.C. Drury: Agrarian Idealist* (Toronto: University of Toronto Press 1986), 152

12 'Second Annual Report of the OMA Commission, 1921–22,' 30

13 This term, 'powers of the weak,' was initially introduced by Elizabeth Janeway. Whereas Janeway associates these powers with all women, Linda Gordon discusses the many ingenious ways that women, as survivors of family violence, have struggled. See Janeway, *Powers of the Weak* (New York: Knopf 1980) and Gordon, *Heroes of Their Own Lives*, esp. chaps 8 and 9.

14 DBW, Mothers' Allowance case files, London, 'Letter from the Local Board, January 20, 1925'

15 'Second Annual Report of the OMA Commission, 1921–22,' 26

16 DBW, Mothers' Allowance case files, London, 'Letter written to the London City Clerk, April 26, 1926'

17 Ibid., 'London City Clerk's account of case,' n.d.

18 Ibid., 'Letter from mother to Local Board, May 10, 1927'

19 See Margaret Hillyard Little, *No Car, No Radio Liquor Permit: The Moral Regulation of Single Mothers in Ontario, 1920–1997* (Toronto: Oxford University Press, forthcoming), chaps 6 and 7.

20 DBW, Mothers' Allowance Case Files, London, 'Letter from City Clerk to investigator, January 31, 1930'

21 Ibid., 'Report from Local Children's Aid Society to Local Board, 1928'

22 Ibid., 'Letter from Relief Department Inspector to City Clerk, April 24, 1931'

23 One local board member charged that the investigators 'seem to be working from a distinctly holier-than-thou point of view and as a result are bringing mixed feelings of fear and gratitude to hundreds of benefactors.' National Archives of Canada (NAC), Kelso Papers, vol. 24, file: Newspaper clippings, Mothers' Allowances, 1925–7, 1933, 'Letter to the Editor,' *Toronto Star*, 13 Dec. 1926

24 Letter from Mrs E. Nolan to *Toronto Star*, 3 Feb. 1926

25 NAC, Kelso Papers, vol. 24, File: Newspaper clippings, Mothers' Allowances, 1925–7, 1933, 'Widowed Waitress Stoutly Defended by Local Laborites: Allegation Rouses Officials to Ask for Government Explanation,' Toronto *Globe*, 13 Dec. 1926

26 DBW, Mothers' Allowance case files, London, 'Letter from Beatty Brothers Manufacturing to Local OMA Board, November 15, 1937'

27 Simcoe County Archives, Simcoe County Local Mothers' Allowance Board minutes, 1920–57, 'Meeting, August 7, 1924'

28 Elgin County Library (ECL), Mothers' Allowance case files, Elgin County, 'Letter to Mrs. B. Graham, investigator, October 26, 1926'

29 This letter includes signatures from two reeves, three councillors, a treasurer, and a

superintendent. ECL, Mothers' Allowance case files, Elgin County, 'Letter from several rate-payers of the Township of Bayham, June 1922.' There are, however, several examples of ratepayers, such as the Danforth Park Ratepayers Association, demanding that the provincial government be more restrictive in OMA administration. OA, RG 49, reel 588, file: Mothers' Pensions, 1920–6, 'Government Is Asked to Revise Widows' Act,' *Toronto Star*, 28 Oct. 1926
30 'First Annual Report of the OMA Commission, 1920–21,' 12

11

Patient Perspectives in Psychiatric Case Files

LYKKE DE LA COUR and GEOFFREY REAUME

... and then that accident happened and I never knew until after my baby was born, when it was four days old the Dr. told me and I got hysterical. I did not care whether I was dead or alive. My brother-in-law took the baby and I never seen it since, I then was taken ... to the General Hospital and I told you what happened there. Dr. Clair I write you out this in case you think I am ashamed of my past life, allow me to tell you I am not ... If you only let me out of here. I am not strong physically but I think I am all right mentally.

Agnes D., Toronto Hospital for the Insane, 1911[1]

Agnes D.'s account provides a perspective rarely found in the field of psychiatric history – the voice and the story of the patient. Despite the literature that has, since the early 1980s, advocated a social history of madness and psychiatric institutionalization, very little historical work has been done on patients.[2] In particular, relatively few studies have examined historical developments in terms of the viewpoints of patients themselves. A considerable amount of research in the field takes a 'top down' approach, examining professional, institutional, and therapeutic developments as they pertain to the advancement of the psychiatric profession.[3] In such studies, the evolution of psychiatry is often presented either as a 'progressive march forward' in the care and management of the mentally ill or, more negatively, as a location for social control. In these types of studies the actual experiences of patients and their responses to institutional and therapeutic developments are generally ignored. More recently, some historians have turned their attention to the study of psychiatric patients.[4] These studies examine themes such as the reasons for committals to psychiatric hospitals, the dominant social, economic, and medical factors characterizing resident psychiatric populations and the therapeutic practices encountered by patients in psychiatric facilities. This research provides valuable details on the collective backgrounds and therapeutic experiences of psychiatric patients. However, few of these studies offer insights into patients' own views on the nature and the meaning of mental 'illness' and psychiatric hospitalization.[5] This paper attempts to expand upon the existing historiography on psychiatric patients by examining the information contained in patient case files.

Psychiatric case files evolved in the early twentieth century as a clinical method for recording extensive personal and medical histories on individual patients. Replacing nineteenth-century casebooks and registers that recorded basic patient data, case files were designed to assist physicians in the diagnosis and treatment of psychiatric patients. These files are an incredibly rich source for historians, as they contain a wide range of documents that provide useful particulars on both the asylum and its resident population.[6] Psychiatric case files generally contain medical dispositions certifying insanity; admission forms detailing the patient's personal, medical, and psychiatric history; clinical charts that note the patient's daily behaviour and any medical treatments given during their stay; psychological reports and IQ tests; conference reports assigning diagnoses; notices of discharge or death; and, in some cases, correspondence by or about patients. The forms located in patient files were written primarily by medical and administrative staff. However, when approached with care and used judiciously, these documents provide important glimpses into the perceptions and viewpoints of psychiatric patients.[7] They also reveal aspects of the actual operations of psychiatric hospitals and the ways in which factors such as class, gender, and race intersect with psychiatric institutionalization.[8]

By drawing on information contained in the case files of patients hospitalized at Ontario Hospitals in Toronto and Cobourg, Ontario, from roughly the 1900s to the 1950s, this paper seeks to demonstrate the value of the case file approach to the retrieval of a patient perspective in psychiatric history.[9] Both the Toronto and the Cobourg Ontario Hospitals treated patients deemed to be suffering from acute and chronic mental illness. However, the Ontario Hospital in Cobourg admitted only women patients to its facilities, and after the mid-1930s it increasingly provided care to women labelled 'mentally deficient.' Whether they were viewed as 'mad' or 'defective,' male and female patients at both institutions had a great deal to say about their experiences of psychiatric hospitalization. By examining three themes – admissions and illness, patient recreation and leisure, and patient labour within psychiatric facilities – this essay seeks to highlight how case files can provide important details on the experiences of patients, details that are crucial to a fuller understanding and analysis of the operations of psychiatric hospitals. Medical historian Steven Noll argues that it is only by utilizing patient records that one can begin to see the true dimensions of the 'human side' of institutionalization.[10] We would add that it is only by using case files that the full historical record emerges, since the men and women who were incarcerated in psychiatric facilities, such as the Ontario Hospitals in Toronto and Cobourg, have an enormous amount to tell historians about what they saw, what they experienced, and how they perceived the events that transpired. As the following discussion demonstrates, patients tried in a variety of ways to exert control and influence over their encounters with the psychiatric system. An awareness of this agency is important for a fuller understanding of the operations of psychiatric facilities.

Admissions and Illness

Most studies of psychiatric hospitals tend to portray patients as passive participants in the processes of psychiatric institutionalization. However, the narratives contained in the case files of the Toronto and Cobourg Ontario Hospitals suggest that many patients actively strove to influence and shape their encounters with the psychiatric system. For example, some patients sought out their own admissions to psychiatric facilities. In 1911, Patrick M., a fifty-three-year-old unskilled labourer, had himself committed to the Toronto asylum because he knew he was 'not all there' mentally and that 'he was of the opinion that something was the matter with his brain.' According to Patrick, he hoped that 'a course of rest and treatment' at the hospital would soon restore him to his normal state of health.[11] Similarly, Munroe F., another Toronto patient, admitted upon his entry to hospital that 'he was very much run down and nervous.'[12] Mildred B., a Cobourg patient, had herself admitted in 1920 when her hallucinations, delusions, and hysterical attacks finally became unbearable. As staff noted in her admission record, 'The reason she gives for coming here is that she is nearly crazy.'[13] Although individuals who sought their own admissions to hospital constituted only a minority of the patients admitted to the Ontario Hospitals at Toronto and Cobourg, stories such as Patrick's, Munroe's, and Mildred's are important, as they suggest that not all patients committed to psychiatric facilities were passive victims of hospitalization. Their accounts illustrate that some patients held the belief or at least the hope that admission to a psychiatric facility would be curative and, hence, beneficial to their mental health.

Another way in which some patients were active participants in the processes of institutionalization was in their opposition to psychiatric hospitalization. Resistance to institutionalization at a psychiatric facility was always a precarious undertaking for patients. On the one hand, patient opposition was interpreted by the medical staff as simply further indication of a patient's disturbed mental state, and patients who resisted their admission to hospital by lashing out at attending staff or by becoming exceedingly agitated found themselves subjected to severe repercussions for their actions. Lorraine J., for instance, who protested 'very strongly' her committal to the Toronto asylum, in 1911, was physcially 'taken' to a ward and then placed in restraints and sedated.[14] Grace S., a Cobourg patient, received similar treatment when she opposed admission to what she perceived as a 'dirty old Asylum.' The admitting doctor noted in her case file: 'says she does not want to be confined in an Asylum as she is not crazy and is afraid some of the patients will hurt her.'[15] On the other hand, evidence in the patient files for the Toronto and Cobourg Ontario Hospitals indicates that opposition to institutionalization worked effectively for some patients and led to their release from hospital. For example, Emma S., a patient who repeatedly maintained that she had been wrongfully confined in the Cobourg hospital, in the early 1920s, secured a discharge from the facility after engaging a lawyer to fight on her behalf.[16] Another Cobourg patient, Elsie M., managed to obtain her release only two months after she was admitted to hospital (and despite opposition by the medical staff) by convincing her family to press for her discharge on the grounds that institutionalization had not produced any positive change in her condition.[17] In 1910, Walter D., a patient at the Toronto asylum who, like Emma S., asserted that he had been wrongfully confined to a psychiatric facility, successfully secured his own release by manipulating a locked door at the hospital with some sort of self-fashioned instrument and escaping.[18] As these stories suggest, when patients had access to the financial resources, the familial supports, or the technical skills needed to help secure a release, they were sometimes successful in their efforts at resisting psychiatric institutionalization.

Patients also strove to influence their encounters with the psychiatric system in terms of the processes associated with medical diagnoses. Comments by patients about their own mental 'illness' appear quite frequently in the case files for the Toronto and Cobourg hospitals and constitute some of the most fascinating aspects of the information contained in these records. Patients definitely had their own views as to what they were feeling and what they believed was causing their distress. However, their claims were more often than not either dismissed by medical staff or simply not acknowledged, even when they were expressed in very clear, non-delusional terms. It is in this dynamic that the full implications of the social imbalances in power relations between those being admitted and those doing the admitting are revealed. Patients themselves generally attributed the causes of their 'illnesses' to actual life traumas. For example, male patients frequently referred to accidents, fights, or stresses associated with the workplace as the chief cause of their mental problems. Women patients

PROVINCIAL LUNATIC ASYLUM.

Relatives or Guardians, with the assistance of the Medical Attendant, are required to give according to the best of their knowledge, precise answers to the following queries, or as many of them as may be applicable to the case of the Patient proposed for admission into the Provincial Lunatic Asylum :

QUERIES. *June 10th 1845*   ANSWERS.

1st. How long has the patient been insane? *2 months*

2nd. If the patient has been oftener than once insane, when did the malady first occur; how often, before this last attack ; in what form, and of what duration? *he was insane about 5 years back, he was affected with brain fever*

3rd. Before the symptoms of lunacy became manifest, was there any unusual depression or elevation of spirits; or was any alteration observed in the temper, disposition, opinions, conduct, sleep, appetite, state of bowels, or health of the patient; and how long before lunacy, were any precursory symptoms observed ?

4th. What have been the prominent features of the malady? Has any obvious change in its form occurred; and does it appear to be increasing, declining, or stationary? *a continuous Excitement; no Change —*

5th. Are there lucid intervals, or any great remissions or exacerbations; and do such changes occur at uncertain times, or at stated periods? *No*

6th. Does the patient rave indifferently on various subjects, or chiefly on one; and what is that subject? Mention particularly any permanent or remarkable illusions. *He raves generally about the fire which happened in London where he suffered some loss*

7th. Has the patient ever made any premeditated or dangerous attempt to injure any other person, and how? *He made some attempt at biting his brother —*

8th. Has the patient ever threatened or attempted to commit any act of self-violence, and by what means? *He has threatened to take some Laudanum —*

9th. Is the patient prone to tear clothes, or to break windows or furniture ? *Yes*

10th. Is the patient married or single; and was any relative of the patient ever insane. *Single , no*

Medical history form and questionnaire, Toronto Asylum, 1845. (Archives of the History of Canadian Psychiatry and Mental Health Services, Griffin-Greenland slides, IV-15) related their emotional and mental debilities more to issues pertaining to unequal gender relations and the domestic sphere. Patients from non-white backgrounds often cited experiences of racism as a contributing factor to their difficulties. However, the medical staff at both the Toronto and Cobourg Ontario Hospitals tended to regard these personal accounts as either 'fabrications' or indications in and of themselves of mental disorders.

Cases where the staff gave no credit to the patient's own perspective on their illness abound in the case files for the Toronto and Cobourg Ontario Hospitals. Take, for instance, Patrick M., who was referred to in the discussion on patient responses to admission. As noted, Patrick began experiencing various mental problems and had himself committed to the Toronto asylum. He attributed his problems directly to a head injury that he had sustained several months before his admission. Upon the advice of his family physician, he had sought out treatment at the Toronto facility. However, following his admission, medical staff at the hospital paid no attention whatsoever to the issue of the accident or how it may have figured into Patrick's illness. Instead, the psychiatrists focused on Patrick's behaviour and his personal history, especially his employment history, which had been fairly unstable. As an unskilled labourer, Patrick had 'knocked from pillar to post' for most of his life through a series of temporary, manual-labour jobs. Staff at the Toronto hospital took this to be a strong indication that he had probably not been normal 'for good many years.' Hence, they diagnosed him as a 'high grade imbecile' and ordered him permanently institutionalized.

Dismissive and discrediting remarks on the part of the medical staff were particularly evident in the files of the women patients, where references to domestic difficulties, violence, and sexual abuse were routinely dismissed as 'hallucinations,' 'delusions of persecution,' or simply 'untrue' fabrications. For example, staff at the Cobourg asylum felt that the 'powers of perception' of Fanny C., who was admitted to the hospital in 1921, were very much impaired, as she 'always harps back to her trouble, first the death of her husband and then the trouble with her sister.'[19] Similar remarks were made by staff members with regards to another Cobourg patient, Marianne H. In her file it was noted: 'Her powers of perception are much impaired ... [O]n carrying on a conversation with her, she invariably returns to the subject of her husband's death. One minute she will be laughing quite heartily and the next speaking about the funeral. It seems impossible for her to get away from it.'[20] In a particularly interesting case, Elsie C. had her claims of domestic violence dismissed by the psychiatrists. Admitted on a lieutenant-governor's warrant, Elsie had been removed from her home to a jail after complaints by her husband and children that she had committed assaults on them and, hence, was a threat to the family.

The doctors who examined her in jail remarked on the medical certifying forms that '[s]he has delusions of persecution claiming that her husband and children have all turned against her and beat and call her vile names, such not being the case.' However, the judge who reviewed her case had a different perspective on Elsie's situation. Apparently, the justice of the peace knew Elsie's family and, while he acknowledged that Elsie was indeed experiencing some mental difficulties, he attributed this condition directly to the 'neglect of a drunken husband causing despair.' He went on to inform the court that Elsie, before her breakdown, had been a 'temperate' and 'industrious' woman of 'good conduct.' In the judge's estimation, she had been 'a quiet woman satisfied with home surroundings.' The judge did finally order Elsie's committal to a psychiatric hospital, but he noted on his official report: 'Not idiotic not imbecile and under proper treatment and good surroundings ought to recover.'[21]

In a similar fashion, patients from non-white backgrounds who attributed the origins of their mental or emotional difficulties to experiences of racism found their claims dismissed or ignored by the psychiatric profession. Non-white patients constituted only a small number of the patients admitted to the Toronto and Cobourg Ontario Hospitals. Generally, they came from Black, Asian, and Native backgrounds and, like their white counterparts, they had their own views as to the causes of their mental debilities. More often than not, non-white patients ascribed their problems to factors related to racial discrimination. But, as with other patients at the Toronto and Cobourg hospitals, their views were not taken seriously by the medical staff. For instance, doctors at the Toronto asylum interpreted as inordinately 'peculiar' the fact that Sandra T., an Afro-Canadian woman, hid pieces of iron and sticks about her 'to use as weapons on the white ... people she calls her enemies.'[22] Mary L., a young Native woman who was admitted to Cobourg in the fall of 1946 as a 'mental defective,' protested her psychiatric committal on the grounds that her limited mental capabilities had to do with the fact that she had received no academic training at the Roman Catholic mission school she had attended.[23] Esther H., the sixteen-year-old daughter of a Jamaican couple, was admitted to Cobourg, in the mid-1950s, following her expulsion from school for chronic misbehaviour and for fighting with other children. After Esther was expelled from classes, the school reported her to the Department of Health, where a psychiatric assessment was done, and she was subsequently committed to Cobourg as a 'high grade moron.' In their admission remarks, doctors at the Cobourg hospital focused on Esther's problematic behaviour – her 'very foolish actions,' her 'irresponsible attitude,' her 'quick and impulsive judgement,' and her 'violent outbursts' - all of which they attributed to her low level of intelligence. However, Esther herself linked her behaviour to experiences of racism at school. As the staff noted in her case file:

'Esther is very sensitive ... to the fact that she is coloured and has become involved in fights with those who have called her a nigger.'[24]

Some patients, then, were active participants in the processes associated with psychiatric institutionalization. However, their ability to control and shape their experiences, once hospitalized, could be influenced by their class, gender, and racial backgrounds. Moreover, patients' own accounts as to the causes of their mental difficulties bespeak the degree to which unequal social relations affected both the mental health of particular men and women and the type of health care they received. While patients undoubtedly constructed their own 'version of events' in the explanations that they gave to doctors as to the origins of their mental illnesses, patients' own perceptions of their health, as the above stories indicate, frequently highlighted problematic social circumstances as the causes of their mental problems. However, in ignoring or dismissing patient perspectives, psychiatric professionals contributed to the perpetuation of problematic social conditions by psychiatrizing, at an individual level, very real social problems and by failing to speak out, at a broader level, about the inequities their patients informed them about.

Patient Recreation and Leisure

References in case files are also useful in providing information on how inmates went about creating their own forms of recreation and leisure while confined, as the following example illustrates. On a summer day in 1918, it was reported in the clinical record for Cindy R., an inmate at the Toronto Hospital for the Insane, that she appeared at one of the front gates all 'dressed up' with her friend and fellow inmate Rochelle W. When asked what they were doing, Cindy said 'they were just going to have a look around,' after which they returned quietly to their living quarters at one of the cottages.[25] In this particular instance, it is possible to show how patients who did not have the good fortune of outside support could nevertheless find ways of enjoying themselves with a sort of self-directed 'internal outing' while still on the grounds of the hospital.

Cindy R., confined at the age of forty in 1897, spent the last thirty-three years of her life at the asylum, during which time no visitors were recorded. It is easy to imagine these two women, Cindy and Rochelle, one of whom it is certain had no outside support, deciding to treat themselves to a leisurely stroll around the grounds, dressed in their best clothes, as if going for a walk in a park. That they went to one of the gates on the edge of the grounds is especially intriguing, and it is worth speculating that the prospect of peering into the forbidden world beyond the mental institution was considered by these two patients as an added attraction to their outing. Such seemingly mundane pursuits would have made life more enjoyable for anyone while institutionalized, let alone for an isolated inmate for whom walking with a friend in their best clothing was something to look forward to while living such a constricted, lonely life.

The recording of leisurely activities in case files presents researchers with numerous possibilities to advance beyond the narrow focus of previous institutional histories, which have only discussed administrative-sponsored activities.[26] This is usually referred to in studies that place such activities within the context of moral therapy, in which organized leisure was intended as a way of helping people with distressed mental states. Patient-initiated forms of recreation and leisure reveal how inmates sought to have more of a say in the world in which they lived and where they tried to find solace from daily routine. In most entries, there tend to be comments about what the inmates did rather than what they said in this regard. Nevertheless, there are case files where the comments of people like Cindy offer a chance to get an idea of what patients were up to or thought about specific leisurely pursuits.

The most well-known inmate at Toronto until her death in 1924 was a well-off patient who called herself Angel Queen XIII. Known for her critical eye for style, Angel Queen extended her leisure activity to events beyond the asylum. Like other inmates, she enjoyed watching nearby parades as a form of entertainment, and one march in particular received her disapproval. Several years before she died, her clinical record noted that Angel Queen was 'very much put out at the Orangemen's parade,' declaring it the worst she had ever seen because they 'had no banners and regalia at all.'[27] In contrast, other inmates were quite satisfied with recreational pursuits they encountered outside of the institution. Patients who were 'trusted' at Cobourg were allowed unescorted town privileges. In references in their case files, their views about leisure are also preserved. Edna A. went every year to the nearby Roseneath Fair, which she enjoyed 'as she meets friends she knew when working out at Hastings.' Edna also went regularly to Salvation Army meetings in town, where she 'has made friends ... [T]hey understand her, and are kind to her.' It was also noted she was 'generous' in donating money to the Army.[28]

In both of these case files, it is possible to see how routine observations have left glimpses of what inmates did to find forms of relaxation. Angel Queen's comments leave us an impression of the type of activity that some inmates engaged in, and also show that even where they had merely a spectator role, supposedly 'insane' patients were active and interested observers of what was happening around them. The references to Edna's social activities in the community show how her desire to enjoy an outing was very much tied into her wish to be with friends. The fact that she was accepted at the Salvation Army would have made attending this group's functions especially welcoming. Thus, engaging in recreational activities could be as much a way of bolstering one's feeling of self-esteem among acquaintances as a form of diversion.

More common are entries that describe the response of patients to leisurely activities, though usually not in their own words. Mary B., confined for over thirty years at various institutions, spent part of her time at Cobourg tending to her garden by the boiler room, in which it was noted, she took a 'great interest.' Mary also wrote poetry. In a particularly telling entry, her medical observers noted that '[o]n the occasion of a slight outbreak of "crawlers," this patient has written a protest in the form of ... [a] poem.'[29] This reference reveals the way in which an inmate could transform a recreational activity - writing poetry - into a political commentary on hygienic conditions at the institution. Thus, leisure was not an exclusively neutral pursuit, but could capture patients' responses to their material circumstances.

Responses to the same form of leisure were not always consistent, but could vary over time or institution. Louise P. kept getting in trouble at Cobourg for smoking cigarettes, even though she was in her twenties. She liked to demonstrate her habit by 'showing off by blowing smoke in the air.' The medical recorder observed that it was 'vulgar to be smoking in the park so openly.'[30] On the other hand, Winston O., confined for over half a century in Toronto, 'knows where to go for tobacco' and was observed to be smoking his pipe in the asylum without interference from hospital staff.[31] It is clear from both these entries that Louise and Winston enjoyed themselves when puffing away. However, while Winston's smoking did not bother the medical recorder at Toronto, two decades later Louise's smoking earned the disapproval of the Cobourg recorder. Whether the latter was due to her being a woman, or to her smoking in public rather than in private, or simply to the reaction of one individual, is not clear.

Oral forms of leisure were another important source of entertainment for some inmates. At Cobourg, staff noted with regard to Mollie B. that she liked 'to gossip very much, will pass all her time this way if not supervised. Is always playing some silly trick on someone, and tells all who will listen about it.'[32] Wallace M. used his imagination to while away the time at Toronto, where he told stories ranging from 'catching whales with hook & line to travelling in far off countries gathering gold chains from trees.'[33] These activities by both patients suggest a desire to create their own imaginative forms of verbal entertainment. Whether this was due to boredom with their situation or a sense of humour, or a combination thereof, will have to remain unknown. However, it is evident from these entries that the entertainment that both of these people enjoyed by using their imagination was, at least in the case of Mollie, very much a response to her environment. She used stories about those around her, and their reactions to her 'silly trick[s]' as a way of relaxing and having what, for her, was a bit of fun. Interestingly, no references to male inmates engaging in 'gossip' have been uncovered for this paper. While it is impossible to know the content of Mollie's conversations that so irritated the hospital staff, the fact that her comments were framed in a way in which no male inmates at Toronto were described suggests the gender definition of discourse that may have been a factor in this description.

The most frequent entries on the subject of leisure and recreation are those that provide a different perspective on patient life without recording an inmate's words or response to events. One of the most active inmates in the pursuit of self-initiated entertainments at the Toronto Hospital for the Insane was Winston O., confined for more than the last fifty years of his life. The masculine nature of asylum leisure is very much in evidence when Winston's enormous output of creations are considered. Well into his seventies and eighties, this man not only played his violin for other patients on the ward, he also created this musical instrument with his own hands out of a box. Furthermore, he built, 'as a joke,' in 1912 a car that he drove around the asylum grounds, constructed an operational snow shovel, wheelbarrows, tubs, and buckets, worked on an airship for at least eighteen months, though it is not clear if it ever flew, made 'shady nooks' for himself to rest in during the warm weather, and skated and sailed an ice-boat on the asylum rink in the winter months.[34]

Winston put his skills to good use in the asylum, for his benefit and for other inmates who could hear his music and watch his latest creation unfold. What is particularly notable is the admiring tone of hospital officials in their observations about Winston. References to his physical resilience, especially as an elderly person, are common: 'He is a remarkably well preserved man of ... seventy-seven ... He is still able to swing an axe with most of the juniors.' Just as Mollie's conversational habits were framed by gender bias in the official records, so too were Winston's activities slanted by a masculine emphasis. Thus, Mollie's efforts to entertain herself were recorded in an unflattering light, whereas Winston was so obviously admired for keeping busy and physically fit during his recreational pursuits.

Yet, the clinical files make it clear that many patients were nowhere near as fortunate as Winston when it came to leisure. These sources also reveal the restrictive nature of recreation among different groups of patients: those who had parole of the grounds, patients who were able to venture out into the community, and inmates who remained confined on locked wards. Winston's creativity was very much tied in with his privileged status as one who could roam the grounds at will. Patients who remained locked up within the hospital had no options to pursue such activities – just what they could find to do on the ward.

This could include sitting in a screened-in verandah on the ward, or enjoying music and drinking large amounts of tea, as with Mavis M., who was noted to be otherwise lethargic while confined at Toronto for thirty-eight years.[35] The only chances that patients considered 'untrustworthy,' like Mavis, had to get out of their restricted environment, to go for a stroll and exercise, were staff-escorted walking parties.

This ability to enjoy freedom from being confined on a locked ward could be extended beyond the asylum grounds, with some patients being taken for trips in the community by staff. This occurred at Toronto with inmates attending the Canadian National Exhibition. As has been noted, at Cobourg, 'trusted' patients could even go into town unescorted by nurses. Mary B. went by herself to picture shows every week, attended church on Sundays, and went to picnics held by local groups as well as with another patient on the beach. Others, such as Laura P., liked to go shopping in town.[36]

Another way in which case files reveal a different perspective on patient life is the manner in which various patients experienced leisure with regard to class divisions within the asylum inmate population. For some patients, obtaining access to privileges made their life less unpleasant. Ellen K., a private wealthy inmate at Toronto for more than the last thirty years of her life, 'went for a little trip to Niagara which she enjoyed very much.'[37] Similarly, Angel Queen was able to indulge her illustrious talent at sewing and crocheting, thanks to a steady and voluminous supply of fabric paid for by her family.[38] For other patients, like Toronto inmate Elaine M., recreational enjoyments were far more difficult to realize, even on a more common level. It was reported that sixty-five-year-old Elaine was 'a great reader, but since breaking her spectacles cannot read,' so she carried with her a 'bundle' of papers that she was no longer able to see clearly.[39] Thus, as these examples from case files suggest, the availability of personal resources to purchase amenities, along with staff perceptions about 'trustworthiness' within the asylum, were both essential for patients to have the chance to pursue recreational and leisurely pursuits inside and outside of the institution.

Patient Labour

While leisure necessarily provides a more easy-going, relaxed impression of patient life, labour illustrates a related but more intense part of their daily existence. Patient labour could be therapeutic and contribute to the self-esteem of confined individuals, just as did leisure. However, patients could also experience work as being exploitative in a way that was less likely with leisure. Medical officials like J.M. Forster, superintendent at Toronto from 1911 to 1920, stated that inmate work was important 'for the taking of patients out of themselves.'[40] The use of patient labour to help encourage mental stability through a regular work routine had been practised among North American and British asylum administrators since the nineteenth century, as Charlotte MacKenzie and S.E.D. Shortt have noted.[41] Yet, while there is a good deal of material about what people who ran the institutions felt about patient labour, there remains a great deal of research to do about what patients themselves thought of their work, which is the focus of this section.

The words of inmates regarding labour practices at Toronto and Cobourg can be uncovered in observations recorded by physicians, nurses, and social workers. Most of the comments in this section relate to what people felt or encountered as patient-labourers. The use of unpaid patient labour at Toronto and Cobourg for the benefit of the internal economy of the asylum could be a double-edged sword. On the one hand, there were patients who very clearly expressed feelings of resentment at being exploited for their work. On the other hand, some inmates found that their toil provided a sense of purpose and self-esteem, and also used their reliability as workers to secure greater freedom. Furthermore, as will be evident in a number of the following references, some women who were incarcerated at Cobourg were sent out into the community to work as domestics, which could be a welcome relief from the confining space of the hospital. Therefore, while people were used as 'free' labour, there was also an important element of agency involved in the work life of patients.

Gender divisions of labour were most obvious in relation to occupations that were traditionally allotted to males and females, though this was not always strictly followed. Men were recorded in clinical files as doing work such as landscaping, coal gathering, painting, carpentry, tinsmithery, and shoe-repair work. Women were listed as having occupations such as sewing, basket making, floor scrubbing, and dusting. There was a certain degree of gender crossover in some occupations at Toronto. This is most notable in reference to both males and females working in the laundry, performing kitchen duties like preparing food, and tidying up such as by washing dishes, sweeping, and polishing floors on the wards in which they resided, helping to care for other inmates who were sick in sex-segregated infirmaries, and keeping their ward dining room clean before and after meals.

Women are not recorded as doing jobs that were usually only available to men in the wider community, such as that of a blacksmith or cabinet-maker, while men are not mentioned as doing work in which women were traditionally segregated, as in the sewing room. Class status before confinement is also reflected in the types of jobs patients had in the institution. It was not uncommon to link up inmates to jobs with which they had previous experience on the

Female asylum patients at work gardening. London, Ontario, 1883. The doctor encouraged patients to work and claimed to have abolished restraint and seclusion in the institution. (Archives of the History of Canadian Psychiatry and Mental Health Services, Griffin-Greenland slides, VII-12)

Women patients housed in the inhospitable cells and bare corridors of an asylum in Newfoundland, 1946. (Archives of the History of Canadian Psychiatry and Mental Health Services, Griffin-Greenland slides, VI-5d)

outside, as occurred with the following Toronto patients. Mathilda I., considered a 'good reliable patient' at her laundry job, had also been a domestic worker before confinement.[42] Stanley L., a shoemaker before admission, was employed on a daily basis in the shoe shop.[43] Wallace S. was listed as a general labourer at the time of his admission in 1888. In 1926 it was noted that this sixty-six-year-old man carried coal to various fireplaces, and had been doing his 'routine work' in the same manner for nearly forty years.[44] The evidence of so many decades of faithful service by patients like Wallace indicates to how crucial certain types of employment could be for some inmates.

For many patients there was an important relationship between their jobs and self-esteem. Mary B. was very proud of the work she did in the ward kitchen at Cobourg, where she began every day at 4 a.m. with a great sense of importance. When the old bread cutter was removed in favour of a new one Mary wrote a poem in which she 'pointed out the advantages of the old machine.'[45] Evelyn B. also revealed this sense of responsibility about her position by stating that she considered herself to be a housekeeper at the Toronto institution. Even while recuperating in the infirmary from an illness, Evelyn inquired 'if everyone is well at the Nurses home and says she would like to be back to work.'[46]

In both of these instances, the recorders emphasize the reliability of the inmates in a way that indicates that their duties were perceived as an integral and welcome part of their lives. It is also obvious that both women worked in areas that were determined by gender and class – kitchen work and house cleaning, positions usually occupied by female domestic servants for those who could afford such hired help. This work provided these patients with a sense of purpose, while it allowed hospital administrators to save money.

Yet this 'sense of purpose' while working for free was clearly not shared by everyone in a similar position. One inmate whose words were recorded by a medical observer show how she insisted on her rights, even though she never received what she wanted. Josie B. was a thirty-three-year-old worker in the Toronto hospital laundry in 1913. It was noted that Josie 'is constantly demanding her wages and by her conduct and conversation shows that she does not realize her position as an Asylum patient. She seems to think she is employed here and is not receiving her pay.'[47] Unlike the comments of patients who appeared ready to work under the existing conditions, these remarks in the clinical record are clearly aimed at driving home the point that Josie's desire for compensation was a sign of her insanity.

The male recorder's comment 'that she does not realize her position as an Asylum patient' says as much about the official attitude towards unpaid patient labour as it does about an angry inmate's advancement of her rights. The emphasis in this quotation is intended to convey an image of Josie being mentally unstable because she is making supposedly irrational demands. Yet, this observation could be read as the unintended record of an inmate putting forward claims that many contemporary union organizers and advocates of women's rights would have seen as entirely justified had Josie been working outside the asylum. The fact that her 'position as an Asylum patient' prevented her arguments from being taken seriously by medical officials illustrates how inmate labour was exploited.

A male inmate at Toronto made similar requests like those that Josie made, though he convinced himself that his demands were met. Jonathan T. was confined from 1890 to 1930, when he was discharged at the age of seventy-eight. During most of the last twenty years of his residence this man was reported to have worked faithfully in the kitchen, but it was also noted on several occasions that Jonathan had definite ideas about getting something for this work. In 1927, he told physicians that he deserved 'a large sum of money for his services.'[48] A few months later, Jonathan was recorded as having claimed that he had been given a total of $7000 for asylum-related work, though this clearly did not happen. By deluding himself in this way, this elderly man was 'rewarding' himself for work that no one had paid him to do. One inmate turned this question around by believing she had to work to earn her keep. Enid W. was said to have a 'mania to scrub floors,' which she believed was required of her to pay for the institutional clothing she received.[49]

Even a patient who was recorded as not working on a regular basis was known to ask for payment after taking on an occasional task. Constance B. spent the last twenty years of her life at the Toronto facility, where she died in 1926. On one of the few occasions in which she is recorded as having done institutional work, this seventy-six-year-old woman had dried the dishes for several days, after which 'she asked the nurse how much she would get for it.'[50] It was also noted that she was 'too deaf' to understand what was said to her, so while this elderly woman was able to communicate her feelings to staff, she was unable to hear any response to her compensation request. After this reference, three years before her death, there is no mention that Constance did any other work. Another Toronto inmate recognized this lack of monetary gain before doing any hospital labour and decided on a course of action that settled matters quite definitively. Marianne B. was a fifty-seven-year-old woman who had refused to do any tasks, since she said 'she is not paid for working in an Asylum.'[51]

As these quotations illustrate, patients sometimes reacted to what they considered unfair labour practices in the asylum. Disappointment at not getting a preferred position could lead to a partial withdrawal of services. Catherine H. was upset at not being accepted after applying for the position of assistant laundress at Cobourg where she cleaned clothes. Thereafter, she would only help out in the dining room.[52] Other patients expressed their dissatisfaction with institutional labour practices by refusing to work. Class-based prejudice influenced Karen S., who said she was 'too much of a lady' to work in the Toronto asylum.[53] On the other hand, an inmate who did not share such prejudices could express opposition to the type of work offered by pointing to an alternative position. Veronica G. was said to have 'hated' laundry work at Cobourg and was also unreceptive to the prospect of working as a domestic servant, a position she 'would much rather not take ... as she wants to go back home and work in one of the factories.'[54] While it is not clear whether this quote means she refused to do any type of work other than that which she requested, Veronica's recorded comments suggest an effort to negotiate a way out of the institution with a job that she found to be more suitable.

A patient's willingness, or not, to accept his or her assigned job in the asylum could influence how he or she was treated. This is made abundantly clear in the clinical record of James M. Though James had threatened to 'knock Mr L.'s brains out with a chair sometime ago,' he was trusted enough on the basis of his abilities as a landscaper to work outside. Eventually, he was even allowed to work in the community unsupervised, and was finally discharged, recovered after eighteen years' confinement on the basis of his reliability as a labourer. This point was repeatedly emphasized in his file.[55]

A number of Cobourg inmates worked outside of the asylum on a regular basis as domestics. Observations from social workers and medical authorities record what domestic workers from Cobourg thought about their situation. Edna A. was considered 'troublesome' while locked up. But after being placed out in the community, Edna 'says she feels like a different person.'[56] Gina S. was reported to have been very happy with her employment as a domestic on a farm. Her file recorded the conditions in which she worked as quite agreeable to her: 'She is very sunburned. She states, "no wonder when I live outside most of the time during the good weather."'[57] The prospect of this work coming to an end also weighed on Gina's mind, as six years after her employment with this family commenced she 'never has any complaints except she is afraid that when calls are made she will someday have to return to hospital ... She feels very thankful to be working and earning her own keep.' Laura P., a seventeen-year-old woman at the time of her admission in 1940, was very enthusiastic about country life and said 'she liked housework all right but working outside suited her best.'[58] For most of the next decade Laura was employed by several different families, shuttling back and forth, with particularly good relations with one woman. However, tensions occurred over relationships and working conditions.

Fed up with being 'chewed at' by one employer, Laura returned to the hospital, after which another position was found for her.

What can be inferred from these comments is an obvious relief at being out in the community, away from the constricted world of the institution. The fact that these women felt 'different' after working at a placement, or were worried at being confined again, suggests how their reactions reflect on the negative memories they had about life 'inside.' At the same time, Laura's response to domestic disputes with her employer, when she returned to the institution, also illustrates how work life 'outside' could be a source of great stress. Cobourg domestic workers, as much as they were relieved to be out of the hospital, expressed similar feelings that those who were confined did about their status: pride in their abilities, a sense of self-worth, using their labour as a way of obtaining greater freedom, and wanting recognition for their efforts. Sixty-nine-year-old Gina S., after working as a domestic for thirteen years, felt undervalued, requested a weekend holiday to which her social worker consented, and 'reminded Worker that she was not so young as she used to be, and may be retiring soon.'[59] Comments like this, and those of other women and men employed inside and outside of asylums, show that there was a real degree of agency among psychiatric patient workers. Yet some patients also understood how much they were taken advantage of and that when it came to advancing their rights, they had to do this primarily on their own initiative.

Preconceived notions about individual ability could also be challenged by the tasks a patient performed, and again offer a completely different perspective on patient life than that provided in histories that emphasize clinical symptoms. Lottie C. was a thirty-one-year-old woman who was labelled a 'moron' when she was admitted to Cobourg in 1939. Her right arm was almost fully paralysed. During her confinement she washed dishes, worked as a maid, could knit, and was considered 'a very fine ironer with one hand. She sometimes manipulates the article she is ironing with her teeth.'[60] This entry illustrates how an otherwise 'silent' patient can speak to later generations through her actions recorded in her medical file. While Lottie's voice is silent, her ability speaks volumes about what kind of a person she was; social and medical impositions could not totally restrict an individual woman considered mentally and physically disabled. The fact that she was confined is an obvious indication of her lack of options in a world that provided few opportunities for a person with what is now called a 'dual diagnosis.' Yet, this medical record shows that Lottie surprised her observers with her skills as a labourer. Like many of the other women and men considered in this section, this inmate was much more than the sum of her labels, a reality that clinical entries on patient labour have, ironically, helped later generations to retrieve and reconstruct.

Conclusion

The use of case files in psychiatric history can offer a unique perspective into the experiences of psychiatric patients and the actual operations of psychiatric hospitals. Most of the literature on asylums emphasizes the custodial and the social-control functions served by psychiatric hospitalization.[61] Focusing on the relationship between the development of psychiatric hospitals and the rise of industrial capitalism, these studies generally tend to suggest that psychiatric facilities operated either as 'holding' institutions for problematic individuals for whom families and communities were unwilling or unable to provide care, or as 'containment' sites where men and women who failed to conform to societal norms, particularly norms associated with class and gender, were placed in order to ensure the maintenance of harmonious and stable bourgeois-patriarchal relations. While not dismissive of the class- and gender-based analyses of these studies, our research on the case files of the Toronto and Cobourg Ontario Hospitals suggests that a more complicated process was involved in terms of both patient encounters with the psychiatric system and the ways in which the dynamics of class, gender, and race structured patients' experiences of hospitalization. As our study shows, far from being passive or 'deranged' victims of hospitalization, many patients tried in a variety of ways to exert control and influence over their encounters with the psychiatric system. Their abilities to shape their experiences were certainly circumscribed by psychiatric professionals, as well as by factors related to class, gender, and race. Nevertheless, within such confines, some patients displayed a considerable degree of agency in responding to their psychiatric hospitalization.

An awareness of such agency is important for a fuller understanding of the operations of psychiatric facilities. The fact that some patients sought out their admissions to psychiatric institutions suggests that contemporaries did not always view asylums as simply 'holding' or 'containment' sites. Similarly, patient responses to institutionalization certainly problematize issues such as why certain management techniques (physical restraints and psychotropic drugs) were used to regulate patient behaviour. The recreational and work cultures that patients were able to forge within the limited constraints of day-to-day living in psychiatric hospitals perhaps indicate the ways in which patients were able to create their own more therapeutic environments. Much more than just adding a 'human side' to the history of psychiatric hospitals, historical perspectives on patients' experiences of institutionalization raise crucial analytical questions about the nature and the meaning of psychiatric hospitalization.

Notes

1 Provincial Archives of Ontario (PAO), Toronto, RG 10, series 20-B-2, Queen Street Mental Health Centre Records, file 11883
2 Bill Lucklin, 'Towards a Social History of Institutionalization,' *Social History* 8 (1983), 87–94; Anne Digby, 'Quantitative and Qualitative Perspectives on the Asylum,' in Roy Porter and Andrew Wear, eds, *Problems and Methods in the History of Medicine* (London: Croom Helm 1987), 153–74; Roy Porter, 'The Patient's View: Doing Medical History from Below,' *Theory and Society* 14 (1985), 175–98; John Woodward, 'Toward a Social History of Medicine,' in John Woodward and Dave Richards, eds, *Health Care and Popular Medicine in Nineteenth-Century England: Essays in the Social History of Medicine* (New York: Holmes and Meier 1977), 15–55; A.M. Brandt, 'Emerging Themes in the History of Medicine,' *Milbank Quarterly* 69 (1991), 199–214
3 T.J.W. Burgess, 'A Historical Sketch of Our Canadian Institutions for the Insane,' *Proceeedings and Transactions of the Royal Society of Canada* 4 (1898), 3–123; Henry M. Hurd, *The Institutional Care of the Insane in the United States and Canada* (Baltimore: Johns Hopkins University Press 1916; repr. New York: Arno Press 1973); F. Allodi, 'The Evolution of the Mental Hospital in Canada,' *Canadian Journal of Public Health* 68 (1977), 219–44; C.A. Roberts, 'Thirty-Five Years of Psychiatry in Canada, 1943–1978,' *Psychiatric Journal of the University of Ottawa* 4 (1979), 35–8; Melvin Baker, 'Insanity and Politics: The Establishment of a Lunatic Asylum in St. John's, Newfoundland, 1836–1853,' *Newfoundland Quarterly* 77 (1981); Melvin Baker, 'Henry Stuart Strubb and the Establishment of a Lunatic Asylum in St. John's Newfoundland, 1836–1855,' *Scientia Canadensis* 8 (1984); Daniel Francis, 'The Development of the Lunatic Asylum in the Maritime Provinces,' *Acadiensis* 6 (1977), 23–38 (repr. in S.E.D. Shortt, ed., *Medicine in Canadian Society: Historical Perspectives* (Montreal: McGill-Queen's University Press 1981), 93–114); Patricia O'Brien, *Out of Mind, Out of Sight: A History of the Waterford Hospital* (St John's: Breakwater Books 1989); Alfred Lavall, 'The Beginnings of the Ontario Mental Hospitals,' *Queen's Quarterly* 49 (1942), 59–67; C. Greenland, 'Services for the Mentally Retarded in Ontario, 1870–1930,' *Ontario History* 54 (1962), 267–74; Cheryl Krasnick, '"In Charge of the Loons": A Portrait of the London, Ontario, Asylum for the Insane in the Nineteenth Century,' *Ontario History* 74 (1982), 138–84; S.E.D. Shortt, *Victorian Lunacy: Richard M. Bucke and the Practice of Late-Nineteenth-Century Psychiatry* (Cambridge: University Press 1986)
4 Wendy Mitchinson, 'Gynaecological Operations on Insane Women, London, Ontario, 1895–1901,' *Journal of Social History* 15 (1982), 467–84; Mitchinson, 'Gender and Insanity as Characteristics of the Insane: A Nineteenth-Century Case,' *Canadian Bulletin of Medical History* 4 (1987), 99–117; Mitchinson, 'Reasons for

the Committal to a Mid-Nineteenth-Century Ontario Insane Asylum: The Case of Toronto,' in Wendy Mitchinson and Janice Dickin McGinnis, eds, *Essays in the History of Canadian Medicine* (Toronto: McClelland and Stewart 1988), 88–109; see also chaps 10 and 11 in Mitchinson, *The Nature of Their Bodies: Women and Their Doctors in Victorian Canada* (Toronto: University of Toronto Press 1991), 278–355; Cheryl Krasnick Warsh, 'The First Mrs. Rochester: Wrongful Confinement, Social Redundacy and Committment to the Private Asylum, 1880–1910,' Canadian Historical Association *Historical Papers*, 1988, 145–67; Warsh, *Moments of Unreason: The Practice of Canadian Psychiatry and the Homewood Retreat, 1883–1923* (Montreal: McGill-Queen's University Press 1989); Mary Ellen Kelm, '"The Only Place Likely to Do Her Any Good": The Admission of Women to British Columbia's Provincial Hospital for the Insane,' *BC Studies* 96 (1992/3), 66–89; Kelm, 'A Life Apart: The Experience of Women and Asylum Practice of Charles Doherty at British Columbia's Provincial Hospital for the Insane, 1905–1915,' *Canadian Bulletin of Medical History* 11 (1994), 335–55; Megan Davies, 'Snapshots: Three Women and Psychiatry, 1920–1935,' *Canadian Woman Studies* 8 (1987), 47–8

5 Geoffrey Reaume, 'Keep Your Labels Off My Mind! or "Now I Am Going to Pretend I Am Craze but Dont Be a Bit Alarmed": Psychiatric History from the Patients' Perspectives,' *Canadian Bulletin of Medical History* 11 (1994), 397–424; Reaume, 'Accounts of Abuse of Patients at the Toronto Hospital for the Insane, 1883–1937,' *Canadian Bulletin of Medical History* 14 (1997), 65–106

6 For details on the potential uses and limitations associated with patient case files as historical sources, see Steven Noll, 'Patient Records as Historical Stories: The Case of Caswell Training School,' *Bulletin of the History of Medicine* 68 (1994), 411–28; Guenter B. Risse and John Harley Warner, 'Reconstructing Clinical Activities: Patient Records in Medical History,' *Social History of Medicine* 5 (1992), 183–205; H. Garfinkel, 'Good Organizational Reasons for Bad Clinical Records,' in H. Garfinkel, *Studies in Ethnomethodology* (Englewood Cliffs, NJ: Prentice-Hall 1967), 186–207; Daphne de Marneffe, 'Looking and Listening: The Construction of Clinical Knowledge in Charcot and Freud,' *Signs* 17 (1991), 71–111; Harriet Nowell-Smith, 'Nineteenth-Century Narrative Case Histories: An Inquiry into Stylistics and History,' *Canadian Bulletin of Medical History* 12 (1995), 47–67; see also the entire issue of *Literature and Medicine* 11 (1992), which is devoted to discussions on the use of case histories as historical sources.

7 For discussions on the possibilities of retrieving the 'voices' of 'ordinary' individuals from case files, see Carolyn Strange, *Toronto's Girl Problem: The Perils and Pleasures of the City, 1880–1930* (Toronto: University of Toronto Press 1995), 12; Joan Sangster, '"Pardon Tales" from Magistrate's Court: Women, Crime, and the Court in Peterborough County, 1920–1950,' *Canadian Historical Review* 74 (1993), 161; Karen Dubinsky, *Improper Advances: Rape and Heterosexual Conflict in*

Ontario, 1880–1929 (Chicago: University of Chicago Press 1993), 7; Linda Gordon, *Heroes of Their Own Lives: The Politics and History of Family Violence* (New York: Penguin Books 1989), 17–18.

8 We take the position, similar to that of Jeffrey L. Geller and Maxine Harris, that psychiatric patients do have a credible story to tell about their experiences with mental illness and psychiatric institutionalization. As Geller and Harris point out, being 'crazy' does not necessarily equate with being 'stupid,' nor does it mean that patients did not have their own valid perceptions of their subjective experiences. Indeed, we would argue that even in cases where patients appear 'deranged,' it is important for analytical and therapeutical purposes to understand their vantage points, however 'strange' they may appear to us. Moreover, in the past, individuals were sometimes confined to psychiatric facilities on the basis of quite questionable diagnoses of mental illness. The views of such patients, often articulated in very clear, non-delusional terms, are particularly revealing and have an enormous amount to tell historians about the reality of patients' past experiences in psychiatric institutions. See Geller and Harris, *Women of the Asylum: Voices from Behind the Walls, 1840–1945* (New York: Doubleday 1994), 7–8; Oliver Sachs, 'Clinical Tales,' *Literature and Medicine* 5 (1986), 16–23.

9 The patient stories presented in this paper are drawn from the following record groups located at the Provincial Archives of Ontario in Toronto: RG 10, series 20-B-2, Queen Street Mental Health Centre Records, and RG 29, series 58, D'Arcy Place Centre, Case Files. Hereafter, only the coded case file number and its location will be indicated in the notes. All the names of the patients who appear in this study have been changed to protect the confidentiality of the individuals involved.

10 Noll, 'Patient Records,' 427–8

11 File 11865 (Toronto)

12 File 7036 (Toronto)

13 File 1177 (Cobourg)

14 File 1004 (Toronto)

15 File 1156 (Cobourg)

16 File 1055 (Cobourg)

17 File 1170 (Cobourg)

18 File 9024 (Toronto)

19 File 1409 (Cobourg)

20 File 1418 (Cobourg)

21 File 1008 (Cobourg)

22 File 7041 (Toronto)

23 File 2973 (Cobourg)

24 File 3253 (Cobourg)

25 File 5029 (Toronto)

26 See, for example, Krasnick, '"In Charge of the Loons,"' 166-7; Shortt, *Victorian Lunacy*, 133-4; Charlotte MacKenzie, *Psychiatry for the Rich: A History of Ticehurst Private Asylum, 1792–1917* (London: Routledge 1992), 71, 74, 147–8; and Ellen Dwyer, *Homes for the Mad: Life Inside Two Nineteenth-Century Asylums* (New Brunswick, NJ: Rutgers University Press 1987), 124, 141–3, 167–8. Dwyer studied patient and staff life at both Willard Asylum and Utica Asylum, though most of her material specifically relating to patient entertainments deal with inmates of Willard Asylum.

27 File 5005 (Toronto)
28 File 1146 (Cobourg)
29 File 1001 (Cobourg)
30 File 2398 (Cobourg)
31 File 2013 (Toronto)
32 File 1117 (Cobourg)
33 File 4009 (Toronto)
34 File 2013 (Toronto)
35 File 2019 (Toronto)
36 Files 1001 and 2398 (Cobourg)
37 File 3037 (Toronto)
38 File 5005 (Toronto)
39 File 7044 (Toronto)
40 File 1002 (Toronto)
41 MacKenzie, *Psychiatry for the Rich*, 26–7; Shortt, *Victorian Lunacy*, 128–9
42 File 2001 (Toronto)
43 File 3017 (Toronto)
44 File 3050 (Toronto)
45 File 2381 (Cobourg)
46 File 7049 (Toronto)
47 File 9009 (Toronto)
48 File 4003 (Toronto)
49 File 2012 (Toronto)
50 File 9029 (Toronto)
51 File 7017 (Toronto)
52 File 1018 (Cobourg)
53 File 7034 (Toronto)
54 File 2381 (Cobourg)
55 File 5033 (Toronto)
56 File 1146 (Cobourg)
57 File 1156 (Cobourg)
58 File 2398 (Cobourg)

59 File 1156 (Cobourg)
60 File 2310 (Cobourg)
61 For example, see Thomas Brown, 'The Origins of the Asylum in Upper Canada, 1830–1839,' *Canadian Bulletin of Medical History* 1 (1984), 27–58; Thomas Brown, '"Living with God's Afflicted": A History of the Provincial Lunatic Asylum at Toronto, 1830–1911,' Ph.D. thesis, Queen's University, 1980; Barry Edginton, 'Moral Treatment to Monolith: The Institutional Treatment of the Insane in Manitoba, 1871–1919,' *Canadian Bulletin of Medical History* 5 (1988), 167–88; Edginton, 'The Formation of the Asylum in Upper Canada,' Ph.D. thesis, University of Toronto, 1981; Harvey Simmons, *From Asylum to Welfare* (Downsview, Ont.: National Institute on Mental Retardation 1982); Simmons, *Unbalanced: Mental Health Policy in Ontario, 1930–1989* (Toronto: Wall and Thompson 1990); see also the studies of Baker, Francis, and Shortt referred to in note 3.

12

Problematic Bodies and Agency:
Women Patients in Canada, 1900–1950

WENDY MITCHINSON

Traditionally, medical historians focused on the history of medical institutions, the rise of the medical profession, and those medical discoveries that shaped our health experience. Overlooked was the dynamic that existed between physician and patient. In recent years, however, many critical analyses have been written about physician–patient and especially physician–female patient interaction.[1] The emphasis has been placed on how physicians treated women, with very little attention being paid to women's participation as patients. One of the reasons for this was the perception by feminist critics that when faced by the medical profession, patients, especially women patients, had little power or agency. The published medical literature of the time provides very little discussion about the involvement of patients in their health care. The assumption of physicians seemed to be that patients should be and would be quiescent. This paper examines a selection of women's gynaecological and obstetrical case files from the Victoria General Hospital (VGH), Halifax, the Montreal General Hospital (MGH), the Royal Victoria Hospital (RVH), Montreal, and the Kitchener-Waterloo Hospital (KWH) for the period 1900 to 1950 in an effort to discern whether such records reveal a patient 'voice' and, if so, the nature of that voice. In doing so, I hope to demonstrate the value of the records as historical documentation. Patient records add to the literature in women's history by exposing the harshness of some women's lives and their resiliency in living them. They suggest that women may have had a different concept of health and view of their bodies than did physicians. The records also serve to remind us that the patient–doctor dynamic was composed of sites of both compliance and resistance, that women patients did have agency even if they did not have much autonomy.[2] Lastly, contacts between physician and patient reveal a profession much more diverse and at times more sympathetic than much of the medical literature on the treatment of women has suggested.

Patient Records as Historical Evidence

The value of using patient records comes largely from what they are and of what they consist. Patient case histories are the medical equivalent of legal precedents, only not as entrenched. Physicians act according to accepted medical practice, which often consists of enacting what they were taught and what they have read in the published medical press. They also treat patients according to their own previous experience, being influenced by personal failures or near failures and acting to avoid repeating them.[3] For the historian, patient records afford the opportunity to examine what doctors did as opposed to what they say they did.

Hospital patient records supply considerable detail about an individual's illness and treatment and about her personal and family history.[4] While the value of patient records perhaps does not need to be stressed, familiarity with them does force the historian to be aware of their fallibility and, at times, of the peculiarities of record saving. Case histories are narratives and stories of experience taken by medical personnel. They are summaries – a distilling of a life, or part of a life – and can never be assumed to represent fully that life.[5] More significant in emphasizing the need for a careful examination of records are the inaccuracies and/or eccentricities of patient files. At times, there are discrepancies between the diagnosis given on the covering sheet of the file and the actual problems experienced by the patient described in the file. Records do not always give the entire diagnosis. Other inconsistencies also occur; for example, the symptom can be put down as the diagnosis. A third problem in using the files concerns the question of representation. The files represent women who were self-selected. The vast majority chose to enter the hospital, and all were there because of some real or perceived health problem. Their experiences cannot be assumed to reflect those of the majority of women or even of those women who experienced health problems. Despite these caveats, the files do open up certain experiences of women and the dynamic between them and the medical profession.

Historians of women have often commented on the hard lives that many women led in the past, and medical records certainly confirm this reality. They are sources for experiences often difficult to access. Two examples illustrate this potential. In 1903, Rebecca Truscott, twenty-one years old and married, came to the RVH suffering from inflammation of the uterine tubes and ovaries (double salpingo-oophoritis) and inflammation of the uterine membrane (endometritis), for which surgeons operated, removing both fallopian tubes. At the young age of twenty-one, Rebecca had already been married for nine years. She had given birth to three children, and all of her labours had been difficult.

As her case record pointed out, she 'has had to work hard for her living – Husband very abusive.'[6] On 24 June 1943, Mrs Frank Holtz, age twenty-nine, entered the KWH suffering from cerebral syphilis. The case record reported that Mrs Holtz was 'infected with syphilis about 18 years ago. Treatment not checked by spinal puncture. Present symptoms began to appear about 1 year ago.'[7] These two examples reveal the issue of violence against women, whether in the form of wife abuse or the horrific reality of an eleven-year-old child being infected with syphilis. Such cases were extreme but they were not rare, and physicians would have been familiar with them through both hospital and private practice. Patient records also remind historians, who are often concerned with finding the 'average' or majority experience, that many people in the past did not 'fit' that experience. Rebecca Truscott, for example, marrying at age twelve, hardly conformed to the mid-twenties average age of marriage for women at the time.

Women and the Experience of Ill Health

One particular aspect of many women's lives that was revealed from the records was their experience of chronic morbidity, that is, of ill health. Both historical demographers and historians of medicine have focused on acute medical problems, especially those linked to mortality, and have downplayed morbidity, perhaps because it is more difficult to define and track. Certainly hospital physicians did not always know what happened to their patients after they received hospital treatment and care. Two examples will suffice to give a sense of how significant morbidity could be for those women experiencing it. Mrs Lilia Howell, age forty-five, entered the RVH on 12 August 1908 suffering from loss of control over her bowel function, incontinence of urine, and soreness in her back and lower abdomen, in addition to loss of weight. Her difficulties had begun twenty-three years earlier with a difficult labour.[8] Mrs Paul (Karin) Hackett, age seventy-two, entered the MGH in 1937 with complete falling of the womb (procidentia). This had begun in 1913. In 1914 she had had a uterine suspension done, but soon after her symptoms gradually returned. For almost a quarter of a century she had endured this aggravation before entering the hospital in 1937.[9]

What are we to make of such cases and others similar to them? From the medical standpoint, the fact that these two women came to the hospital reveals a certain amount of faith in the science of medicine. But that they waited so long also suggests that medical treatment in a hospital was not their first choice. There could be many reasons for this. For one, a hospital stay was expensive. Most of the patient records do not indicate whether the individual was a paying patient or not, but general hospital statistics suggest that non-paying patients or those who paid minimal fees represented a significant number of admissions. For example, in 1920 public patient days at the MGH constituted over three times the total patient days represented by private and semi-private patients. In 1935, of the 9753 patients admitted, 6064 were public.[10] In addition to the actual cost of being in the hospital, whether a woman was a paying or charity patient, she had to make arrangements to ensure that her home and/or family was cared for while she was gone. For many women, a hospital stay meant separation from friends and family, and for those who lived out of town the separation was even more wrenching. Also it is not surprising that some women would be reluctant to seek out gynaecological treatment in particular. Gynaecology was very much a surgical specialty, and the prospect of undergoing surgery was understandably frightening, even more so when it is remembered that gynaecologists did not just repair but often removed. Almost all aspects of a woman's reproductive system could be and were 'taken out' – uterus, ovaries, fallopian tubes.

Physicians tended to see such women as victims of their own bodies. Doctors were part of a professional culture that pathologized some of the normal physiological processes of women. The conventional medical wisdom was that women's bodies were more problematic than male bodies, the result of 'natural' weakness. Women's bodies, especially their reproductive systems, were much more complex than men's and thus more could go wrong with them; this was the fundamental premise of gynaecology as a separate specialty. In addition, the complicating factors of menstruation, pregnancy, childbirth, and menopause were stresses that men simply did not experience. It was not women's fault, but they did pay the price. As Percy Ryberg in his popular health manual made clear regarding menstruation, 'since the beginning of time women have been afflicted in this way. It is the price to pay for the creation of new life, which never can come into existence without pain.'[11] It is also understandable why physicians saw women's bodies as problematic; they only saw bodies that were not 'working properly.'

It is difficult to know what women thought of their bodies. If they internalized some of the attitudes represented by Ryberg's quote, they may have been quite fatalistic about them. For whatever reason, women clearly were willing to undergo years of discomfort and sometimes pain before seeking out hospital medical help. These women had learned how to adjust their lives to their situation, but clearly something had altered to make them overcome the factors inhibiting hospital choice. The following examples suggest what had changed. Mrs Martha McMullin, a young wife, had always had painful menstruation. However, the pain had been increasing, and by 1902 she 'had to resort to morphia & chloroform for alleviation.'[12] Since the birth of a child, Mrs Stewart Patton had experienced menstrual difficulties, which had continued for seven years. Only when she began to feel very tired and feel 'she could not carry on' did she enter MGH.[13] In 1945, Mrs A. Reich sought hospital help in the form of a vaginal hysterectomy for her prolapsed uterus, which she had had for twenty-seven years. During that time she had been able to push her uterus back into place when it descended but now she no longer could.[14] Fifty-nine-year-old Mrs Gaeton Laforce had a similar problem. By 1950 she had had falling of the womb for nineteen years. What finally brought her in was 'urgency and frequency [of the bladder] for 1 month.'[15]

The ability of many women to endure discomfort for so long before seeking medical help implies that women accommodated their bodies to discomfort or pain. Only when the accommodation broke down, when women lost what control they had over their bodies, were they willing to relinquish even more control and face the cost of hospital care, the danger it represented, and the separation from home and perhaps loved ones. When a chronic situation transformed itself into an acute situation, they sought medical help. Pain was acute, discomfort was not. Being able to do one's tasks, even with pain, was chronic, not being able to do so acute. Once the discomfort became too great or the time spent dealing with it too much, then the women reached a turning point. But they made the decision, and clearly when they did would vary depending on their circumstances and concepts of their bodies.

Women's Views of Their Bodies

It is these concepts about which we know so little, whether we are referring to a specific woman or women generally. Women obviously had some knowledge about their bodies that came from living with them; that is, they had embodied knowledge that they could interpret. They had access to other sources of knowledge about their health as well. Although popular health manuals did not seem to have been as evident during this period as they had been in the nineteenth century,[16] women's magazines did provide a certain amount of health coverage. Patent medicines still existed. Public-health nurses, too, were sources of information as were midwives, who continued to practise in certain parts of the country. Women could also talk to one another, and older women especially could pass on their experience. Physicians frowned on these information networks and advised women not to listen to friends and relations but to depend on their doctors for information that would be medically scientific. This advice had significant consequences; if followed, the patient became very much dependent on her physician, since for most non-medical people the language of medicine was inaccessible.

While health was significant, it was only one part of a woman's life, and we cannot assume that she gave it the same priority as the medical profession. What is clear from some of the records is that women's knowledge of their bodies was different than that of physicians and that they simply did not prioritize health information in the same way. For example, women could be quite vague about what specific medical treatment they had received. Jane Granger, when in the MGH in 1902, remembered that some years previously she had 'had some' operation in 1899 and thought 'an ovary was removed and the uterus ventrofixed.' When Mrs Mavis Denton entered the VGH in 1930, she reported that she had had twins who had died and that after the birth of her last child she had been sick for seven days. However, she did not know 'if instruments were used or if she was torn.' Miss Deborah Kelly, age forty-two in 1950 when she entered the MGH, detailed how she had gone to a physician for help about her menstrual difficulties, but she could only remember that he had given her white pills and when they didn't work she was given yellow pills.[17] The kind of detail a physician wanted from his patients was not always forthcoming. Their interest in the details of treatment was clearly quite different from his.

Both women and physicians often focused on the nature of women's bodies as problematic. At times, however, women patients would give their own twist. Mrs Linda McCarthy, suffering from chronic endometritis, entered the VGH in November 1920. Twenty-five years of age, she claimed that her periods had been 'normal until after she was married 6 years ago when dysmenorrhoea [painful menstruation] commenced.'[18] In her view, her body had been functioning fine until marriage at age nineteen. McCarthy's was not an uncommon perception, but it raises the question of how women viewed marriage if some saw it as a source of health problems.[19] Physicians, too, often blamed marriage for gynaecological difficulties in women owing to their being infected with VD by their husbands. Marriage, and the sexual relations that went with it, exposed women to the potential dangers of pregnancy and childbirth, and one of the strongest themes in the patient records was the belief of many women that their health problems were very much linked to childbirth trauma.[20] How did such experiences affect the way these women faced subsequent pregnancies? Historians have pointed out the dangers of dying in childbirth and how women in the past, as a result, viewed childbirth with mixed emotions, but they have overlooked the fear of being injured based on previous experience in labour. Neither should historians accept uncritically the cause-and-effect relationship women often saw between marriage or childbirth and ill health. Marriage and childbirth are life markers and often used as reference points in situating the timing of events.[21]

The physicians who often saw the repercussions of childbirth injury were the

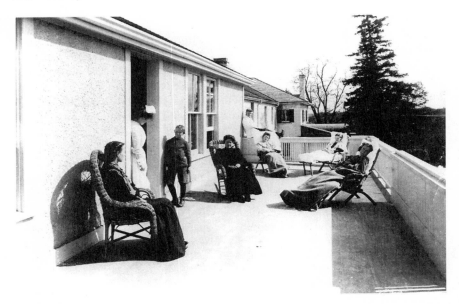

Toronto Hospital for Consumptives: porch of new women's building, 1905. (Archives of Ontario, ACC 14662-14)

gynaecologists, who did not blame women's bodies so much as they blamed the mishandling of pregnancy and labour by other physicians.[22] But gynaecologists themselves were often blamed by women for their health problems. In November 1920, Mrs Amy Hutter, age thirty-three, came to the VGH with cancer of the cervix uteri. Her history revealed that her menstruation had been regular until she underwent surgery in 1914 for a cystic ovary. For the next five years she did not menstruate. In September 1920 she started to feel a 'dull pain in lower part of "stomach." Had severe pain during coitus blood coming from vagina after completing the act.' She then thought there was something wrong and went to a doctor who told her she was experiencing the 'change of life.' She continued to bleed and finally her physician sent her to the hospital.[23] For Mrs Hutter, the origin of her ill health was her gynaecological surgery in 1914. It was how *she* measured its beginnings – her life was fine until surgery. It had cured whatever she had gone in for, but had left her with another problem. Similarly, Mrs Linda Craton, age thirty-two, had undergone surgery in 1922, which in 1930 she saw as the source of pain in her lower left abdomen, dysmenorrhoea, menorrhagia, and frequency of micturition.[24] For these two women, sur-

This photo of a robust, outdoors woman contrasts sharply with the fragile images of women featured in hospital, sanatorium, and asylum photographs. (National Archives of Canada, PA 112889)

gery was a very mixed blessing. It removed one problem, but apparently left them with another. This raises issues about how success rates in hospitals were measured. Both women, according to their hospital records, had their original problems solved – they did not die and thus would have been a success from the medical standpoint. From their standpoint the outcome was much more ambivalent.

Women Patients and Agency

The above scenario is very bleak. There emerges a view of the morbidity of women, seemingly caused by their bodies, that at times the medical profession was unable to offset and, indeed, from the perspective of some women and some physicians, could compound. Other factors such as poverty or family circumstances also restricted women's ability to control their health. As well, once they came under hospital purview, the medical system as it existed placed limits on patient autonomy, especially that of women patients.[25] Two examples of these limits are found in the meaning of consent and in how married women were often seen as part of a marital unit rather than as individuals in their own right. When ethicists write today about consent, they mean informed consent.[26] This was not the case in the past. Doctors generally told patients what was going to occur, but there was little emphasis placed on making sure that the patients understood or were aware of all the options available to them. Even if they had been, they were still dependent on the physician, who was part of the system that constructed the knowledge. Consent did not have to be written or even verbal – it could be implied.[27] We know very little about the history of consent in the medical profession or the history of medical ethics generally in the Canadian context. In the case of married women, their consent was often not even sufficient. For example, at the MGH in 1950, there is in the record of Mrs Galabin an examination treatment and operation consent form. At the bottom it states, 'In all cases of patients under 21 years of age. This consent must be signed by the father, if alive otherwise by the mother of the patient. If neither parent is living the nearest relative who is of age must sign. A wife, although 21 years of age, must have her husband's consent.'[28] When Mrs James Hewitt entered the KWH on 2 January 1943 because of extreme pain, the result of pregnancy, it was her husband who signed the consent form for the Caesarean section.[29] It appears to have been an elective C-section, as Mrs Hewitt had been in bed for several months during the pregnancy. In two other cases the issue of consent revolved around sterilization. Mrs Ginette Kelly, age thirty-eight, entered the RVH for surgery to provide uterine support. Her record stated 'husband consulted, wanted more children, did not tie tubes. It did seem as though it would have been better to ligate them out and fix uterus rather than suspend.'[30] Whether the couple, in fact, made the decision together is unknown. All the record indicates is that a procedure that was deemed medically superior was not done because the husband expressed the desire to have more children. In the same year, when Martha Kauffer underwent sterilization at the KWH, she had to consent to the procedure, as did her husband.[31] With respect to childbearing a couple was seen as a unit. What would have occurred if a wife had wanted the procedure and her husband refused consent is unclear. However, one legal text designed for medical practitioners suggested that in that situation the sterilization would not have occurred.[32]

Given the constraints on women at the time, the culture of hospitals, and the society of which they were a part, it is difficult to access patient agency through the patient records. After all, the records reflect the view of the attending physician and other medical personnel who came into contact with the patient. Also, the infrastructure of a society at any particular time may be such that it is difficult to maintain some semblance of patient control. In the context of the first half of the twentieth century, we are looking at a period when the status of the medical profession was on the rise, when gynaecology was becoming a major surgical specialty, and when childbirth was increasingly becoming medicalized. The pressure was on women to seek medical help when their bodies seemed to give them difficulties. While this limited the number of choices they had in responding to bodily changes, they were not without the ability to select among the choices, make decisions among the options, and either positively or negatively react to proposals made by their physicians.

Patient case histories reveal that there were several sites of resistance for women when faced with the medical profession. We have already seen two examples of this resistance. First it was evident in a patient's decision to seek medical help or not to seek it. Many women chose not to go to physicians, and if they did decide to go they were the ones who determined *when* that would occur. Whether their decision was taken in consultation with family and friends, their personal physician, or on their own is unknown, but the decision finally was the woman's. Second, women had their own perception of the origin of their medical problems. It has already been noted that many women felt that marriage and subsequent childbearing were the cause of their ill health. Others dated it to previous medical treatment. Still others blamed different factors. Mrs Eliza Barron came to the VGH in December 1930. Diagnosed as suffering from nervous prostration (neurasthenia), she described experiencing sinking spells, feeling not right in the head, numbness in her left arm, spells of depression, a lump in her throat, and stomach troubles. It is unknown what Eliza felt about the diagnosis of neurasthenia; she did, however, have a very firm idea of what was causing her symptoms. According to her, she 'had been brooding over questions involving her married life such as birth control which she has been practising against her religious [United Church] convictions. She also state[d] that in her sexual relations of recent months that she [had been] "frigid." '[33] That this was a problem for Eliza is understandable. Getting access to birth control was difficult because of its illegality. The irony was that in the interwar years the advice manuals directed at men and women were urging the glories of marital sexuality and the responsibility of each partner to ensure the satisfaction and enjoyment of the other.[34] Fear of pregnancy could certainly curtail that enjoyment, especially in times of economic downturn when an additional child could place severe economic strains on a family. It would seem perfectly reasonable for Mrs Barron to 'brood.' Mrs Alvin Southard, age forty-three, linked her loss of energy, easy fatiguability, nervousness, and so on to her approaching menopause.[35] And this is understandable, since these were characteristics of menopause that were part of both conventional and medical wisdom at the time.[36] What these examples reveal is that women often had their own view of what was wrong with them; at times this conformed to the medical view of the problematic female body, at others it did not.

Once in the hospital, patients could exert some control over their treatment. Most acquiesced in what their physicians recommended; they had acknowledged that something was wrong and that the medical profession could 'fix' it, so it only made sense to accept what the physicians had to say. Some women, of course, had no choice but to accept treatment. One of those women was a Mrs Ruggoso, a patient who had already had five full pregnancies and, at the age of forty-one, was faced by a sixth, which was complicated by a heart condition. According to her friends she was terrified that she would die if her pregnancy went to term, and attempted to abort the fetus. The attempt failed, and she was taken to the RVH on 6 November 1901. On admission, she 'was very angry when told that everything was being done to prevent [the loss of the fetus].' The doctors were trying to save her four-to-five month fetus after she had gone to the trouble to take 'all manner of drugs to bring on abortion' in order, from her point of view, to save her own life. No wonder she was angry – her physicians were not doing what *she* wanted them to.[37] Mrs Ruggoso's condition was grave when she entered the hospital and, given the illegality of abortion, she was in no position to resist efforts to save the fetus. Ultimately, physicians failed in their attempts and lost both the fetus and the mother. Other women, however, were in a better position to exert their will.

Some patients simply refused the proffered therapy. Medical professionals tended to view this response as non-cooperation and to see it as blameworthy. From the patient's perspective, however, it may have been more positive. Martha Quint, at the age of eighty, had been 'troubled by a lump in rt breast. Always refused to have it attended to surgically.' In 1921, at the age of eighty-five, she entered the VGH dying from breast cancer.[38] At best, surgery would have extended her life somewhat, but at what cost to an eighty-year-old? Mrs Quint made her decision – an understandable one, given her circumstances. Miss Ann Valoux, aged forty-two, entered the MGH as a private patient in April 1935. In her case file there is a letter from her surgeon to her physician in Ste-Agathe, Quebec, thanking him for the referral and noting that 'I feel this patient, at her age and with her condition would be very much better if she had the uterus removed.' His mention of her age was a reference to the fact that she was not likely to bear children, since she was coming to the end of her childbearing years. What was not functional, then, was deemed expendable. Although it was unlikely that a spinster lady was going to give birth, Ann decided that she wanted to keep her uterus and refused to have it removed. Thus, her surgeon 'removed the polypi from the fundus by curettage and suspended the uterus.'[39]

Another area in which patients exhibited some control was in the patient history they provided. In some cases these life stories were at odds with how the attending physicians viewed the patient. For example, when Mrs Mavis Denton entered the VGH with threatened abortion, she was willing to admit that she had taken pills to bring about her periods, but denied having 'any discharge p.v. [per vagina] at any time.' She may have denied it, but physicians discovered 'from other sources ... that she ... had [had] gonorrhoea and syphilis for some time.'[40] Similarly, Myrtle McGinnis, single and pregnant at age eighteen, entered the same hospital in 1930 complaining of aches and pains and feeling cold all the time. Her record reports that she '[w]orked at Halifax Hotel and was not out with any men since June. Her boyfriend has been with her until she came to V.G.H.' Myrtle had to admit her unmarried state, and her pregnancy, but she denied that she had syphilis despite the fact that she was to be treated with neosalvarsan.[41] Most patient denials about their conditions revolved around the suggestion of immorality. Women simply differed from one another as to where they drew the line. For some, as with the above cases, it was denial of venereal disease; for others it was denial of self-induced abortion, even in the face of evidence to the contrary.[42] The stubbornness of the denials suggests the ability of patients to reshape aspects of their lives that they could not face or about which they did not want others to know. An extreme case was that of Private Moira Chouinard, who entered the KWH on 17 January 1945 suffering from an incomplete abortion. The record that accompanied her from the military hospital revealed that she had been admitted on 13 December suffering from absence of menstruation (amenorrhoea) for six months with recent severe menstrual bleeding. On 14 December she passed a clot that 'was apparently products of conception,' which was confirmed by a Toronto lab. Nonetheless, '[p]atient denied any possibility of pregnancy ... and she did not change her story.' She finally entered the KWH because, after her discharge from the military hospital on 22 December, she started to bleed again.[43] Whether it was her own self-image that forced Moira to deny the possibility of pregnancy or her desire to remain in the military, she was willing to maintain her stance in the face of 'scientific' evidence to the contrary.

Not only did some women negotiate their own medical history, but they determined when their hospital record would end. Unhappy with their hospital stay, they simply discharged themselves. This was often noted with a very strong sense of disapproval in the case files. It is not always clear why such women made the decision or whether they made it at the urging of family and friends. However, any stay in the hospital was expensive, even for charity patients who had to consider the cost of being away from home and what that might mean for their family. For others, home may have been where they wanted to be even if they were very ill. On 14 June 1903 Mrs Stewart Hamilton, age thirty, had given birth to her first child after a long and somewhat complicated labour. The child only lived a few seconds. Mrs Hamilton's recovery was slow and she experienced abdominal pain, weakness, and feverishness as a result of puerperal septicaemia. By 5 July she started to improve, and on 5 August she decided to leave;[44] why is unclear, but it would seem safe to assume her decision was linked to the loss of her first child and to being separated from her family for a considerable time.

The most extreme example of women exerting control over the direction of their lives reflected in these medical records was their decision whether or not to carry a pregnancy to term. Much research has been done on the history of abortion, usually based on court cases against abortionists.[45] More often than not, something went wrong with the abortion (often the death of the woman) to bring it to the attention of the authorities.[46] If the incidence of abortion is seen as an iceberg and the court cases are the tip, and often the result of a woman dying, then the hospital cases are the next layer down, since women entered the hospital only when their abortion went wrong but when they were still alive. These records reveal the ordinariness of abortion, the apparent frequency with which women induced it in themselves, or often with the help, knowingly or not, of physicians. The ordinariness of it is also revealed by the reaction of some hospital doctors who, when faced with a woman who had self-aborted, at times suspended moral judgment despite abortion's illegality and their responsibility to alert the authorities.

All sorts of women self-induced abortions. Young, single women were clearly a major group. For example, Martha McNamara, a single twenty-two-year-old waitress from Newfoundland, entered the VGH on 9 January 1931. In September 1930 she had missed her period and so in early October she took some pills to encourage menstruation. She began to bleed in mid-October and assumed that this was her regular period since the timing was right. She stopped bleeding and then began again two days later. On Monday 5 January she obtained more pills from her physician and took a large dose (seven or eight) for the next three days. She began to bleed again and entered the hospital, whose record notes, 'Patient admits having had opportunity to become pregnant.' Part of a foetus was found in the vagina and removed.[47] Several themes emerge from this record. The fact that Martha was young and single and from outside the province suggests a person away from family and friends with few people to whom she could turn for help. Her narrative of what was wrong with her, namely irregular menstruation, indicates the ability of individuals to reshape what was happening to them. Of course, this may have been a story she concocted for her physician in order to get abortifacients, fearing that if he suspected she was pregnant little help would be forthcoming. The fact that her physician gave her the pills without testing her for pregnancy, however, is suggestive of complicity. The narrative suggests some agency on her part – she went to a physician for a problem that she diagnosed, she presented him with the diagnosis, and she expected help. When she first took the pills she was very early in her pregnancy. However, when she returned for more pills she was approximately four and one-half months pregnant and there could have been little doubt about her condition; still there was no suggestion that the physician was suspicious. Perhaps he did not have to be; he knew very well what the pills were for and had his own reasons for helping her. In either case, it reveals a physician willing to accept a lay diagnosis; he gave power to the patient or connived with her in the fiction of missed periods and gave her something to bring about an abortion.

Married women, too, resorted to abortion. Mrs Joanna Southern was married with one child age seven when she entered the VGH in August 1921. She was thirty-one years of age and in addition to her one child she had had two abortions in three years, although according to her statement they were not self-induced. The same could not be said for the one that brought her into the hospital, for she admitted 'passing a white bone knitting needle ... into the uterus.' This caused her 'considerable' pain and left her with a painful left side, which had been getting worse.[48] Mrs Southern was Roman Catholic. Whatever was prompting her to abort was viewed by her as much more significant than the beliefs of her church. This reveals the real difficulties that women had when their religious beliefs and the needs of their daily lives were at odds, something already seen with Mrs Barron and her anxiety over the use of birth control.

Why were women willing to do such harm to themselves? For those who were single, the answer is obvious. Societal disapproval was a harsh thing to face.[49] For married women, historians have pointed to the cost of bearing more children when a family could barely support the ones it already had. The case records suggest other reasons as well. Elizabeth Molawyz, for example, had only been married just over three months when she aborted at age nineteen in 1912. Perhaps she simply decided it was too soon after marriage to give birth.[50] In the case of Mrs Mavis Denton, although she already had one child, that child was only one and one-half years old and its birth had been a difficult one. Perhaps the memory of the birth trauma was such that Mavis Denton could not face another pregnancy, at least not yet. Certainly Mrs Ruggoso with her heart condition did not think she could. While it is impossible to know what was in the minds of these women, their records suggest that historians need to examine what women themselves thought of childbirth and their own bodies, especially the limits they placed on what those bodies could withstand.

Physician Sympathy

These case files reveal the apparent lack of difficulty in accessing abortifacients. We know very little about the control of drugs in this period, but what is clear is the ease with which some women patients received pills from physicians to bring on their periods. As a consequence, historians need to rethink views of physicians' public opposition to abortion since these cases suggest that some physicians identified with the women rather than the law.[51] When faced with the reality of attempted abortion, they saw their responsibility was to help their patients and not be moral arbiters. This was especially the case when faced with a woman who, for whatever reason, was felt to need a therapeutic abortion. Protestant medical ethics had long given priority to the life of the mother over the life of the child, and so when faced with a woman with severe TB or heart disease, many physicians had few qualms about providing abortions.[52] Yet the patient files reveal that some physicians were willing to broaden the reasons for therapeutic abortion. Mrs Wallace Williams, age thirty-eight, was two and one-half months pregnant with her first child when she entered the KWH on 20 January 1945. Her record reads: 'Patient has been very nervous because of family responsibilities she has worried a great deal, and has slept poorly ... and it was thought a therapeutic abortion was indicated.'[53] Thus, an abortion was to be provided for emotional reasons not medical ones. Clearly, some physicians could be much less dogmatic in their treatment than historians have suggested and also than the public medical literature suggests. But was this well known in the wider population? The sad case of Mrs Ruggoso, who felt compelled to self-abort because of her heart condition, suggests that it was not. She would have been a prime candidate for a therapeutic abortion, but she clearly did not feel that this was something she could hope to receive.

Conclusion

This overview of a selection of women's patient files has revealed the wealth of information included within them. These patient records have exposed to public scrutiny the lives of women who, in the normal course of their existence, would have remained unknown. In doing so, aspects beyond their medical care, such as domestic violence, are revealed. A close examination of these records has illuminated three aspects central to historians of women and medicine. The first is the strength that many women exhibited in their lives, and the discomfort of morbidity they endured before they sought relief from it. Physicians, however, could look at this same morbidity and conclude that women's bodies were problematic. Women, however, did not necessarily view their bodies in the same way, and at times focused on other factors, including medical treatment, to account for their medical problems. This suggests a site of disjunction when physicians and women patients met that needs much more investigation. Second, women patients were not without agency. Although limited by circumstances in their lives, by societal mores, and by the unequal power relationship they had with physicians, individual women did exert their will. They decided if and when they would seek medical help and how long they would undergo treatment. At times they were able to direct the nature of the medical treatment they received. They often diagnosed the origin of their ill health and indeed fashioned their own medical history. Lastly, the medical profession emerges from these records, not as a monolith, but as diverse in its treatment of women and more sympathetic on certain issues than the published historiography has suggested.

Notes

Research for this essay has been funded by the Social Sciences and Humanities Research Council of Canada (SSHRC) and the Hannah Institute for the History of Medicine. The Program for Scholars and Artists in Residence funded by the Rockefeller Foundation in 1994 and participation in a SSHRC Network grant 1993–6 provided me with the opportunity to develop many of the ideas in this essay.

1 See, for example, Wendy Mitchinson, *The Nature of Their Bodies: Women and Their Doctors in Victorian Canada* (Toronto: University of Toronto Press 1991); Gena Corea, *The Mother Machine: Reproductive Technologies from Artificial Insemination to Artificial Wombs* (New York: Harper and Row 1966); Corea, *The Hidden Malpractice: How American Medicine Mistreats Women* (New York: Harper Colophon Books 1985); Judith Walzer Leavitt, *Brought to Bed: Child-Bearing in America, 1750–1950* (New York: Oxford University Press 1986); Deborah McGregor, *Sexual Surgery and the Origins of Gynecology: J. Marion Sims, His Hospital, and His Patients* (New York: Garland Publishing 1989); Barbara Katz

Rothman, *In Labour: Woman and Power in the Birthplace* (London: Junction Books 1982); and Margarete Sandelowski, *Pain, Pleasure, and American Childbirth: From Twilight Sleep to the Read Method, 1914–1960* (Westport, Conn.: Greenwood Press 1984).

2   As Margaret Little has pointed out in her paper in this volume, agency is often individual rather than collective. Linda Gordon in *Heroes of Their Own Lives: The Politics and History of Family Violence: Boston, 1880–1960* (New York: Penguin Books 1988), 18, maintains that although women as a group may be subordinate in power to men, this does not mean that an individual woman cannot have agency or that her life is predetermined. In recent years, historians have been seeing agency as positive and heroic, but there is no necessary reason why it should be. Agency is limited, confined, influenced, and shaped by so many different factors that it is impossible for any person to have total agency. Thus, what historians need to discuss is degree of agency or types of agency.

3   On this topic see Patricia A. Kaufert and John O'Neill, 'Analysis of a Dialogue on Risks in Childbirth: Clinicians, Epidemiologists, and Inuit Women,' in Shirley Lindenbaum and Margaret Lock, eds, *Knowledge, Power and Practice: The Anthropology of Medicine and Everyday Life* (Berkeley: University of California Press 1993), 32–54.

4   For example, the forms kept by the obstetrics service of the RVH contain an admission sheet that has the usual information of name, address, marital status of the patient, the number of pregnancies she has had, her age, when admitted, date of confinement, discharge date, previous admissions, husband's name, his occupation, which doctor referred her, where she was born, her condition on admission, what doctor's service she is on, and the diagnosis – under which are listed her pelvic measurements, information on her pregnancy, labour, puerperium, whether there was operative interference, the foetal result, and the maternal result. Another sheet provides her medical history, including a section for the history of previous pregnancies and a history of the present one. Also included are the results of a physical exam, the results of a perineal exam and the expected date of birth. Another sheet describes the actual labour. Not all hospital records are as detailed as the RVH obstetrical records or collected in one file. In non-obstetrical records, for example, what often survives is just the admission records, the history of the patient, and a summary of treatment. In some hospitals surgical records were kept separate from the admission records: anaesthesia records could also be separate, as could detailed autopsy reports. For an excellent description of the development of hospital record keeping, see Barbara Craig, 'Hospital Records and Record Keeping, c. 1850–c.1950 Part I: The Development of Records in Hospitals,' *Archivaria* 29 (Winter 1989–90), 57–87, and Part II, *Archivaria* 30 (Summer 1990), 21–38. See also Guenter B. Risse and John Harley Warner, 'Reconstructing Clinical Activities: Patient Records in Medical History,'

Social History of Medicine 5:2 (August 1992), 183–206. Case histories as a form of medical discourse go back to the period of Hippocrates. The form the case history takes, however, changes with the particular concerns and medical doctrines of the period. Harriet Nowell-Smith, 'Nineteenth-Century Narrative Case Histories: An Inquiry into Stylistics and History,' *Canadian Bulletin of Medical History* 12:1 (1995), 51

5 This distillation is more detailed than what is provided in medical texts and journals, which tends to be a summary of the case history. The case histories are framed by the patient and other medical personnel in addition to the physician. Stanley Raffel, *Matters of Fact: A Sociological Inquiry* (London: Routledge and Kegan Paul 1979), 89

6 All the names of patients have been changed to protect their confidentiality. I have maintained the same initials and have substituted names suggestive of the same ethnicity. McGill University Archives, Royal Victoria Hospital Papers (RVH), RG 95, vol. 5, Gynaecology case charts, 1903, patient no. 1499, Rebecca Truscott, admitted 22 July 1903

7 Kitchener-Waterloo Hospital Archives (KWH), patient no. 1865, Mrs Frank Holtz, admitted 25 June 1943

8 RVH, RG 95, vol. 45, Gynaecology case charts, 1908, patient no. 3464, Mrs Lilia Howell, admitted 12 Aug. 1908

9 McGill University Archives, Montreal General Hospital Papers (MGH), RG 96, vol. 186, Patients casebook 3190–239, 1937, patient no. 3230, Mrs Paul Hackett, admitted 7 June 1937, discharged 2 July 1937

10 McGill University Archives, Annual reports of the Montreal General Hospital, 1920 and 1935

11 Percy E. Ryberg, *Health, Sex and Birth Control* (Toronto: Anchor Press 1942), 33

12 RVH, RG 95, vol. 1, Gynaecology case charts 1250–99, patient no. 1265, Mrs Martha McMullin, admitted 15 Oct. 1902

13 MGH, RG 96, vol. 186, Patients casebook 3190–239, 1937, patient no. 3213, Mrs Stewart Patton, admitted 6 June 1937, discharged 26 June 1937

14 KWH, patient no. 1748, Mrs A. Reich, admitted 16 May 1945

15 MGH, RG 96, vol. 200, Patients casebook 45–95, 1950, patient no. 59, Mrs Gaeton Laforce, admitted 3 Jan. 1950, discharged 19 Jan. 1950

16 Manuals existed, but the advice they gave was more general, whereas in the nineteenth century, especially at mid-century, the manuals tended to be very specific and used as a substitute for medical care, since many people would not have had access to physicians.

17 MGH, RG 96, vol. 163, Patients casebook, Gynaecology, 1902–4, patient no. 2, Jane Granger, admitted 6 Jan. 1902, discharged 19 Feb. 1902; Victoria General Hospital Archives (VGH), patient no. 1024, register no. 957, Surgical Dept., Mrs Mavis Denton, admitted 30 Dec. 1930, discharged 4 Jan. 1931; MGH, RG 96, vol. 199, Patients

casebook 893–936, 1950, patient no. 912, Miss Deborah Kelly, admitted 3 Feb.
1950, discharged 8 Feb. 1950

18 VGH, patient no. 334, register no. 241, Mrs Linda McCarthy, admitted 23 Nov.
1920, discharged 16 Dec. 1920

19 This was true in the nineteenth century as well. See Mitchinson, *The Nature of Their
Bodies*, 60–1.

20 MGH, RG 96, vol. 163, Patients casebook, Gynaecology 1902–4, patient no. 7, Mrs
Bernier, admitted 11 Jan. 1902, discharged 12 Feb. 1902; RVH, RG 95, vol. 88,
Obstetric casebook, patient no. 295, Mary Cord, admitted 1 Feb. 1902, discharged
1 Feb. 1901; VGH, patient no. 801, register no. 700, Mrs Martha Beacon, admitted
1 Mar. 1921, discharged 24 Mar. 1921

21 For a discussion of women's sense of time see Margaret Conrad, '"Sundays Always
Make Me Think of Home": Time and Place in Canadian Women's History,' in
Veronica Strong-Boag and Anita Clair Fellman, eds, *Rethinking Canada: The Prom-
ise of Women's History* (Toronto: Copp Clark Pitman, 1986), 67–81.

22 *Canadian Medical Association Journal* 10:10 (1920), 901; *Public Health Journal*
14:6 (1923), 243; *Canadian Medical Association Journal* 19:2 (1928), 228; *Canadian Public Health Journal* 23: 12 (1932): 566; *Canadian Medical Association Journal* 56: 2 (1947): 170

23 VGH, patient no. 274, register no. 212, Mrs Amy Hutter, Surgical Dept., admitted
18 Nov. 1920, discharged 3 Dec. 1920

24 VGH, patient no. 412, register no. 143, Mrs Linda Craton, admitted 12 Oct. 1930,
discharged 3 Nov. 1920

25 Autonomy has become one of the goals of modern medical ethicists (see Susan
Sherwin, *No Longer Patient: Feminist Ethics and Health Care* [Philadelphia: Temple University Press 1992]). By this is meant patient control over decision making
and their lives. However, this was never a major goal for the years 1900 to 1950.
Indeed, physicians seemed rather upset when patient agency was exerted.

26 See also Ruth R. Faden and Tom L. Beauchamp, *A History and Theory of Informed
Consent* (New York: Oxford University Press 1986).

27 Kenneth George Gray, *Law and the Practice of Medicine* (Toronto: Ryerson Press
1955), 33

28 MGH, RG 96, vol. 200, Patient casebook 45–95, 1950, patient no. 69, Mrs Galabin,
admitted 3 Jan. 1950, discharged 12 Jan. 1950

29 KWH, patient no. 19, Mrs James Hewitt, admitted 2 Jan. 1943

30 RVH, RG 95, vol. 112, Gynaecology case charts, patient no. 19276, Mrs Ginette
Kelly, admitted 25 Aug. 1921

31 KWH, patient no. 3230, Martha Kauffer, admitted 14 Oct. 1943

32 Gray, *Law and the Practice of Medicine*, 33

33 VGH, Medical Dept., patient no. 230, register no. 221, Mrs Eliza Barron, admitted

31 Dec. 1930, discharged 8 Jan. 1931. Mrs Barron's hospital record is a bit confusing since it discusses her marital relations, yet lists her as a widow. If marital relations is a euphemism for sexual relations, then the tension Mrs Barron felt between her religious convictions and her need for birth control would be even greater.

34 See Alfred Tyrer, *Sex, Marriage and Birth Control* (Toronto: Marriage Welfare Bureau 1943), 142, and Ryberg, *Health, Sex and Birth Control*, 25.

35 MGH, RG 96, vol. 190, Patients casebook 4725–69, 1945, Mrs Alvin Southard, patient no. 4756, admitted 17 July 1945, discharged 2 Aug. 1945

36 See *Ontario Journal of Neuro-Psychiatry* 1:2 (July 1922), 23; *Canadian Journal of Medicine and Surgery* 61:2 (February 1927), 4; *Canadian Medical Association Journal* 34:5 (May 1936), 597; Ryberg, *Health, Sex and Birth Control*, 185–6; *Manitoba Medical Review* 24:4 (April 1944), 104; *Alberta Medical Bulletin* 13:1 (January 1948), 64.

37 RVH, RG 95, vol. 88, Obstetric casebook, patient no. 252, Mrs Ruggoso, admitted 6 Nov. 1901, discharged (death) 12 Nov. 1901

38 VGH, Medical Dept., patient no. 131, register no. 138, Mrs Martha Quint, admitted 20 Jan. 1921, discharged (died) 22 Jan. 1921

39 MGH, RG 96, vol. 181, Patients casebook 1901–50, 1935, patient no. 1906, Miss Ann Valoux, admitted 24 Apr. 1935, discharged 13 May 1935

40 VGH, patient no. 1024, register no. 957, Surgical Dept., Mrs Mavis Denton, admitted 30 Dec. 1930, discharged 4 Jan. 31

41 VGH, patient no. 940, register no. 622, Surgical Dept., Myrtle McGinnis, admitted 24 Nov. 1930, discharged 2 Dec. 1930

42 For example, VGH, patient no. 3882, register no. 3742, Surgical Dept., Maureen Heffaus, admitted 5 Sept. 1931, discharged 14 Sept. 1931

43 KWH, patient no. 196, Moira Chouinard, admitted 17 Jan. 1945

44 RVH, RG 95, vol. 5, Gynaecology case charts, 1903, patient no. 1474, Mrs Stewart Hamilton, no date of admission, discharged 5 Aug. 1903

45 See Constance Backhouse, 'Involuntary Motherhood: Abortion, Birth Control and the Law in 19th Century Canada,' *Windsor Yearbook of Access to Justice* 3 (1983), 61–130; Angus McLaren and Arlene Tigar McLaren, *The Bedroom and the State: The Changing Practices and Politics of Contraception and Abortion in Canada, 1880–1980* (Toronto: McClelland and Stewart 1986).

46 Tracy Penny, '"Getting Rid of My Trouble": A Social History of Abortion in Ontario, 1880–1929,' M.A. thesis, Laurentian University, 1995, 45–6.; Susanne Klausen, 'Doctors and Dying Declarations: The Role of the State in Abortion Regulation in British Columbia,' *Canadian Bulletin of Medical History* 13:1 (1996), 53–82

47 VGH, patient no. 1205, register no. 1087, Surgical Dept., Martha McNamara, admitted 9 Jan. 1931, discharged 20 Jan. 1931

48 VGH, patient no. 1628, register no. 1465, Surgical Dept., Mrs Joanna Southern, admitted 21 Aug. 1921, discharged 28 Sept. 1921

49 For one study of how unwed mothers were treated see Andrée Lévesque, 'Mères ou malades: Les Québécoises de l'entre-deux-guerres vues par les médecins,' *Revue d'histoire de l'Amérique française* 38:1 (Summer 1984), 23–37.

50 RVH, RG 95, vol. 85, Gynaecology case charts, 1912, patient no. 5579, Elizabeth Molawyz, admitted 7 Sept. 1912

51 See McLaren and McLaren, *The Bedroom and the State* (1986).

52 For example, Mrs Harriet Scott, age 40, had TB and entered the RVH for 'emptying of the uterus' of a three-month foetus, after which she went to a sanatorium. RVH, RG 95, vol. 108, Gynaecology case charts, 1914, Mrs Harriet Scott, admitted 18 June 1914. Note the use of the terms: she is not in for an *abortion* but the *emptying of the uterus*. Physicians were able to distance themselves from what they were doing, in this case, by the language used. Not all physicians did so, however. In the case of Mrs Madeleine Knox from French Village, Nova Scotia, the VGH record was very blunt. She had TB and it was advised 'to terminate the pregnancy.' VGH, patient no. 3705, register no. 3517, Surgical Dept., Mrs Madeleine Knox, admitted 17 Aug. 1931, discharged 31 Aug. 1931. The institutions examined here were not Catholic ones, so the situation would have been quite different in such hospitals.

53 KWH, patient no. 217, Mrs Wallace Williams, admitted 20 Jan. 1945

PART FIVE
'PROBLEM' FAMILIES: ARENAS OF CONFLICT,
TARGETS OF REFORM

13

Uncovering and Reconstructing Family Violence: Ontario Criminal Case Files

ANNALEE GOLZ

The problems of domestic violence and other manifestations of violence against women remain central political concerns within the contemporary feminist movement. They have also become the subject of growing interest among feminist historians both internationally and in Canada.[1] Inspired in part by current struggles to raise awareness about violence against women, feminist historians are re-examining the internal dynamics of marital and familial relations in the past. Legal documents, especially criminal case files, have proved to be critical sources for probing and reconstructing the more obscure and often conflictual dimensions of family and personal life, especially since there are few other written sources available on the subject. At the same time, criminal court records pose very real interpretive challenges: they are, like many historical documents, often frustratingly incomplete, and court transcripts are riddled with gaps and silences that require cautious analysis and contextual explanation.

This paper will explore some of the analytical challenges and the enormous research potential of criminal case files involving various forms of family violence (for example, wife abuse, non-support, criminal neglect, and spousal murder). The cases were gleaned from the late-nineteenth- and early-twentieth-century Ontario court records available at four levels of court: the Police or Magistrates Court, the County Court Judges' Criminal Court, the Court of General Sessions, and the High Court of Justice or the Criminal Assizes.[2] These historical records, I argue, reveal a great deal about how family violence 'crimes' were adjudicated by the legal system, and how the institutions of marriage and the family, as well as the courtroom itself, constituted sites of a complex series of negotiations, antagonisms, and struggles. At the same time, the court testimonies, as written down through the medium of the police magistrate / court recorder and, in some cases, as presented through the voice of a paid interpreter, constitute historical 'texts' that were created within specific systems of meaning and relations of power. This process of re/construction makes it difficult to locate what could be termed the 'originator of meaning' or an 'authorial voice,' and renders problematic the endeavour of women's historians to gain access to the 'voices' and/or 'experiences' of those women who had been abused, neglected, and, indeed, murdered by husbands or other male family members.

A central premise of feminist historiography has long been to recover the historical experiences of women and recount how they themselves described and defined them. Despite my initial, naive excitement at having discovered the 'voices' of battered and neglected wives, it became increasingly evident, after reading hundreds of wife-battering and non-support cases, that women's court testimonies could not necessarily be read as literal renditions of their experiences. The particulars of each case, as recorded in the trial records, were certainly distinct in terms of the specific context and patterns of husbandly violence and neglect, but equally striking is the degree of rhetorical sameness and the structured and scripted narratives that recurred in the testimonies of wives (and indeed husbands). Thus, while criminal case files offer one of the few means of gaining some understanding of the 'experiences' of battered and neglected wives historically, or at least of how women constructed them, it is necessary to examine the gendered, social, and legal context as well as the relations of power within which wives articulated their grievances. In addition, the narrative strategies they (and their accused husbands) frequently employed in the courtroom must also be scrutinized.[3]

The Law, Criminal Case Files, and Uncovering Family Violence

When I began my research – at first I was mainly interested in wife-battering – I assumed that I was embarking on an impossible journey; impossible in the sense that if contemporary Canadian women encounter various socio-economic, legal, and ideological obstacles that inhibit them from prosecuting their abusive and violent husbands, then women in the past must have suffered in comparative isolation and silence. One Toronto *Globe* reporter in 1881 even suggested that the very commonness of wife abuse helped to explain the lack of extensive public discussion of this issue. 'Instances of wife-beating,' he wrote, 'are of every day occurrence, and cause little or no excitement.'[4] It soon became apparent, however, that apart from the connection made by temperance reformers between alcohol consumption and marital/familial discord, relative public silence on the issue of domestic violence in general and wife battering in particular was not necessarily matched on the level of married women's personal practice. The evidence shows that abused and battered wives, particularly those of Anglo-Celtic rural and urban working-class backgrounds, did seek some form of protection and redress through the courts. In the process, they attempted (though often unsuccessfully) to defend, assert, and/or negotiate their rather ambiguously defined right not to be beaten and abused by their husbands. Given the incompleteness and at times vagueness of the court records, however, accurately quantifying the number of wife-abuse cases heard before a particular court or even assessing conviction rates and sentencing patterns is difficult.

The vagueness of the court records stems partly from the fact that 'wife battering' per se did not constitute a discrete criminal category until 1909, when 'wifebeating' was first mentioned in the Canadian Criminal Code under an amendment that introduced whipping as a discretionary punishment for husbands convicted and imprisoned for assault causing bodily harm.[5] Both before and after this amendment, acts of verbal or physical aggression by husbands were usually prosecuted under more general offences ranging from threats and intimidation to various degrees of assault, wounding, and attempted murder. Consequently, one of the most consistent sources for quantifying the number of wife-abuse cases heard and adjudicated before a particular court – the criminal docketbooks and minutebooks in which the name of the plaintiff and the defendant, the nature of the charge, and the verdict and sentence were meticulously recorded[6] – are still problematic. This is principally because the precise relationship between the plaintiff and the defendant (as well as other potentially pertinent information related to class and race/ethnicity) remained unspecified, and because the terms 'wifebeating' and 'assault' were used interchangeably and inconsistently.

While the absence of distinct criminal sanctions against wife abuse has posed certain limitations, this relative 'invisibility' has also proved to be quite beneficial. Through the process of sifting through the available criminal case files in search of possible wife-battering cases, my understanding of the nature and extent of physical violence against female members within the institution of the family broadened incrementally (involving not only relationships between husbands and wives, but also between sons and mothers, and fathers and daughters). So did my sense of how struggles around masculine authority within the household were also profoundly gendered (extending to the often volatile relations between fathers and sons, and between brothers).[7] This more extensive research into a wider spectrum of criminal case files also resulted in a growing sense of the pervasiveness of verbal and physical violence against married women, and particularly of the various contexts within which wife battering or habitual abuse had occurred, but did not necessarily reach the legal system. In some criminal trials involving men charged with offences ranging from larceny to arson, the introduction of evidence indicating a history of intemperance coupled with abusive and/or neglectful behaviour was generally viewed by legal authorities as a further indication of 'bad character,' and was often taken into account when sentences were imposed.[8] In other instances, what initially appeared to be a rather routine criminal case involving an assault between two unrelated men, between a father and son, or between other family members quickly unravelled to reveal a violent dispute over the prerogative of a third party to intervene in a husband's self-perceived right 'to do as he pleased' in ruling his own household.[9] While these manly and familial contests between abuser and protector disclosed a great deal about how tenaciously husbands defended their position of authority within the institution of marriage, how crucial outside intervention was in halting excessive violence against wives, and how the courts viewed this form of violent third-party interference, they did not necessarily translate into husbands themselves being arrested on charges of wife assault. Thus, unlike the more interventionist methods of the church discipline courts or extralegal forms of community discipline like charivaris in the early nineteenth century,[10] the onus for laying a formal legal complaint, despite the interference of neighbours, relatives, or police constables, and depending on the extent of her injuries, tended to rest on the shoulders of the abused wife involved.

The degree to which incidents of wife abuse and the varied responses to them surfaced vicariously in the courts is further underscored by a relatively unusual case[11] involving Adam F. of Reach Township, who in 1904 was charged with attempted suicide. According to several witnesses who testified at the preliminary hearing, Mr F. had clearly tried to take his own life by cutting his throat with a butcher knife. His son Edward stated that he had discovered his father on the floor of his house lying in a pool of blood, with a bloody knife lying nearby. Although not necessarily essential to the prosecution of the case, the nagging question that seemed to linger throughout the trial was why Mr F. had committed this seemingly desperate act. According to another witness, the accused had claimed to have 'done it' because 'he wanted to get out of trouble.' The meaning of this ambiguous phrase did not become evident until Mr F. took the stand on his own behalf. He candidly informed the judge that on the day in question, he had, for reasons he did not disclose, taken an axe and broken the stove, and then had proceeded to assault his wife by slapping and kicking her. 'My wife cried murder,' he added. '[M]y wife went over to Mrs Clevertons place. Mrs Cleverton came to our House and she threatened the Law, and I thought to get out of trouble I would take my life without a minutes thought. I took my knife now produced in Court and cut my throat with it. I intended to kill myself at the time.' Mrs Cleverton, his sister-in-law, offered additional details, suggesting that Mr F. had not only been 'drinking a good deal' and was generally 'dissatisfied with his marriage,' but also had abused his wife for years and to such an extent that she was afraid to live alone with him. Unfortunately, the recorded testimonies did not provide any possible explanation for why threatening Mr F. with 'the Law' would have precipitated his attempted suicide. Did it represent an act of remorse? Did he fear a loss of reputation should his abusive behaviour became public? Or did he indeed suffer from 'bad spells' and 'convulsions' as hinted at during the trial? Interestingly, no medical evidence was included. Despite all the unanswered questions associated with this case, Mr F. was eventually convicted of attempting to commit suicide. For want of another feasible explanation for his act, the Whitby County Court judge concluded that Mr F. had been insane at the time, and this warranted his detainment in custody until the lieutenant-governor had decided his fate.[12]

Although Adam F. constructed his suicide attempt as a response to the possibility of criminal prosecution, sentencing patterns, based on a sample of 431 wife-abuse cases that surfaced in the lower and higher criminal courts between 1857 and 1920, indicate that abusive husbands generally had little to fear in terms of severe punishments if convicted of wife assault. When husbands were convicted, the sentences imposed tended to vary according to the nature of the charge and the severity of the crime. It was not entirely uncommon for the courts to find excessively brutal and murdering husbands/fathers not guilty by reason of insanity or other apparent 'mental disorders.'[13] Some desperate wives or other family members also attempted to ensure the long-term removal of extremely and habitually violent husbands/fathers from the household by charging them with being insane, and hence dangerous to both family and community. In 1882, for example, James H. of Hibbard Township was eventually deemed insane after evidence at his trial indicated a steady escalation of violent behaviour. He had kicked and assaulted his daughter with an iron poker, accused his wife of trying to poison him and then threatened to murder her, and tried to strike his older son with a chair – all the while asserting that 'he was in his own house and he could do as he pleased.' Fearful for their lives, Mr H.'s wife and children testified to his increasingly violent 'bad turns,' and declared that he was 'not a fit subject to be about and unless he is incarcerated, the family is in danger.'[14]

Nevertheless, according to my sample, the most common sentences imposed by the criminal courts included a monetary fine (ca. 19 per cent), a term of imprisonment (ca. 21 per cent), and, most often, a suspended sentence with or without a recognizance and sureties binding a husband to keep the peace, usually for a term of between six months and two years (ca. 59 per cent). What these general patterns suggest is that in the majority of cases, the criminal courts were less inclined to punish violent husbands than to endeavour to mediate marital relations and restore order within the community by attempting to regulate their behaviour. One of the underlying premises of binding a husband to keep the peace was the extraction of a promise, often reinforced by a bond and sureties, of better conduct towards his wife in the future. The outcome of one 1897 assault case involving Cornelius B. was typical. The judge ruled that if the accused would 'take back his wife' and treat her 'properly,' the court would suspend sentence. When the defendant agreed to the conditions by entering into his own recognizance to keep the peace for one year and to appear for sentence when called upon, he was discharged from custody.[15] The same happened to John W. of Pickering Township, convicted in 1905 of pointing a loaded firearm at his wife and threatening to murder her after she attempted to leave him for the eleventh time because of his abusive behaviour. The conditions of his suspended sentence included paying a bond of $300 and signing the following statement: 'I John W[ ] am to in future use [my] wife properly or she is to leave with out any disturbance, that [I] must [do] everything desireable of a husband towards his wife, Lizzie Y[ ] W[ ].' An additional clause specified that Lizzie, who was evidently perceived as equally culpable, 'must [also] be a proper wife towards her husband.'[16]

Particularly for poor and working-class wives with children, this form of mediation could potentially serve to modify a husband's violent behaviour without risking the economic difficulties that his imprisonment would entail. Given the structural dependency of many wives on a male wage and their economic vulnerability more generally, even the temporary absence of the male breadwinner could seriously threaten the often precarious working-class and rural family economy. Moreover, some husbands, like William M. of Toronto, greeted their prison sentence with, what one Toronto *Globe* reporter described as, 'a number of blasphemous threats as to what he would do when he was released.'[17] After 1909, although the punishment was rarely implemented, there was at least the further possibility that whipping would be added to a term of imprisonment. The severity of this additional punishment carried even greater risks of retaliation.[18] Given these various considerations, it is not surprising that many married women specifically requested that the courts bind their husbands to keep the peace. Other wives, however, particularly those compelled to return to the courts to lay further complaints, were more sceptical about the effectiveness of peace bonds in preventing further assaults. As Catharine B. of Galt told the magistrate, '[w]hen he was bound over last year to keep the peace towards me, he has been worse since, [I] do not want him bound over to keep the peace again, it is no use.'[19]

In some instances, court decisions were shaped by the perceived economic needs of the particular family involved as opposed to the potential benefits of imposing harsher penalties. In 1913, Nathan K., a Whitby junk dealer, was convicted of beating his nineteen-year-old daughter, Solphie, and was released on a suspended sentence, on the condition that he keep the peace for two years. Two years later, he was back in court on charges of assaulting his wife, Etta, occasioning her actual bodily harm for which he received another suspended sentence. In the period between the two trials, and during the year after his second conviction, a series of letters between Solphie, the Attorney-General's Office, the local justice of the peace, and the Oshawa Police Department revealed that Mr K. was not fulfilling the conditions of his suspended sentences, a situation that created a dilemma among legal authorities as to whether or not a harsher sentence should be imposed. What these various communiques offer is a relatively rare glimpse into the actual deliberations of legal authorities in family-violence cases, particularly since they were under considerable pressure from members of Mr K.'s immediate family.

Solphie, acting on behalf of the family and particularly her non-English-speaking mother, requested that the Attorney-General's Office intervene in the case by writing a series of complaints and a lengthy letter that recounted nightmarish stories of the brutality her father was inflicting on the family. 'The same thing happens nearly every day and night,' she wrote. 'My father treats us so harshly we cannot stand it any longer. Oh! God have mercy on my poor mother.' Soon afterwards, a briefly worded telegram declared: 'No protection here – Father ill-treating Mother.' In her complaints, Solphie also strongly intimated that local police constables were condoning her father's behaviour. She noted that their lame attempts at reasoning with him using 'gentle words' were largely ineffective in preventing further abuse. These latter accusations prompted a stern letter from the Attorney-General's Office to the crown attorney in Whitby, which stated, 'Once more Miss K[ ] has complained about the treatment of her mother. She alleges that on Thursday last ... her mother was assaulted and seriously injured by her father, but that the Police will not take the matter up. I think it would be well to enquire as to this and insist if necessary that the Police shall do their duty in the matter.' Oshawa's acting chief constable hastily denied these allegations, depicting Mrs K. as a volatile and hysterical woman of questionable character, and strongly implying that there was little indication that her husband's behaviour warranted more direct police intervention. The more pressing issue raised in the correspondence, however, was whether the mounting evidence of Mr K.'s habitually abusive behaviour over what amounted to a three-year period warranted imposing a stiffer sentence. According to the Attorney-General's Office, there were at least two considerations involved: 'I need not remind you that for wife beating when the assault is serious, the man is liable to be whipped ... [but] there is some hesitation about imprisoning K[ ] because it would leave his family destitute.' By December

1916, the County Court judge had apparently come to a similar conclusion, indicating that the economic stability of the family in question should take precedence. In his final verdict on the case, he stated, '[N]othing has been brought before me to cause me to think that matters would be improved by imposing sentence at present. Sentence is further suspended.'[20]

What the details of this case suggest, then, is that the economic well-being of the family unit that required the presence of a functioning (albeit habitually abusive) male breadwinner was the foremost consideration in the decision of the court. Like many abused wives and daughters, Etta and Solphie also had to weigh their economic survival against their desire for personal safety and freedom from physical violence. But their repeated appeals to the legal system for some form of protection went largely unheeded, and given their apparent persistence, they were probably more discouraged than heartened by the eventual outcome. In effect, the verdicts and sentences handed down by the courts offered few guarantees that patterns of abuse would abate or cease.

The economic reliance on a male breadwinner relates to another pattern that surfaced in the criminal-court records, particularly in those cases involving non-support or the failure to provide necessaries. What the criminal cases prosecuted under these legal provisions indicate is that violence against married women and children could manifest itself in various forms that went beyond the more commonly identified acts of overt verbal and/or physical aggression, suggesting that both the meaning and boundaries of what constituted family violence require some historical reconsideration. Unlike the generic criminal categories under which wife abuse was prosecuted, desertion, non-support, and criminal neglect were tried under specific and widening legal provisions during the late nineteenth and early twentieth centuries. Within an industrializing economy, these broadening criminal sanctions reflected an attempt to deter husbands from reneging on their marital and familial obligations, to prevent male breadwinners from leading 'idle lives,' and to ensure that the costs of maintaining wives and children would remain the economic responsibility of husbands, rather than a social burden on the municipality or local charities.[21] Thus, beginning in 1869, the legal responsibility of husbands to provide for the support and maintenance of their wives and children, as originally defined and enforced under common law, was subject to further regulation under two separate sections of the Criminal Code. In one section, an 1869 act respecting vagrants included a stipulation that all persons who were able to work, but wilfully refused or neglected to maintain themselves and their families, were subject to a fine of up to fifty dollars or a prison term of up to two months. In 1874, the maximum term of imprisonment was extended to six months.[22] In the more widely used section, a husband's refusal to provide his wife and children with 'necessary food, clothing, and lodging' without 'lawful excuse,' if it caused bodily harm, life endangerment, or permanent injury to health, carried with it a maximum penalty of up to three years' imprisonment. (In 1913, the definition of criminal non-support was substantially broadened, going beyond the afore-mentioned categories to include 'destitution' and 'necessitous circumstances' as grounds for prosecution).[23] Given these widening legal sanctions and the economic expectations of wives, one of the most frequent reasons that husbands appeared in the criminal courts was for breaches of their financial responsibilities either during marriage or after marital separation.[24]

Many criminal cases prosecuted under the provisions against criminal non-support involved fairly common situations in which a husband had deserted or was neglecting to provide adequately for his wife and children, forcing wives to seek some form of economic support elsewhere.[25] Other more serious cases, however, revolved around the refusal by husband/fathers to obtain medical attention for their wives or children during childbirth or illness, or to provide basic necessities for family members, situations that could have life-threatening or even fatal consequences. In some instances, this refusal could be attributed to poverty or destitution, or to religious beliefs, such as those adhered to by Christian Scientists, who prescribed faith and prayer rather than the solicitation of medical attention; in others involving criminal neglect and even manslaughter, the court transcripts often revealed motives that were more calculated and intentional. As indicated by the case of Armetta M., whose infant died shortly after childbirth because her spouse refused to assist her or to obtain the aid of a doctor or nurse,[26] her husband's actions reflected how patriarchal authority could be exercised through the tight and at times malicious control of the economic resources within the household. In other words, family violence and the unequal relations of power underlying it emerged in various guises, which included the physical violence and life endangerment resulting from the deliberate denial and withdrawal of sufficient food, clothing, and medical assistance.

While criminal cases involving non-support and especially criminal neglect strongly suggest the need for redefining the meaning and parameters of domestic violence, a closer scrutiny of the kinds of physical abuse inflicted on married women tends to indicate the necessity to rethink the boundaries between physical and sexual violence. In their court testimonies, some wives did imply, often in veiled language, that marital rape or other forms of sexual coercion were linked to the physical mistreatment meted out by their husbands. Emma S. of Ellice Township, who charged her husband with assault in 1905, was perhaps the most frank in this regard. In her court testimony, she described a series of incidents, in which she was physically punished and violently threatened by her husband because she 'objected [to] sleeping with him' when he was drunk: 'He was drunk – He wanted me to go to bed with him – I refused going with him – He threw me on the bed ... He took hold of my left arm with force ... He pulled me around the room and swore at me – He told me I might keep my damned hole to my self and that he would break my back – that scene lasted for an hour or hour and a half – My arm was bruised and he bit me on the arm and it was discolored – it was black and blue then yellow ... My leg was marked – either kicked or done by his throwing himself on me ... On Friday and Thursday of last week he abused me again ... I went upstairs, he followed me, locked me in the room and was going to throw me on the bed – He said he should break my damned neck, he had the butcher knife in his hand ... I was very much afraid of him.'[27]

On a more symbolic level, court transcripts, which often consisted of medical reports in wife-assault cases and post-mortem examinations in wife-murder cases, also indicated that at times a husband's kicks and blows targeted specific areas of the female body. In 1916, Yustena B.'s doctor testified that the wounds she sustained at the hands of her husband included not only 'chunks of skin knocked off her neck and face as though taken off by finger nails,' but, more seriously, a 'large red bruise [or lump] on her left breast,' apparently caused by her husband's knee.[28] A more ominous case involved Almeda S., who in 1886 was brutally beaten by her enraged husband on a village street in Kenyon Township. Several members of the small community, who attempted to intercede on her behalf but were averted when Mr S. threatened to shoot anyone who interfered, informed the court that, despite Almeda's pleas 'for mercy' as she knelt before him, her husband's repeated kicks were directed at her 'private parts.' One witness concluded his testimony by stating, '[I]t was the most brutish act I ever saw.'[29] Similarly, the post-mortem examination of Jane W.'s body, after she died of injuries sustained in being beaten by her husband, concluded that, in addition to contusions over her entire body, there was 'no doubt that Jane W[] died from the effects of an external injury received on or about the private parts.' Jane's neighbour, who cared for her before her death, declared that 'the private parts were so black and swelled, I could hardly look at it.'[30] As these and other similar cases suggest, the various intersections between physical and sexual violence cannot be understood when considered as discrete or disconnected issues. Rather, the sexual intimidation of wives or the scripts found on their bruised and dead bodies tend to disclose how some husbands' expressions of masculine entitlement, their sense of husbandly proprietorship, and, indeed, their rage were concentrated on those parts of their wives' bodies that most signified their femaleness and their sexuality.

Despite my initial scepticism about the feasibility of uncovering extensive evidence of wife abuse in the Ontario criminal case files of the late nineteenth and early twentieth century, my excursion into these historical records has generally been highly fruitful. It has been a process of constant re/discovery, of shedding certain preconceptions about the nature of family violence, of broadening my understanding of its pervasiveness, complexities, and parameters, and of redefining what constituted violence within the institutions of marriage and the family during this period. Reconstructing and interpreting the various meanings associated with domestic violence and the workings of patriarchal authority, however, does not end with considering the diversity and richness of the criminal case files. As court narratives of abused wives and violent husbands indicate, the courtroom itself became a site in which other battles were fought.

Wives and Husbands: The Courtroom as a Site of Struggle

While the criminal-court records suggest that incidents of wife abuse were by no means an uncommon phenomenon, it is, of course, arguable that many such cases remained undetected. Various social and ideological pressures could inhibit wives from launching criminal proceedings against their husbands. As one married woman put it, she 'didnt like to expose him or herself.'[31] Other considerations, such as fear, self-blame, or the possible loss of economic support, may also have accounted for the failure of some wives to appear in court or for their sudden withdrawal of complaints. Class and ethnicity also seemed to influence whether or not abused wives were inclined to turn to the criminal-justice system. For instance, Anglo-Celtic rural and urban working-class women demonstrated the strongest sense of entitlement to legal protection by their active presence on their own behalf in the criminal courts. This presence may have been partially based on a sense of ethnic affinity with legal authorities, a common language, and a familiar British-based system of justice; a connectedness that non-English-speaking immigrant women or, for that matter, Aboriginal women might not so readily have shared. Moreover, the comparative absence of battered Anglo-Saxon middle-class women in the criminal as opposed to the more discrete and expensive civil courts[32] was not so much due to men of the middle and professional classes being less likely to abuse their wives, as some social commentators argued, but was more the outgrowth of strengthening Anglo-Protestant bourgeois notions of companionate marriage, domestic privacy, and class propriety. The flip side of these ideals, particularly for white middle-class women, was the desire to avoid the glare of community scandal.[33] In 1878, one newspaper commentator claimed that unlike the artisan and labouring classes, where 'we are chiefly, if not exclusively, to look for the dangerous wife-beater,' wife abuse among the upper and middle classes never exceeded 'an occasional blow or two of a not dangerous kind.' He also noted positively that even though the latter incidents might become a source of 'gossip in the particular circles concerned, or as things whispered ... by aggrieved domestics,' the prudent protection of 'family honour' necessitated that they 'rarely if ever' came to 'public discussion in a Court of law.'[34]

When instances of wife abuse did reach the legal system, most cases, especially if classified as relatively 'minor' offences such as verbal threats or common assault, were tried summarily before the local justice of the peace or in the community-based Police Magistrate's Court. It was here, at the lowest level of the judicial hierarchy, that abused wives first encountered the criminal-justice system and confronted the wide discretionary powers wielded by the presiding justice of the peace or police magistrate, and where particularly working-class family (and community) members appeared to settle a wide range of disputes and conflicts. Unfortunately, there are few surviving detailed records of the daily adjudication and mediation of familial and community matters in the lower courts.[35] Beyond the local courts, and as was the case with other indictable offences, more serious wife-assault cases involving grievous bodily harm, wounding, and attempted murder were referred either to the County Court Judges' Criminal Court for trial before a judge, or to the Court of General Sessions or the Criminal Assizes for trial by jury, depending on the declared wishes of the defendant. Since the criminal case files gathered and produced in the higher courts have been preserved and tend to be more detailed, it is these trial records that most clearly illustrate the kinds of marital tensions and struggles that emerged in the courtroom.

Once in the courtroom, an abused wife was placed in a position in which she was forced to confront not only the ambiguities of the law, but also either the stony silence of her husband or his litany of denials, justifications, and counter-accusations. In these marital battles, as presided over by judge or jury, both the plaintiff and the defendant tended to employ various strategies to gain or to divert the attention of the courts. While wives sought, in various ways, to defend their right to a degree of physical safety and to assert their sense of entitlement to legal protection, husbands used various rhetorical means to elicit the empathy of the legal authorities. At times, the confrontation and struggles between husbands and wives over, for example, divergent interpretations of the incident in question would erupt into heated exchanges and mutual recriminations, particularly when the accused invoked his legal prerogative to cross-examine all witnesses.

The most common response of husbands to charges of wife abuse or indeed wife murder was silence. Given the rules of evidence, and the fact that many pled not guilty or guilty to a lesser charge such as common assault, it is not surprising that husbands felt it prudent, or their legal counsel advised them, to say nothing lest they provided potentially self-incriminating evidence. While this silence on the part of husbands makes it difficult to grasp how they interpreted and constructed their own actions, the silent, even unnerving presence of a husband in the courtroom could exude and reflect a degree of power and control over the proceedings. More specifically, given the dynamics of these particular trials, in which wives were largely responsible for providing the burden of proof and in which their wifely conduct often came under intense scrutiny, the strategy of silence could effectively deflect the court's attention away from the accused, and divert its focus more directly on the plaintiff.

When husbands did formally respond to the charge, their statements tended to fall into a number of fairly predictable patterns. Some husbands, especially when their wives appeared in court with visible signs of ill treatment, simply denied that they were responsible for the injuries, insisting that the wounds were the consequence of accidental or drunken falls, or had in some manner been self-inflicted. Other married men appeared more remorseful, but their regret was often constructed around certain external causes that had either justified or precipitated their violent behaviour. The most notable justifications included the effects of alcohol and, particularly in cases when husbands strongly suspected or had caught their wives committing adultery, intense sexual jealousy and even temporary insanity. Given that marital infidelity signified one of the gravest offences a married woman could commit, this latter defence, often described in terms of 'exceptional' or 'mitigating' circumstances, tended to elicit considerable sympathy from judges, juries, and members of the community.[36]

Generally, however, drunkenness served as a central explanatory justification for a husband's abusive behaviour, and remained the most pervasive social explanation for wife abuse and familial disharmony at the turn of the century. While this connection between intemperance and family violence tended to divert attention from the hierarchical relations of power that structured relations between husbands and wives, the symbolic importance of the brutish drunken husband/father as the principal cause of the disintegration of the family unit did create a space, as Kathryn Harvey has argued, for wives 'to publicly name the crime of wife-battering.'[37] At the same time, husbands did attempt to appropriate the discourse of the temperance movement and use it for their own purposes, a strategy that could potentially displace and immobilize the efficacy of their wives' complaints. In 1882, Patrick L. of Gananoque attempted to absolve himself of any responsibility for brutally assaulting and beating his wife by explaining to the judge, 'I don't remember striking my wife ... I think liquor was the cause of it.' In responding to her husband's claim, however, Sarah L. remained adamant, insisting that even though her husband had been drunk when 'he hammered me from room to room,' he was certainly 'not as drunk as he pretended to be.'[38] In 1905, a more appropriately repentant Conrad S. of Ellice Township also blamed alcohol for what amounted to sixteen years of habitual abuse, when he stated, 'I did not intend to hurt, I did not intend to break her back ... I think I would get on all right if it were not for whiskey ... So far as drinking I intend to quit ... and become a sober man.' In this instance, Emma, his wife, rather acutely attributed his excessive violence to another factor, which had little to do with his intemperate habits: 'All his abuse is carried on in anger and wickedness, but with the intent to boss me and control.'[39]

Other husbands, however, employed a more direct approach as a way of gaining the empathy of the male judge or all-male jury, particularly by launching into a litany of complaints about their wives' alleged intemperate habits and aggressive conduct, their flagrant disobedience of husbandly authority, or their consistent failure to fulfil assigned tasks or to provide expected services in the household. And these various deficiencies were constructed as nothing less than legitimate marital grievances and instances of undue provocation. John H., an Oshawa storekeeper, on the other hand, responded to the wife-beating charge launched against him simply by emphasizing his wife's personal failures: 'My wife is not very smart. Whatever anyone comes to tell her she believes it and she get mad at me and I never have a good time with her.'[40]

Countering the various claims made by their husbands, or simply establishing the legitimacy of their own complaints, accounted for certain recurring characteristics that surfaced in the testimonies of married women. When swearing their depositions or while undergoing (often gruelling) cross-examination, wives frequently assured the magistrate or judge that they had not, for example, been intoxicated at the time of the beating, that they had in no way verbally or physically provoked their husbands' violence, or that they had found themselves in the untenable position of attempting to protect their children from being beaten.[41] They also went to great lengths to indicate that they were good, hardworking, and respectable wives and mothers, undeserving of their husbands' ill treatment. In 1912, Ethel W. of Oshawa charged her husband with beating her and attempting to strangle her. During the trial, her husband, an ironworker, did admit that he had taken 'hold of her by the arms and shook her' because he 'found fault with the fish she was cooking,' but he quickly went on to suggest that the main source of his marital grievance was not necessarily her lack of culinary skills. Rather, his central complaint was what he described as his 'wretched life' because, as he put it, 'she dont look after me.' He also insisted that during marital disputes, 'she can pound me as well as I pound her.' In her own testimony, Ethel responded to each of these claims, first by adamantly denying that she had struck her husband, and second by repeatedly disavowing that she had neglected her wifely duties. 'I keep my own house clean as I can,' she stated. 'I always get his meals ready for him ... My house is clean, you can go down and see it. Mrs A[ ] was down and undoubtedly looked around a bit.'[42]

Given intensifying social and legal concerns about the problems of non-support at the turn of the century, this issue also became an integral part of the arsenal of grievances that wives invoked in their struggles with their husbands, emphasizing that their spouses were not only violent and abusive, but also less than adequate economic providers. After laying a complaint against her husband, William, for aggravated assault in 1881, Emma R. of St Thomas told the local police magistrate that on the previous day the accused had come home 'the worse of liquor' and had struck her repeatedly 'on the head and face with the potato masher' because she had reprimanded him for selling the last two chickens they possessed. Emphasizing that this was 'not the first time the defendant has assaulted and threatened [her],' Emma went on to explain that her shiftless husband was equally guilty of reneging on his responsibilities as a breadwinner and on his labour duties within the household. 'The defendant is a shoemaker,' she stated. 'I have not received a dollar of his money since Christmas. I have of my own labor had to provide for myself, pay rent and buy fire wood. Yesterday while I was out washing the defendant instead of cutting wood to burn broke up two of the chairs for fuel.'[43] Alvina T. of Stratford presented a very similar series of grievances in 1903, after charging her husband, David, a Grand Trunk railway worker, with assaulting, threatening, and putting her 'out of doors.' While her principal aim was to 'have him bound over to keep the peace,' since, in her words, 'I am afraid of him,' she sought to reinforce the legitimacy of her complaint, by exposing his other failures as a husband and father: 'Deft has assaulted me very often since our marriage 13 years ago ... He has on several occasions threatened to kill me ... I am a strictly sober hard-working woman. I do the best I can for my family of 5. Deft does not supply me with sufficient means to keep the house and I have had to take in washing and go out to work to earn enough to buy clothes for self and children ... I have been informed that he gets $2 a day ... Deft does not pay rent – we have been served with [a] notice to quit if the rent [is] not paid.'[44]

In addition, the testimonies of neighbours, letters containing character references, and petitions from members of the community could potentially bolster or undermine a wife's claim for justice or protection from the legal system. During the 1916 trial of Wasil B., charged with assaulting and beating his wife, a neighbour attested to the good character of Yustena, his wife, when she stated, '[T]his woman is a good woman, not drunken or quarrelsome.' When asked about the rather suspicious cut on Mr B.'s forehead, she corroborated Yustena's own statement by indicating that 'she would not hurt her husband, only to defend herself.'[45] Similarly, the 1898 case involving Ellen W. of Pickering Township, who charged her husband with aggravated assault, was assisted considerably by a series of letters submitted by neighbours and members of the community. Emphasizing that she was not only an 'honest, hardworking, and respectable woman,' but also a 'good and faithful wife and mother ... worthy of the confidence of her husband,' the community tended to stress those ideal traits that the County Court judge would conceivably interpret as those of a woman deserving the protection of the courts.[46]

By contrast, in the 1895 case involving Sarah S. of Port Perry, who charged her husband with wounding when he fired four shots at her, seventy-four citizens of the community, including the reeve and the chief constable, signed a petition outlining the reasons why the defendant, Mr S. should be treated with 'deep sympathy' and leniency. In their collective statement, it was Mrs S., who was directly implicated, by having 'persecuted, betrayed and provoked the man beyond endurance' and through the 'inhuman manner in which he has been treated and the unbearable provocation which he had to bear for the last few years.' The petition concluded by emphasizing, '[W]e ... know him to be a sober industrious and loyal citizen, somewhat excitable but perfectly harmless and obliging.'[47]

For many wives, however, what motivated them to lay complaints against their husbands and what often shaped their narratives in the courtroom was the fear that, if their husbands were allowed to act on the self-perception that they had the right to 'do as they pleased,' and unless they obtained some form of legal protection, they or their children would eventually become the fatal victims of their husbands' violence. In many instances, their testimonies not only included accounts of the brutal and often gruesome details of the physical violence they had endured, but also evoked a sense of desperation that their lives were in imminent danger. Many wives, for example, echoed the sentiments of Hanora C. of Merrickville, when she told the County Court judge that after her husband attempted to choke her and threatened to kill her, 'I have not slept in my house for a week for fear that he would carry out his threats to murder me.'[48] Perhaps more ominously, the concerns of some married women were articulated in terms of their husbands' intentional attempts to ensure a degree of privacy before proceeding to assault them, a situation that would potentially deter outside intervention. As Johanna R. of the Village of Iroquois stated in 1880, when her husband came home drunk and began to assault her brutally, the problem was not simply that there was 'no one present at the time,' but that he 'made me hook the door before he commenced to abuse me.'[49] While it is certainly possible that some wives sought to bolster their complaints by constructing the abuse and the beatings they had received as exceptionally severe or inhuman, and by depicting themselves as victims in imminent peril, this should not necessarily lead us to discount the anxieties, be it from verbal threats or physical violence, that these women undoubtedly felt. For as criminal trials involving wife-murder cases clearly suggest, it was indeed often a fine line between being a battered wife and being a dead one.

While most husbands charged with murdering their wives did not provide written or verbal statements, those who did often utilized the same explanations and justifications for killing their wives as they did for abusing them. Moreover, the degree of culpability of wives for their own deaths often became a central component in the subsequent murder and manslaughter trials, the main difference being that they had been rendered permanently silent and no longer had the opportunity to defend their status as 'good, dutiful, and respectable wives and mothers.' Rufus W. of Smiths Falls, who in 1910 was charged with strangling his wife to death, provided a whole list of marital grievances, which he maintained had incited his murderous act. In his unusually detailed statement, he explained that he had been angry that his wife had, 'on a lot of lies and a pack of other women,' been responsible for his conviction and imprisonment on charges of non-support. He further stated that she had also consistently failed to fulfil her wifely obligations, and had ultimately provoked him: 'My wife did not treat me right. She would go to hotels and work. She also drank beer and whiskey. She was intemperate for years ... I never lived agreeably with my wife ... [and] I have frequently charged my wife with misbehaviour ... She brought it on herself. I spoke roughly to her. She said "Go to Hell" ... She threw a tea pot at me, then I grabbed her and choked her to death, and I guess she got her dues.' He also admitted that he had been 'wanting to do it for this last three or four days,' and then congratulated himself on his efficiency, having 'done a good job of it ... that's the way to do it, do it right and be done with it.'

During the subsequent trial, both the prosecution and especially the defence felt it necessary to investigate at least some of the allegations Mr W. had made against his wife. While the defence attorney attempted to prove that Mr W.'s addiction to liquor had caused irritability and 'weakening tendencies on [his] mental as well as moral faculties,' he also consistently asked the witnesses a series of probing questions about the conduct and character of the deceased. These queries typically revolved around whether Mrs W. had been drinking on the evening of the murder and to what extent she may have incited her husband's violent actions. The following cross-examination of Ella, one of the daughters, suggests the direction of his interrogation:

Q. I suppose your mother, as far as the talk was concerned gave your father just as much as he gave her?

A. Yes sir.

Q. And that was pretty often?

A. Yes sir.

Q. I suppose further, that your mother jawed your father pretty well, pretty often?

A. Not that I can think of.

Q. Well, when the row started, she held her own as far as the talk was concerned?

A. No reply.[50]

In a somewhat similar vein, John B. of East Whitby Township, after fracturing his wife's skull with an axe and then setting fire to their dwelling house, also offered a statement, in which he directly implicated his spouse for her own exceptionally brutal death. While the testimony at the trial revealed that he had not only habitually abused her, but had also threatened 'to do the old woman in' ever since they had been married eight years previously, he nonetheless offered the following statement: 'The 8 years I [was] with the late Mrs B[ ] should have been the most useful part of my life but her obstinacy discouraged out everything ... I think she was suffering from recurrent insanity ... I think in this case I should be acquitted, [I] have always been a peacemaker ... I never had any intention to kill Mrs B, only to frighten her from keeping such a flock of cats, the said cost as much to keep them as ourselves. These cats frequently evacuated between the sheets and on top of bed clothing, vomited there, also exasperating me frequently to an uncontrollable state of mind.'[51]

While both Rufus W. and John B. were convicted and sentenced to be executed for murdering their wives (the latter obtaining a reprieve largely owing to his advanced age), other husbands were treated with greater leniency. This was particularly the case when any real or alleged moral indiscretion on the part of their wives was introduced into evidence, circumstances that were considered by judges and juries as extenuating enough to warrant the lesser charge of manslaughter or even acquittal. In 1921, for example, Fred K. of Oshawa was charged with killing his wife, after she died of injuries sustained when he struck her on the face and head during a marital dispute. According to the testimony of several witnesses, the main source of the dispute revolved around Mr K.'s accusations that his wife was having 'improper relations with a man named John,' who had temporarily boarded at his house. Angered by the allegation, Mrs K. apparently began to quarrel and use profane language, and then attempted to strike her husband several times with a chair. Ultimately, the defendant's acquittal was at least partially based on the suggestion that it was Mrs K. who had been 'making trouble' by verbally and physically provoking her husband, and partially because she had incited him by going to the movies one evening with the boarder while her husband was out of town. Even though going to the movies together seemed to have been the extent of their so-called 'improper relations,' the defence attorney summed up one of the main issues raised by the trial, when he stated, '[W]e are discussing the question of whether or not this man has ... or had a right to strike his wife; was provoked ... that this man was justified in any way ... Surely a married man would take offense at any improper conduct of this kind.'[52]

Conclusion

The Ontario criminal case files on wife abuse and other forms of family violence at the turn of the century, while fragmentary, are enormously important sources in the recovery of particular aspects of marital and familial relations in the past. But even though these criminal records are as close as feminist historians are going to get to the 'voices' and 'experiences' of battered and neglected wives, they need to be approached with interpretive caution, especially given the socio-legal context within which they were produced and constructed. What they do reveal, however, is the extent to which the courtroom itself became a site of struggle between husbands and wives, in which various meanings associated with domestic violence were fought out. The ways in which these protagonists fashioned their narratives emerged not only from their varying expectations and sense of entitlements within marital relations, but also from their attempts to gain the attention and/or empathy of the courts. In the end, however, the practices of the courts and the ambiguities of the law tended to reproduce rather than challenge the unequal distribution of power and privilege, and the sense of male prerogative that structured relations between husbands and wives. While abused wives struggled in various ways for their right to physical safety and their entitlement to legal protection (however ineffective), it was often their character and their conduct, alive or dead, that was ultimately scrutinized and called into question in the courts.

Notes

1 In Canada, see, for example, Kathryn Harvey, '"To Love, Honour and Obey": Wife-beating in Working-Class Montreal, 1869–1879,' *Urban History Review* 19:2 (October 1990); 'Amazons and Victims: Resisting Wife-Abuse in Working-Class

Montreal, 1869–1879,' *Journal of the Canadian Historical Association*, new series, 2 (1991); Erin Breault, 'Educating Women about the Law: Violence against Wives in Ontario, 1850–1920,' M.A. thesis, University of Toronto, 1986; T.L. Chapman, '"Till Death Do Us Part": Wife-beating and the Criminal Justice System in Alberta, 1905–1920,' *Alberta History* 36:4 (1988); Judith Fingard, 'The Prevention of Cruelty, Marriage Breakdown, and the Rights of Wives in Nova Scotia, 1880–1900,' *Acadiensis* 22:2 (Spring 1993); Constance Backhouse, *Petticoats and Prejudice: Woman and Law in Nineteenth-Century Canada* (Toronto 1991); Karen Dubinsky and Franca Iacovetta, 'Murder, Womanly Virtue and Motherhood: The Case of Angelina Napolitano, 1911–1922,' *Canadian Historical Review* 72:4 (1991); Karen Dubinsky, *Improper Advances: Rape and Heterosexual Conflict in Ontario, 1880–1929* (Chicago 1993); and Annalee Golz, '"If a Man's Wife Does Not Obey Him, What Can He Do?" Marital Breakdown and Wife Abuse in Late Nineteenth- and Early Twentieth-Century Ontario,' in Susan Binnie and Louis Knafla, eds, *Law, State and Society: Essays in Modern Legal History*, (Toronto 1995).

2 In my research, all criminal cases that directly or indirectly revealed instances of physical violence, non-support, and/or neglect within marital and familial relations were compiled from the following records found in RG 22 at the Archives of Ontario (hereafter AO): Waterloo County Police Court Minutebooks (Galt), 1857–1920; Perth Police Court Dockets (Stratford), 1893–1906; Police Court Minutebooks and Justice of the Peace Returns of Convictions for Belleville (1874–7), Picton (1851–82, 1887–1919), Galt (1900–11), Sarnia (1910–23), and Sault Ste Marie (1907–20); County Court Judges' Criminal Court (hereafter CCJCC) Minutebooks and Case Files for Carleton (1908–20), Grey (1869–1920), Elgin (1879–1908), Haldimand (1869–1920), Niagara North (1869–1919), Perth (1872–1901), Ontario (1881–1920), Leeds and Grenville (1882–94), and Stormont, Dundas, and Glengarry (1870–1919); Crown Attorney Case Files for Algoma (1916–20), Carleton (1910–20), and York (1902–20); and Criminal Assizes Indictment Case Files (hereafter CAI) available for 46 counties and districts from 1859 to 1920. I have not included additional cases culled from local Ontario newspapers in my analysis in this paper.

3 For more discussion of these interpretative issues, see the debate between Joan Scott and Linda Gordon in *Signs* 15:4 (Summer 1990), 848–60.

4 Toronto *Globe*, 11 Apr. 1881

5 (1909) 8 & 9 Edward VII, c. 9, s. 2 (c). This amendment prompted considerable debate among federal parliamentarians and was strongly supported by the Ontario Woman's Christian Temperance Union. Canada, House of Commons, *Debates*, 12 Mar. 1883, 287; 25 Jan. 1909, 94; 4 Feb. 1909, 556–70; *Debates of the Senate*, 18 May 1909, 678–9; S.G.E. McKee, *Jubilee History of the Ontario Woman's Christian Temperance Union, 1877–1927* (Whitby n.d.), 87

6 See, for example, Police Court Minutebooks and Justice of the Peace Returns of

Convictions for Sarnia (1910–23), Belleville (1874–7), Picton (1851–82, 1887–1919), Galt (1900–11), and Sault Ste Marie (1907–20); and CCJCC Minutebooks for Haldimand (1869–1920), Elgin (1879–1908), Carleton (1908–20), and Grey (1869–1920).

7 An analysis of these gendered and generational patterns of 'family' violence are beyond the parameters of this article, but they receive full attention in my Ph.D. dissertation, 'Dis/membering the Family: Marital Breakdown and Family Violence in Ontario, 1830–1920' (Queen's 1998), chap. 6.

8 See, for example, 1891–8, Hiram T., Ontario Crown Attorney / Clerk of the Peace CCJCC Case Files, box 6 (1898–1901).

9 See, for example, 1920, Clayton R., Algoma Crown Attorney (Sault Ste Marie) Case Files, box 1 (1916–20)

10 Lynne Marks, 'Christian Harmony: Family, Neighbours, and Community in Upper Canadian Church Discipline Records' (in this volume); Bryan D. Palmer, 'Discordant Music: Charivaris and Whitecapping in Nineteenth-Century North America,' *Labour / Le Travail* 3 (1978), 5–62

11 In examining the available testimonies in attempted-suicide cases tried in the criminal courts, this was the only one directly linked to wife battering. On the other hand, out of a total sample of 118 suspected wife murders that occurred between 1857 and 1920, at least 17 husbands attempted to commit or successfully committed suicide immediately or shortly after completing their homicidal acts. See Golz, 'Dis/membering the Family,' chaps 6 and 7.

12 1904, Adam F., Ontario County CA/CP CCJCC Case Files, box 8 (1904–6)

13 See, for example, 1895, Oliver M., Carleton County CAI, box 20 (1892–6); and 1916, Charles B., Peterborough County CAI, box 124 (1896–1918). Moreover, 13 of the 118 married men suspected of wife murder in my sample were declared insane by the courts.

14 1882, Alexander H., Perth County CCJCC Case Files, box 1 (1872–84)

15 1897, Cornelius B., Elgin County CCJCC Docketbook, 1879–1908

16 1905, John W., Ontario County CA/CP CCJCC Case Files, box 8 (1904–6)

17 Toronto *Globe*, 11 Apr. 1881

18 Two of the few cases in which this form of punishment was imposed involved Wasil B. of Whitby Township, who was sentenced to one month in prison and five lashes with 'the usual cat on the fifth day after imprisonment,' and William W. of Oshawa, who was sentenced to three months in prison and 'to be whipped six stripes with the cat o nine tails at the end of the second month.' See 1916, Wasil B., Ontario CA/CP CCJCC Case Files, box 16 (1916); 1912, William W., Ontario CA/CP CCJCC Case Files, box 12 (1912).

19 1873, Francis B., Waterloo County Police Court Minutebooks (Galt), vol. 3 (1871–3)

20 1913 and 1915–16, Nathan K., Ontario County CA/CP CCJCC Case Files, box 13 (1913) and box 15 (1915)

21 For a discussion of these issues, see, for example, (1910) *Rex v. Fred Y.*, AO, RG 4–32, Ontario Attorney General Files, no. 1490.

22 (1869) 32 & 33 Vict., c. 28, s. 1; (1874) 37 Vict., c. 43

23 (1869) 32 & 33 Vict., c. 20, s. 25; (1913) 3 & 4 Geo. V, c. 14, s. 242a

24 The criminal records I researched yielded 365 cases of wife desertion, non-support, and criminal neglect, in addition to 15 cases of manslaughter that were directly linked to the failure to provide necessaries. See Golz, 'Dis/membering the Family,' chap. 5.

25 See, for example, 1897, Edward R., Essex County CAI, box 37 (1895–1901).

26 1916, N. Peter M., Algoma Crown Attorney (Sault Ste Marie) Case Files, box 1 (1916–20)

27 1905, Conrod S., Perth Police Court Dockets (Stratford), 1893–1906

28 1916, Wasil B., Ontario County CA/CP CCJCC Case Files, box 16 (1916). The word 'lump,' as a description of the same injury, surfaces later in the testimony of a female neighbour.

29 1886, Samuel S., Stormont, Dundas and Glengarry CCJCC Case Files, 1870–89

30 1862, James W., Lambton County CAI, box 69 (1859–62)

31 1862, James W., Lambton County CAI, box 69 (1859–62)

32 For an analysis of middle-class married women's civil litigation in the Court of Chancery on the grounds of marital cruelty, see Anne Lorene Chambers, 'Married Women and the Law of Property in Nineteenth-Century Ontario,' Ph.D. diss., Toronto, 1993, 38–67.

33 For a more detailed discussion of these patterns, see my article '"Murder Most Foul": Spousal Murders in Ontario, 1870–1915,' in Nancy Erber and George Robb, eds, *Disorder in the Court: Trials and Sexual Conflict at the Turn of the Century* (New York, forthcoming).

34 Toronto *Globe*, 20 Apr. 1878

35 The most notable exceptions are the 14-volume Galt Police Court Minutebooks (1857–1920) and the Stratford Police Court Dockets (1893–1906), in which detailed testimonies were recorded.

36 See, for example, 1877, Joseph S., York County CAI, box 207 (1877).

37 Harvey, 'Amazons and Victims,' 138

38 1882, Patrick L., Leeds and Grenville CCJCC Case Files, 1882–94

39 1905, Conrad S., Perth Police Court Dockets (Stratford), 1893–1906

40 1912, John H., Ontario County CA/CP CCJCC Case Files, box 12 (1912)

41 1901, John S., Grey County CAI, box 47 (1896–1907)

42 1912, William W., Ontario County CA/CP CCJCC Case Files, box 12 (1912)

43 1881, William R., Elgin CAI, Box 29 (1880–2); Elgin County CCJCC Docketbook, 1879–1908

44 1903, David T., Perth Police Court Dockets (Stratford), 1893–1906. Some married

women also laid formal charges of assault and non-support simultaneously. See, for example, 1880 and 1881, John H., Elgin County CCJCC Docketbook, 1879–1908; and 1906, Jessie W., Grey County CCJCC Minutes, 1869–1920.

45 1916, Wasil B., Ontario County, CA/CP CCJCC Case Files, box 16 (1916)
46 1898, Frederick W., Ontario County CA/CP CCJCC Case Files, 1881–98
47 1895, Arthur S., Ontario County CA/CP CCJCC Case Files, 1881–98
48 1890, Charles C., Leeds and Grenville CCJCC Case Files, 1882–94
49 1880, William R., Stormont, Dundas, and Glengarry CCJCC Case Files, 1870–89
50 1910, Rufus W., Lanark County CAI, box 76 (1880–1918)
51 1912, John B., Ontario County CA/CP CCJCC Case Files, box 11 (1910–12); Ontario County CAI, box 110 (1898–1923)
52 1921, Fred K., Ontario County CA/CP CCJCC Case Files, box 18 (1918–28); Ontario County CAI, box 110 (1898–1923)

14

Parents, Daughters, and Family Court Intrusions into Working-Class Life

FRANCA IACOVETTA

In April 1945, thirteen-year-old Nellie entered the York County Family Court in Toronto to face charges of juvenile delinquency. Her parents had laid the charges, claiming that for the past year Nellie had been staying out 'all night' and 'acting up with boys.' 'She leaves home,' testified an exasperated father to Judge Douglas Webster, 'and we just can't keep her in the house at all.' This was not Nellie's first time in court. In late March, she had received a twelve-month probationary sentence with supervised visits with the Big Sister Association. Webster had ruled out harsher options because, despite her 'incorrigible' behaviour, Nellie had remained a virgin. That trial had focused on her late-night escapades with a man, first in his rooming house bedroom and then in a lake-shore tourist cabin. Under questioning, Nellie admitted to kissing the man but insisted she had not had sex with him. She responded similarly to questions about another incident in which she spent three nights in a motel with two boys, 'French and Cooke.' She swore she had slept on the couch while they had shared the bed. The medical report confirmed Nellie's sexual status, noting that 'the hymen is stretched but not completely ruptured.'[1] During sentencing, Webster had declared that her virginity had worked 'a great deal in her favour.'

But even an intact hymen could not ultimately protect an apparently unrepentant girl from serious penalty. When, in April, Nellie returned to court, Webster declared that her parents had tried 'everything' but she had failed to 'act good.' 'Well, Nellie,' he pronounced, 'I have to send you to the Ontario Girls' Training School at Cobourg ... to save your life, your reputation.'

Are bad girls[2] like Nellie best viewed as non-conformists resisting suffocating conventions and demanding greater autonomy and self-determined pleasure? In some respects, young working-class women like Nellie did courageously transgress dominant codes of female respectability and contest the right of a patriarchal, bourgeois state to dictate their lives. Such resistance, historians have shown, helped carve out alternative sexual practices. As the judgments of court officials suggest, these young women's curved hips, painted lips, and developed breasts literally embodied a sassy, defiant sexuality. Yet, as scholars of sexuality have also shown, we cannot interpret the actions of misbehaving girls solely in these terms. Hardly a monolithic group, delinquent girls attached different meanings to their actions. Others were silent, leaving parents and experts to debate cause and cure. Exaggerating the agency of rebellious teenagers would also distort the complex class, gender, racial-ethnic, and familial dynamics involved, and erroneously downplay the power of the state, as illustrated by the range of penalties and punishments that the courts could impose.[3]

Families emerged as sites of conflict between parents and daughters over the issue of female sexual and social autonomy. The Ontario family court had as its aim the supervision of working-class and marginal populations, but working-class parents were not merely its passive victims.[4] Parents who used the juvenile-delinquency laws[5] endeavoured to empower themselves in their battles at home. Most did not initially or eagerly adopt this strategy, though their actions indicate some acceptance of the dominant, indeed hegemonic, sexual and moral codes regarding female respectability.[6] Working-class parents did not necessarily expect their daughters to be paragons of virtue and even showed a degree of permissiveness that drew criticism from court officials. We know too that in the past rural and working-class families tolerated premarital sex between youths when marriage was anticipated, and indeed enforced, by kin and community. But if such tolerance suggests some important differences between plebian and middle-class mores, there is inadequate evidence to support bold claims for the alternative sexual politics of the working classes.[7] Indeed, patriarchal codes of female honour that placed a premium on obedient and marriageable daughters could cross class and racial-ethnic barriers. Working-class and immigrant parents might forgive a certain amount of 'acting up,' but many drew the line at what they considered flagrantly promiscuous or uncontrollable behaviour.[8]

Neither girls nor parents, however, could match the power of the courts. Daughters were thrust into a labyrinth of legal and non-legal institutions. The regulatory power of the state also rebounded on the parents, as they too became subject to the gaze of legal, medical, and social authorities. The experts applied a mixed-bag repertoire of social and psychological theories of behaviour, a casework approach based on data gathering, and a pro-family framework favouring resocialized children and eventual reconciliation. Yet this professional apparatus only thinly masked much conventional moralizing about bad girls, and the experts' actions usually ruptured, rather than reunited, families.[9]

This paper explores the themes of female delinquency, parental responses, and court intrusions by examining 114 cases involving minor girls (under sixteen) who came before the York County Family and Juvenile Court on delinquency charges during the period from 1945 to 1956. The court's jurisdictional territory was geographically expansive, covering suburban and ex-urban locales surrounding Toronto, particularly to the north of the city.[10] Although many infractions occurred in the city, most defendants hailed from suburban places such as Scarborough or North York.[11] The predominant profile, drawn from available data,[12] is of Anglo-Celtic, heterosexual girls from struggling but not destitute families.[13] Fathers' occupations include truck driver, construction worker, and travelling salesman. Most mothers were homemakers, but a minority held jobs as waitresses, factory workers, and store clerks. A few households were headed by a lone parent or were reconfigured families composed of remarried or unwed couples and stepchildren and stepsiblings. That a minority of parents were homeowners attests perhaps to the rising expectations and living standards of some working-class families in the post-1945 era.[14] The fragility of this status is also revealed by the court files, which document people preoccupied with jobs, house bills, and hefty mortgages on recently purchased suburban bungalows. Evidently, the daughters were not critical family wage earners, though some had part-time jobs, suggesting that in some of the cases under study parental responses to rebel daughters were provoked less by material scarcity and more, perhaps, by a frustration with behaviour that threatened their own hard-earned position in the ranks of the post-war respectable working classes.[15] Although these years witnessed heavy immigration, cases involving immigrants are in a minority, a pattern that probably reflects their residential concentration during this period in the city rather than its suburbs and newcomers' concern to avoid any entanglement with the law. But though few in number, such cases show how mainstream racial chauvinism was replicated in and reinforced by the justice system.

Bad Girls: Case and Context

The pursuit of pleasure by working-class girls and women has involved risks and dangers, including exposure to manipulative and abusive men and the moral condemnation of family and neighbours. It has also made women vulnerable to the regulatory powers of the state.[16] Beyond actually punishing transgressors, the processes of moral regulation have profoundly affected the wider society by making certain behaviours, namely middle-class and Anglo-Celtic standards of conduct, appear normal and moral, while stigmatizing other conduct as abnormal and immoral. As Marxist, Foucauldian, and feminist scholars of such processes observe, the naturalizing of bourgeois standards, such as female premarital chastity, reflected the ascendancy of the middle classes and was integral to how they could govern without persistent recourse to force. Class-based power is especially effective when it also operates as ideology: it limits individual desire and choice by cultivating a situation in which many (though never all) citizens willingly conform to the dominant social norms because they cannot imagine alternatives or because they hope to reap the rewards that acquiescence promises. Such ideological pressures, if need be, could be bolstered by repression and punishment. The legal, medical, and psychological professions have played a prominent role in both realms.[17] The delinquent-girl case files, I argue, are ideologically saturated records that reflect predominant class, gender, and racial norms and contemporary professional categories of knowledge, treatment, and punishment. Yet, they are not so exclusively the products of bourgeois experts that we cannot learn anything about the clients. The files are simultaneously the product of a 'dialectic of power and resistance'[18] between the court authorities and the girls and parents, whose marginal power within the legal system and wider society did not preclude their efforts to influence outcomes. Their very creation attests to the complex power relations at play. Thus, rather than presenting discourse and materialist analyses as mutually exclusive – the one confined to decoding linguistic meanings, the other seeking material causes and the recovery of experience – I have tried to integrate insights from both approaches while maintaining a focus on the centrality of class and gender power at work in these female delinquency dramas.[19]

Any analysis of female delinquency should consider the wider social and political contexts. Historical studies of transgression have focused on earlier eras,[20] but recently scholars have turned to the early post-1945 period to consider youth and sexuality during the Cold War, a time of heightened domesticity, repressive political and moral codes, and pro-family values associated with the much-celebrated white, middle-class, preferably suburban, household consisting of a breadwinner husband and a stay-at-home monogamous mother. Contrary to conventional portraits of a widespread political and sexual conformity, the emerging social histories of the era suggest more a period of insecurity, if also rampant conspiracies and surveillance, as well as resistance. New work in women's and gay history has captured contemporary critiques, as well as actual defiance, of the prevailing class, gender, and political norms.[21] Studies have documented the tremendous anxiety of political and social elites regarding perceived threats to post-war reconstruction and bourgeois standards of morality, including 'reds,' divorced persons, immigrants, homosexuals, and working mothers. They have shown how restrictive attitudes towards sex and gender roles became institutionalized within a national-security state that equated the 'good' nuclear family as a moral arsenal in the fight for democracy.[22]

The celebration of North American bourgeois family values was rooted in class-biased, racial-ethnic, patriarchal, and heterosexist assumptions regarding decent behaviour, with its predictable sanctions against non-conformists, be they gays or promiscuous heterosexual girls. Such sanctions were hardly new to the post-1945 world; elite angst over allegedly falling health and moral standards, fracturing families, and other threats to social order are familiar historical occurrences. So is the concern to uphold notions of female premarital chastity and the ideals of marriage, and motherhood.[23] It is not entirely surprising that post-war idealization of the family, and of women's role as wife, mother and moral guardian, followed a period of comparatively greater economic and social independence. Still, the early post-1945 years in Canada did witness some distinguishing features, including our own Cold War discourse of containment applied to political and moral dissidents alike. Indeed, the period saw a moral panic[24] with regard to juvenile delinquency. Journalists, educators, and child and welfare experts in Canada, as elsewhere, declared an alarming rise, even an epidemic, in 'deviant morality' among urban young people. They made much of the occasional lurid newspaper story of a pregnant girl seeking an illegal abortion, the murder of two immigrant women by 'the DP strangler,' an alcoholic mother who temporarily abandoned her children to be with her lover, or girl gang members committing petty theft.[25] Even a cursory glance at the Toronto *Star* for the years 1948 to 1951 suggests the lurid narratives and dire predictions that helped give shape to the panic. Headlines dubbed juvenile delinquency a pressing 'social challenge,' and 'a social barometer' of the times, and warned that 'hoodludism' was 'on the rise.' News columns told of 'outbreaks of delinquency,' of 'girl spies' used in youth gang wars, and expressed concern for the fate of children from divorced families. Reporters routinely quoted child experts who blamed 'fool parents' for delinquent children, and advised parents and school teachers alike to plan social activities in order 'to avoid teenage trouble.'[26] The experts equated inappropriate gender and sexual conduct among boys and girls as symptomatic of the fragility of post-war democracy and morality, and linked anti-delinquency reforms to the project of building a brave new world.[27]

As recent studies reveal,[28] post-war discourses on juvenile delinquency revealed a distrust, even disdain, for poor and working-class parents, who were portrayed as incapable of inculcating respectable gender identities into their children. Child activists also proposed numerous remedies, such as supervised sports and leisure programs, that legitimated the role of experts in shaping the sound moral character of young women and men. These expert discourses also equated misbehaving girls with sexual promiscuity, or predicted it as an eventual outcome, even where there were no clear signs of sexual misconduct. Older and familiar moral explanations of juvenile delinquency as symptomatic of

Protect Law, Youths Claim: Tell of Girl Spies, War

Stories of teenage troubles in Toronto and its surrounding areas like the one reproduced here appeared regularly in the Toronto media during the delinquency panic of the 1940s and 1950s.

Newmarket, July 10 – Prospect of a 'war' between the 'Beanery Gang,' and the 'Junction Boys,' two west-end Toronto groups, was openly talked about here Friday as a side-light to a trial of 15 Toronto youths on charges of disorderly conduct and trespassing at Lake Wilcox on July 3.

They spoke of an impending big blow-up and told of the intergang battle that was to have taken place last week but which didn't come off when one side failed to show up.

They told, too, of girl spies and of trucks used to cart the gangs to each other's territory.

Police alleged at the time of their arrest they were members of the 'Beanery Gang' which has caused trouble at teen-age dances. But this was denied by spokesmen who said most of the 15 were members of the 'Junction Boys' whose headquarters is at Dundas and Keele Sts. Others among the 15 denied membership in either faction.

All 15 were fined $10 and costs or 10 days for petty trespassing by Magistrate O. S. Hollingrake and the boys dug deep into their own – or their parents' pockets – to pay up ...

The same fine was meted out to 21 boys and nine girls convicted of trespassing on the Shadow Lake girls' camp property at Musselman's lake on various dates in June. Reaching into their pockets for their own wallets, or glancing at their parents to come forward, the youths in this case also paid up.

The line-up in front of the clerk's desk was so long as they paid their fines that the front rows had to be cleared of spectators to provide waiting space.

One father said: 'My boy is up north on a job but I'll pay his fine and take over from here.' Magistrate Hollingrake nodded his head approvingly.

Some of the accused said the 'beanery gang' began about a year ago and now has a membership between 25 and 50 regulars plus about 100 'pickups' available for major engagements. They said they had a number of girl spies to look over the situation in the Keele-Dundas district – headquarters for the Junction gang.

On the other hand the Junction boys admitted their numbers had been increased with the addition of two lesser street gangs for the Wilcox trip last week. They rode to Wilcox lake by truck and car. The Junction group has about 25 regulars.

Source: Toronto *Star*, 10 July 1948

poor spiritual health coexisted with environmental assessments regarding, for example, alcoholic parents and broken homes, but also with a growing (though not new) penchant for psychological and psychiatric approaches to the issue. As the reports of professionals assessing girls up on delinquency charges in York county suggest, post-war youth and behavioural experts set a demanding, indeed, rigid standard for the good adolescent girl, one based on narrowly defined Christian and bourgeois notions of feminine respectability. A 'well-adjusted' girl attended church, participated in church- and school-organized activities, and belonged to volunteer youth organizations, such as the Girl Guides, that offered healthy supervised recreation. She helped her mother with house chores, enjoyed healthy hobbies, such as sewing and sports, supervised younger siblings, and earned respectable if not stellar grades in school. She read character-forming novels, not 'trashy' dime-store magazines and pulp novels that romanticized loose behaviour.[29] Of course, the good girl was also defined by what she refrained from doing: she did not venture far from home, stay out 'very late' or all night, skip school, or disobey or steal from her parents. More-over, she practised premarital celibacy as a prerequisite to a good marriage and motherhood.[30] Given such lofty standards of 'goodness,' court officials could deem in need of supervision virtually every girl brought to court.

Professional evaluations of delinquency also drew heavily on theories of child development, including those of Piaget and Freud, that posited the view that 'normalcy' in young adulthood was achieved by successfully completing a series of physical, psychological, and sexual stages of development. Failure to do so, warned Canadian psychologists, could produce 'crippled personalities.'[31] The influence on the family-court personnel of these models and other allegedly diagnostic tools is evident in the case files on delinquent girls. The caseworkers who interviewed family members and conducted home visits religiously recorded the stages of the girl's psycho-sexual development. The psychiatrists evaluated her mental capacity, using, for example, IQ tests, and her communi-cation skills, and they assessed the quality of her family's interpersonal dynam-ics. The role that psychologists and psychiatrists played in the assessments reflects, in part, the growing incursion of psychiatric approaches into post-war social and rehabilitative work.[32] But their assessments, based as they were in evaluations about mental or psycho-emotional capacity, could also serve to pathologize the delinquent girl by attributing her behaviour to mental inferiority or a 'poor' family environment.

Notwithstanding the hand of experts in producing them, these case files permit us to discern actions, conflicts, and consequences, if not motives or subjectivi-ties. They help document for the early post-war era the gap between prescriptive norms for respectable female conduct and the reality of young, single women

News of the Week in Toronto Schools:
'Fool Parents' Bear Blame for Bad Behaviour – Expert

Post-war child experts drew on a large repertoire of explanations for juvenile delinquency, including inadequate parenting.

Fathers and mothers who worry over the ideas that their child may be 'emotionally maladjusted' will be interested in the report brought back from San Francisco by Trustee Mrs. May Robinson. She attended the conference of the International Council for Exceptional Children there, and heard the famous Dr. Holman of Duke University speak on children who are behaviour problems.

His reply to a question – 'Why so much antisocial behaviour in the world today?' – was in three terse words: 'Darn-fool parents.'

Dr. Holman has spent many years in research on this problem, and he is definitely opposed to the self-expression school of thought.

Source: Toronto *Star*, 2 April 1949

daring to be bad. They reveal that Toronto and its surrounding suburbs and communities offered the adventuresome (or unhappy) teenager numerous opportunities for, quite literally, cheap thrills and diversions. Suburban girls headed down to the city's better-known recreational areas, such as the Yonge Street taverns. They went also to the local parks and beaches of inner city and suburb, the dirt roads and wooded areas of suburbia and ex-urbia, and neighbouring towns.[33] The suburban Scarborough Bluffs offered a scenic backdrop for fifteen-year-old Catherine C's sexual encounters with an eighteen-year-old man she had met at a beach party. In March 1946, it landed both of them in court and brought both a twelve-month probationary sentence.[34] House parties, cinemas, and coffee shops offered alternative gathering places. In October 1956 under-age party girls Barbara, Lynda, and Myra were arrested for attending a house party with liquor. They had been invited there by some older boys they had met earlier that night at a restaurant. The arresting police officer dubbed the party 'the worst he had ever seen, girls upstairs were in all stages of undress, windows broken, there were 55 people in this 4 roomed bungalow, 173 empty beer bottles had been consumed [and] about 12 quart liquor bottles, 8 or 10 '"mickies."' The girls got away with $5 fines, no doubt because the officer testified that he did not think they had been drinking and 'they all looked like decent girls.'[35]

Dance halls have long held a sexual reputation, and racism has long informed sexual discourses regarding white women and black men. These themes converged in the case of fifteen-year-old Lynda B. of North York, a white girl whose mother contacted the court authorities in the winter of 1954 because Lynda was not only skipping school and staying out late, but had taken to attending the downtown dance clubs 'where the coloured boys go.' A defiant Lynda stated plainly in court that she went to the 'coloured dances to have fun and to dance.' Her mother objected, telling the court-appointed social worker preparing the family history that she was 'very threatened by Lynda's behaviour with coloured boys, fears above all that Lynda will get pregnant with a "black baby" ... Deals with this by nagging and tearing Lynda down.' Lynda admitted she was not a virgin, a fact confirmed by the MD report, but said 'it happened before' her dance-hall days. Interestingly, the case worker was unsympathetic to the mother's anxieties because she was far from being an exemplary parent. As an incorrigible, Lynda ended up in training school, but as much because the authorities considered Lynda's home dysfunctional.[36]

The workplaces that employed some of the girls, such as restaurants and dime stores, also offered semi-supervised meeting places.[37] In 1947, fourteen-year-old teenagers Elaine and Shirley turned their after-school job in a city hospital into an adventure by sneaking into the room of a patient – a married soldier who, along with his friends, offered the girls alcohol and got them drunk. Elaine passed out at home and her parents called the police. While the girls admitted to drinking and 'acting stupid' while intoxicated, they defended the men involved, declaring that they had 'conducted themselves in a gentlemanly manner and did not act improper.' [38]

The importance of the car to urban and suburban living, and to sexual adventure, is amply illustrated. Fifteen-year-old Jeannie S. was hauled into court in May 1956 after police caught her twice having intercourse with an 18-year-old boy in a parked car. Her declarations that they were in love and planned to marry apparently did not impress the magistrate, particularly since the boy's mother disapproved of the relationship and Jeannie's own checkered past hurt her credibility. Police testified she had given birth to an illegitimate child earlier that year, 'keeps very late hours and does not hold a job altho [sic] looks after children while her mother works.' Both received suspended sentences and were told to 'refrain from seeing one another in the future.'[39]

The 1946 case of the two Joyces – Joyce B. and Joyce K. – shows suburban teenagers exploring midnight fun in moving vehicles. Every time the police caught them out late with boys, they were in a car, a truck, or, on one occasion, a railway handcart left unguarded in a railroad yard. One evening they met some boys at a local baseball game and then spent the night with them in a car on a lonely stretch of highway in Etobicoke. When police found them the next day, the girls confessed to having had sexual intercourse. They told police that the boys had promised to call a taxi to take them home if they first had sex with them, but then reneged on the promise. If police considered at all the possibility that the girls had been raped, they never recorded it. Soon afterwards, the girls were picked up while joyriding with four boys in a pick-up truck in a neighbouring suburb. Next evening occurred the railway handcart episode, which landed them in court. The judge sentenced them to one year's probation. It appears that class, rather than virginity, kept these girls out of training school. The case histories prepared for the judge stressed their respectable middle-class backgrounds, that they had 'good homes,' went to Sunday school, and had pledged to lead a 'clean life' in future.[40]

Police reports, trial transcripts, and other materials contained in the case files reveal the varied ways that teenaged girls found adventure. An evening saw girls move from one spot to another, as planned or chance meetings resulted in an invitation to a wiener roast on the beach, a house party, or even a night spent in a cheap motel. 'Hanging out' could mean hours sipping coffee and smoking cigarettes in a doughnut shop, but in the anticipation of something happening. If there was nothing doing at the burger joint, the girls moved on to a local ball game, pool room, or swimming pool. Take the case of fifteen-year-old Sharon B., described as a 'tall, *attractive* girl who could pass for 17 years of age' and 'dated boys from Working Boys Homes.' She frequented a downtown greasy spoon, Harry's Grill. The first time she was picked up there by police late at night, a gang of youths had been 'playing crap' in the back room and been arrested. The next time she was arrested, she had spent the night with her boyfriend at a downtown hotel. Claiming she was too scared to go home, Sharon had covered costs by pawning her grandmother's watch. She was also considered a serious flight risk who hated school, though, ironically, she did well. A heavily supervised twelve-month probation sentence was the judge's response.[41]

Neighbouring towns and cities, such as Hamilton, Peterborough, and Lindsay had an appeal as getaway places, including for hitchhikers. Joyriding with boys could turn into a getaway weekend for girls, unless they got caught.[42] They ran off to find out-of-town friends, attend a circus, and for adventure. In 1949, Joanne B. took off to Lindsay with a friend, stayed with a distant relative, visited the local fair, and landed a job at a doughnut shop. According to her father, who charged her with delinquency, Joanne had been unduly influenced by a girlfriend with 'a superior mind' and 'a fellow' of 'very questionable character.' The police constable involved agreed. In exchange for a suspended sentence, Joanne agreed not to see the boy unless her father permitted it.[43]

In pursuing adventure, girls took risks, though whether they recognized fully the potential dangers involved is unclear. Whether Marlene accepted the possibility that partying with boys late at night might place her in physical danger is impossible to say for certain. But we know that the night after she was punched by a drunken boy to whom she said she had refused sex, she was right back on the street, drinking and cussing with the same gang.[44] Even when girls offered explanations for a judge or caseworker, determining motives is a tricky enterprise. Yet, it is clear that these delinquent girls were not a monolithic group. Whether truthful or not, the girls' testimonies and interviews suggest that most understood that they were defying parents and otherwise 'breaking the rules.'[45] But while their actions reveal similar patterns – sneaking out after curfew, smoking in boxcars, drinking liquor in the park, having sex in a car, poor attendance and declining grades at school, persistent squabbles with parents – the explanations that girls offered for their behaviour ranged widely. Some girls, including Nellie of our opening story, got 'into trouble with boys' yet remained virgins and strenuously defended their sexual reputation. A minority of the girls appeared decidedly defiant, claiming unabashedly to the authorities that they liked to party. The case of June M., a fifteen-year-old girl who boldly declared to police that 'she would rather do it than eat' is a graphic example. Her file details several episodes of gang sex – in the woods in West Hill, in a field near Oshawa, in a 'shack' near her home, and in a parked car – that she appears to have initiated. Her sexual partners included teenaged boys and young men on leave from the air force. By contrast, one judgmental runaway stated that she could no longer live with her divorced mother after catching her having sex with a man. She took up with a boy and claimed to be living a 'respectable' life away from Toronto.[46] But most girls did not blurt out their sexual or other predilections. Their explanations revolved around complaints about strict parents, boredom, and the allure of fun and friends. On occasion caseworkers acknowledged that a girl might be trying to escape an abusive situation, though their comments refer almost exclusively to physical beatings by a father, leaving unexplored the possibility of incest or emotional forms of torment.

Other girls defy easy categorization, as they were themselves abusive or destructive, swearing at parents repeatedly, smashing objects around the house, and even slapping and kicking their mothers. The daughter of Ukrainian immigrants, June A., for example, not only broke curfews, brought home unwelcome friends, and stole money. She also threw hot water at her mother and threatened to hit her with a chair.[47] Gwen B. had been kicked out of the house by her parents after several out-of-town sexual escapades involving men. But, claimed her mother, she returned home frequently and scared the family by cursing and swearing 'violently,' bringing strangers into the house, and threatening to kill herself and the entire family.[48] That a few of these nasty girls were diagnosed with serious mental and emotional problems is not surprising and, of course, further complicates the picture. Gwen B., for example, was committed to a psychiatric hospital, though whether it was her incorrigibility or mental capacity that actually decided matters for the psychiatrist involved remains uncertain. Notwithstanding the penchant of psychiatric specialists to probe for mental deficiencies, at least a few girls clearly appeared to be suffering serious mental anguish.[49] Their apparently 'out of control' behaviour, in turn, provoked frustrated, even terrified, parents to find ways to contain them. One such case involved a girl who, according to her mother, went 'hysterical' when menstruating, throwing temper tantrums, smashing up the house, disappearing from home, and staying out with boys. Another case involved Violet C., who by the 1950s had, in the caseworker's estimation, developed a reputation 'for being a class bad girl.' Her thick case file reveals a long history of parental abuse and a litany of foster homes and emotional troubles.[50]

While we cannot easily determine motives or truth, the case files do permit us rare glimpses of the familial disputes and generational conflicts fought over a teenaged girl's demand for social and sexual freedom. The file created on June A. and her Ukrainian parents, for instance, records the competing accusations, claims, and recriminations between mother and daughter. It thereby reveals competing notions of June's right to determine her own standard of conduct. When her mother first charged June with delinquency in the fall of 1949, she provided a long list of complaints, including late nights out, boys, truancy, and disreputable friends. In the recordings of the Children's Aid Society (CAS) social worker assigned to the case, we find the mother's version of June's descent into delinquency. For three years, she claimed, a 'sweet happy obedient child' had become a terror, refusing to go to school even though she was academically capable; secretly working underage at a fish-and-chips shop until she was caught; constantly being out at dances, movies, lakeshore wiener roasts, and restaurants; staying out late or all night; refusing to help out at home; corresponding with an inmate of the Bowmanville Boys Training School; refusing to introduce her friends to her parents; and socializing with 'older' girls who had got 'into trouble' and had had to leave school. She accused June of spending money foolishly on her friends, buying them lunches with her mother's money and giving away things, including two heavy coats and a pair of Oxfords. She could not afford to buy herself clothes or badly needed dentures, the mother added, because she 'buys for June.'

Refusing to give ground, June countered with serious charges of her own, telling the CAS worker that her mother was a snoop who invaded her privacy, was rude to her friends, and intercepted the letters that arrived from her boyfriend. Her mother, June claimed, locked up her clothes, pestered her friends' parents, and tried to break up her friendships. June also blamed her late-night escapades on her mother's intolerable behaviour, claiming that she was reduced to sneaking out at night because of her mother's constant prying. She had given up bringing friends home, June added, because her mother constantly badgered them about being on her furniture and scuffing the hardwood floor. June also used her medical exam, which confirmed her virginity, to discredit her mother's insinuations and thereby her credibility.

The mother-daughter battle was not the only household battle. June's mother complained about her husband, an out-of-town cook, for his absences from home and his failure in disciplining their daughter. She accused him of encouraging June to 'shirk housework' while expecting her 'to be a slave.' She resented him for refusing to let her work outside the home and generally driving her 'crazy.' As if to further discredit him, she added gratuitously that her husband's siblings were communists. The father's only recorded response was to say his wife had been 'too strict' with June. But if parents grappling with defiant daughters did not always agree on where to draw the line, it took only one of them to go to court.

Parental Responses and Court Intrusions

The parents' role in these dramas was both complex and ambiguous. Their decision to lay charges against a daughter brought the force of the state and its legal and non-legal authorities into their lives.[51] The tribunal hearings that transpired in family court were not especially awe-inspiring or majestic,[52] but the seemingly informal procedures or the magistrate's colloquial style of address could not mask the serious matter at hand: the effort to corral misbehaving girls into a complex network of penal and rehabilitative institutions and social-welfare services aimed to constrain and change them. One intrusion could lead to another: minor probationary infractions or further complaints by parents, police, or court officials could result in harsher penalties and extended terms in boarding and industrial training schools.[53]

The parents also became the target of expert assessments and court intrusions. If they had meant to intimidate a daughter into obedience, they soon found that they too were being judged and admonished. Nor could they undo what their actions had prompted. This is not to suggest that parents were simply duped into using court injunctions against rambunctious daughters or that they knowingly surrendered their authority to the courts. Most were fully capable of defining the boundaries of their tolerance and their preferred punishment. Still, their decision to use the courts, though a pragmatic one, may not have been an entirely autonomous one. There were plenty of opportunities for police, court officers, and counsellors to advise, even cajole, parents to take this route. Once parents laid the charge, things moved swiftly. Normally, the girl was sent to an observation or detention home for a medical exam and for interviews with a social worker or psychologist. The number of courtroom witnesses varied, but usually the girl, at least one parent, and perhaps a police officer gave testimony. So might caseworkers who had had previous contact with her, such as CAS or Big Sisters staff or truancy officers. The trial might be remanded a few times to allow for follow-up reports, but a case could be decided within a few weeks.

In considering parental responses, we should take into account the obvious bias that they likely tried to present themselves in the best possible light, as reputable people caught in an unbearable situation. Still, the main image to emerge in these files is of tremendously frustrated working-class parents using the law 'as a last resort' in their ongoing battles to rein in an unruly daughter or to save a promiscuous daughter before she got pregnant, contracted VD, or had her reputation permanently ruined. By the time parents went to court, there had already been much squabbling, issuing of threats, door-slamming, hollering, name-calling, and noisy late-night police visits. Parents claimed to be at their wit's end, after having tried various strategies to control their daughter, such as sending her to an out-of-town relative or new surroundings. Significantly, many parents depicted their daughter not as a criminal but, rather, as an impressionable girl led astray by others, usually boys, married men, and sassy girlfriends. In making such claims, they were also defending their own integrity as respectable folks. But they were also expressing firm disapproval of the girl's continuing misconduct, even going so far as to approve of the punitive powers the justice system could wield over her. Some even showed some hope in the rehabilitative powers of the system to reform their daughter and thus restore her chance for marriage and family. In that regard, working-class parents accepted the dominant, restrictive codes of femininity, even while they might tolerate other forms of misconduct. Even permissive parents who allowed very late curfews or tolerated a daughter's occasional 'lip' drew the line at sexual promiscuity.

These patterns are evident in cases involving parents who took daughters to court, including our opening story. Before the magistrate, Nellie's father testified against his daughter and, significantly, on her behalf. During the first court appearance, he stressed that Nellie had only started acting up recently, after turning thirteen, but also insisted that she could no longer 'be handled,' that 'her mother and I couldn't keep her at home.' 'We never licked her,' he added, on his own behalf. The next time in court, he defended Nellie's respectable attendance at school, adding that he permitted her go out at night but opposed her staying out very late or all night. When Judge Webster asked, 'Any trouble at home? he replied, 'No, Nellie is a nice child in the home, fairly good, can't kick on that, but it is this going out, she is going to head into some obstacle that we are not going to be able to overcome.' Described by caseworkers as hard-pressed people raising four children in a 'crowded' house, Nellie parents also went to some lengths to try to salvage their daughter's 'reputation' and 'future.' When the court advised them to move farther away from the city, the father found a new job at a soup-making factory in New Toronto and bought a house. In his words, 'I sunk everything I had for her good.' When that strategy failed, her parents wanted a tough form of justice, even rejecting the idea of a foster home as it would permit Nellie too much freedom.

Similar patterns characterize the mother's responses in a 1956 Scarborough case involving twelve-year-old Trudy A. Trudy, her mother, stepfather, and stepbrother lived on the stepfather's wages, some modest family-assistance benefits, and occasional support payments from Trudy's birth father. According to her mother, Trudy had been acting up for a year and efforts to help her, including a temporary stay with an out-of-town woman friend, had failed. The list of infractions is familiar: broken curfews, a sassy girlfriend, 'boys in the box cars,' running away, and, eventually, being interested in men 'regardless of age or type.' Even while hauling her daughter into court, Trudy's mother defended her daughter's reputation and her own. Mrs A. explained how alarmed she had been to find at home a book of boys' names and addresses, but added that Trudy was not a truant, had never been caught stealing, and was always willing to 'help out' with the dishes, make beds, and run errands. She attested to Trudy's good shopping habits: she saved her money carefully, was 'never wasteful,' and not a 'foolish spender.' Mrs A. admitted to her daughter's habit of hanging out with gangs, but also drew an ethical distinction: Trudy herself had never lit fires or caused property damage. Trudy, she added, was well-liked but had a knack for choosing 'under-dog' friends, girls who were having 'problems' at home. Indicating her own generosity as a mother, Mrs A. added that Trudy had never been ill treated and was allowed to invite friends home and play 'her' music (western and rock-and-roll).[54]

Whatever their intentions, working-class parents who entered the family-court system were often judged harshly by the caseworkers assigned to investigate their family. Parents praised for their sincerity and concern were accused of dimwittedness, 'lack of insight,' and poor parenting techniques. The probation officer assigned to supervise Catherine C., the teenager caught out on the Scarborough Bluffs, criticized the mother for 'attempt[ing] to cover up' for her daughter's mistakes rather than closely monitoring her. The psychiatrist assigned to Nellie's case condescendingly assessed her mother as well intentioned but 'probably not very capable.'[55] Similarly, the female caseworker assigned to the case of Trudy A., the gang girl, was sympathetic but paternalistic towards the mother, whom she described as 'a plain looking' and 'shy' woman of 'average intelligence,' who was 'very concerned' but 'obviously puzzled by her daughter's behaviour.' She was 'an excellent housekeeper,' but incapable of handling the situation. Indeed, the parents' earlier efforts to help Trudy were criticized. They had let Trudy work at a restaurant even though she was underage, as it had 'kept her off the streets.' For that, the court chastised them for breaking the law.

Class and racial-ethnic prejudice underlined even sympathetic portraits of parents. In the reports prepared on the Ukrainian girl, June A., the mother gained sympathy for the abuse she had endured, but was dismissed as an uneducated immigrant subjecting her daughter to a poor environment. In sifting through the barrage of allegations launched by June and her mother, the caseworker relied heavily on her impressions of the personalities involved. Personal indictments of the warring parties abound. Like many other girls, June was described in sexualized language that focused on her prematurely mature body: she was 'well-built' though 'sullen-looking'; shapely but with 'a tendency to be overweight'; 'nicely dressed' but 'uses more makeup than the average girl her age.' The caseworker's negative diagnosis of the mother drew on a mix of expert opinion, ethnic prejudice, and gratuitous criticism about her physical appearance: a 'short stocky woman who wears slacks constantly,' has 'blunt' features, hair in an 'upsweep,' and 'a discontented expression,' and 'speaks in a constant flow of broken English, usually dissolving in tears.' In an ironic twist to the usual complaints of middle-class home visitors about the supposedly inadequate housekeeping skills of their clients, the caseworker criticized June's mother for overdoing it. The report praised the quality of the house, describing it as 'well built,' 'immaculately kept,' 'very tastefully furnished,' and located in a 'good neighbourhood,' but supported June on the question of the home's unwelcoming feel and chastised the mother for being so overly concerned with keeping a pristine house that visitors did not feel welcome. The father did not fare much better: the caseworker dubbed him a 'swarthy-medium-built man wearing a rather helpless, bewildered look. He has difficulty in speaking and understanding English and appears dull,' she added, and can neither 'cope' with his wife nor 'take a definite stand with June.'

More than merely nasty swipes or indicators of class snobbery, these judgments affected people's lives. For example, though the case history produced on June A. and her parents actually lacked much substantiated information about June's alleged activities, it became the basis on which the courts constrained her. Without interviewing the mother, the psychiatrist involved drew primarily on the CAS caseworker's report to reach his conclusions: that the mother was an 'emotional, unstable person' lacking insight into her daughter's problems, and that June's problems stemmed from a very poor 'interpersonal relationship' with her mother and her deep resentment of her parents' Ukrainian background. Significantly, though the patterns exhibited in this case resembled closely those involving Anglo-Celtic girls, he attributed the problems to immigrant maladjustment. As the situation between June and her mother worsened considerably, the experts offered no new insights and never accepted any responsibility for the deteriorating relations. But they did recommend escalated punishments and remedies. When June broke the terms of her initial probationary sentence by running off with some girls, she was placed in a Catholic girls' boarding home. By the time she was expelled from there, for breaking curfews, she had turned sixteen and was no longer a minor. The caseworker's response was to advise June's parents of their rights to incarcerate their daughter under a different law, the Ontario Female Refuges Act, which covered older girls.[56]

Only a tiny minority of parents mentioned in my sample of cases were highly manipulative, negligent, or abusive. A few did try to use the courts for their own selfish ends. One widowed father was accused by caseworkers of wanting to send his daughter to an institution 'so he'd have no responsibility.' A divorced mother apparently tried to have her daughter sent away because the teenager did not fit into her plans to remarry.[57] Among the most notorious parents were the divorced parents of dance-hall girl Lynda B. According to his ex-wife, the father was a drug trafficker with numerous convictions – police dubbed him one of Canada's 'top criminals in narcotics' – and a wife-beater who hit her in front of the children and brought home prostitutes. Yet, the mother received no sympathy from the caseworker, who noted her own police record on narcotics charges and described her as self-interested, manipulative, untrustworthy, and 'lacking any insight' into or genuine concern for her daughter's problems. 'One cannot help but be impressed,' the report reads, 'with the deplorable environmental conditions the girl has had to cope with ... [T]hat she has retained an intact personality under these conditions is difficult to explain.' Nor did the caseworker sympathize with the mother's concern about her daughter's Black boyfriends, even though we might well have expected caseworkers to frown upon mixed-race relations.[58] This response reflected less a liberal attitude than the caseworker's personal dislike and disapproval of the mother. He dismissed her concerns as hypocritical in light of the 'deplorable conditions' to which she had subjected her daughter.

The experts themselves did not always agree on causes and cures. Generally, their aim was to catch the girls in various stages of moral degeneration and arrest the decline, discerning the root of the problem through an individualized case-history approach, and implementing remedies for rehabilitation, all with the intention, at least theoretically, of reuniting the reformed girl with her family. While couched in the scientific or social-work vocabulary of their profession, the reports reflected the familialist ideology and conventional bourgeois morality of the day. Whether they thought the girl was emotionally unstable or the parents inefficient disciplinarians, whether they considered the family dysfunctional or temporarily under stress, they advocated a strategy of family reconciliation. But the strategy often involved the temporary removal of the girl to what was considered a more controlled, and rehabilitative, environment. Industrial schools, for example, offered a training in education and domestic skills within a strict, disciplined environment. Moreover, the heavily bureaucratized nature of the juvenile justice system, where many decisions were made outside the judicial arena, gave non-legal authorities wide discretionary power to extend original sentences, subject the inmate to further medical or intelligence tests, or transfer her to new foster-home placements. Girls sentenced to the industrial training schools, for instance, were given indeterminate sentences that could be extended until age eighteen. While most did not stay the full term, the decision to release or detain them further did not require judicial hearing but was an extra-legal administrative decision made by appropriate personnel.[59]

The assessments produced for the family-court magistrate deciding on a particular girl's fate could contain a paradoxical mix of expert opinion. Some obvious differences marked the approach of social workers and psychiatrists. Predictably, the reports of the social workers (whether probation officers or social-agency staff) tended to offer more-environmental explanations, focusing on the home situation and documenting the girl's childhood history. On the surface, they appear less judgmental than the psychiatrist's assessments, in part because of their descriptive detail. By contrast, the psychiatrists used more specialized, clinical language specific to their training, and their reports focused on both diagnosis and prognosis. A common prognosis was that without a supervised recreation program administered by qualified personnel, a disobedient girl lacking solid parental guidance could become sexually promiscuous. Such distinctions cannot be considered hard and fast, however, since the same caseworker's report could provide elements of both approaches.

Two recurring patterns – divergent expert opinion and parental loss of authority to the courts – are captured in the files prepared on Pauline B., a Catholic girl eventually sent to a training school. Pauline's mother charged her daughter in 1953, following a year of truancy and frequent runaway escapades, including to Hamilton, where she took up with a boy. Pauline's mother made her preference for a foster home clear to the court, but said she would settle for Maryvale, a Catholic boarding school. What complicated the case enormously was the possibility that Pauline was mentally ill. She suffered from 'moodswings.' The runaway attempts had occurred following depressive episodes, during which Pauline was, according to her mother, 'irritable, impatient, unreasonable, also lies and can't be trusted.' Also complicating matters was a rift between mother and grandmother, the grandmother offering to take in Pauline on a foster-case basis, the mother claiming that the grandmother was mentally incapable of doing so.

In trying to get at the root of the problem, this case file follows familiar procedures. The social summary prepared for the court and resident psychiatrist contain much biographical material, including details about the mother's divorce and her two husbands. Just before Pauline's birth, Pauline's mother had left her father, described as a 'former Barnardo boy' and a 'good-natured man,' who nevertheless had a 'quick temper, gambled, and didn't provide.' She then married Pauline's stepfather, a mechanic suffering from ulcers, which Mrs B claimed had caused him to 'regress' mentally over the years. On the advice of an Ontario Provincial Police officer, the mother had recently quit her job to devote more attention to Pauline, whom, she added, got along with her stepfather largely because he didn't 'bother with her' – an ambiguous statement at best.

Turning to Pauline's psychosexual development, the report recorded that Pauline's mother had harboured 'very bitter' feelings toward her father during pregnancy and had nursed Pauline 'only' a few weeks before turning to bottle-feeding. Pauline started teething at seven, standing at eighteen months, took her first step at twenty months, was more than two years before she spoke, and was four years old before she was fully toilet-trained. Evidently, she used to vomit, because of a bowel condition, and she had endured rickets, measles, rheumatic fever, chicken pox, mumps, a broken arm, and gall-bladder problems. She also occasionally threw 'temper tantrums,' and had a poor appetite, refusing to eat meat or vegetables unless forced, enjoying fried foods, especially fish and chips, that made her 'very sick' afterwards, and sweets. The mother claimed to have given Pauline a frank training in sex education. In detailing the girl's fall from grace, the report stressed the change in personality. Once a good student, Pauline now played hooky and forged signatures. Once a 'nice' person who 'liked shows, dancing and watching TV' and had 'lots' of friends, Pauline's interests had declined to trashy 'True Story magazines or pocket novels.' Pauline's numerous runaway attempts are also recorded in minute detail, as are the jobs she landed during these episodes. The report ends with the caseworker's recommendation – training school. Although impressed by Pauline's ability to find work, the caseworker was swayed by the mother's insistence that Pauline could not support herself, that when she was away she came back 'dirty' and in 'poor health.' Indeed, the mother now favoured a training-school term on the grounds, she argued, that Pauline would 'have a chance of becoming a respectable citizen.'

The summary went to the psychiatrist, whose report judged the mother harshly. Blaming the working mother for neglecting her children is combined with a negative psychological profile of the woman: 'her own problems have been so great that she has only been able to direct a limited degree of attention to this girl.' He was kinder to Pauline, saying that 'she seems capable of getting work and looking after herself.' While noting that she had 'demonstrated poor judgment in many areas,' he was impressed with her maturity, adding that in interviews she had discussed her plans 'with considerable insight and intelligence,' showing no sign of any 'serious personality disorder.' Thus, he recommended against training school, saying that the disciplined regime would not offer a long-term solution to her 'adjustment.' He preferred Maryvale Catholic Girls Boarding School on the grounds that its 'more academic training' would better help a mature girl with job placement afterwards. His second choice was a foster home.

How much Judge Webster was influenced by any of the reports is uncertain. He chose the training-school option, though he did so in part because in the time that the case was remanded Pauline became 'more' delinquent. She had run away twice, including, it was claimed, to a Hamilton 'bawdy house,' got caught with a young man on a boat, and boasted about the growing number of men she had slept with. As with Nellie, persistently defiant and unrepentant girls could provoke the courts to incarcerate them.

Conclusion

When Nellie's parents hauled her before the York County Family Court on delinquency charges, they exposed her and themselves to the prying eyes of legal, medical, and social authorities. Like other forms of socialized justice operating within modern welfare states, the juvenile justice system blurred the lines between punishment and protection. It punished girls like Nellie for their transgressions while also claiming to be protecting their badly tattered, if not entirely ruptured, reputations and their reduced, if not entirely eliminated, chances at marriage and family. As scholars note, such processes served to legitimate precisely those norms and mores that the dominant classes decreed as appropriate. By corralling and confining minor girls who defied prevailing codes of the good adolescent girl, the family court reflected and reaffirmed the legitimacy of a bourgeois, patriarchal morality.[60]

But we need also to avoid what one feminist criminologist has called 'essentialist feminist' arguments that acknowledge patriarchy but ignore the class and racial-ethnic contours of juvenile justice. When attributing motives to the experts and judges who decided the girls' fate, we cannot simply assert that the most offensive misconduct is always non-marital sex.[61] Virgins like Nellie went to training school while some deflowered girls received less harsh penalties. Persistent disobedience of a non-sexual kind could invite a coercive response, though it might be justified on the grounds of pre-empting future sexual misconduct. The magistrates and experts recommended solutions that also reflected their distrust in the parenting capacity of working-class and immigrant parents. Such observations suggest the need to pay close attention to the convergence of critical factors, such as class and race, as well as patriarchy, and to the details and differences of each case. Comparative work on the regulation of boys and girls, and of heterosexual and homosexual offences, would also prove helpful. Still, the sexualized language used to describe bad girls is striking and alone suggests how sexual and non-sexual definitions of misconduct could be blurred.

The oppressive penalties and repressive remedies taken by the family court against misbehaving teenage girls illustrate how female transgressors seriously rankled the legal and non-legal experts committed to building 'anti-delinquent communities.' Whatever their motives or state of health, the bad girls of Toronto's post-war suburbs engendered strong rebuke both from their working-class parents and from the courts and their related agencies. In examining how such unruly acts provoked censure from parents and the courts we need to understand the processes of moral and social regulation. In so doing, we also catch glimpses of how the state could wield enormous power over ordinary people's lives.

Notes

Thanks to the Toronto Labour Studies Group and my co-contributors to this volume for their helpful comments on earlier versions of this paper.

1 The report added that Nellie had supplied a logical explanation – 'her girlfriend had inserted her fingers into her vagina' – but there was no reference indicating that caseworkers suspected Nellie of being a lesbian. This is case no. 31 in a sample of 114 files on female juvenile delinquency isolated for scrutiny here from a general sample of 315 cases culled from the Archives of Ontario (hereafter AO), RG 22, series 5829, York County Family Court (Jarvis St), Domestic Case Files, 1945–56.
2 Quotation marks around value-loaded terms such as bad, delinquent, and respectable, should be understood.
3 My observations have been influenced by such important studies as Kathy Peiss,

Cheap Amusements: Working Women and Leisure in Turn-of-the-Century New York (Philadelphia 1986); Karen Dubinsky, *Improper Advances: Rape and Heterosexual Conflict in Ontario* (Chicago 1994); and Carolyn Strange, *Toronto's Girl Problem: The Perils and Pleasures of the City* (Toronto 1995).

4 It was part of a social-welfare justice system established at the turn of the century and designed to punish and rehabilitate deviants. See Dorothy Chunn, *From Punishment to Doing Good: Family Courts and Socialized Justice in Ontario, 1880–1940* (Toronto 1992).

5 Under the federal juvenile-delinquency acts (1908; revised 1952), minor girls who engaged in unacceptable adult behaviour (drinking, sexual relations, vagrancy) could be charged with delinquency, a category that included those deemed 'about to become' or 'in the process of becoming' a delinquent. Co-defendants could face related offences, such as 'contributing to delinquency.' This paper focuses on cases of parents who charged daughters under the JD acts, but police, school authorities, and others could also press charges. Many, probably most, girls never had a formal hearing; their cases were bureaucratically processed. Consult *Revised Statutes of Canada* (Ottawa 1952), chap. 160; Chunn, *From Punishment to Doing Good*; and Lorne Stewart, *The History of the Juvenile and Family Court of Toronto* (Toronto 1971).

6 On Gramsci's concept of hegemony, and Foucauldian and Marxist notions of moral regulation, see the introduction to this volume and the references in note 17, below.

7 For this interpretation see Lori Chambers, 'Courtship, Condoms, and Getting Caught: Working-Class Sexual Behaviour in Ontario, 1921–61,' paper presented to the Canadian Historical Association, Montreal, August 1995. For findings similar to mine regarding parental responses, see Joan Sangster, 'Incarcerating "Bad Girls": The Regulation of Sexuality through the Female Refuges Act in Ontario, 1920–1945,' *Journal of the History of Sexuality* 7:2 (October 1996), which considers parents taking older daughters (16–35) to court.

8 Mary Odem, *Delinquent Daughters: Protecting and Policing Adolescent Female Sexuality in the United States, 1885–1920* (Chapel Hill, NC, 1995), draws similar arguments for Los Angeles, California, 1880s–1920, and shows how working-class and immigrant notions of female honour provoked similar parental responses.

9 Annalee Golz, 'Family Matters – The Canadian Family and the State in Postwar Canada,' *left history* 1:2 (Fall 1993); James Struthers, *The Limits of Affluence: Welfare in Ontario, 1920–1970* (Toronto 1994), esp. chap. 5; Mona Gleason, 'Normalizing the Ideal: Psychology, the School, and the Family in Post–World War II Canada, 1945–1960,' Ph.D. thesis, University of Waterloo, 1996; John Graham, 'A History of the University of Toronto School of Social Work,' Ph.D. thesis, University of Toronto, 1995; Franca Iacovetta, 'Gossip and Hearsay in Delinquent Girl Case Files,' paper presented to the Canadian Historical Association, St Catharines, 1996.

10 The Toronto Family Court had jurisdiction over the City of Toronto.

11 Occasionally, defendants from Toronto, and more distant rural locales such as Aurora and Stouffville, appear.

12 Many cases offer little or no biographical information, and for each category of information a different set of cases had to be considered. My qualitative assessments are based on the following rough guidelines: 'most' means more than 75 per cent of those cases that record the information; 'majority' means more than 50 per cent; 'some' means between 15 and 30 per cent; and 'few' or 'minority' means less than 10 per cent.

13 None of the cases in my sample involve girls suspected of being lesbians (though the larger sample of 315 files includes cases of boys charged with delinquency for alleg-edly committing homosexual acts.) On lesbian bad girls, see Becki Ross, 'Street Haven at the "Corners," 1965–69,' paper presented to Gender, Race and the Con-struction of Canada Conference, Vancouver, Fall 1995.

14 Alvin Finkel, Margaret Conrad, and Veronica Strong-Boag, *History of the Canadian Peoples*, vol. 2 (Toronto 1993), chap. 10; on persistent poverty, see Struthers, *Limits of Affluence*.

15 These women thus differ significantly from the turn-of-the century women from impoverished urban or rural backgrounds who have captured much attention in recent works on sexuality and leisure, including those cited below. On working-class respectability and sexual regulation of daughters, see Odem, *Delinquent Daughters*.

16 Peiss, *Cheap Amusements*; Dubinsky, *Improper Advances*; Strange, *Toronto's Girl Problem*; Christine Stansell, *City of Women: Sex and Class in New York, 1789–1860* (New York 1986); Joanne Myerowitz, *Women Adrift: Independent Wage Earners in Chicago, 1880–1930* (Chicago 1988); Odem, *Delinquent Daughters*; Rickie Solin-ger, *Wake Up Little Susie: Single Pregnancy and Race before Roe v. Wade* (New York 1992); Mariana Valverde, 'Building Anti-Delinquent Communities: Morality, Gender and Generation in a City,' in Joy Parr, ed., *A Diversity of Women: Ontario, 1945–1980* (Toronto 1995)

17 See, for example, the introduction to this volume; Mariana Valverde, ed., *Studies in Moral Regulation* (Toronto 1994); Michel Foucault, *History of Sexuality* (3 vols, New York 1978–86), vol. 2; Philip Corrigan and Derek Sayer, *The Great Arch: Eng-lish State Formation as Cultural Revolution* (London 1985); Biddy Martin, 'Femi-nism, Criticism, and Foucault,' in Irene Diamond and Lee Quinby, eds, *Feminism and Foucault: Reflections on Resistance* (Boston 1988); Carol Smart, ed., *Regulat-ing Womanhood: Historical Essays on Marriage, Motherhood and Sexuality* (Lon-don 1992); Linda Gordon, *Heroes of Their Own Lives: The Politics and History of Family Violence* (New York 1988); and Mary Louise Adams, *The Trouble with Nor-mal: Postwar Youth and the Making of Heterosexuality* (Toronto, 1997). Studies that illustrate the class, racial-ethnic, and patriarchal biases of the Canadian legal system

include Constance Backhouse, *Petticoats and Prejudice: Women and the Law in Nineteenth-Century Canada* (Toronto 1991); Dubinsky, *Improper Advances*; Strange, *Toronto's Girl Problem*; and Sangster, 'Incarcerating "Bad Girls."'

18 The quotation is from Eric Sager's essay in this volume.

19 I reject the extreme relativism of some postmodernist theories, but see insights regarding the social production of knowledge, decentred nature of power, and competing meanings of understanding as compatible with Marxist and feminist analyses of class, patriarchy, hegemony, oppression, resistance, and accommodation. On addressing the representation/reality divide, see Regina Kunzel, 'Pulp Fictions and Problem Girls: Reading and Rewriting Single Pregnancy in the Postwar United States,' *American Historical Review* 100:5 (December 1995); Kathleen Canning, 'Feminist History after the Linguistic Turn: Historicizing Discourse and Experience,' *Signs* 19:2 (Winter 1994); and Maynard, in this volume.

20 Important exceptions include work on homosexuality and state repression during the Cold War, including Gary Kinsmen, '"Character Weaknesses" and "Fruit Machines": Towards an Analysis of the Anti-Homosexual Security Campaign in the Canadian Civil Service,' *Labour/Le Travail* 35 (Spring 1995).

21 Differing perspectives are offered in Elaine Tyler May, *Homeward Bound: American Families in the Cold War Era* (New York 1988); Joanne Meyerowitz, 'Beyond the Feminine Mystique: A Reassessment of Postwar Mass Culture, 1946–1958,' *Journal of American History* 79 (March 1993); Wini Breines, *Young, White, and Miserable: Growing Up Female in the Fifties* (Boston 1992); Adams, *The Trouble with Normal*; Parr, *Diversity of Women*.

22 Geoffrey S. Smith, 'National Security and Personal Isolation: Sex, Gender, and Disease in the Cold-War United States,' *International History Review* 14:2 (May 1992); May, *Homeward Bound*. On Canada, see Ruth Roach Pierson, *'They're Still Women After All': The Second World War and Canadian Womanhood* (Toronto 1986); essays in Parr, ed., *Diversity of Women*; Adams, *The Trouble with Normal*; Franca Iacovetta, 'Making New Canadians: Social Workers, Women Clients and the Reshaping of Immigrant Families,' in Iacovetta and Mariana Valverde, eds, *Gender Conflicts: New Essays in Women's History* (Toronto 1992); Veronica Strong-Boag, 'Home Dreams: Women and the Suburban Experiment in Canada, 1945–60,' *Canadian Historical Review* 72:4 (1991); and Reg Whitaker and Gary Marcuse, *Cold War Canada* (Toronto 1994).

23 To take one example, the post–World War One era in Canada, consult Cynthia Comacchio, *'Nations Are Built of Babies': Saving Ontario Mothers and Children, 1900–1940* (Montreal/Kingston 1990); Andrée Lévesque, *La Norme et les déviantes: Les Femmes au Québec pendant l'entre-deux-guerres* (Montreal 1989).

24 The term is Jeffrey Weeks's and refers to a historical moment when deep-seated social fears and anxieties (in which sexuality usually figures prominently) crystallize

around and are displaced onto an identifiable target. *Sex, Politics and Society: The Regulation of Sexuality since 1800* (London 1981), 14

25 Valverde, 'Anti-Delinquent Communities'; Elise Chenier, 'Every Parent Trembles: The Construction of Sexual Danger in the Toronto News Media, 1954–1956,' Graduate History research paper, Queen's University, 1994; Toronto *Star*, 18 Sept. 1948

26 Toronto *Star*, 28 Aug. 1948, 11 Dec. 1948, 24 Feb. 1951, 10 July 1948 and 13 Aug. 1949, 1–3 June 1948, 2 Apr. 1949, and 15 Jan. 1949

27 Valverde, 'Anti-Delinquent Communities'

28 Ibid., Adams, *The Trouble with Normal*; Gleason, 'Normalizing the Ideal,' esp. chaps 2 and 3

29 For the U.S. see Kunzel, 'Pulp Fiction.'

30 For post-war Canada see also Sherene Razak, 'Schools for Happiness: Instituts Familiaux and the Education for Ideal Wives and Mothers,' in Katherine Arnup, Andrée Lévesque, and Ruth Roach Pierson, eds, *Delivering Motherhood: Maternal Ideologies and Practices in the 19th and 20th Centuries* (London 1990).

31 Gleason, 'Normalizing the Ideal,' chaps 3 and 4

32 For example, see ibid.

33 Mary Louise Adams, 'Almost Anything Can Happen: A Search for Sexual Discourse in the Urban Spaces of 1940s Toronto,' in Valverde, ed., *Moral Regulation*

34 Case no. 23

35 Case no. 43

36 Case no. 50. It remains unclear why foster-home and boarding-school options were rejected, however.

37 These were usually part-time jobs, but a few girls obtained work permits that allowed them to leave school before the legal age of 16.

38 Case no. 11

39 Case no. 38

40 Both mothers were housekeepers; one father was an interior designer, the other an engineer. Case no. 17

41 Case no. 46

42 Only a few such cases involved auto theft.

43 Case no. 12

44 Case no. 7

45 I have borrowed the phrase from Andrée Lévesque's *La Norme et les déviantes*, translated in English as *Making and Breaking the Rules* (Toronto 1994).

46 Case no. 52

47 Case no. 24

48 Case no. 13

49 I accept both the reality of mental illness / mental anguish and the view that the process of labelling certain deviants as mentally incompetent and other repressive

acts condoned by medical authorities have reflected class, gender, and racial-ethnic biases. See the essay by Lykke de la Cour and Geoffrey Reaume in this volume.

50 Case no. 97; case no. 50

51 Information on the complainant is available for 94 of 114 cases: 27 cases, or 29 per cent, involve parents who laid charges. In 12 of the 46 cases in which a police officer is named as complainant, the file shows that parents had contacted police to find their daughter. A generous estimate of parent-influenced cases would therefore be 39 cases or 32 per cent of the total sample. Other complainants included social workers (12 cases), school authorities (6), and neighbours (3).

52 On the ideological impact of the law see Douglas Hay, 'Property, Authority, and the Criminal Law,' in D. Hay, Peter Linebaugh, and E.P. Thompson, eds, *Albion's Fatal Tree: Crime and Society in Eighteenth-Century England* (London 1975). Socialized justice relied on allegedly de-criminalized proceedings: rules of evidence were 'relaxed' and social experts were recruited to diagnose problems and recommend rehabilitative remedies. Chunn, *From Punishment to Doing Good*.

53 For example, until 1951, girls (like boys) in training schools could be held there at the discretion of the authorities until age 21; after 1951, the maximum age was 18. See Valverde, 'Anti-Delinquent Communities,' who also describes the strict regime inside the female industrial schools.

54 Trudy received a suspended sentence with supervised visits with the Big Sisters, but it is not clear that the parents' views mattered. Caseworkers stressed Trudy's young age: as the social worker wrote, since Trudy was only twelve, she had not yet formed 'serious delinquent behaviour' and should be 'developing a better organized social recreation program.' Case no. 36

55 Case no. 23; case no. 1

56 Case no. 36. On the Ontario Female Refuges Act see Sangster, 'Incarcerating "Bad Girls"'

57 Case no. 7; case no. 58

58 Gleason, 'Normalizing the Ideal'

59 The average stay of girls at the Catholic St Mary's school was one and one-half years, at the Protestant Galt school one year. Many of the girls and boys sent to industrial schools had never gone to trial. Valverde, 'Anti-Delinquent Communities'

60 For example, see Smart, *Regulating Womanhood*; Chunn, *From Punishment to Doing Good*; and Odem, *Delinquent Daughters*.

61 Kerry Carrington, *Offending Girls: Sex, Youth and Justice* (Sydney 1993) is a contemporary Australian study that considers the disproportionate number of Aboriginal girls convicted under juvenile-delinquency laws and also the criminalization of boy's deviant behaviour.

15

The 'Grab Bag' Mennonite Refugee Family in Post-War Canada

MARLENE EPP

When Mary Rempel immigrated to Canada in 1948 as a refugee from war-torn Europe, her first job was in the laundry at a small, private hospital in north Winnipeg. It is not surprising that Mary described the matron and other employees at the hospital as 'a family' since, over the course of the past decade, she had repeatedly been forced to redefine – however subconsciously – the form and function of family in her own life. Mary was born in 1932 in a village in the Mennonite settlement of Khortitsa in Ukraine.[1] As was the case for many other Soviet German families, Mary's father and grandfather were arrested by the Soviet secret police in 1937 and 1938 respectively; neither was seen or heard from again. Mary's family then moved in with her grandmother. Mary's mother, a young woman at the time, met and was courted by a German soldier who was part of the occupation forces in Ukraine from 1941 to 1943. They married in secret and, together with Mary and her younger brother, left the Soviet Union with the retreating German army in the fall of 1943. Mary gained another brother from this new union, but lost her stepfather when he was killed in action towards the end of the war. After living for a time in eastern Germany with her step-grandparents, Mary's family was reunited with her grandmother, two of her aunts, and an uncle, all of whom had trekked out of Ukraine by a different route. Finding themselves in Soviet-occupied territory at the end of the war, the entire family group made a dramatic escape across the border to western Germany.

As displaced persons in the British zone of occupied Germany, Mary and her family investigated their prospects for immigration to North or South America. In 1947 Mary and her two brothers tragically lost their mother when she died after undergoing surgery for varicose veins, an operation intended to ensure their eligibility for immigration. The three orphaned children then became the responsibility of one of Mary's aunts, Justina, who was only a few years older than Mary herself. Justina, a young woman in her late teens, became a mother of sorts to the children of her late sister as well as caring for her own mother and second sister, both of whom were in ill health. Because the rest of the family had to remain in Europe an extra year to pass medical screenings, Mary and her brothers immigrated to Canada alone in 1948. Given that the three were without parents, some Canadian relatives made attempts to adopt the younger boys. Mary, however, insisted that her family stay together and she resolutely went about securing housing for them and employment for herself.

A year later, Justina, with Mary's grandmother and other aunt, arrived in Canada and before long was able to purchase a house for the entire family group. Mary's family changed once again when she married at the age of nineteen; the newlywed household included her two brothers, a situation that caused no small amount of annoyance for her new mother-in-law. Mary herself claimed that marriage at a young age was for her a way to bring a father figure back into her life.

Creating 'Grab Bag' Families

Although Mary's story is pieced together from several oral interviews, rather than from documented case files, I have used her experience to provide a vivid illustration of the themes that this paper will address. Using a variety of case files, which will be described further on, supplemented by oral accounts and other memory sources,[2] I will analyse the family structure and sex ratio in a migrant group of Mennonite refugees. Two issues drawn from case files – remarriage and illegitimacy – illustrate some of the particular difficulties faced by immigrant families whose form and function did not fit the idealized version of either Canadian society or Mennonite communities. This paper focuses on Mennonites as a case study, yet the questions raised and conclusions offered are, I believe, relevant to the history of refugee populations generally. By examining family fragmentation and reconfiguration within the Mennonite refugee community, this study aims to contribute to the historical understanding of families in 'their various configurations' and to an awareness of their 'diversity of form and function.'[3] Furthermore, this study will add a new perspective to characterizations of the Canadian immigrant family that have rarely included either refugee migrants or female-headed families.[4] At a methodological level, the findings presented here demonstrate that the case file does not provide a pure form of historical information, but must be read with attention to the subjectivity of the creators of the file as well as to how it has been classified and utilized by subsequent users. When juxtaposed against other sources such as written memoirs and oral interviews, the case file can be seen, on the one hand, to be incomplete and at times misleading. On the other hand, it is able to substantiate details that are only hinted at in other sources.

Between the years 1947 and 1952, approximately 8000 Mennonites were admitted to Canada as refugees, having been displaced from their homes in the Soviet Union and eastern Europe during the course of the war. Most notable about this immigrant group was a high percentage of female-headed families as well as an almost universal problem of missing family members. The sex imbalance in this migrant group was created not only by the absence of men who were fathers and husbands, but also by the fact that many young, single men had been arrested and exiled in the Soviet Union or were killed or lost in action as soldiers conscripted into both Soviet and German armed forces.[5] Beyond the fact that many immigrant households had few or no adult males in them, family units almost without exception had experienced separation and fragmentation and could name many missing members from either the nuclear and/or extended circle. Most families in fact fit historian Sheila Fitzpatrick's definition of a 'grab bag family' – one in which individuals with or without a blood relationship come together to share housing, food, and other resources for the purpose of survival under wartime conditions.[6] The life histories of refugees also provide a vivid illustration of Diana Gittins's thesis that families are 'infinitely variable and in a constant state of flux.'[7]

In order to understand the historical context in which Mary's family collectivity was formed, some chronology is necessary. The inauguration of forced collectivization in the Soviet Union in the late 1920s and the subsequent arrest and deportation of 'kulaks' and others considered subversive to the state all brought severe hardship to Soviet Mennonite communities.[8] The breakdown of Mennonite culture included the closure of churches and the banning of religious meetings and public ritual during the first half of the 1930s. Mennonites were targeted for persecution because of their status as a cultural minority, their strong religious orientation and consequent lack of sympathy for communist ideology, and because of their economic prosperity vis-à-vis the Russian peasantry.

The initial wave of deportations under the program of de-kulakization continued into the early 1930s and saw mainly men, but also entire families, sent into exile. In the middle of the decade the number of arrests declined, but this brief lull in terror was short-lived. The years 1936 to 1938 are frequently referred to as those of the 'great purges' because of the massive number of arrests, disappearances, and exiles that were ordered by Stalin's government.[9] Entire truckloads of men were taken from a village in any one night. Several sources state that by the outbreak of the Second World War, an average of 50 per cent of Mennonite families were without a father.[10] A family that was intact was a rarity. Further family fragmentation occurred after the Soviet Union entered the war, as men and youth were conscripted into the Red army, and as others – men, women, and youth – were recruited into work armies mainly to dig trenches to stall advancing German tanks. Fearing that German-speaking minorities, including Mennonites, would collaborate with German forces, Soviet authorities ordered another wave of deportations in the summer of 1941. In this case, most of the remaining adult males and boys over sixteen years were evacuated eastward, with machinery and livestock, ahead of the advancing German forces. By the time the German forces had completely occupied the Mennonite colonies of Ukraine, an estimated 65,000 of the entire Soviet Mennonite population of 100,000 had been deported eastward or otherwise removed from their homes.[11]

The German occupation of Ukraine brought a sense of stability to the Mennonite colonies for a two-year period (1941–3). Public religious practice was resumed, German educational institutions were opened, and a move was made towards privatizing agriculture. Among German colonists, there were strong hopes that Germany would win the war and that exiled family members might return home. These hopes declined along with Germany's diminishing fortune on the war front and, when German forces began their westward retreat from the Ukraine in the fall of 1943, they took with them approximately 350,000 Soviet Germans, of which about 10 per cent were Mennonites.

After a westward trek by horse and wagon and train, the refugees were resettled in that part of Poland now under German control. Germany's decreasing fortunes in the war as well as a severe labour shortage meant that the influx of ethnic Germans was a valuable personnel commodity. Young men in their late teens as well as older men who had escaped deportation in the Soviet Union were now conscripted into various departments of the Nazi military. This meant further separation for families and for women, the painful knowledge that sending one's father, son, or brother into the German army at that point could mean goodbye forever. Many of those who did manage to escape death during the war found themselves in prisoner-of-war camps, their fate or whereabouts unknown to their families for several years.

Of the 35,000 Mennonites who had left Ukraine in 1943, approximately 23,000 went missing in the war or were repatriated to the Soviet Union in accordance with the terms of the Yalta agreement. In the five years following war's end, the remaining 12,000 Mennonite refugees scattered throughout Europe found their way to displaced-persons camps or otherwise connected with relief and immigration agencies operating in the Allied zones.[12] Almost all of these eventually immigrated to Canada and South America.

Defining the Refugee Family

The organization that took on the challenge of assisting Mennonite refugees to immigrate to Canada was the Canadian Mennonite Board of Colonization

(CMBC), based in Saskatchewan.[13] The CMBC worked together with the U.S.-based Mennonite Central Committee (MCC), which held the responsibility of administering relief to Mennonite refugees in post-war Europe, and through the Canadian government's Department of Citizenship and Immigration and Department of Labour. Each refugee would eventually be assisted and processed by a range of individuals, from volunteers to paid professionals, from church workers to government officials.

Canada's immediate post-war priority was the transport and rehabilitation of Canadian service personnel and their families, and thus prospects for the large-scale movement of displaced persons and refugees from Europe seemed dim. With the threat of repatriation to the Soviet Union facing all Soviet-born Mennonites in Allied and Russian zones of occupation, the MCC was anxious to move its refugee population off the continent. Since Paraguay was already home to several thousand Mennonites and was opening its doors with relatively few restrictions, the first large transports of Mennonite refugees went to South America, beginning in February 1947.[14] Canada was the preferred country, however, and with the passage of Orders in Council in early 1947 that expanded the admissable classes of close relatives and contract labourers, the movement of Mennonite refugees turned from South to North America. The CMBC then took on the role of matching potential immigrants in Europe with sponsoring relatives or employers in Canada under the various provisions of an expanding post-war immigration policy.[15] By the end of 1947, 542 Mennonite refugees had arrived in Canada. The year 1948, however, represented the height of the migration, when 3838 Mennonites immigrated, the majority making their homes in Manitoba and British Columbia.

On arrival in Canada, the CMBC recorded information about each immigrant household on a *Familienverzeichnis* (family register). Although the nature of the registration form changed slightly over the years, and there is inconsistency in the amount of detail provided, one can obtain a broad range of information about family units that came under the sponsorship of the CMBC.[16] Some discrepancies are due to the fact that in certain cases immigrants themselves completed the forms, while in others the handwriting indicates that they were filled out by an official with the CMBC. In its most detailed version, the family register offered the following data: full name; birth date; birthplace; marital status; last place of residence; place names and dates regarding the refugee trek and migration to Canada; information about sponsors; and lists of missing family members, including where and why they were left behind. Each form included all the members of a family unit, however defined at that moment by the CMBC or by the family itself. Extended family linkages could sometimes be established between consecutive forms; in addition, numerous forms represented families that were not strictly nuclear: single parents with children, three-generation family units, older children without parents, and so forth. Any given 'family' was thus defined by virtue of the individuals grouped together on a registration form.

Analysing these files at a quantitative level produces a demographic portrait of this group of refugees. The 1948 group represented the largest number of Mennonites immigrating and is probably the most representative of those originating in Ukraine, and thus will be the sample used for illustrative purposes here. For the year 1948, the number of females migrating to Canada was 2224, which represented 58 per cent of the total compared with 1613 males, or 42 per cent.[17] Given that these totals include immigrants of all ages, a further breakdown by age and position within the family (at the time of arrival in Canada) is necessary for a better understanding of the group's demographics.

It is evident from table 15.1 that the ratio of male to female was fairly even up to the age of twenty, an age cohort that I have subdivided into children (up to age 16) and young adults (age 16 to 19). Among adults (age 20 and above) an imbalance begins to occur; most striking is the difference in the numbers of widows (592) versus widowers (98). Furthermore, a very small percentage of widowers immigrated with dependents (children under age 16), while slightly over half the widows arrived with young families. Most widowers had in fact been separated from their families during the war, frequently because they had been conscripted into the German military or workforce, only to discover that their wives and children had been overtaken by the Red Army in Poland or repatriated to the Soviet Union at war's end. Women, on the other hand, were more likely to remain with their younger children throughout the war.

Beyond generating statistics that illustrate sex ratios over generations, the CMBC registers raise questions and suggest interpretations regarding family fragmentation and reconfiguration. The case files are themselves constructed from the perspective of what an ideal or normative family type is. As a result, they can be somewhat deceptive regarding the actual linkages between individuals who are listed together on a registration form as a family group. Other sources, such as memoirs, can reveal surprising additional information about the nature of the relationships in the family. For instance, one record lists a widow and seven children or dependents, aged twenty-five to one year. There is no information on the record to indicate that all seven are other than the widow's own children. However, the 1946 birthdate of the youngest child – ten years after the family's father was arrested and exiled – raises questions, and in searching for other information about this family through oral interviews, it is learned that the eldest daughter in fact gave birth to the one-year-old.[18] Thus, this family group contained within it two single-parent groupings. The manner in which the identity of the child's mother is not obvious on the form parallels the way in which the child's very existence is masked in oral narratives of the

TABLE 15.1
Mennonites immigrating to Canada as defined by
position within the family (1948)

Children (under age 16)	F	533
	M	627
		1160
Young adults (age 16 to 19)	F	183
	M	186
	Unknown	1
		370
Single adults (age 20 & older)	F	547
	M	332
		879
Widows* (with dependants under age 16)		592
		(313)
Widowers (with dependants under age 16)		98
		(6)
Married**		723
Divorced		3
Unknown		13
Total		3838

*I defined an individual as a widow (widower) on the following basis: if, under the question regarding marital status, it was explicitly stated or indicated that the spouse was missing; if a woman is listed without a spouse (with or without children) and a maiden name appears in brackets or if she is designated *Frau*; if a woman is accompanied by children but no father is listed.
**The number of married is an odd number and therefore does not represent an equal number of men and women. In some cases spouses appeared on separate forms for a variety of reasons; e.g., one may have been detained in Europe for processing reasons or a couple may have arrived at different times. It is possible that one-half of the couple may not have been sponsored by the CMBC and therefore would not appear in their records, or that marital status was assumed to be single among groups of male contract workers when in fact some may have been married.

family's story and suggests that illegitimacy was indeed problematic, to the point of denial, both for the Canadian Mennonite community and for the family itself.

In other cases, the self-perception of new immigrants themselves was a factor in the way they were defined on paper. The uncertainty over their own marital status caused some women to identify themselves as widows while others declared themselves to be married, even though their situations were identical. In both cases, husbands had gone missing either during the purges of the late 1930s or during the war itself, and no confirmation of death had been received. One might easily put these two into different categories were it not for additional information regarding missing family members. Some women specifically stated *Mann vermisst* – husband missing – under the section on marital status.

Other questions that seemingly called for simple, factual answers also raised questions of definition. Although birth date and place were relatively straightforward, questions regarding former residence, intended place of residence, and missing family members prompted a variety of different responses depending on how an immigrant her/himself answered What is my home? Who is my family? Even personal name was not an absolute, since some Mennonites had changed or modified their names at various times in order to be less Jewish-sounding, to avoid repatriation, or to unify a family group under one name to ease the process of immigration. The individuals that a registrant chose to list in the section on missing family members is especially interesting in demonstrating the way in which family was constructed from the standpoint of an individual (the registrant) at any given point in time. While one individual might list as many members of their extended family as would fit in the space provided, including those who had disappeared already in the late 1920s and early 1930s, another person might list only those known to be alive, such as family members left behind in displaced-person camps or men known to be in prisoner-of-war camps.

The case files of the CMBC, together with selected Department of Immigration Department files, combined with cases drawn from Mennonite congregational records, reveal particular issues surrounding the integration of refugee families. The 'problems' of remarriage and of illegitimacy are significant, but rarely spoken of, subtexts in the life stories of post-war Mennonite immigrants. While memory sources provide either vivid illustration or veiled reference, depending on the narrator, to questions of sexuality, institutional records offer additional information and perspectives – not necessarily any more true – to certain characteristics of the fragmented refugee family. What both issues suggest is that the refugee family, in its multiple forms, was at odds with the 'happy united family' that was central to discourse surrounding the family in Canadian society and Mennonite communities in the post-war era.[19]

The Problem of Illegitimacy

One family type that was not initially admissible under the close-relative scheme of Canadian immigration policy was that of an unmarried woman with a child, termed 'illegitimate.' The main official of the CMBC, J.J. Thiessen, wrote to the director of the Department of Immigration, A.L. Jolliffe, on several occasions requesting the admission of 'unmarried women with children.' In response to Jolliffe's initial refusal, Thiessen asked for consideration on 'compassionate grounds,' since many of the young women were 'war casualties' (victims of rape). He assured Jolliffe that there were Canadian sponsors willing to take such women as domestic workers and that the CMBC would assume responsibility for the 'unfortunates.' Subsequently, Thiessen stressed that the CMBC would assume responsibility for providing for the children and 'not allowing the immigrants to become public charges in Canada.'[20]

Certain Mennonite leaders in fact seemed to have less trouble than government officials did in integrating unmarried mothers and their children into notions of family. For instance, in July 1949, C.F. Klassen, MCC's relief and immigration ambassador in Europe, wrote to J.J. Thiessen, expressing his distress over the government's stance: 'That Ottawa applies such a narrow interpretation to the term "dependents" and that illegitimate children are only permitted to come if the father is present, shuts out quite a lot. This is very, very unfortunate! The fathers of these children are, in the case of rape, first of all unknown. We are only glad that the mothers were not infected by the monsters. Ottawa must be yielding in this case. These unwed mothers with their guiltless charges must be given the opportunity to make a new beginning. They are not bad people and when sponsors on the other side are ready to receive them, Ottawa should let them in. It is cruel to do otherwise! [translation]'[21] It seemed that the immigration department was willing to admit the women as labourers, but not together with their children, suggesting that without fathers present, unwed mothers with dependents did not constitute a family unit. One high-level official with the Department of Labour in fact suggested that 'a good many' of the women with children who had entered Canada already may have 'manufactured stories that their husbands were behind the iron curtain, thus concealing illegitimacies.'[22]

Owing to the persistent lobbying efforts of the CMBC, the government reversed its stance on particular cases, albeit without changing its overall policy. As far as can be established, all the unmarried mothers for whom special petitions were made were subsequently admitted to Canada with their children, usually under the Farm Labour or Domestic Workers contract.

Although tabulations drawn from the 1948 CMBC family registers reveal twenty-six cases specifically defined as single mothers, in other situations there

is ambiguity surrounding the parentage of a child. As in the case described earlier, the existence of an unmarried mother with a child is not immediately
apparent from the way in which individuals were grouped together on a form.
There are at least twenty-five additional cases in which a woman in her forties
or fifties (widowed or not) is listed together with one or more single adult
daughters, possibly with several other teenagers or children, and then a very
young child (less than five years). In these cases, uncertainty arises as to who is
the mother of the young child – the middle-aged family matriarch or her daughter. Although Mennonite religious beliefs condemned premarital sex (it is
impossible to determine its actual occurrence), the fact that Mennonite women
were victims of wartime rape, and were also compelled to reconstruct traditional morality to meet the exigencies of wartime survival, suggests that pregnancies outside of marriage may have been more common in this group than
would otherwise have been the case.[23]

The point here is not to determine with certainty which were cases of illegitimacy, but to illustrate the way in which families could be defined on paper so as
to create such ambiguities. Certain memory sources more vividly illustrate the
way in which illegitimacy cast a cloud of deviancy over the immigrant family.
One woman living in the Soviet zone of occupied Germany at the end of the
war gave birth to a daughter after trading sex with a Soviet officer for food and
protection for herself and her three other children. When the 'illegitimate' child
grew up in Canada, negative rumours surrounded her own morality – she was
thought to be 'loose' and 'easy' – simply because she was born out of wed-
lock.[24] In another case, following the Mennonite practice of adult baptism, a
young immigrant woman asked to be baptized, but was refused by two Mennonite churches in Alberta and Ontario. As an unmarried mother with a young
son, it was expected that she repent of her sins before being baptized. The
woman had in fact married the child's German father during the war, but had
sought an annulment when she discovered that he already had a wife from
whom he was separated but not divorced. The complicated circumstances of her
marriage and her own stubborn personality prompted her to withhold this information from the church, allowing them instead to think of her as an unwed
mother.[25]

While there was an element of genuine sympathy behind the efforts of
CMBC officials to bring unmarried mothers with children to Canada, and
although there were instances of community acceptance to offset the negative
anecdotes given above, the general attitude towards these women was that they
added a dimension of immorality to the immigrants, who in their very fragmentation represented a discomfiting aberration to the ideal family of the post-war
era. With respect to unmarried mothers specifically, Canadians feared that 'the
moral fibre of the nation and of the nuclear family unit was at risk' owing to

perceptions that illegitimacy was escalating during the war and post-war era.[26] Although there has been little historical analysis of family ideology within Mennonite communities, limited research suggests a discourse similar to that of secular society, which included an idealization of domesticity as the proper role for women.[27]

Reconfiguring Families through Remarriage

As women without men in Canadian Mennonite communities, the new immigrants were somewhat of an anomaly. Particularly for those who had lost their husbands in the Soviet purges of the 1930s, marital status was ambiguous. Most of these women never received any official confirmation of their husbands' fate, although it was common to obtain second-hand accounts of starvation in a Siberian labour camp or violent death on the war front. Although the women functioned for all intents and purposes like widows and were treated as such for the most part, their official marital status remained in a grey area – a fact that became most obvious when the option of remarrying presented itself. Many women alone took the position that if the slightest possibility existed that their husbands were alive, then remarriage was out of the question. Indeed, the emotional attachment that women continued to feel for men who had been absent from their lives for several decades and with whom they had lived for a relatively short time – in some cases only a matter of months – was quite striking. Annemarie Tröger, who has analysed the stories of German women in the Second World War, observes that the 'myth of marriage as the warm and secure refuge in difficult and unsafe times' was ironically sustained most strongly by war widows and single women who idealized the missing men in their lives. These women in particular tried to justify their marriageless state by placing marriage on such an ideal plane that finding an adequate partner was out of the question.[28]

For other women who had survived successfully without a spouse and were quite happy with their emotional and economic independence, remarriage was not a desirable option. Katja, who immigrated to Canada as a single mother, chose not to marry because exposure to violence against women during the war had turned her against men. In her words: 'Already when I was young I decided there would be no men in my life ... I saw too many women raped and killed by men when they were with them. No. I just don't like them.'[29] Maria, a widowed mother of six children, expressed her ambivalence about men in a more humorous way. According to her daughter, Maria received regular visits from a single man (possibly a widower) who lived across the street from her at her new home in British Columbia. When the visits became a little too frequent, Maria had said: 'If I married him, I would have to sleep with him. Oh No!'[30] The son of another widow observed that his mother was focused on 'making it' economically, rather than finding a husband, and that she often spoke of men with disdain, saying 'they don't know what life is all about.'[31]

For yet another group of women, loneliness, the yearning for physical intimacy, and the quest for greater economic stability made remarriage a desirable option. The ambiguity of her marital status quickly became apparent, however, when a widow indicated her intentions to marry again. The problem that this presented came to the attention of Mennonite churches in North America when it was learned that a significant number of common-law marriages existed amongst the scattered refugees in Europe and also in the newly established Mennonite colonies in Paraguay, where the first large movements of post-war refugees had settled.

The problem of 'family disorganization,' as one Mennonite sociologist put it, was dealt with by two Mennonite conferences in North America in 1947.[32] Both the General Conference Mennonites and the Mennonite Brethren Conference took the position that it was impossible to permit a church member to remarry as long as there was uncertainty whether the first partner had died or not.[33] A remarriage that took place contrary to this ruling meant that a church member would automatically be excommunicated. The General Conference position was modified somewhat two years later when the Conference of Mennonites in Canada decided that those who chose to remarry could not be received as members into the church, though they also could not be refused communion, if they chose to partake of it.[34] Although the Canadian and Paraguayan governments, as well as Mennonite leaders in Paraguay, allowed for remarriage following a seven-year separation and no word from the missing partner during that time, Canadian Mennonites held that no marriage could take place where any doubt remained.

At the level of congregations, where action against erring members was to take place, the issue was less clear-cut. The official conference policies notwithstanding, some congregations chose to weigh each individual situation on its own merit. In some congregations, an initial attitude of rigidity and condemnation with respect to standards of morality that seemed to be compromised by problematic remarriages gave way to greater tolerance and situational decision making as the complexity of the issues and emotions involved became apparent. In a church context, problem cases were dealt with, not by a professional body officially constituted to hand down a ruling based on specific guidelines and regulations, but usually by a committee or council consisting of (male) ministers and deacons who were elected to deal with all church matters, whether administrative, theological, or moral. Information on remarriage is thus drawn from cases that appear randomly, and in more or less detail depending on the recorder, within church minutes, rather than systematic case files.

One case from Sargent Avenue Mennonite Church in Winnipeg revealed how complex family fragmentation and reconfiguration could become. The story of Heinrich and Elizabeth (not their real names) was repeated many times elsewhere in Canada. Born in the Soviet Union in 1909, Heinrich had married a Russian woman in 1930. They had two children, born in 1933 and 1940. Heinrich immigrated to Paraguay in 1946, his family left behind in the Soviet Union. Elizabeth, also a Soviet Mennonite, was born in 1911 and married in 1933. Her husband was arrested and exiled in 1937, the year that their only child was born. Elizabeth also immigrated to Paraguay after the war. In Paraguay Elizabeth and Heinrich met and were married in 1952, then immigrated to Canada. At the time of their marriage, neither Elizabeth nor Heinrich had received any word of their first spouses, although shortly thereafter Heinrich learned that his first wife and children were still living in the Soviet Union.[35]

In the early fall of 1960 their case first came to the attention of the Sargent church council, from whom they were seeking acceptance as church members. Although the congregation had dealt with individuals who were intending to remarry without confirmation of a previous spouse's death, this was the first instance in which the second marriage had already taken place. Now the church was faced, not with the decision of excluding a member, but with the question of whether to accept as church members a married couple, one of whom had a spouse still living. After appearing before the church council, Heinrich and Elizabeth's petition came before a meeting of the congregation. A vote was taken, resulting in 147 for and 3 against the acceptance of the couple as members at Sargent. Not all of the membership approved of the congregational decision and several months later a husband and wife announced their withdrawal from Sargent after indicating they believed that the marriage of Heinrich and Elizabeth was unbiblical.

At one level, this was a highly definitive statement of affirmation for Heinrich and Elizabeth and the reality of their new family formation. It also demonstrated the dilemma facing the church, given that the marriage was already eight years old. If Sargent did not accept them, another congregation probably would; thus, church growth was also a motivating factor. In fact, some couples who were refused remarriage, or were excluded by Mennonite churches, left for other denominations altogether, such as the Lutheran church.[36] Nor was it uncommon for individuals and couples to continue attending a congregation even after being excluded as members. The acceptance of Heinrich and Elizabeth was also in keeping with a long-standing tradition of remarriage among

Mennonite widows and widowers resulting from the 'hardships of disease, war, immigration, and religious persecution.'[37]

At another level, the church's decision was an affirmation of the happy united family that was normative for that community. In Canadian churches with a significant number of female-headed households from the post-war migration, the presence of so many widows was frequently cited as a problem and their very existence was a painful reminder of the dislocation and tragedy experienced by the Mennonite settlements in the Soviet Union. By tacitly allowing remarriages to take place, churches were diminishing the number of potentially burdensome widows in their midst, and also putting behind them a past history of community disintegration that was almost too painful to acknowledge. Remarriages offered the approximation, if not the complete restoration, of the ideal family configuration.

The rigid stance held by the conference was obviously problematic at the congregational level when it appeared that couples were going ahead with remarriages, even if it meant forfeiting official membership. While some couples gravitated towards other denominations where they could be married, others simply went ahead and married and continued to attend, without membership, the Mennonite church that had refused their official acceptance.

The case files drawn from church records reveal a number of issues that were central to the remarriage debate: the question of whether one-half of a separated couple could be considered innocent if the other half had already remarried; the apparent hypocrisy in a church position that sympathized with the need for couples to remarry yet rejected them as church members; the highly doctrinaire attitude of much of the church's leadership versus the situational approach that immigrants had taken throughout much of their lives.

For women who did remarry, with or without opposition from their churches, the outcome could vary. Some cases of remarriage were undoubtedly happy and no more problematic than any other marriage; however, there is substantial evidence, particularly in the memory sources of post-war immigrants, that the choice to remarry had not been a good one. Katie, who immigrated to Canada in 1948 with four daughters, decided to remarry in 1955. Confirmation of her first husband's death in 1942 arrived just before her wedding, though she had decided to go ahead even without official word. Initially her daughters, all but one of whom had left home, felt good about the marriage, expecting that 'now she would be taken care of.' However, their opinions began to change as time went on. In one daughter's words: 'For my mother it was very hard. She somehow expected a little more. She found out later on that the husband she married didn't really have anything. He had debts too because he had bought a farm. She worked very hard on the farm. He was a widower with two children. It didn't work out too well with the children either.'[38] In another case, a widow living in Ontario met a man who had been from the same village in the Soviet Union. At the age of seventy she married (her first husband had been arrested during the Stalin purges) and moved with him to British Columbia. According to one of her three daughters: 'It turned out very sad. He was everything we girls had feared. He didn't look after her. All he wanted was a housekeeper.' When it became apparent that her health was in danger, the daughters retrieved their mother from British Columbia and took legal action to prevent her second husband from trying to take her back.[39] The sentiments expressed in these two stories, which are shared in other accounts, indicate that, for some widows, the decision to remarry brought neither emotional nor financial comfort, an especially sad ending to their lives given the many other tragedies they had faced.

In choosing to remarry, with or without knowledge of a first spouse's death, some widows may have been trying to create a 'normal' family, either one that existed in memories of the past or one that emulated the families of their relatives and neighbours in Canada. That individual congregations had difficulty enforcing conference regulations against remarriage suggests that a high degree of sympathy existed for couples who, out of whatever motivation, wanted to live together as husband and wife. The increasing tolerance towards remarriage may also point to a desire, on the part of the church's officials and members, to incorporate widows and their children into a traditional family structure of which the husband was properly the head. The widow who remarried ceased to be a sexual threat and was also viewed as less likely to become a financial or emotional burden on the community. The self-sufficiency and independence displayed by women who had delivered themselves and their families through horrendous wartime situations may have posed a dilemma, if not an actual threat, to the notions of familial hierarchy held by Canadian Mennonites.

Another means of restoring the family was through reunification efforts. Shortly after the war ended, the Mennonite Central Committee established a tracing service to locate missing relatives of Mennonites in North America and hopefully bring about reunions. These brief, but extensive case files – called *Suchkartei* – contained 15,000 to 17,000 names of missing persons and were cross-referenced with the tracing services of other organizations. The service remained active well into the 1960s. An MCC employee said that initially those working with the tracing service would be very excited when they located a lost one and would immediately send telegrams to both sides of the family. Later they became more low-key when they realized that such news created mixed emotions, especially when new marriages had occurred and children been born of those new unions.[40] In some of these cases, the decision was made not to reunite. In a few cases, a husband and wife, separated for possibly thirty years, found that reunification was a problem, even if neither had remarried. In one instance, a woman living in Canada travelled to Germany to be reunited with her husband who had emigrated there from the Soviet Union. They were together several weeks, but decided that they had 'drifted too far apart' and were 'not compatible any longer.' In another case, great happiness accompanied the reunification of a couple in Canada; however, about a year later they separated, one remaining in Winnipeg while the other moved to Ontario. The couple, both in their sixties, found that 'each had learned to cope on his and her own' and 'living together just didn't work out anymore.'[41]

Conclusion

The refugee families who were integrated into Canadian Mennonite communities after the Second World War carried with them stories and experiences that would set them apart from their co-religionists in Canada for decades to come, despite the shared church and associational life, despite the occurrence of marriages between the different migrant groups, and despite the fact that blood relationships existed between the Canadian Mennonites and the post-war immigrants. What set them apart the most perhaps was the fact that most families had been transformed – through deaths, disappearances, and other losses – from a traditional family to a family composed of those who survived. While each 'grab bag' family unit undoubtedly longed for the return of its missing members, the remaining individuals nevertheless developed strategies for adapting and making their way in a new land. For some widows, remarriage was an opportunity to create a new family, one that offered comforts of economy and companionability, and that allowed them to escape the stigma of widowhood attached to them. Churches, in their growing lenience towards the issue of remarriage, also demonstrated a desire to bring normalcy to the family life of the recent immigrants. The fact that some remarriages didn't work well suggests that for some individuals, women especially, the traditional family was no longer a comfortable fit. The history of this particular group of refugee immigrants demonstrates above all that the discourse of the happy united family did not, and possibly never could, reflect their own lived experience of family.

Notes

I am grateful for the helpful comments on an earlier draft of this article offered by participants at the 'On the Case' workshop, April 1995. I would also like to acknowledge the financial support of the Social Sciences and Humanities Research Council, the University of Toronto, and the Quiring-Loewen Trust.

The descriptor 'grab bag' family used in the title of this paper is borrowed from historian Sheila Fitzpatrick's book *Stalin's Peasants: Resistance and Survival in the Russian Village after Collectivization* (New York: Oxford University Press 1994).

1 The story of Mary and Justina – not their real names – is told in oral interviews (nos. 21 and 25) conducted by the author in Winnipeg, Manitoba, in 1993 and 1994. In order to maintain the anonymity of those interviewed, I will use pseudonyms and refer to these and subsequent interviews by number only.
2 This paper is drawn from my larger study examining the post-war migration of Mennonite refugees and displaced persons. See 'Women without Men: Mennonite Immigration to Canada and Paraguay after the Second World War,' Ph.D. thesis, University of Toronto, 1996. I use the descriptor 'memory sources' to refer to oral interviews, published and unpublished written memoirs, and works of historical fiction based on true life stories.
3 See review essay by Cynthia R. Comacchio, 'Beneath the 'Sentimental Veil': Families and Family History in Canada,' *Labour / Le Travail* 33 (Spring 1994), 279–302.
4 For an especially helpful historiographical review of Canadian writing on immigration, see Franca Iacovetta, 'Manly Militants, Cohesive Communities, and Defiant Domestics: Writing about Immigrants in Canadian Historical Scholarship,' *Labour / Le Travail* 36 (Fall 1995), 217–52. An important exception to the paucity of historical writing on refugee women is Janice Potter-MacKinnon, *While the Women Only Wept: Loyalist Refugee Women in Eastern Ontario* (Montreal and Kingston: McGill-Queen's University Press 1993); see also Isabel Kaprielian, 'Creating and Sustaining an Ethnocultural Heritage in Ontario: The Case of Armenian Women Refugees,' in Jean Burnet, ed., *Looking into My Sister's Eyes: An Exploration in Women's History* (Toronto: Multicultural History Society of Ontario 1986), 139–53; and Franca Iacovetta, 'Remaking Their Lives: Women Immigrants, Survivors, and Refugees,' in Joy Parr, ed., *A Diversity of Women: Ontario, 1945–1980* (Toronto: University of Toronto Press 1995), 135–67.
5 The sex imbalance among Mennonite displaced persons was quite different than for other DP communities. For instance, almost two-thirds of Ukrainian adults immigrating to Canada from 1947 to 1951 were male. See Ihor Stebelsky, 'Ukrainian Population Migration after World War II,' in Wsevolod Isajiw, et al., eds, *The Refugee Experience: Ukrainian Displaced Persons after World War II* (Edmonton: Canadian Institute of Ukrainian Studies Press 1992). Among Polish refugees immigrating during the same years, there were three times as many men as women. See Henry Radecki with Benedykt Heydenkorn, *A Member of a Distinguished Family: The Polish Group in Canada* (Toronto: McClelland and Stewart 1976), 33–4.

6 Fitzpatrick, *Stalin's Peasants*, 221. Fitzpatrick states that the 'grab bag family' was not at all uncommon in the Soviet Union during the 1930s.

7 Diana Gittins, *The Family in Question: Changing Households and Familiar Ideologies* (London: Macmillan 1985), 4

8 A 'kulak' was broadly defined as a wealthy farmer. Given their general economic prosperity vis-à-vis the Ukrainian peasantry, Mennonites were prime targets for de-kulakization. Studies that examine developments within the Mennonite colonies under the Soviet regime include John B. Toews, *Czars, Soviets and Mennonites* (Newton, KS: Faith and Life Press 1982), chaps, 11–12; Toews, 'Early Communism and Russian Mennonite Peoplehood,' and Victor G. Doerksen, 'Survival and Identity in the Soviet Era,' in John Friesen, ed., *Mennonites in Russia, 1788–1988: Essays in Honour of Gerhard Lohrenz* (Winnipeg: CMBC Publications 1989), 265–87, 289–98; and Colin Peter Neufeldt, 'The Fate of Mennonites in Soviet Ukraine and the Crimea on the Eve of the 'Second Revolution' (1927–1929),' M.A. thesis, University of Alberta, 1989. Useful for a broader perspective is Ingeborg Fleischhauer and Benjamin Pinkus, eds, *The Soviet Germans: Past and Present* (London: C. Hurst 1986).

9 For background on the Stalin purges, see Robert Conquest, *The Great Terror: A Reassessment* (London: Pimlico 1992; original ed. 1968).

10 'World War II,' *Mennonite Encyclopedia* (Hillsboro, KS: Mennonite Brethren Publishing House, 1955–9), 5: 941–2; George K. Epp, 'Mennonite Immigration to Canada after World War II,' *Journal of Mennonite Studies* 5 (1987), 110

11 These statistics are from T.D. Regehr, *Mennonites in Canada, 1939–1970: A People Transformed* (Toronto: University of Toronto Press, 1996). The ratio among the Mennonites was comparable to that of the German population generally. See Fleischhauer and Pinkus, *Soviet Germans*, 101.

12 Statistics are from Frank H. Epp, *Mennonite Exodus: The Rescue and Resettlement of the Russian Mennonites since the Communist Revolution* (Altona, MB: D.W. Friesen and Sons 1962), 363.

13 The Canadian Mennonite Board of Colonization was established in 1922 with the initial purpose of arranging the emigration of approximately 21,000 Mennonites from the USSR to Canada before 1930. The organization dissolved in the early 1960s and its large archival collection was deposited in Winnipeg at the present Mennonite Heritage Centre.

14 For more detail on these transports see Peter and Elfrieda Dyck, *Up from the Rubble: The Epic Rescue of Thousands of War-Ravaged Mennonite Refugees* (Scottdale, PA: Herald Press 1991); also Epp, *Mennonite Exodus*, chaps 24, 27.

15 For a brief summary of Canadian immigration policy for this period see, for instance, Reg Whitaker, *Canadian Immigration Policy since Confederation* (Ottawa: Canadian Historical Association 1991); and Valerie Knowles, *Strangers at Our Gates:*

Canadian Immigration and Immigration Policy, 1540–1990 (Toronto: Dundurn Press 1992). The legalities and negotiations involved in establishing the Mennonites' status as displaced persons or refugees eligible for immigration are discussed in T.D. Regehr, 'Of Dutch or German Ancestry? Mennonite Refugees, MCC and the International Refugee Organization,' *Journal of Mennonite Studies* 13 (1995), 7–25.

16 There are approximately 5000 forms for the post–Second World War period. Because of their deteriorating condition, they were microfilmed ca. 1990, and these sets were deposited at the Mennonite Heritage Centre (MHC), Winnipeg, and Manitoba Archives. See Canadian Mennonite Board of Colonization Collection, RG XXII-A.1, vol.3403–12, MHC microfilm nos. 553–68.

17 Calculations are based on the entry of all the CMBC family registrations for 1948 in a computer database. My total of 3838 (the sex of one is unknown) differs by 10 from the standard 3828 given in CMBC records and in Epp, *Mennonite Exodus*. The discrepancy most likely results from individuals who appear on more than one record but for whom insufficient information was given to detect such repetition.

18 Interview no. 9, as well as informal conversation with others who knew about this situation

19 The phrase 'happy, united family' is borrowed from Annalee Gölz, 'The Canadian Family and the State in the Post-war Period,' *left history* 1 (Fall 1993), 9–49.

20 See correspondence between J.J. Thiessen and A.L. Jolliffe on the following dates: 5 July 1949, 19 Sept. 1949, 4 Oct. 1949, 27 Feb. 1950, and 6 March 1950. National Archives of Canada (NAC), RG 76, vol. 855, file 544–22.

21 C.F. Klassen to J.J. Thiessen, 1 July 1949. MHC, XXII-A.1, CMBC (166), 1328/983

22 William T. Snyder to C.F. Klassen, 29 Sept. 1949. Snyder is referring to A. MacNamara, Deputy Ministry of Labour. MHC, XXII-A.1, CMBC, 1328/982

23 I have examined the issue of wartime rape in more detail elsewhere. See 'The Memory of Violence: Soviet and East European Mennonite Refugees and Rape in the Second World War,' *Journal of Women's History* 9:1 (Spring 1997), 58–87.

24 Interview no. 28

25 Interview no. 6

26 Margaret Little, 'The Blurring of Boundaries: Private and Public Welfare for Single Mothers in Ontario,' *Studies in Political Economy* 47 (Summer 1995), 100–1

27 For more detail, see chaps 5–7 of my thesis, 'Women without Men.' For a discussion of Mennonite women's roles during the 1950s and 1960s, see also Gloria Neufeld Redekop, *The Work of Their Hands: Mennonite Women's Societies in Canada* (Waterloo, ON: Wilfrid Laurier University Press 1996), 57–79. For analyses of Canadian family ideology in the post-war era, see for instance the essays in Joy Parr, ed. *A Diversity of Women: Ontario, 1945–1980* (Toronto: University of Toronto Press 1995).

28 Annemarie Tröger, 'Between Rape and Prostitution: Survival Strategies and Chances

of Emancipation for Berlin Women after World War II,' in Judith Friedlander et al., eds, *Women in Culture and Politics: A Century of Change* (Bloomington: Indiana University Press 1986), 115.

29 Katja's story is told in Pamela E. Klassen, *Going by the Moon and the Stars: Stories of Two Russian Mennonite Women* (Waterloo, ON: Wilfrid Laurier University Press 1994), 55.

30 Interview no. 9

31 Interview no. 1

32 See J. Winfield Fretz, *Pilgrims in Paraguay* (Scottdale, PA: Herald Press 1953); also Dyck and Dyck, *Up from the Rubble*, chap. 15.

33 Epp, *Mennonite Exodus*, 453

34 *Conference of Mennonites in Canada Yearbook* (1949), 10–11

35 The story of Heinrich and Elizabeth is pieced together from brief entries in the Family and Member Registers, and also from church-council minutes of Sargent Avenue Mennonite Church. MHC, III-62, microfilm 190 and 191

36 Interview no. 28

37 John F. Peters, 'Traditional Customs of Remarriage among Some Canadian Mennonite Widow(er)s,' *Journal of Mennonite Studies* 10 (1992), 119

38 Interview no. 13

39 Interview no. 16

40 Robert Kreider, *Interviews with Peter J. Dyck and Elfrieda Klassen Dyck: Experiences in Mennonite Central Committee Service in Europe, 1941–1949* (Akron, PA: MCC 1988), 187–8

41 Both of these cases are described by Peter Dyck in Kreider, *Interviews*, 188.

Afterword

Telling Stories about Dead People

KAREN DUBINSKY

This volume has given a diverse group of Canadian historians the opportunity to do something we don't usually do in public: express the joys, frustrations, and vast doubts we harbour about the sources we use to tell our stories. Thus, this book reads rather differently than most other studies in the social history of Canada. Here historians have told some new and extremely interesting tales, but they are accompanied by a unique commentary; how, these authors are asking, do I know what I just said? Whose story am I telling? What stories am I not telling in the process of choosing this one? Raising such questions, out loud, is a bit like the scene in *The Wizard of Oz* when we discover that the most powerful being in the land is really a frail old man manipulating machinery behind the curtain. 'What is history?' is a question that has, of course, amused historians for generations, but rarely do we examine – publicly – what goes on behind the curtain. So, far from being a dry excursion through methodology (as such discussions often are), this book raises fascinating questions about how we know what we historians brazenly claim to know about the past.

My favourite answer to this question – What is history? – came from a student some years ago. History, he declared, is simply 'telling stories about dead people.' This book is concerned with the process of telling stories about dead people who, in a certain sense, never really 'lived,' at least as far as the historical record is concerned. As many of these articles point out, there is a tremendous satisfaction in finding the stories of those who did not set pen to paper (or carefully preserve such writings in archival boxes): wartime refugees, poor mothers, battered wives, and political dissidents, to name just a few. And it's not just the fact that these historical actors were on the losing end of nineteenth- and twentieth-century Canadian power relations – which they were – that makes these stories unique. Some of them, most notably the patients incarcerated in Ontario's psychiatric hospitals and asylums, were deemed not to possess a subjectivity at all. It's hard to make a dent in the historical record when you don't really exist.

I too was drawn to the case file – in my case, criminal case files – for many of the same reasons described by these authors. I began looking at criminal case files initially to test what I suspected was the gap between the discourse of seduction constructed by the Ontario branch of the Knights of Labour in the 1880s and the way prosecutions for this crime were carried out. The Knights – a union that was known for its relatively progressive thinking about women workers – were as interested in a curious crime they called 'seduction' as they were about women's suffrage, temperance, and the other 'traditional' feminist issues. Yet they constructed the issue completely as a problem of class power, in which aristocratic libertine capitalists seduced the maidenly working girls in their employment. I suspected that it probably wasn't overfed, sensuous capitalists who were charged under this law, so my first foray into legal records was to investigate how the seduction law, which I had learned about through the eyes of the Knights, was applied.[1] This, by coincidence, occurred in the mid-1980s, the same time that the 'sex debates' or 'sex wars' were being waged in feminist theory and politics. Feminist fur was flying around issues such a pornography (Was it the root cause of patriarchy? What was the relationship between representation and reality? Was censorship an appropriate political response?), prostitution (Was it wholly exploitative of women or just work by another name?), and the place of sexual politics generally in the grand schema of women's liberation (Was heterosexuality inherently oppressive? Was male violence inherent or inevitable?). I liked the nuanced, complicated, and generally 'sex positive' answers to these questions that were being advanced by people such as Ann Snitow, Joan Nestle, and Varda Burstyn, and, armed with Carol Vance's 'pleasure danger' analysis of female sexuality, I began to think about the origins of contemporary sexual discourses. What would female sexual agency look like historically? What were the historical roots of the association, which seems so easily made, between male sexuality and conquest? The work of American historians Christine Stansell and Kathy Peiss, who were among the first feminists to bring these questions to the archives, provided compelling evidence *for* female sexual agency and autonomy in what were very often bleak and brutal settings.[2]

From this perspective, criminal case files began to look like a newly opened window, through which I fancied I could hear snatches of arguments from the past. This analogy has become so hackneyed that I use it advisedly here (and perhaps only in its historical context). Historians have learned a great deal in the decade or so since I began my research, and, as this volume attests, approach case file research with a great deal of theoretical sophistication. So while it is now a bit shopworn to speak quite so enthusiastically and innocently about historical sources, I can vividly remember the thrill I experienced at the beginning of my research into sex-crime prosecutions, because it felt to me like I had actually 'found sex' in the Canadian past. (In 1986 this came as a bit of a revelation). I 'found' arguments between women and men and, to a certain extent, between parents and children, about issues we historians rarely get a chance to observe: heartbreak, broken promises, passion, and emotional, and sometimes physical, pain. It's worth remembering that 'finding sex' – or any other topic that has been similarly obscured from history – can also have a powerful impact on the students we teach. To quote from the final exam of a second-year student of my acquaintance: 'For anyone who is against pro-choice today, I suggest you read the case files of the Hôpital de la Miséricorde.'[3]

Historians find case file records endlessly interesting and useful because, I think, we imagine they grant us admission to the historical party. In them we can hear private conversations, often ones no one else was intended to hear, and often between people – or groups of people – we would not hear from otherwise. We are not simply silent observers of the goings-on, however, for clearly we have some interpretive work to do. We try to read through the generally hostile eyes and ears of those who recorded these conversations. This strategy, reading 'against the grain,' has enormous potential in the history of sexuality, since I can think of few historical sources that do not require it. There is some interesting evidence of people who exposed their sex lives and longings to their diaries, but not nearly so often as we snoopy historians wish they had, and not nearly in such numbers as those who were forced to tell all to the prying eyes of police, Indian agents, social workers, court reporters, doctors, or judges.

Not all people, of course, were forced to 'tell all' to the authorities. That working-class people and immigrants turn up disproportionately in legal records didn't bother me initially, for I came at this from labour history, and was frankly more interested in the lives of marginal people. So, ironically, the class and ethnic bias of the legal system, medical system, or social-welfare system works to the social historian's advantage, as many of this book's authors have found as well. But when we are researching the lives of the working class, or of immigrant populations, through the hostile eyes of one of the systems that helped to sustain class and ethnic hierarchy, some very complicated questions emerge.

Careful readers will have noted that American historian Linda Gordon turns up quite a bit in many of the articles in this book. Her study *Heros of Their Own Lives* is a book that many historians consider to be one of the bibles of case file research. But this was not a universally praised work, and a trenchant critique came from Joan Scott, another historian of some note. Scott, in an often-cited *Signs* debate, chided Gordon for naivety, for too easily or unproblematically reading case file records for agency and resistance, when, in Scott's view, the agency of battered women was 'not outside of but fully constructed by social welfare institutions, and specific to the contexts in which it was observed and documented: the case reports of client behaviour written by social workers.'[4]

At the time of this debate, I was drawn to Gordon's polemical response, which was basically to argue that 'a fist is a fist is a fist.' In other words, she suggested, there is a material and indeed political reality to the lives of, in her case, abused women. I could, of course, make a similar argument about criminal case files for sexual offences. (Indeed, I often have.) But there is a way in which that response sidesteps an important issue that Scott raises, which is relevant to all those working with records of state agencies or institutions of regulation.

How, for example, do we understand the racial dynamics of regulation? It was widely believed at the turn of the century that racial and ethnic minorities in Canada had a distinct set of sexual practices, attitudes, rules, and systems of regulation. Most Anglos believed this to be a very bad thing indeed. But was it true? When we try to answer this question using the stories of sexual conflicts that caught, or were brought to, the attention of the criminal courts, we can see how complicated this apparently simple question really is. It is extremely difficult to separate this question from the various ways in which perceptions of race and sex combined to mobilize racial prejudice. How do we determine where distinct cultural practice leaves off, and racism or ethnocentrism begins? Did Finnish immigrants in Canada, for example, really practise 'free love,' or was this widely held assumption simply the product of Anglo-Saxon worries about immigrant Bolsheviks? The sexual habits of immigrant groups evolved in a climate of hostility and regulation, which makes the assessment of immigrant sexual mores extremely difficult. We cannot separate the propensity of an immigrant woman to take the risk involved in taking on a second lover, performing an abortion, or leaving town with her boyfriend from the question of state examination of immigrant morality and the use of sexuality as an instrument of domination. As many of the articles in this volume make clear, non-Anglo immigrants were particularly vulnerable to scrutiny.

Recent explorations in lesbian and gay history might help us understand more about the complexities of 'deviant' behaviour, sexual and otherwise. There is some interesting work, for example, being done by an American historian, Jennifer Terry, who uses a psychiatric study of homosexuality in the late 1930s to investigate what she calls 'the production of deviant subjectivity.' As Steven Maynard's contribution to this collection also indicates, such psychiatric studies are not transparent sources through which historians can discover some fully crafted gay or lesbian identity. Rather, Terry's approach is to find where the subjects of this medical study were compliant with, and where they resisted, pathological characterizations of themselves. She tries to locate the sites of conflict, tension, and resistance between the doctors and their subjects.[5]

This method strikes me as a useful one for the investigation of a range of 'deviant' people historically, for, as Margaret Little and others have suggested in this collection, case files are really 'sites of contestation' between the observers and the observed. In this respect, social historians using case file research can learn from other analyses of power relationships, on topics that seem far away from the police court or social worker's office in twentieth-century southern Ontario. Scholars of imperialism and colonialism, for example, are also trying to come to grips with the power relationships in texts such as travel and exploration writing. In her book *Imperial Eyes: Travel Writing and Transculturation*, Mary Louise Pratt tries to understand how travel and exploration writing produced 'the rest of the world' for European readerships at particular points in Europe's expansionist trajectory. One of her most insightful contributions is the notion that travel and exploration writing creates what she calls 'contact zones,' that is, social spaces where disparate cultures 'meet, clash, and grapple with each other, often in highly asymmetrical relations of domination and subordination, like colonialism or slavery.'[6] This formulation of imperialism is a relational one; it treats relations among colonizers and colonized not in terms of separateness but of interaction, in a context of unequal power relations. Here we have a way of addressing the issues that were, in my view, too starkly drawn in the Gordon/Scott debate. An African under the tourist gaze is not the same as an African before tourism – in the same way that a battered woman changes under the social worker's gaze, or a runaway immigrant girl changes under the gaze of the police. The challenge for historians here is twofold: one is to see how the African, the battered woman, or the runaway immigrant has been shaped by the gaze, and here Terry's method of investigating compliance and resistance is useful. The second challenge is to consider how the tourist, the social worker, or the police officer themselves have been recast by such interactions.

Many of the articles in this collection are written from a feminist perspective, and many are contributing to the project of Canadian women's history. What happens when we use case file evidence to explore the men who were, very often, the primary reason why women became 'cases'? I discovered in subsequent research on the history of sexual crime that, while there was no single surefire defence that a man charged with sexual assault could invoke to make his version of events more believable, men who were able to harness prevailing stereotypes about women's sexuality and morality had a greater chance of raising doubts about the character, and hence veracity, of the complainant's story.[7] That the behaviour or character of the woman involved was scrutinized more intensively than the actions of men makes it that much more difficult to write men into the story of sexual assault historically. A turn-of-the-century rape trial revealed far more about the history, life circumstances, and specific behaviour of the female complainant than of the male accused. Here we have a new twist on an old feminist story, for, ironically, men are the ones who are 'hidden from history,' precisely because of their power. As Annalee Golz has suggested in her study of wife abuse in this volume, the more successful men charged with abuse or murder were (and remain) at deflecting attention to their female accusers, the more likely they were to walk away from both the courtroom and the historical record. That men had such power to define the issues in a rape or abuse trial leads to a vexing methodological problem. The contemporary convergence of interest in case file research and the history of masculinity poses some unanticipated problems that are in many ways different from the challenges faced by women's historians in the past. Silence, as AIDS activists remind us, equals death. Sometimes, however, silence also equals power. Interrogating that silence – which was rendered natural in the day-to-day workings of the criminal-justice system – will be a challenging issue facing those who try to explore the history of masculine identities.

Finally, another important feature of this project is its interdisciplinary, or inter-regulatory focus. This book gives us a strong sense of how broadly case files can be used; criminal files, for example, tell us about much more than the law, medical files tell us about more than the medical system. This project, by bringing together such a wide variety of sources, broadens the scope that much more. Bettina Bradbury and Lynne Marks each note the differences between records generated by religious institutions and those generated by bureaucratic state agencies; but their work raises interesting possibilities concerning the origins of 'bureaucratic' reform. The fascinating overlapping mechanisms of regulation collected in this book – religious, medical, legal, commercial, social-work, political – illustrate how partial our studies have been up to now. Perhaps this collection will inspire other historians to examine the past through the medium of the case file in a much more holistic fashion. There is great potential, for example, for a community study in which legal, medical, and religious records, and whatever else is available for a given community, could be used to reconstruct a more complete version of the 'private lives' and (likely private miseries) of its residents. Such a project would also add an important geographic dimension, for it matters whether relationships between doctors and patients, poor people and social workers, women and men were forged in big cities or small towns; whether the social worker was located in an imposing government building in Toronto or drove into the village from far away each month.

So case files have a great potential to reveal much more than we know now about the history of power relations in Canada, and especially the subtleties of power as it was exercised and confronted by those who have been written out of the story of big 'P' power in the past; vote-less nuns and equally vote-less elderly women, for example. But case file research is, and will remain, promising also for a much more mundane reason: these documents simply reveal a lot of obscure, fascinating information. Ellen Ross's recent study of nineteenth- and early-twentieth-century working-class London mothers, *Love and Toil*, is a great example of the kind of richly textured study I hope we will see more of in Canada – the kind that integrates material from case files seamlessly with other, more conventional, historical sources: newspaper research, autobiographies, and the like. The result is a book that lets the reader into the world of working-class mothers on what often feels like extremely intimate terms; 'almost like fiction,' as some of my students have commented, which is, in this context, high praise. Thus, by using case files broadly, to explore a given event or social phenomenon – the Depression, for example, or motherhood, childhood, or immigration – historians can also tell more complete, and more interesting, stories.

This collection will, one hopes, encourage others to take a closer look at these documents. Rather than presenting a 'how to' model, this book suggests the vast potential of explorations in the contact zone between the powerful and the marginal in Canadian history, and the diverse approaches one can take in doing so.

Notes

1 This research was published as 'Maidenly Girls or Designing Women? Prosecutions for Seduction in Ontario,' in Franca Iacovetta and Mariana Valverde, eds, *Gender Conflicts: Essays in Women's History* (Toronto: University of Toronto Press 1992).

2 See, for example, Carol Vance, ed., *Pleasure and Danger: Exploring Female Sexuality* (Boston: Routledge 1984); Ann Snitow, Christine Stansell, and Sharon Thompson, eds, *Powers of Desire: The Politics of Sexuality* (New York: Monthly Review Press 1983); and Varda Burtsyn, ed., *Women against Censorship* (Toronto: Douglas and McIntyre 1985). Early feminist historical works on power, pleasure, and agency are Christine Stansell, *City of Women: Sex and Class in New York, 1789–1860* (New York: Alfred A. Knopf 1986) and Kathy Peiss, *Cheap Amusements: Working Women and Leisure in Turn-of-the-Century New York* (Philadelphia: Temple University Press 1986).

3 Andrée Lévesque, 'Deviants Anonymous: Single Mothers at the Hôpital de la Miséricorde in Montreal, 1929–1939,' in Veronica Strong-Boag and Anita Clair

Fellman, eds, *Rethinking Canada: The Promise of Women's History*, 2nd ed. (Toronto: Copp Clark 1992). The Hôpital de la Miséricorde was a home for unwed mothers and, as my student correctly saw it, is an excellent illustration that the acquisition of the choice to either abort or carry a pregnancy to term is one of the most important changes in the lives of women in the twentieth century.

4 Linda Gordon and Joan Scott debate, *Signs* 15:4 (Summer 1990) 848–60

5 Jennifer Terry, 'Theorizing Deviant Historiography,' *differences* 3:1 (Summer 1991), 55–74

6 Mary Louise Pratt, *Imperial Eyes: Travel Writing and Transculturation* (New York: Routledge 1992), 5. See also Patricia Jasen, *Wild Things: Nature, Culture and Tourism in Ontario, 1790–1914* (Toronto: University of Toronto Press 1995); George Robertson et al., eds, *Travellers' Tales: Narratives of Home and Displacement* (London: Routledge 1994); David Spurr, *The Rhetoric of Empire: Colonial Discourse in Journalism, Travel Writing, and Imperial Administration* (Durham: Duke University Press 1993); Anne McClintock, *Imperial Leather: Race, Gender and Sexuality in the Colonial Contest* (New York: Routledge 1995); and Marianna Torgovnick, *Gone Primitive: Savage Intellects, Modern Lives* (Chicago: University of Chicago Press 1990).

7 Karen Dubinsky and Adam Givertz, '"It Was Only a Matter of Passion": Masculinity, Race and Sexual Danger,' in Nancy Forestell, Katherine McPherson, and Cecilia Morgan, eds, *Gender in Canada* (in progress)

Contributors

Bettina Bradbury teaches history and women's studies at York University, is editor of *Canadian Families* (1992), and is the author of many articles on working-class families. Her *Working Families: Age, Gender and Daily Survival in Industrializing Montreal* (Toronto 1993) won the John A. Macdonald prize for best book in Canadian history. Her current research is on nineteenth-century marriage and widowhood.

Robin Brownlie has a Ph.D. in history from the University of Toronto and is a postdoctoral fellow at York University. A specialist in Native–white relations, her articles have appeared in the *Canadian Historical Review* and *Journal of the Canadian Historical Association*. Her current research is on lesbians in post-war Canadian prisons.

Lykke de la Cour has taught history and women's studies at York and Trent Universities, and has published articles in women's, gender, and medical history. She is currently completing her dissertation on women and the asylum in Ontario.

Karen Dubinsky teaches history at Queen's University. The author of *Improper Advances: Rape and Heterosexual Conflict in Ontario, 1880s–1920s* (Chicago 1993), she is completing a book on the history of the tourist industry at Niagara Falls.

Marlene Epp received her Ph.D. in history at the University of Toronto. The author of numerous articles on immigration, women, and oral history, she is completing a book on post-1945 Mennonite female migration to Canada and Paraguay.

Annalee Golz teaches women's studies at the University of Victoria. She is completing her doctoral thesis on marital breakdown and domestic violence in nineteenth- and early-twentieth-century Ontario. Her work has appeared in several legal-history collections and *left history*.

Franca Iacovetta, of the University of Toronto, is the author of *Such Hardworking People: Italian Immigrants in Postwar Toronto* (Montreal and Kingston 1992) and co-editor of several books, including, from University of Toronto Press, *Gender Conflicts* (1992) and *A Nation of Immigrants* (1998). Her current work is on 'delinquent girls,' and immigrant/refugee reception work in Cold War Canada.

Gregory S. Kealey, Dean of Graduate Studies at Memorial University, Newfoundland, recently resigned as long-time editor of *Labour / Le Travail*. He is the author of many articles and several books in Canadian working-class history, including, most recently, *Workers in Canadian History* (Montreal 1997).

Margaret Hillyard Little teaches women's studies and political science at Queen's University. Her book on welfare policy, moral regulation, and single mothers in Ontario will be published by Oxford University Press.

Angus McLaren is Professor of History at the University of Victoria. He is the author of several books, including *The Trials of Masculinity: Policing Sexual Boundaries, 1870–1930* (Chicago 1997); *A Prescription for Murder: The Victorian Serial Killing of Dr. Thomas Neill Cream* (Chicago 1993); and *Our Own Master Race: Eugenics in Canada* (Toronto 1990).

Lynne Marks is Associate Professor of History at the University of Victoria and has published widely on women's, gender, and working-class history. She is the author of *Revivals and Roller Rinks: Religion, Leisure, and Identity in Late-Nineteenth-Century Small-Town Ontario* (Toronto 1996). Her current research is on church regulation, and on religion and madness.

Steven Maynard's work has appeared in the *Canadian Historical Review* and *Journal of the History of Sexuality*. His book *Toronto the Gay: Sex, Men, and the Police in Urban Ontario, 1890–1940* will be published by University of Chicago Press.

Wendy Mitchinson, Professor of History at the University of Waterloo, has written widely in women's history. The author of *The Nature of Their Bodies:*

Women and Their Doctors in Victorian Canada (University of Toronto Press 1991) and co-editor of *Essays in the History of Canadian Medicine* (Toronto 1988), she is writing a book on women and illness in modern Canada.

Geoffrey Reaume holds a Ph.D. in history from the University of Toronto, and has published in the field of medical history, specializing in psychiatric patients' perspectives. His doctoral dissertation, on the Toronto asylum, is a social history of the male and female patients.

Eric W. Sager is Professor of History at the University of Victoria and Director of the Canadian Families Project. He is the author of *Seafaring Labour: The Merchant Marine of Atlantic Canada, 1820–1914* (Montreal and Kingston 1989), and co-author with Gerry Panting of *Maritime Capital: The Shipping Industry in Atlantic Canada, 1820–1914* (Montreal and Kingston 1990).

Carolyn Strange is with the Centre of Criminology at the University of Toronto. She is the author of *Toronto's Girl Problem: The Perils and Pleasures of the City, 1880–1930* (Toronto 1995) and co-author with Tina Loo of *Making Good: Law and Moral Regulation in Canada, 1867–1939* (Toronto 1997). She is also the editor of *Qualities of Mercy: Justice, Punishment, and Discretion* (Vancouver 1996).

James W. St.G. Walker teaches history at the University of Waterloo and has published widely in the area of Black history and race relations. He is the author of *The Black Loyalists: The Search for a Promised Land in Nova Scotia and Sierra Leone, 1783–1870* (2nd ed., Toronto 1992) and *'Race,' Right and the Law in the Supreme Court of Canada: Historical Case Studies* (Waterloo, ON, 1997).